No Differences?

How Children in Same-Sex Households Fare

Studies from Social Science

**Edited by Ana Samuel
with an Introduction by
John Londregan**

Published by the Witherspoon Institute
2014

Articles on page 1, "Same-Sex Parenting and Children's Outcomes: A Closer Examination of the American Psychological Association's Brief on Lesbian and Gay Parenting," *Social Science Research* 41 (July 2012): 735–751, http://dx.doi.org/10.1016/j.ssresearch.2012.03.006; page 21, "How Different Are the Adult Children of Parents Who Have Same-Sex Relationships? Findings from the New Family Structures Study," *Social Science Research* 41(4) (July 2012): 752–770, http://dx.doi.org/10.1016/j.ssresearch.2012.03.009; and "Parental Same-Sex Relationships, Family Instability, and Subsequent Life Outcomes for Adult Children: Answering Critics of the New Family Structures Study with Additional Analyses," *Social Science Research* 41(6) (November 2012): 1367–1377, http://dx.doi.org/10.1016/j.ssresearch.2012.08.015; page 61, "Methodological Decisions and the Evaluation of Possible Effects of Different Family Structures on Children: The New Family Structures Study (NFSS)," *Social Science Research* 41 (November 2012): 1357–1366, http://dx.doi.org/10.1016/j.ssresearch.2012.08.011; page 79, "Nontraditional Families and Childhood Progress through School: A Comment on Rosenfeld," *Demography* 50 (June 2013): 955–961, http://dx.doi.org/10.1007/s13524-012-0169-x; "Normal Progress through School: Further Results (white paper, June 2, 2014), used with permission of Douglas W. Allen, Catherine R. Pakaluk, and Joseph Price; page 107, "High School Graduation Rates Among Children of Same-Sex Households," *Review of Economics of the Household* 11 (December 2013): 635–658, http://dx.doi.org/10.1007/s11150-013-9220-y; page 141, "Comparative Relationship Stability of Lesbian Mother and Heterosexual Mother Families: A Review of Evidence," *Marriage & Family Review* 46:8 (2010): 499–509, http://dx.doi.org/10.1080/01494929.2010.543030; and page 157, "Nontraditional Families and Childhood Progress through School," *Demography*, Volume 47-Number 3, August 2010: 755–775.

John Londregan, professor at the Woodrow Wilson School of Public and International Affairs, Princeton University, *editor*
Ana Samuel, research scholar at the Witherspoon Institute, *editor*

Alicia Grimaldi, *director of publishing, the Witherspoon Institute*

Betsy Stokes, *assistant editor*
Margaret Trejo, *book design and layout*
Diego Samuel, *cover design*
Printing by Thomson-Shore

Published in the United States by the Witherspoon Institute
16 Stockton Street, Princeton, New Jersey 08540

Library of Congress Control Number: 2014953091

ISBN 978-0-9851087-2-4

Printed in the United States of America

Contents

Introduction
v

Summary and Reprint of Loren Marks's
"Same-Sex Parenting and Children's Outcomes: A Closer Examination of the
American Psychological Association's Brief on Lesbian and Gay Parenting"
1

Summary and Reprint of Mark Regnerus's
"How Different Are the Adult Children of Parents Who Have Same-Sex
Relationships? Findings from the New Family Structures Study"
and
"Parental Same-Sex Relationships, Family Instability, and Subsequent
Life Outcomes for Adult Children: Answering Critics of the
New Family Structures Study with Additional Analyses"
21

Summary and Reprint of Walter R. Schumm's
"Methodological Decisions and the Evaluation of Possible Effects of Different
Family Structures on Children: The New Family Structures Survey (NFSS)"
61

Summary and Reprint of Douglas W. Allen, Catherine R. Pakaluk, and Joseph Price's
"Nontraditional Families and Childhood Progress through School:
A Comment on Rosenfeld"
and
"Normal Progress through School: Further Results"
79

Summary and Reprint of Douglas W. Allen's
"High School Graduation Rates Among Children of Same-Sex Households"
107

Summary and Reprint of Walter R. Schumm's
"Comparative Relationship Stability of Lesbian Mother and Heterosexual
Mother Families: A Review of Evidence"
141

Appendix
Michael J. Rosenfeld's "Nontraditional Families
and Childhood Progress through School"
157

Introduction

John Londregan

The papers included and summarized in this volume all study the nexus between children's well-being and the structure of the families in which they are raised. In particular, the authors focus on the efficacy of families in which the adults are involved in a physically intimate same-sex relationship. This is an increasingly important topic, as many countries have extended their definition of marriage to encompass same-sex couples, while others are considering doing so. Because of their policy relevance, the papers in this volume will be read by many for their importance to the approval of particular referenda, or to the outcome of a specific Supreme Court test case. That is unfortunate. A reading of the sometimes apoplectic reactions in the press, and even among some academics, to the papers by professors Marks and Regnerus reminds one of Samuel Johnson's aphorism that "prejudice, not being founded on reason, cannot be removed by argument." It is clear that for some people, scientific research on this subject is irrelevant. This volume is meant for those who still approach the topic of parenting and sexuality with open minds.

The first question someone not immersed in the empirical social-science literature might ask is, "Why is this so complicated? Aren't there enough studies already for us to have settled these questions?" Two of the main reasons we still have a lot to learn on this subject have to do with the technical issues of *bias* and *power*. These are statistical terms of art with somewhat misleading names.

A biased statistical estimator for a population characteristic will tend to take on a value that is unrepresentative of the characteristic it is meant to estimate. To give an example, in 1936, *Literary Digest* magazine conducted a massive opinion poll about the November presidential election. They collected responses from readers and supplemented their data with a survey of telephone subscribers and automobile owners. Their prediction? A landslide win for Alf Landon. They were half right; there was a landslide, but it was for Roosevelt, not for Landon, a man whom you may have never even heard of. Technically speaking, their polling was biased. Why? Their readers tended to be Republicans, as did, in 1936, telephone subscribers and the owners of automobiles—so they oversampled Republicans and undersampled Democrats.

What about power? When we conduct a hypothesis test, we assemble the statistical evidence relevant to the hypothesis and its alternative and then come to a verdict, very much as a court might do.[1] So let's think about "trying" the case of our hypothesis against the alternative. To make matters concrete, suppose we test the *null hypothesis* that women and men are equally likely to identify as Democrats against the *alternative hypothesis* that women are more likely to be Democrats than are men. In this case, we can potentially commit two sorts of errors. We commit a so-called type I error if we falsely reject our hypothesis, whereas we commit a type II error if we falsely accept it.

Now for the complicated part. The rules of hypothesis testing give the benefit of the doubt to the null hypothesis, just as criminal law embodies a presumption of innocence. So, analysts will proceed by choosing a probability of a type I error (corresponding to false rejection). Typical choices include a 10-percent probability of false rejection, a 5-percent probability of falsely rejecting, and a 1-percent probability. Most of the authors of the studies in this volume follow a common convention of indicating coefficient estimates that are significantly different from zero at 5 percent with an asterisk, and those for which they can reject the hypothesis with a 1-percent chance of a type I error with two asterisks. The probability of a type I error is called the *size* of the hypothesis test. However, while this approach controls the probability of false rejection (a type I error) it can leave one with a very high probability of falsely accepting an incorrect null hypothesis (a type II error). The *power* of a test is the probability that it does not make a type II error by falsely accepting the null hypothesis.

Power calculations are made more complicated by the fact that most of the alternative hypotheses we are interested in are in fact composite hypotheses. So if we test the null hypothesis that women and men are equally likely to identify as Democrats against the alternative that women are more likely to be Democrats, we are really testing against a whole series of alternatives: that women are twice as likely to be Democrats, that they are but 1 percent more likely, and so forth. The smaller the difference between the null hypothesis and the alternative, the lower the power—that is, the more likely we are to falsely accept the null hypothesis when in fact the alternative is true. The power of a test is also affected by how large a sample we have; all else equal, large samples will give us more power.

Of course, all of these probability calculations are made with respect to a standard set of assumptions that are at best only approximately correct, but this is the state of the art, and the same tool kit is used by pretty much everyone doing quantitative sociological studies of the family.[2]

The first paper, by Loren Marks, examines the foundations of the position taken by the American Psychological Association (APA) on what it calls "lesbian and gay parenting." The 2005 APA monograph setting forth that organization's position asserts that the question of whether the child rearing efficacy of parents in same-sex relationships is at least the equal of that of heterosexual couples is settled and that the serious academic literature speaks with a single voice on the matter. Marks reviews an extensive literature on the topic and finds that most of the studies on the subject rely on convenience samples, which can provide a useful window on the experience of parents in same-sex relationships. However, Marks notes that the convenience samples, a staple of this literature, suffer from two generic problems. First, the sample sizes are very small, and so the power of their findings of "no difference" is very weak. Secondly, the samples are unrepresentative, and so the findings suffer from a bias. Both problems prevent the studies from being conclusive.

Why the problems with convenience samples? The bias of such studies in the literature emerges because researchers recruit parents unrepresentative of the wider population of parents in same-sex relationships, for example by contacting relatively well-educated and affluent lesbian parents. The low power of most studies stems from their small sample sizes. One of the better studies might include a dozen or two lesbian families and a comparable number of heterosexual families. In such a small sample, only enormous differences in children's outcomes will rise to the level of statistical significance.

Marks also notes that many of the small studies either fail to identify a comparison group of heterosexual parents, or they compare educated and affluent lesbian couples to single heterosexual parents. He suggests that better comparison groups might consist of married heterosexual parents or of all heterosexual parents. Certainly that would be the case if one wanted to sustain that there was no difference between the status quo outcomes for children of parents in same-sex relationships and those of heterosexual married parents, as some have seemed to want to do.

Marks highlights three studies that avoid small convenience samples and work with much larger random samples, two of which can be found in this volume, in the chapter by Mark Regnerus and the chapter by Douglas Allen, Catherine Pakaluk, and Joseph Price.

Mark Regnerus's much bruited study takes an innovative approach to solving the difficulties of generating a large sample of parents in same-sex relationships. Working with the internet-polling firm Knowledge Networks, now acquired by GfK, Regnerus contacted over 15,000 young and early-middle-aged adults and asked them about their childhoods, including whether at least one of their parents had been involved in a same-sex relationship while they were growing up.[3] Regnerus notes in his chapter that this retrospective definition of having had a parent in a same-sex relationship overlaps with, but is not identical with, having had a parent who self-identified as gay or lesbian. Some critics have objected to his use of "gay and lesbian parents" as shorthand for "the parents of the adults in his sample who had been involved in a same-sex romantic relationship," but he is very clear about his definition.

Even after having cast such a wide net, Regnerus finds but a few hundred adults who had grown up in households with a parent in a same-sex relationship (for 163 cases, it was their mother; in 73 cases, it was their father). Professor Regnerus finds that there are numerous dimensions on which adults whose parents had had same-sex relationships encountered worse life outcomes than those raised by both biological parents who were married to each other. The outcomes for the children of parents who had had same-sex relationships more closely resembled those for children of single-parent heterosexual households than the outcomes for those who grew up under the protection of an intact heterosexual marriage. Regnerus suggests that much of the reason for this is the instability of the partnerships of the parents who had had same-sex relationships. On the one hand, this does not tell us much about what happens in lesbian households in which both adults have advanced degrees, earn high incomes, and manage to stay together for decades. On the other hand, it may reflect reality for the majority of children who grow up with parents who have had same-sex relationships.

Of course, even with the reach of a professional internet-polling firm and a survey of over 15,000 individuals, sampling bias can intrude itself. People cannot be compelled to respond, and given the relative rarity of parents in same-sex relationships, even a sample size in the tens of thousands of individuals will yield a relatively small set of parents in same-sex relationships. The only way you could avoid these problems would be to get the Census Bureau to conduct your survey as part of the decennial census, to which individuals are required by law to respond. This is exactly what the other two studies mentioned in Loren Marks's chapter do. Michael Rosenfeld accessed the 5-percent random sample from the 2000 decennial census, and he compared the outcomes for children of same-sex couples with those of married heterosexual couples. His performance variable was grade retention—whether a child was reported to be at least a grade behind. The cost of using the census data comes in the form of being able to access relatively few variables as compared with the Regnerus survey.

In their chapter, Douglas Allen, Catherine Pakaluk, and Joseph Price look at the same dataset considered by Michael Rosenfeld, who failed to reject the null hypothesis that the children in the sample with same-sex parents (there were 8,632 in the 5-percent sample) are more likely to be retained than are the sampled children who were being raised by married heterosexual parents, of whom there were 1,189,893 in the 5-percent sample. Firstly, the authors show that Rosenfeld's data-analysis strategy had low power. In particular, while one cannot reject that the children of same-sex parents are not statistically significantly more likely to be retained than are the children of married heterosexual parents, neither do they differ in a statistically significant way from the sampled children of never-married women (there were 77,879 in the entire sample). Indeed, the parameter estimates for the children with same-sex parents are very similar to those of the children of the never-married women, which in turn are statistically significantly worse than the outcomes for the children with married heterosexual parents.

Allen, Pakaluk, and Price then go on to show that Rosenfeld's finding of no difference hinges on two critical decisions: firstly he eliminated geographically mobile children who had changed domicile during the preceding five years, and secondly he excluded children who had been adopted. Including either group, even with a control variable for the group mean, expands the sample size and increases the power of the tests.

In either case, the result is that the sharper estimates reveal that the children of same-sex parents more closely resemble the children of single heterosexual parents than they do the children of married parents. In the companion piece, the same authors further hone their analysis by considering only the children (in fourth and eighth grade) whose grade level is expressly asked about in the census. Again the sharper data leads to a more statistically significant difference between the children of parents in same-sex relationships and those of heterosexual married parents.[4]

Rosenfeld argues strenuously for the need to exclude the data for mobile and adopted children, on the grounds that mobility is a proxy for family instability, while he contends that same-sex couples are more likely to adopt troubled children. Yet when the data is included along with controls for these variables, the same-sex parenting variable again becomes significant. The picture that emerges from this exercise is that familial instability may be an important *mechanism* by which the children of parents in same-sex relationships fare worse than those with married heterosexual parents.

Douglas Allen continues the quest for a large probability sample by working with a 20-percent sample from the 2006 Canadian Census. By 2006, gay and lesbian marriage was legal throughout Canada, and the census question only identified a child as having gay or lesbian parents if she (or he) responded affirmatively to the question, "Are you the child of a (male/female) same-sex married or common-law couple?" This survey provides a glimpse of what society might look like immediately after the legalization of same-sex marriage. For both children of gay and of lesbian parents, Allen finds significant deficits in high-school completion. Moreover, while he generally finds that late-adolescent children of lesbian parents have high-school completion rates that resemble those of the children of single women, and overall the late-adolescent children of gay parents resemble children raised by single men, there is an additional feature to the data—the daughters of gay male parents fare worse than the sons,[5] whereas no similar gender disparity emerges in any of the other family structures he studies. Allen ends by calling for the research community to distinguish between gay and lesbian couples raising children, rather than aggregating them into the same category.

Finally, there are two chapters by Walter Schumm. In the first, he notes that while a different researcher might have made different research-design choices than did Mark Regnerus, the choices Regnerus opted for are all within the range of standard practice for the sort of research he is doing. Indeed, the sample design shortcomings of the Knowledge Networks survey are less severe than for any of the widely cited studies based on convenience samples.

The papers in this volume follow a trajectory, from the concerns raised by Loren Marks about small convenience samples, to the large survey conducted by Mark Regnerus, to the gigantic census samples analyzed by Douglas Allen, Catherine Pakaluk, and Joseph Price. A picture emerges: in a cross-section of children raised by parents in same-sex relationships, life outcomes tend to resemble those of children raised by single and divorced parents. So perhaps the mechanism for this process is the instability of the families headed by parents in same-sex relationships?

The second Schumm chapter follows up on this question, combing the literature for references to the instability of lesbian households (gay parents are less-studied, and the census samples suggest that lesbian couples raising children are less-rare than gay couples doing the same). The point of departure is the claim by Biblarz and Stacey that lesbian parents are more likely to separate than are married heterosexual parents. While the Biblarz and Stacey conjecture is based on the sort of convenience samples that much of this volume succeeds in transcending, Schumm compares study after study of lesbian parents to population data on heterosexual marriages. He concludes that lesbian couples are about twice as likely to split as are heterosexual married couples.

The research papers each contribute to our understanding of the relationship between family structure and the welfare of children. Though of course none of them provides the last word on the subject, they collectively show us that family structure does matter for children's outcomes and that we are not justified in maintaining an *a priori* assumption that parents in same-sex relationships do as well at raising children as do married heterosexual couples.

While all of this research is interesting, and while it contributes to our store of knowledge, many questions remain. These papers do not settle the question of parents in same-sex relationships, but they do warn us that the matter is still in doubt. Some have suggested that the instability of lesbian couples is due to the absence of a marriage option, though the Canadian study and work by Andersson and colleagues on lesbian registered partnerships in Sweden indicate that there, too, the risk of divorce is over twice that for heterosexual marriages.[6]

How public policy proceeds from here is, of course, a political matter. Some see same-sex marriage as the centerpiece of individual freedom and want to push it into law by any means necessary, while the deeply held religious beliefs of others lead them to oppose it as profoundly sinful. Pragmatists might note that several countries have recently volunteered their next generation as guinea pigs in the huge social experiment of same-sex marriage. The papers in this volume suggest that we really don't yet know how that experiment is going to turn out.

Notes

1. To be sure, there is a branch of statistics, named for the Reverend Thomas Bayes, that views this approach as wrongheaded and prefers that analysts confronted with alternative hypotheses provide what amount to betting odds on the options, but this is not the approach that has come to dominate the sociological literature on family structures that concerns us here.
2. The followers of Thomas Bayes, who call themselves Bayesians, are also tied to their own set of approximately correct and more-or-less standard assumptions.
3. This interesting vantage on family structure has come in for its share of criticism. Some have questioned the stature of the polling firm. While GfK is perfectly adept at publicizing itself, the reader is invited to visit the list of academic journals that have published papers based on the surveys of Knowledge Networks: www.knowledgenetworks.com/ganp/docs/KN-Journals-List.pdf. It is an extensive roster including *NATURE*, *American Economic Review*, *American Political Science Review*, *Harvard Law Review*, and among other sociological journals, *Journal of Marriage and Family*.
4. In their unpublished addendum, the authors further probe the data to find differences in the child-rearing outcomes of same-sex male couples and same-sex female couples.
5. Oddly, in their further analysis of the 5-percent sample of the 2000 U.S. Census, Allen, Pakaluk, and Price find the opposite disparity, with girls raised by same-sex male couples faring better than the boys, while boys and girls were equally disadvantaged when raised by same-sex female couples.
6. See Gunnar Andersson, Turid Noack, Ane Seierstad, and Harald Weedon-Fekjær, "The Demographics of Same-Sex Marriages in Norway and Sweden," *Demography* 43 (February 2006): 79–98, p. 95.

Summary of Loren Marks's

"Same-Sex Parenting and Children's Outcomes: A Closer Examination of the American Psychological Association's Brief on Lesbian and Gay Parenting"

Social Science Research 41 (July 2012): 735–751,
http://dx.doi.org/10.1016/j.ssresearch.2012.03.006

In 2005, the American Psychological Association (APA) published a brief on lesbian and gay parenting, which claimed, "Not a single study has found children of lesbian or gay parents to be disadvantaged in any significant respect relative to children of heterosexual parents."

Marks finds the confidence of the APA surprising, in light of the small size of the convenience samples used to conclude "no significant differences" among the children as well as the history of social science research on family structures, which has found that departures from the intact biological family are associated with negative child outcomes. He reviews the research cited by the APA to verify that their claim was backed by sound scientific evidence. After careful analysis, he concludes that the evidence does not warrant the claim made by the APA.

To begin, Marks screens the sixty-seven cited manuscripts and finds that eight of these were unpublished disertations. Since unpublished work has not passed peer review, he discounts these and focuses on the remaining fifty-nine published studies. He finds seven difficulties with the APA claim.

First, the APA makes suggestions about the *general experience* of children of lesbian and gay parents, while the samples in the cited studies were not representative of the *general population* of kids from lesbian and gay homes. The APA suggests that "children of lesbian or gay parents" are not disadvantaged *on the whole*, when compared to children of opposite-sex parents. However, Marks explains, the vast majority of the fifty-nine studies—77 percent—relied not upon random samples but upon convenience samples.

Convenience samples are distinguished from random samples because the former only gather data from people who actively volunteer to provide it—for example, folks who offer their own personal stories about same-sex parenting or who give reports or anecdotal evidence about their experience with children of same-sex parents. This information, while valuable, is not randomly selected data, and it can introduce bias. People who are highly motivated to see changes in marriage laws, for example, may be the most willing to volunteer information about their same-sex parenting experiences. Moreover, convenience samples tend to recruit data from clusters of homogenous people, informants who tend to have the same social background, interests, economic situations, and/or behavioral patterns. One cannot make generalizations about the whole population of children living with same-sex parents by relying on data gathered from and reflective of the experience of a small, homogenous group of people. For the APA to speak about the "children of lesbian or gay parents" without explaining the limitations of its sources is misleading.

Second, the fifty-nine studies were not based upon samples that were racially, socioeconomically, or gender diverse. They relied exclusively on all-white or almost-all-white samples of predominantly middle- to upper-class, well-educated women.[1] Only three papers studied gay-father households with comparisons to heterosexual households—and *none* of these studied the outcomes of the children of gay fathers, but rather of the gay fathers themselves. So although the APA made a claim about "children of lesbian or gay parents," the actual studies referenced were only about outcomes of children parented by middle- to upper-class, well-educated, white lesbian women. These studies did not account for the mothers' distinct advantages in wealth, race, and education. Clearly, the experiences of these children cannot reasonably be said to represent the *average* experiences of children from all same-sex parents in the United States.

Third, although the APA claim made a comparison between the children of lesbian and gay parents and the children of heterosexual parents, Marks found that only thirty-three of the fifty-nine studies involved a heterosexual comparison group at all. Of those thirty-three studies, thirteen used a heterosexual comparison group that consisted exclusively of single-parent families, most of which were single mothers. (The other twenty studies did not specify the makeup of the heterosexual comparison group, a failing in its own right.) One would expect that when the APA speaks of "children of heterosexual parents," it refers at least in part to children from intact married mother-and-father families, the family structure in which social scientists typically expect children to perform the best. However, such children were *never* the comparison group in the cited studies. In effect, the studies cited by the APA compared a select sample of one group (the children of wealthy, two-white-mother families) to a select sample of another group (children of diverse-background, one-mother-only families), and the APA made a sweeping claim of no differences between the children of lesbian or gay families relative to heterosexual families.

Fourth, the APA claimed that "not a single study" had found children of lesbian or gay parents to be disadvantaged. However, Marks finds that there had been a study published prior to 2005 that should have been noted: the Australian study by Sotirios Sarantakos (1996). The Sarantakos study compared children from heterosexual married couples, homosexual couples, and cohabiting couples, using data from the largest comparative sample available at the time (*N=174).*[2] Based upon teacher reports, child test scores, and school assessments of the children's performance (rather than on parental reports of children's progress), Sarantakos found that the children from married heterosexual households outperformed their peers from homosexual households in significant respects. The APA, however, only cited the Sarantankos study in a footnote and criticized it, arguing that it contradicted the no-differences findings of the majority of the research and was published in a lesser-known Australian journal. Marks points out, though, that the important thing to note about the Sarantakos Study was that the children from same-sex families were compared to children from *married heterosexual families* and that significant differences in child outcomes came to the surface. Moreover, the APA's awareness of the existence of this study damages the credibility of the claim that "not a single study" had found children of lesbian or gay parents to be disadvantaged when compared to children from heterosexual families.

Fifth, the APA claimed that the children of same-sex parents were not disadvantaged "in any significant respect." However, when Marks looks at the kinds of child outcomes examined by the fifty-nine papers, he finds that most of them studied *gender-related outcomes*, which are not of great general interest to society. Marks explains that social-science work on child outcomes typically focuses on greater societal concerns, such as "intergenerational poverty, collegiate education and/or labor force contribution, serious criminality, incarceration, early childbearing, drug/alcohol abuse, or suicide."[3] By contrast, the papers cited by the APA studied outcomes such as "sexual orientation; behavioral adjustment, self-concepts and sex-role identity; sexual identity; sex-role behavior; self-esteem; psycho-sexual and psychiatric appraisal; socio-emotional development; and maternal mental health and child adjustment."[4] So, for the APA to claim that the children were not disadvantaged "in any significant respect" was misleading, based upon what the discipline of social science normally identifies as the most significant respects.

Marks further points out that Sarantakos had published a longer, book-length study in 2000 through Harvard University Press that had reported significant and upsetting differences between children from same-sex households and children from opposite-sex households in areas such as "drug and alcohol abuse, education (truancy), sexual activity, and criminality."[5] The APA did not even cite this Harvard, peer-reviewed book in a footnote, although it did cite eight unpublished dissertations in support of its claim.

Sixth, Marks notes that none of the fifty-nine studies looked at the long-term outcomes of the children. He explains that scientists working on child outcomes know that many children do not exhibit problems until later in life, when it is time for adolescents and young adults to form their own romantic relationships, enter the labor force, contribute to society, and eventually form their own families. For the APA to omit studies of child outcomes in adolescence and early adulthood, cite primarily early-child outcomes, and declare that there were no disadvantages for the children of same-sex households was a premature declaration.

Finally, and seventh, Marks warns the APA of having violated its own standards of statistical research as outlined in its *Publication Manual*. Repeatedly, the APA has published directions to the effect that research claiming to establish no differences between groups had to take seriously "statistical power considerations" of the research, pay close attention to sample sizes and effect sizes, and provide evidence of the strength of relationships in its reported results. Marks finds that only four of the fifty-nine studies provided statistical tests that passed these standards. As a result, fifty-one of the studies fall into a type-II error, a false negative claim of "no differences."

Marks ends his review with suggestions for future researchers of same-sex parenting:

1. Move away from small convenience samples, and use large representative samples.
2. Move away from gender-related child outcomes, and focus on outcomes of greater interest to society, which exhibit themselves later in the life of a child (during adolescence and early adulthood).
3. Include *diverse* same-sex families in the samples (at least gay-father families, but also racial minorities and those with lower socioeconomic status).
4. Include *intact* opposite-sex married families in the comparison group.
5. Respond carefully to criticisms from experts about sample sizes, sampling strategies, statistical power, and effect sizes.

The 2005 APA brief on lesbian and gay parenting claimed, "Not a single study has found children of lesbian or gay parents to be disadvantaged in any significant respect relative to children of heterosexual parents." However, Marks's review reveals that the studies cited by the APA rather provide evidence for a substantially narrower view: *Some* children raised by two well-educated, white, lesbian women of middle-to-high socioeconomic status show no differences in mostly gender-related outcomes when compared to children raised by single mothers from diverse racial and socioeconomic backgrounds.

Notes

1. Michael Rosenfeld explains: "Among the convenience sample studies, several of the most important have been based on samples of women who became parents through assisted reproductive technology (ART; Brewaeys et al. 1997; Chan, Raboy, and Patterson 1998; Flaks et al. 1995). Because individuals who become parents through assisted means can be identified through reproductive clinics—and are therefore easier to recruit than the general population of same-sex couple parents—the literature on same-sex couple parenting has tended to feature studies of the kind of women who can afford ART: white, upper-middle-class women. Nationally representative data tend to paint a different picture: in the U.S. Census, same-sex couple parents tend to be more working class and are much more likely to be nonwhite compared with heterosexual married couples." See appendix: Michael Rosenfeld, "Nontraditional Families and Childhood Progress through School," *Demography* 47 (August 2010): 755–775, p. 757.
2. The Sarantakos study did not use a large, random representative sample in the way the Regnerus study did in 2012.
3. Marks, 743.
4. Ibid.
5. Ibid., 744.

Social Science Research 41 (2012) 735–751

Contents lists available at SciVerse ScienceDirect

Social Science Research

journal homepage: www.elsevier.com/locate/ssresearch

ELSEVIER

Same-sex parenting and children's outcomes: A closer examination of the American psychological association's brief on lesbian and gay parenting

Loren Marks *

Louisiana State University, 341 School of Human Ecology, Baton Rouge, LA 70803, United States

ARTICLE INFO

Article history:
Received 3 October 2011
Revised 8 March 2012
Accepted 12 March 2012

Keywords:
Same-sex parenting
Lesbian
Gay

ABSTRACT

In 2005, the American Psychological Association (APA) issued an official brief on lesbian and gay parenting. This brief included the assertion: "Not a single study has found children of lesbian or gay parents to be disadvantaged in any significant respect relative to children of heterosexual parents" (p. 15). The present article closely examines this assertion and the 59 published studies cited by the APA to support it. Seven central questions address: (1) homogeneous sampling, (2) absence of comparison groups, (3) comparison group characteristics, (4) contradictory data, (5) the limited scope of children's outcomes studied, (6) paucity of long-term outcome data, and (7) lack of APA-urged statistical power. The conclusion is that strong assertions, including those made by the APA, were not empirically warranted. Recommendations for future research are offered.

© 2012 Elsevier Inc. All rights reserved.

1. Introduction

Over the past few decades, differences have been observed between outcomes of children in marriage-based intact families and children in cohabiting, divorced, step, and single-parent families in large, representative samples.[1] Based on four nationally representative longitudinal studies with more than 20,000 total participants, McLanahan and Sandefur conclude:

> Children who grow up in a household with only one biological parent are worse off, on average, than children who grow up in a household with both of their biological parents...regardless of whether the resident parent remarries.[2]

Differences have recurred in connection with myriad issues of societal-level concern including: (a) health,[3] mortality,[4] and suicide risks,[5] (b) drug and alcohol abuse,[6] (c) criminality and incarceration,[7] (d) intergenerational poverty,[8] (e) education and/or labor force contribution,[9] (f) early sexual activity and early childbearing,[10] and (g) divorce rates as adults.[11] These outcomes represent important impact variables that influence the well-being of children and families, as well as the national economy.

---

* Fax: +1 225 578 2697.
E-mail address: lorenm@lsu.edu
[1] See Table 2; McLanahan and Sandefur (1994) and Wilcox et al. (2005).
[2] McLanahan and Sandefur (1994), p. 1 (emphasis in original).
[3] Waite (1995).
[4] Gaudino et al. (1999) and Siegel et al. (1996).
[5] Wilcox et al. (2005, p. 28) and Cutler et al. (2000).
[6] Bachman et al. (1997), Flewelling and Bauman (1990), Horwitz et al. (1996), Johnson et al. (1996), Simon (2002), Waite and Gallagher (2000), Weitoft et al. (2003), and Wilcox et al. (2005).
[7] Blackmon et al. (2005), Harper and McLanahan (2004), Kamark and Galston (1990, pp. 14–15), Manning and Lamb (2003), and Margolin (1992, p. 546).
[8] Akerlof (1998), Blackmon et al. (2005), Brown (2004), Oliver and Shapiro (1997), Rank and Hirschl (1999).
[9] Amato (2005), Battle (1998), Cherlin et al. (1998), Heiss (1996), Lansford (2009), Manning and Lamb (2003), McLanahan and Sandefur (1994), Phillips and Asbury (1993), and Teachman et al. (1998).
[10] Amato (2005), Amato and Booth (2000), Ellis et al. (2003), and McLanahan and Sandefur (1994).
[11] Cherlin et al. (1995) and Wolfinger (2005).

By way of comparison, social science research with small convenience samples has repeatedly reported no significant differences between children from gay/lesbian households and heterosexual households. These recurring findings of no significant differences have led some researchers and professional organizations to formalize related claims. Perhaps none of these claims has been more influential than the following from the 2005 American Psychological Association (APA) Brief on "Lesbian and Gay Parenting".[12,13]

> Not a single study has found children of lesbian or gay parents to be disadvantaged in any significant respect relative to children of heterosexual parents.

Are we witnessing the emergence of a new family form that provides a context for children that is equivalent to the traditional marriage-based family? Many proponents of same-sex marriage contend that the answer is yes. Others are skeptical and wonder—given that other departures from the traditional marriage-based family form have been correlated with more negative long-term child outcomes—do children in same-sex families demonstrably avoid being "disadvantaged in any significant respect relative to children of heterosexual parents" as the APA Brief asserts? This is a question with important implications, particularly since the 2005 APA Brief on "Lesbian and Gay Parenting" has been repeatedly invoked in the current same-sex marriage debate.

2. Statement of purpose

The overarching question of this paper is: *Are the conclusions presented in the 2005 APA Brief on "Lesbian and Gay Parenting" valid and precise, based on the cited scientific evidence?*[14] In the present paper, seven questions relating to the cited scientific evidence are posed, examined, and addressed.[15]

Two portions of the APA Brief are of particular concern to us in connection with these questions: (a) the "Summary of Research Findings" (pp. 5–22), and (b) the first and largest section of the annotated bibliography, entitled "Empirical Studies Specifically Related to Lesbian and Gay Parents and Their Children" (pp. 23–45). In the latter section (pp. 23–45), the APA references 67 manuscripts. Eight of these studies are "unpublished dissertations".[16] The 59 published studies are listed in Table 1 of this paper, providing clear parameters from which to formulate responses to the seven outlined questions, next.

2.1. Question 1: how representative and culturally, ethnically, and economically diverse were the gay/lesbian households in the published literature behind the APA brief?

In response to question 1, more than three-fourths (77%) of the studies cited by the APA brief are based on small, non-representative, convenience samples of fewer than 100 participants. Many of the non-representative samples contain far fewer than 100 participants, including one study with five participants (Wright, 1998; see Table 1). As Strasser (2008) notes:

> Members of the LGBT community…vary greatly in their attitudes and practices. For this reason, it would be misleading to cite a study of gay men in urban southern California as if they would represent gay men nationally (p. 37).

By extension, it seems that influential claims by national organizations should be based, at least partly, on research that is nationally representative.

Lack of representativeness often entails lack of diversity as well.[17] A closer examination of the APA-cited literature from the "Empirical Studies" (pp. 23–45) section of the APA Brief reveals a tendency towards not only non-representative but racially homogeneous samples. For example:

---

[12] The APA Brief's stated objective was primarily to influence family law. The preface states that "the focus of the publication…[is] to serve the needs of psychologists, lawyers, and parties in family law cases…. Although comprehensive, the research summary is focused on those issues that often arise in family law cases involving lesbian mothers or gay fathers" (APA Brief, 2005, p. 3). Redding (2008) reports that "leading professional organizations including the *American Psychological Association*" have issued statements and that "advocates have used these research conclusions to bolster support for lesbigay parenting and marriage rights, and the research is now frequently cited in public policy debates and judicial opinions" (p. 136).

[13] Patterson, p. 15 (from APA Brief, 2005).

[14] Kuhn (1970/1996) has stated that there is an "insufficiency of methodological directives, by themselves, to dictate a unique substantive conclusion to many sorts of scientific questions" (p. 3). To draw substantive conclusions, a socially and historically influenced paradigm is needed. Research is then "directed to the articulation of those phenomena and theories that the paradigm already supplies" (p. 24). Indeed, paradigmatic biases, and other influences, can make us vulnerable to "discrepancies between warranted and stated conclusions in the social sciences" (Glenn, 1989, p. 119; see also Glenn, 1997).

[15] Kuhn (1970/1996) has noted that "when scientists disagree about whether the fundamental problems of their field have been solved, the search for rules gains a function that it does not ordinarily possess" (p. 48).

[16] These unpublished dissertations include Hand (1991), McPherson (1993), Osterweil (1991), Paul (1986), Puryear (1983), Rees (1979), Sbordone (1993), and Steckel (1985). An adapted portion of one of these dissertations (Steckel, 1985) was eventually published (Steckel, 1987) and is included in the present examination; the other unpublished work is not included in Table 1 of this paper.

[17] Of the 59 published "Empirical Studies Specifically Related to Lesbian and Gay Parents and Their Children", no studies mention African-American, Hispanic, or Asian-American families in either their titles or subtitles. The reference list in the APA Brief's "Summary of Research Findings" (pp. 15–22) is also void of any studies focusing on African-American, Hispanic, or Asian-American families. None of the "Empirical Studies Specifically Related to Lesbian and Gay Parents and Their Children" (pp. 23–45) holds, as its focus, any of these minorities. (*Note:* Three years after the 2005 APA Brief, Moore (2008) published a small but pioneering study on African–American lesbians.)

Table 1
Publications Cited in APA brief on lesbian and gay parenting (pp. 23–45).

Author and year	GayLes N	Hetero N	Stat used	Cohen N	Stat power	Outcome studied	Hetero compar group
Bailey et al. (1995)	55par; 82chl	0	T-test/Chi	393	N/A	Sexual orientation	None
Barrett and Tasker (2001)	101	0	T-test/Chi	393	N/A	Child responses to a gay parent	None
Bigner and Jacobsen (1989a)	33	33	T-test	393	No	Parents reports of values of children	Fathers
Bigner and Jacobsen (1989b)	33	33	T-test	393	No	Parent reports of parent behavior	Fathers
Bos et al. (2003)	100	100	MANOVA	393	No	Parental motives and desires	Families
Bos et al. (2004)	100	100	MANOVA	393	No	Parent reports of couple relations	Families
Bozett (1980)	18	0	Qualitative	N/A	N/A	Father disclosure of homosexuality	None
Brewaeys et al. (1997)	30	68	ANOVA	393	No	Emotional/gender development	DI/Non-DI Couples
Chan et al. (1998a)	30	16	Various	393	No	Division of labor/child adjustment	DI Couples
Chan et al. (1998b)	55	25	Various	393	Reported	Psychosocial adjustment	DI Couples
Ciano-Boyce and Shelley-Sireci (2002)	67	44	ANOVA	393	No	Division of child care	Adoptive Parents
Crawford et al. (1999)	0	0	MANOVA	393	N/A	388 Psychologists' attitudes	N/A
Flaks et al. (1995)	15	15	MANOVA	393	No	Cognitive/behavioral/parenting	Married Couples
Fulcher et al. (2002)	55	25	T-test/Chi	393	Reported	DI/adult-child relationships	Parents
Gartrell et al. (1996)	154	0	Descript.	N/A	N/A	Prospective Parent Reports	None
Gartrell et al. (1999)	156	0	Descript.	N/A	N/A	Reports on parenting issues	None
Gartrell et al. (2000)	150	0	Descript.	N/A	N/A	Reports on parenting issues	None
Gartrell et al. (2005)	74	0	Descript.	N/A	N/A	Health, school/education	None
Gershon et al. (1999)	76	0	Reg.	390	N/A	Adolescent coping	None
Golombok et al. (1983)	27	27	T-test/Chi	393	No	Psychosexual development	Single mother families
Golombok et al. (2003)	39	134	Various	393	No	Socioemotional dev./relations	Couples & singles
Golombok and Rust (1993)	N/A	N/A	N/A	N/A	N/A	Reliability testing of a pre-school gender inventory	
Golombok and Tasker (1996)	25	21	Pearson	783	Reported	Sexual orientation	Children of single mothers
Golombok et al. (1997)	30	83	MANOVA	393	No.	Parent–child interactions	Couples & singles
Green (1978)	37	0	Descript.	N/A	N/A	Sexual identity	None
Green et al. (1986)	50par; 56chl	40par; 48chl	Various	390	No	Sexual identity/social relations	Single mothers
Harris and Turner (1986)	23	16	ANOVA/Chi	393	No	Sex roles/relationship with child	Single moth. & fath.
Hoeffer (1981)	20	20	ANOVA	393	No	Sex-role behavior	Single mothers
Huggins (1989)	18	18	T-test	393	No	Self-esteem of adolescent children	Divorced mothers
Johnson and O'Connor (2002)	415	0	Various	N/A	No	Parenting beliefs/division of labor/etc.	None
King and Black (1999)	N/A	N/A	F	393	N/A	338 College students' perceptions	N/A
Kirkpatrick et al. (1981)	20	20	Descript.	N/A	No	Gender development	Single mothers
Koepke et al. (1992)	47 couples	0	MANOVA	393	N/A	Relationship quality	None
Kweskin and Cook, 1982	22	22	Chi-Sqr	785	No	Sex-role behavior	Single mothers
Lewis, 1980	21	0	Qualitative	N/A	N/A	Child response to m. disclosure	None
Lott-Whitehead and Tully, 1993	45	0	Descriptive	N/A	N/A	Adult reports of impacts on children	None
Lyons, 1983	43	37	Descriptive	N/A	No	Adult self-reports	Divorced mothers
McLeod et al., 1999	0	0	Mult. regr.	N/A	No	151 College student reports	N/A
Miller, 1979	54	0	Qualitative	N/A	N/A	Father behavior & f-child bond	None
Miller et al., 1981	34	47	Chi-Sqr	785	No	Mother role/home environment	Mothers
Morris et al., 2002	2431	0	MANCOVA	N/A	N/A	Adult reports on "coming out"	None
Mucklow and Phelan, 1979	34	47	Chi-Sqr	785	No	Behavior and self-concept	Married mothers
O'Connell, 1993	11	0	Qualitative	N/A	N/A	Social and sexual identity	None
Pagelow, 1980	20	23	Qual/Descr.	N/A	N/A	Problems and coping	Single mothers
Patterson (1994)	66	0	T-test	393	No	Social/behavioral/sexual identity	Available norms
Patterson (1995)	52	0	T-test/Chi/F	393	No	Division of labor/child adjustment	None

(continued on next page)

Table 1 (*continued*)

Author and year	GayLes *N*	Hetero *N*	Stat used	Cohen *N*	Stat power	Outcome studied	Hetero compar group
Patterson (2001)	66	0	Various	393	No	Maternal mental health/child adjustment	None
Patterson et al., 1998	66	0	Various	393	No	Contact w/grandparents & adults	None
Rand et al. (1982)	25	0	Correlations	783	No	Mothers' psychological health	None
Sarantakos, 1996	58	116	F-test	393	N/A	Children's educational/social outcomes	Married/non-married
Siegenthaler and Bigner, 2000	25	26	T-test	393	No	Mothers' value of children	Mothers
Steckel (1987)	(Review)	N/A	N/A	N/A	No	Psychosocial development of children	None
Sullivan, 1996	34 couples	0	Qualitative	N/A	N/A	Division of labor	None
Tasker and Golombok, 1995	25	21	Pearson/T	783	No	Psychosocial/sexual orientation	Single mothers
Tasker and Golombok (1997)	27	27	Various	393	Reported	Psychological outcomes/family rel.	Single mothers
Tasker and Golombok (1998)	15	84	ANCOVA/Chi	785	N/A	Work and family life	DI & NC couples
Vanfraussen et al. (2003)	24	24	ANOVA	393	No	Donor insemination/family funct.	Families
Wainwright et al. (2004)	44	44	Various	393	No	Psychosocial/school/romantic	Couples
Wright (1998)	5	0	Qualitative	N/A	N/A	Family issues/processes/meaning	None

N/A = Not applicable (e.g., In connection with statistical power, qualitative studies and studies without heterosexual comparison groups are coded as N/A).

1. "All of [the fathers in the sample] were Caucasian" (Bozett, 1980, p. 173).
2. "Sixty parents, all of whom were White" comprised the sample (Flaks et al., 1995, p. 107).
3. "[All 40] mothers...were white" (Hoeffer, 1981, p. 537).
4. "All the children, mothers, and fathers in the sample were Caucasian" (Huggins, 1989, p. 126).
5. "The 25 women were all white" (Rand et al., 1982, p. 29).
6. "All of the women...[were] Caucasian" (Siegenthaler and Bigner, 2000, p. 82).
7. "All of the birth mothers and co-mothers were white" (Tasker and Golombok, 1998, p. 52).
8. "All [48] parents were Caucasian" (Vanfraussen et al., 2003, p. 81).

Many of the other studies do not explicitly acknowledge all-White samples, but also do not mention or identify a single minority participant—while a dozen others report "almost" all-white samples.[18] Same-sex family researchers Lott-Whitehead and Tully (1993) cautiously added in the discussion of their APA Brief-cited study:

> Results from this study must be interpreted cautiously due to several factors. First, the study sample was small (*N* = 45) and biased toward well-educated, white women with high incomes. These factors have plagued other [same-sex parenting] studies, and remain a concern of researchers in this field (p. 275).

Similarly, in connection with this bias, Patterson (1992), who would later serve as sole author of the 2005 APA Brief's "Summary of Research Findings on Lesbian and Gay Families", reported[19]:

> Despite the diversity of gay and lesbian communities, both in the United States and abroad, samples of children [and parents] have been relatively homogeneous.... Samples for which demographic information was reported have been described as predominantly Caucasian, well-educated, and middle to upper class.

In spite of the privileged and homogeneous nature of the non-representative samples employed in the studies at that time, Patterson's (1992) conclusion was as follows[20]:

> Despite shortcomings [in the studies], however, results of existing research comparing children of gay or lesbian parents with those of heterosexual parents are *extraordinarily clear*, and they merit attention... There is no evidence to suggest that psychosocial development among children of gay men or lesbians is compromised *in any respect* relative to that among offspring of heterosexual parents.

---

[18] Examples of explicit or implicitly all-White (or nearly all-White) samples include, but are not limited to: Bigner andJacobsen (1989a,b), Bozett (1980), Flaks et al. (1995), Green (1978), Green et al. (1986), Hoeffer (1981), Huggins (1989), Koepke et al. (1992), Rand et al. (1982), Siegenthaler and Bigner (2000), Tasker and Golombok (1995, 1998), Vanfraussen et al. (2003).
[19] Patterson (1992, p. 1029).
[20] Patterson (1992, p. 1036) (emphasis added).

Patterson's conclusion in a 2000 review was essentially the same[21]:

> [C]entral results of existing research on lesbian and gay couples and families with children are *exceptionally clear. . . .* [The] home environments provided by lesbian and gay parents are just as likely as those provided by heterosexual parents to enable psychosocial growth among family members.

Although eight years had passed, in this second review, Patterson (2000) reported the continuing tendency of same-sex parenting researchers to select privileged lesbian samples. Specifically, she summarized, "Much of the research [still] involved small samples that are predominantly White, well-educated [and] middle-class" (p. 1064).[22] Given the privileged, homogeneous, and non-representative samples of lesbian mothers employed in "much of the research", it seems warranted to propose that Patterson was empirically premature to conclude that comparisons between "gay or lesbian parents" and "heterosexual parents" were "extraordinarily clear"[23] or "exceptionally clear".[24]

There is an additional point that warrants attention here. In Patterson's statements above, there are recurring references to research on children of "gay" men/parents. In 2000, Demo and Cox reported that "children living with gay fathers" was a "rarely studied household configuration".[25] *In 2005, how many of the 59 published studies cited in the APA's list of "Empirical Studies Specifically Related to Lesbian and Gay Parents and Their Children" (pp. 23–45) specifically addressed the outcomes of children from gay fathers?* A closer examination reveals that only eight studies did so.[26] Of these eight studies, four did not include a heterosexual comparison group.[27] In three of the four remaining studies (with heterosexual comparison groups), the outcomes studied were:

(1) "the value of children to. . .fathers" (Bigner and Jacobsen, 1989a, p. 163);
(2) "parenting behaviors of. . .fathers" (Bigner and Jacobsen, 1989b, p. 173);
(3) "problems" and "relationship with child" (Harris and Turner, 1986, pp. 107–8).

The two Bigner and Jacobsen (1989a,b) studies focused on fathers' reports of *fathers'* values and behaviors, not on children's outcomes—illustrating a recurring tendency in the same-sex parenting literature to focus on the parent rather than the child. Harris and Turner (1986) addressed parent–child relationships, but their study's male heterosexual comparison group was composed of two single fathers. Although several studies have examined aspects of gay fathers' lives, none of the studies comparing gay fathers and heterosexual comparison groups referenced in the APA Brief (pp. 23–45) appear to have specifically focused on children's developmental outcomes, with the exception of Sarantakos (1996), a study to which we will later return.

In summary response to question 1 ("How representative and culturally, ethnically, and economically diverse were the gay/lesbian households in the published literature behind the APA Brief?"), we see that in addition to relying primarily on small, non-representative, convenience samples, many studies do not include any minority individuals or families. Further, comparison studies on children of gay fathers are almost non-existent in the 2005 Brief. By their own reports, social researchers examining same-sex parenting have repeatedly selected small, non-representative, homogeneous samples of privileged lesbian mothers to represent all same-sex parents. This pattern across three decades of research raises significant questions regarding lack of representativeness and diversity in the same-sex parenting studies.

2.2. Question 2: how many studies of gay/lesbian parents had no heterosexual comparison group?

Of the 59 publications cited by the APA in the annotated bibliography section entitled "Empirical Studies Specifically Related to Lesbian and Gay Parents and Their Children" (pp. 23–45), 33 included a heterosexual comparison group. In direct response to question 2, 26 of the studies (44.1%) on same-sex parenting did not include a heterosexual comparison group. In well-conducted science, it is important to have a clearly defined comparison group before drawing conclusions regarding differences or the lack thereof. We see that nearly half of the "Empirical Studies Specifically Related to Lesbian and Gay Parents and Their Children" referenced in the APA Brief allowed no basis for comparison between these two groups (see Table 1). To proceed with precision, this fact does not negate the APA claim. It does, however, dilute it considerably as we are left with not 59, but 33, relevant studies with heterosexual comparison groups.

2.3. Question 3: when heterosexual comparison groups were used, what were the more specific characteristics of those groups?

We now turn to a question regarding the nature of comparison samples. Of the 33 published "Empirical Studies Specifically Related to Lesbian and Gay Parents and Their Children" (APA Brief, pp. 23–45) that did directly include a heterosexual

---

[21] Patterson (2000, , p. 1064) (emphasis added).
[22] Patterson (2000, p. 1064).
[23] Patterson (1992, p. 1036).
[24] Patterson (2000, p. 1064).
[25] Demo and Cox (2000, p. 890).
[26] Bailey et al. (1995), Barrett and Tasker (2001), Bigner and Jacobsen (1989a,b), Bozett (1980), Harris and Turner (1986), Miller (1979), Sarantakos (1996).
[27] Bailey et al. (1995), Barrett and Tasker (2001), Bozett (1980), Miller (1979).

Table 2
Brief overview of 15 intact/divorce/step/single family studies.

(N)	Number of reported participants
Probability	Is the study based on a probability sample?
Comp Grp	Is a probability sample used as a comparison group?
Long	Does the study employ measurements across time?
Key	! = Yes; X = No

	(N)	Probability	Comp Grp	Long
Amato (1991)	9643	!	!	!
Aquilino (1994)	4516	!	!	!
Brown (2004)[a]	35,938	!	!	X
Chase-Lansdale et al. (1995)[b]	17,414	!	!	!
Cherlin et al. (1998)[c]	11,759	!	!	!
Ellis et al. (2003)	762	!	!	!
Harper and McLanahan (2004)[d]	2846	!	!	!
Hetherington and Kelly (2002)[e]	1400	!	!	!
Jekielek (1998)	1640	!	!	!
Lichter et al. (2003)[f]	7665	!	!	X
Manning and Lamb (2003)	13,231	!	!	X
McLanahan and Sandefur (1994) (based on four data sets)				
PSID[g]	2900	!	!	!
NLSY[h]	5246	!	!	!
HSBS[i]	10,400	!	!	!
NSFH[j]	13,017[k]	!	!	!
Mitchell et al. (2009)[l]	4663	!	!	!
Nock (1998)[m]	3604	!	!	!
Page and Stevens (2005)[n]	2023	!	!	!
Total	148,667			

[a] National Survey of America's Families (NSAF).
[b] United Kingdom study and sample.
[c] United Kingdom study and sample.
[d] National Longitudinal Survey of Young Men and Women (NLSY).
[e] Virginia Longitudinal Study (VLS).
[f] National Survey of Family Growth (NSFG).
[g] Panel Study of Income Dynamics (PSID).
[h] National Longitudinal Survey of Young Men and Women (NLSY).
[i] The High School and Beyond Study (HSBS).
[j] National Survey of Families and Households (NSFH).
[k] This is the total original sample. The sub-sample is unlisted but is likely smaller.
[l] National Longitudinal Study of Adolescent Health (Add Health).
[m] National Longitudinal Survey of Young Men and Women (NLSY).
[n] Panel Study of Income Dynamics (PSID).

comparison group, *what were the more specific characteristics of the groups that were compared?* The earlier examination and response related to question 1 documented that, by Patterson's reports, "Despite the diversity of gay and lesbian communities...in the United States",[28] the repeatedly selected representatives of same-sex parents have been "small samples [of lesbians] that are predominantly White, well-educated [and] middle-class" (p. 1064).[29]

In spite of homogeneous sampling, there is considerable diversity among gay and lesbian parents. Considerable diversity exists among heterosexual parents as well. Indeed, the opening paragraph of the present article noted recurring differences in several outcomes of societal concern for children in marriage-based intact families compared with children in cohabiting, divorced, step, and single-parent families.[30] Many of the cited findings are based on probability samples of thousands (see Table 2).

Because children in marriage-based intact families have historically fared better than children in cohabiting, divorced, step, or single-parent families on the above outcomes, the question of what "groups" researchers selected to represent heterosexual parents in the same-sex parenting studies becomes critical. A closer examination of the 33 published same-sex parenting studies (APA Brief, pp. 23–45) with comparison groups, listed chronologically, reveals that:

1. Pagelow (1980) used "single mothers" as a comparison group (p. 198).
2. Hoeffer (1981) used "heterosexual single mothers" (p. 537).
3. Kirkpatrick et al. (1981) used "single, heterosexual mothers" (p. 545).
4. Kweskin and Cook (1982) used women from Parents without Partners (p. 969).

---

[28] Patterson (1992, p. 1029).
[29] Patterson (2000, p. 1064).
[30] See Footnotes 2–10 for documentation.

5. Lyons (1983) used "heterosexual single mothers" (p. 232).
6. Golombok et al. (1983) used "single-parent households" (p. 551).
7. Green et al. (1986) used "solo parent heterosexual mothers" (p. 175).
8. Harris and Turner (1986) used 2 "male single parents" and 14 "female single parents" (p. 105).
9. Huggins (1989) used "divorced heterosexual mothers"[31] (p. 123).
10. Tasker and Golombok (1995) used "heterosexual single mothers" (p. 203).
11. Tasker and Golombok (1997) used "single heterosexual mothers" (p. 38).

We see that in selecting *heterosexual* comparison groups for their studies, many same-sex parenting researchers have not used marriage-based, intact families as heterosexual representatives, but have instead used single mothers (see Table 1). Further, Bigner and Jacobsen used 90.9 percent single-father samples in two other studies (1989a, 1989b).[32] In total, in at least 13 of the 33 comparison studies listed in the APA Brief's list of "Empirical Studies" (pp. 23–45) that include heterosexual comparison groups, the researchers explicitly sampled "single parents" as representatives for heterosexual parents. The repeated (and perhaps even modal) selection of single-parent families as a comparison heterosexual-parent group is noteworthy, given that a Child Trends (2002) review has stated that "children in single-parent families are more likely to have problems than are children who live in intact families headed by two biological parents".[33]

Given that at least 13 of the 33 comparison studies listed in the APA Brief's list of "Empirical Studies" (pp. 23–45) used single-parent families as heterosexual comparison groups, what group(s) did the remaining 20 studies use as heterosexual representatives? In closely examining the 20 remaining published comparison group studies, it is difficult to formulate precise reports of the comparison group characteristics, because in many of these studies, the heterosexual comparison groups are referred to as "mothers" or "couples" without appropriate specificity (see Table 1). Were these mothers continuously married—*or* were they single, divorced, remarried, or cohabiting? When couples were used, were they continuously married—*or* remarried or cohabiting? These failures to explicitly and precisely report sample characteristics (e.g., married or cohabiting) are significant in light of Brown's (2004) finding based on her analysis of a data set of 35,938 US children and their parents, that "regardless of economic and parental resources, the outcomes of adolescents (12–17 years old) in cohabiting families...are worse...than those...in *two-biological-parent* married families".[34] Because of the disparities noted by Brown and others, scientific precision requires that we know whether researchers used: (a) single mothers, (b) cohabiting mothers and couples, (c) remarried mothers, or (d) continuously married mothers and couples as heterosexual comparison groups.

Due to the ambiguity of the characteristics of the heterosexual samples in many same-sex parenting studies, let us frame a question that permits a more precise response, namely: *How many of the studies in the APA Brief's "Empirical Studies" section (pp. 23–45) explicitly compare the outcomes of children from intact, marriage-based families with those from same-sex families?* In an *American Psychologist* article published the year after the APA Brief, Herek (2006) referred to a large, national study by McLanahan and Sandefur (1994) "comparing the children of intact heterosexual families with children being raised by a single parent". Herek then emphasized that "this [large scale] research literature does not include studies comparing children raised by two-parent same-sex couples with children raised by two-parent heterosexual couples".[35] Isolated exceptions exist with relatively small samples (as discussed shortly in response to question 4 and as listed in Table 1), but they are rare.

Given what we have seen regarding heterosexual comparison group selection, let us revisit three related claims. First, in 1992, Patterson posited that[36]:

[N]ot a single study has found children of gay and lesbian parents to be disadvantaged in any respect relative to children of heterosexual parents.

Patterson's (2000) claim was similar[37]:

[C]entral results of existing research on lesbian and gay couples and families with children are exceptionally clear.... [The] home environments provided by lesbian and gay parents are just as likely as those provided by heterosexual parents to enable psychosocial growth among family members.

Lastly, and most significantly, we turn to the APA Brief's "Summary of Research Findings on Lesbian and Gay Parenting", also single-authored by Patterson (see p. 5)[38]:

Not a single study has found children of lesbian or gay parents to be disadvantaged in any significant respect relative to children of heterosexual parents.

---

[31] "Four of the 16 [divorced] heterosexual mothers were either remarried or currently living with a heterosexual lover" (p. 127).

[32] "Of the 66 respondents, six were married, 48 were divorced, eight were separated, and four had never been married" (Bigner and Jacobsen (1989a, p. 166). This means the sample was 90.9% single.

[33] Moore et al. (2002); for an extensive review, see Wilcox et al. (2011).

[34] Brown (2004, p. 364) (emphasis added).

[35] Herek (2006, p. 612).

[36] Patterson (1992, p. 1036) (emphasis added).

[37] Patterson (2000, p. 1064) (emphasis added).

[38] Patterson, p. 15 (from APA Brief, 2005), (emphasis added).

In all three of these claims (including that latter from the 2005 APA Brief), Patterson uses the broad and plural term "heterosexual parents", a term that includes marriage-based, intact families. This broad claim is not nuanced by the information that, with rare exceptions, the research does not include studies comparing children raised by two-parent, same-sex couples with children raised by marriage-based, heterosexual couples. Further, no mention is made that in at least 13 of the 33 extant comparison studies referenced in the Brief (pp. 23–45), the groups selected to represent "heterosexual parents" were composed largely, if not solely, of single parents. We now move to another related examination of the APA Brief.

2.4. Question 4: does a scientifically-viable study exist to contradict the conclusion that "not a single study has found children of lesbian or gay parents to be disadvantaged"?

There is at least one notable exception[39] to the APA's claim that "Not a single study has found children of lesbian or gay parents to be disadvantaged in any significant respect relative to children of heterosexual parents".[40] In the "Summary of Findings" section, the APA Brief references a study by Sarantakos (1996),[41] but does so in a footnote that critiques the study (p. 6, Footnote 1). On page 40 of the APA Brief's annotated bibliography, a reference to the Sarantakos (1996) article is offered, but there is no summary of the study's findings, only a note reading "No abstract available".

Upon closer examination, we find that the Sarantakos (1996) study is a comparative analysis of 58 children of heterosexual married parents, 58 children of heterosexual cohabiting couples, and 58 children living with homosexual couples that were all "matched according to socially significant criteria (e.g., age, number of children, education, occupation, and socio-economic status)".[42] The combined sample size (174) is the seventh-largest sample size of the 59 published studies listed in the APA Brief's "Summary of Research Findings on Lesbian and Gay Parenting" (see Table 1). However, the six studies with larger sample sizes were all adult self-report studies,[43] making the Sarantakos combined sample the largest study (APA Brief, pp. 23–45) that examined *children's developmental outcomes.*

Key findings of the Sarantakos study are summarized below. To contextualize these data, the numbers are based on a teacher rating-scale of performance "ranging from 1 (very low performance), through 5 (moderate performance) to 9 (very high performance)".[44] Based on teacher (not parent) reports, Sarantakos found several significant differences between married families and homosexual families.[45]

Language Achievement	Married 7.7, Cohabiting 6.8, Homosexual 5.5
Mathematics Achievement	Married 7.9, Cohabiting 7.0, Homosexual 5.5
Social Studies Achievement	Married 7.3, Cohabiting 7.0, Homosexual 7.6
Sport Interest/Involvement	Married 8.9, Cohabiting 8.3, Homosexual 5.9
Sociability/Popularity	Married 7.5, Cohabiting 6.5, Homosexual 5.0
School/Learning Attitude	Married 7.5, Cohabiting 6.8, Homosexual 6.5
Parent-School Relationships	Married 7.5, Cohabiting 6.0, Homosexual 5.0
Support with Homework	Married 7.0, Cohabiting 6.5, Homosexual 5.5
Parental Aspirations	Married 8.1, Cohabiting 7.4, Homosexual 6.5[a]

[a] Sarantakos, 1996, pp. 24–27.

Sarantakos concluded, "Overall, the study has shown that children of married couples are more likely to do well at school in academic and social terms, than children of cohabiting and homosexual couples".[46]

The APA's decision to de-emphasize the Sarantakos (1996) study was based, in part, on the criticism that "nearly all indicators of the children's functioning were based on subjective reports by *teachers*".[47] The Sarantakos study was based, in part, on teacher reports. However, teacher reports included "tests" and "normal school assessment" (p. 24). Subsequently, it may be

---

[39] Other arguably contradictory studies are reviewed by Schumm (2011).

[40] Patterson, p. 15 (from APA Brief, 2005).

[41] Among the diverse types of gay/lesbian parents there are at least two major categories that warrant scholarly precision: (a) two lesbian or gay parents raising an adopted or DI (donor insemination) child from infancy with these and only these two parents; and (b) two lesbian or gay parents raising a child who is the biological offspring of one of the parents, following a separation or divorce from a heterosexual partner. The Sarantakos sample is of the latter (b) type. In terms of scholarly precision, it is important to differentiate and not draw strong implications from 'a' to 'b' or 'b' to 'a.' Indeed, the author would posit that adopted versus DI children may also warrant separate consideration. The core issue is that precision is essential and overextension of findings should be avoided. This same issue is of serious concern in connection with the tendency to overextend findings regarding lesbian mothers to apply to gay fathers (see Regnerus, this volume).

[42] Sarantakos (1996, p. 23).

[43] In order, these six studies include: (1) Morris et al., 2002 (*N* = 2431), who addressed adults' reports of "coming out"; (2) Johnson and O'Connor (2002) (*N* = 415), who addressed adults' reports of parenting beliefs, division of labor, etc.; (3) Crawford et al. (1999) (*N* = 388), who addressed psychologists' self-reports of gay adoption; (4) King and Black (1999) (*N* = 338), who addressed college students' perceptions of gay parents; (5) Bos et al. (2003) (*N* = 200), who addressed parental motives and desires; and (6) Bos et al. (2004) (*N* = 200), who addressed parental reports of couple relations. These foci are not *children's* outcomes.

[44] Sarantakos (1996, p. 24).

[45] Social Studies Achievement is significant at the $p = .008$ level; the eight other differences are significant at the $p = .000$ level.

[46] Sarantakos (1996, p. 30).

[47] APA Brief (2005), Footnote 1, p. 6 (emphasis added).

argued that Sarantakos' decision *not* to rely solely or extensively on parent reports, as is done in most same-sex parenting studies, is a strength, given parents' tendencies towards bias when reporting on their own children.[48] Sarantakos[49] also drew data from school aptitude tests and observations, thereby modeling a research ideal of *triangulation of sources*.[50] In fact, the study integrated not only three data sources to triangulate; it featured at least four (i.e., teachers, tests, observations, and child reports). Further, the study controlled for "education, occupation, and socio-economic status" and then, based on teacher reports, compared marriage-based families with gay/lesbian families and found nine significant differences—with children from marriage-based families rating higher in eight areas. By objective standards, compared with the studies cited by the APA Brief, the 1996 Sarantakos study was:

(a) *The largest comparison study to examine children's outcomes,*[51]
(b) *One of the most comparative* (only about five other studies used three comparison groups),[52] and
(c) *The most comprehensively triangulated* study (four data sources) conducted on same-sex parenting.[53]

Accordingly, this study deserves the attention of scientists interested in the question of homosexual and heterosexual parenting, rather than the footnote it received.

As we conclude the examination of question 4, let us review a portion of APA's published negation of Sarantakos' (1996) study[54]:

[*Children Australia*, the journal where the article was published] cannot be considered a source upon which one should rely for understanding the state of scientific knowledge in this field, particularly when the results contradict those that have been repeatedly replicated in studies published in better known scientific journals.

For other scientists, however, the salient point behind the Sarantakos findings is that the novel comparison group of marriage-based families introduced significant differences in children's outcomes (as opposed to the recurring "no difference" finding with single-mother and "couple" samples). We now turn to the fifth question.

2.5. Question 5: what types of outcomes have been investigated?

With respect to the APA Brief's claim that "not a single study has found children of lesbian or gay parents to [have] disadvantaged [outcomes]", *what types of outcomes have been examined and investigated*? Specifically, how many of the same-sex parenting studies in Table 1 address the societal concerns of intergenerational poverty, collegiate education and/or labor force contribution, serious criminality, incarceration, early childbearing, drug/alcohol abuse, or suicide that are frequently the foci of national studies on children, adolescents, and young adults, as discussed at the outset of this paper?

Anderssen and colleagues cataloged the foci of same-sex parenting studies in a 2002 review and reported[55]:

Emotional functioning was the most often studied outcome (12 studies), followed by sexual preference (nine studies), gender role behavior (eight studies), behavioral adjustment (seven studies), gender identity (six studies), and cognitive functioning (three studies).

Examination of the articles cited in the 2005 APA Brief on Lesbian and Gay Parenting yields a list of studied outcomes that are consistent with Anderssen's summary, including: "sexual orientation"[56]; "behavioral adjustment, self-concepts, and sex-role identity"[57]; "sexual identity"[58]; "sex-role behavior"[59]; "self-esteem"[60]; "psychosexual and psychiatric appraisal"[61]; "socioemotional development"[62]; and "maternal mental health and child adjustment".[63]

---

[48] It is well replicated that individuals tend to rate the group with which they most identify more positively than they do other groups. This positive bias includes within-family ratings Roese and Olson (2007).

[49] Sarantakos is the author of several research methods textbooks (2005, 2007b) and the author/editor of a four-volume, 1672-page work in Sage Publications' Benchmarks in Social Research Series (2007a).

[50] "Triangulation is a means of checking the integrity of the inferences one draws. It can involve the use of multiple data sources, …multiple theoretical perspectives, multiple methods, or all of these" (Schwandt, 2001, p. 257). In effect, the standard of triangulation is advocacy for checks and balances.

[51] Six of the 59 studies listed in the 2005 APA Brief (pp. 23–45) had larger samples, but, as discussed earlier, they all focused on adult reports of adult perceptions and outcomes.

[52] For example, Brewaeys et al. (1997), Golombok et al. (2003, 1997), MacCallum and Golombok (2004), and Tasker and Golombok (1998).

[53] In spite of the strong design with respect to triangulation, the Sarantakos study does not appear to be based on a true probability sample, nor is it or a *large* sample (although it is a subsample of a 900-plus study). The study is rigorous by comparison to other same-sex parenting studies, but is limited compared with most of the nationally representative studies on intact families listed in Table 2.

[54] Patterson (2005) in APA Brief, p. 7, Footnote 1.

[55] Anderssen et al. (2002, p. 343).

[56] Bailey et al. (1995) and Golombok and Tasker (1996).

[57] Patterson (1994).

[58] Green (1978).

[59] Hoeffer (1981) and Kweskin and Cook (1982).

[60] Huggins (1989).

[61] Golombok et al. (1983).

[62] Golombok et al. (1997).

[63] Patterson (2001).

With these focal outcomes identified, it is noteworthy that all of the aforementioned outcomes of societal-level concern are absent from the list of "most often studied outcome(s)" as identified by Anderssen et al.[64] In response to the present article's question 5 (what *types* of outcomes have been investigated for children of gay/lesbian families?), it may be concluded: In the same-sex parenting research that undergirded the 2005 APA Brief, it appears that gender-related outcomes were the dominant research concern. To be more precise, Table 1 lists several categories of information regarding the 59 published empirical studies; one of these categories is the "outcome studied". More than 20 studies have examined gender-related outcomes, but there was a dearth of peer-reviewed journal articles from which to form science-based conclusions in myriad areas of societal concern.[65]

One book-length empirical study[66] entitled *Same-Sex Couples* (Sarantakos, 2000, Harvard Press) did examine several issues of societal concern. In connection with the questions raised in the present article, this study:

(1) includes a diverse sample of lesbian *and gay* parents instead of focusing on privileged lesbian mothers (question 1);
(2) uses not only one but two heterosexual comparison samples; one married parent sample and one cohabitating parent sample (questions 2 and 3);
(3) examines several outcomes of societal concern (question 5); and
(4) is unique in presenting long-term (post-18 years old) outcomes of children with lesbian and gay parents (question 6, addressed later).

This study's conclusion regarding outcomes of gay and lesbian parents reads, in part:

If we perceive deviance in a general sense, to include excessive drinking, drug use, truancy, sexual deviance, and criminal offenses, and if we rely on the statements made by adult children (over 18 years of age)…[then] children of homosexual parents report deviance in higher proportions than children of (married or cohabiting) heterosexual couples (Sarantakos, 2000, p. 131).

The 2005 APA Brief does not cite this study, again leaving us to more closely examine the claim that "Not a single study has found children of lesbian or gay parents to be disadvantaged in any significant respect relative to children of heterosexual parents" (p. 15).

The Sarantakos (2000) study also includes the report that "the number of children who were labeled by their parents as gay, or identified themselves as gay, is much higher than the generally expected proportion" (p. 133). However, the study also notes areas of no significant heterosexual–homosexual differences (i.e., "Physical and emotional well-being", p. 130), consistent with the 2005 APA Brief's claims. All of these findings warranted attention in the 2005 APA Brief but were overlooked. Of most interest to us here, however, is the novel attention of Sarantakos (2000) on multiple concerns of societal importance, including drug and alcohol abuse, education (truancy), sexual activity, and criminality.

In any less-developed area of empirical inquiry it takes time, often several decades, before many of the central and most relevant questions can be adequately addressed. This seems to be the case with same-sex parenting outcomes, as several issues of societal concern were almost entirely unaddressed in the 2005 APA Brief.

2.6. Question 6: what do we know about the long-term outcomes of children of lesbian and gay parents?

In the preceding response to question 5, the outcomes of intergenerational poverty, criminality, college education and/or labor force contribution, drug/alcohol abuse, suicide, early sexual activity, early childbearing, and eventual divorce as adults were mentioned. Close consideration reveals that the majority of these outcomes are not "child" outcomes. Indeed, most of these outcomes are not optimally observable until (at the earliest) mid-late adolescence or early adulthood (and in the case of divorce, not until middle adulthood). As discussed in question 5, virtually none of the peer-reviewed, same-sex parenting comparison studies addressed these outcomes.[67]

Additionally, of the 59 published studies cited by the APA 2005 Brief (pp. 23–45), it is difficult to find comparison studies of any kind that examine late adolescent outcomes of any kind. The few that utilize comparison groups have comparison groups of 44 or fewer.[68] Let us further explore the importance of a lack of data centered on adolescents and young adults.

Table 2 identifies 15 of the hundreds of available studies on outcomes of children from intact families (as contrasted with comparison groups such as cohabiting couples and single parents). One of these studies included a data set of 35,938 children—one of "the largest…nationally representative survey[s] of US children and their parents".[69] Based on analysis of this

---

[64] Anderssen et al. (2002, p. 343).

[65] Including: intergenerational poverty, criminality, college education and/or labor force contribution, drug/alcohol abuse, suicide, sexual activity and early childbearing, and eventual divorce.

[66] This study is a later, larger, and more detailed report on the earlier mentioned Sarantakos (1996) study. The sample of that study was larger than the other comparison samples in Table 1.

[67] Gartrell and colleagues (1999, 2000, 2005) have commenced to do so, but in 2005 they were reporting on children who were only 10 years old (with a sample size of 74 and no heterosexual comparison group).

[68] I.e. Wainwright et al. (2004).

[69] Brown (2004), p. 355.

nationally representative sample, Susan Brown emphasized, "The findings of this study...demonstrate the importance of separately examining children and adolescents". She then explained[70]:

> Although the outcomes of children (6–11 years old) in cohabiting families...are worse...than those of children in two-biological-parent married families, much of this difference...is economic.... In contrast, regardless of economic and parental resources, the outcomes of adolescents (12–17 years old) in cohabiting families...are worse...than those...in two-biological-parent married families.

In short, in the case of cohabiting families and "two-biological-parent married families" the differences in children's outcomes *increase in significance as the children grow older*. The likelihood of significant differences arising between children from same-sex and married families may also increase across time—not just into adolescence but into early and middle adulthood. For example, research indicates that "[d]aughters raised outside of intact marriages are...more likely to end up young, unwed mothers than are children whose parents married and stayed married", and that "[p]arental divorce increases the odds that adult children will also divorce".[71]

Longitudinal studies that follow children across time and into adulthood to examine such outcomes are comparatively rare and valuable. We briefly turn to a key finding from one such study that followed children of divorce into middle adulthood. Based on a 25-year longitudinal study, Wallerstein and colleagues (2001) state:

> Contrary to what we have long thought, the major impact of divorce does not occur during childhood or adolescence. Rather, it rises in adulthood as serious romantic relationships move center stage. When it comes time to choose a life mate and build a new family, the effects of divorce crescendo (p. xxix).

Wallerstein's research, like nearly all of the studies in the same-sex parenting literature, is based on a small, non-representative sample that should not be generalized or overextended. Her longitudinal work does, however, indicate that "effects [can] crescendo" in adulthood. Did any published same-sex parenting study cited by the 2005 APA Brief (pp. 23–45) track the societally significant long-term outcomes into adulthood? No. Is it possible that "the major impact" of same-sex parenting might "not occur during childhood or adolescence...[but that it will rise] in adulthood as serious romantic relationships move center stage"? Is it also possible that "when it comes time to choose a life mate and build a new family" that the effects of same-sex parenting will similarly "crescendo" as they did in Wallerstein's study of divorce effects? In response to this or any question regarding the long-term, adult outcomes of lesbian and gay parenting we have almost no empirical basis for responding. An exception is provided by the findings from self-reports of adult "children" (18 + years of age) in Sarantakos' (2000) book-length study, but those results not encouraging. This is a single study however—a study that, like those cited by the APA Brief, lacks the statistical power and rigor of the large, random, representative samples used in marriage-based family studies (see Table 2). We now move to a final related empirical question regarding the same-sex parenting literature.

2.7. Question 7: have the studies in this area committed the type II error and prematurely concluded that heterosexual couples and gay and lesbian couples produce parental outcomes with no differences?

The Summary of Research Findings in the APA brief reads, "As is true in any area of research, questions have been raised with regard to sampling issues, statistical power, and other technical matters" (p. 5). However, neither statistical power nor the related concern of Type II error is further explained or addressed. This will be done next.

In social science research, questions are typically framed as follows: "Are we 95% sure the two groups being compared are different?" ($p < .05$). If our statistics seem to confirm a difference with 95% or greater confidence, then we say the two groups are "significantly different". But what if, after statistical analysis, we are only 85% sure that the two groups are different? By the rules of standard social science, we would be obligated to say we were unable to satisfactorily conclude that the two groups are different. However, a reported finding of "no statistically significant difference" (at the $p < .05$ level; 95%-plus certainty) is a grossly inadequate basis upon which to offer the science-based claim that the groups were conclusively "the same". In research, incorrectly concluding that there is no difference between groups when there is in fact a difference is referred to as a Type II error. A Type II error is more likely when undue amounts of random variation are present in a study. Specifically, small sample size, unreliable measures, imprecise research methodology, or unaccounted for variables can all increase the likelihood of a Type II error. All one would have to do to be able to come to a conclusion of "no difference" is to conduct a study with a small sample and/or sufficient levels of random variation. These weaknesses compromise a study's "statistical power" (Cohen, 1988).

It must be re-emphasized that a conclusion of "no significant difference" means that it is unknown whether or not a difference exists on the variable(s) in question (Cohen, 1988). This conclusion does not necessarily mean that the two groups are, in fact, the same on the variable being studied, much less on all other characteristics. This point is important with same-sex parenting research because Patterson (1992, 2000) and the 2005 APA Brief seem to draw inferences of sameness based on the observation that gay and lesbian parents and heterosexual parents appear not to be statistically different from one another based on small, non-representative samples—thereby becoming vulnerable to a classic Type II error.

---

[70] Brown (2004), p. 364.
[71] Wilcox et al. (2011), p. 11.

To make the APA Brief's proposition of sameness more precarious, in a review published one year after the APA Brief in the flagship APA journal, *American Psychologist*, Herek (2006) acknowledged that many same-sex parenting studies have "utilized small, select convenience samples and often employed unstandardized measures".[72] Anderssen et al. (2002) similarly indicated in their review of same-sex parenting studies, "The samples were most often small, increasing the chance to conclude that no differences exist between groups when in fact the differences do exist. This casts doubt on the external validity of the studies".[73] With these limitations noted, the 2005 APA Brief explicitly claimed that findings of non-significant differences between same-sex and heterosexual parents had been "repeatedly replicated" (p. 7, Footnote 1).

Reasons for skepticism regarding the APA Brief's claim that findings have been "repeatedly replicated" rest in Neuman's (1997) point that "the logic of replication implies that different researchers are unlikely to make the same errors".[74] However, if errors (e.g., similarly biased sampling approaches employing "small, select convenience samples"[75] and comparison groups) are repeated by different researchers, the logic behind replication is undermined. As has been previously detailed in the response to question 1 in this article, same-sex parenting researchers have repeatedly selected White, well-educated, middle- and upper-class lesbians to represent same-sex parents. This tendency recurred even after this bias was explicitly identified by Patterson (1992, 2000).[76] Further, repeated sampling tendencies in connection with heterosexual comparison groups (e.g., single mothers), were documented in response to Question 3 in this paper. These repeated (convenience) sampling tendencies across studies that employed different measures do not seem to constitute valid scientific replication.

An additional scientific question raised by the above information regarding "small, select convenience"[77] samples is framed by Stacey and Biblarz (2001) who reveal that "many of these [comparative same-sex parenting] studies use conventional levels of significance…on miniscule samples, substantially increasing their likelihood of failing to reject the null hypothesis".[78] Was the APA's claim that "Not a single study has found children of lesbian or gay parents to be disadvantaged…"[79] based on clear scientific evidence or (perhaps) Type II errors? In response, we now turn to the APA-acknowledged but unexplained critique of low "statistical power" in these studies (p. 5).

The last three editions of the APA Publication manual (1994, 2001, 2010) have urged scholars to report effect sizes and to take statistical power into consideration when reporting their results. The APA 5th Publication manual (2001) in use at the time of APA's 2005 Brief on Lesbian and Gay Parenting stated:

> Take seriously the statistical power considerations associated with your tests of hypotheses. Such considerations relate to the likelihood of correctly rejecting the tested hypotheses, given a particular alpha level, effect size, and sample size. In that regard, you should routinely provide evidence that your study has power to detect effects of substantive interest (e.g., see Cohen, 1988). You should be similarly aware of the role played by sample size in cases in which not rejecting the null hypothesis is desirable (i.e., when you wish to argue that there are no differences [between two groups])… (p. 24).

This awareness of statistical power in cases "when you wish to argue that there are no differences" bears directly on same-sex comparative research. The APA 5th Publication manual (2001) continues:

> Neither of the two types of probability [alpha level or *p* value] directly reflects the magnitude of an effect or the strength of a relationship. For the reader to fully understand the importance of your findings, it is almost always necessary to include some index of effect size or strength of relationship in your Results section (p. 25).

Let us review three statements from the *APA 5th Publication Manual* for emphasis:

(1) The APA urges researchers to: "Take seriously the statistical power considerations" and "routinely provide evidence" (p. 24).
(2) The APA identifies a specific concern with sample size and statistical power in connection with cases where authors "wish to argue that there are no differences" between compared groups (p. 24).
(3) The APA concludes: "It is almost always necessary to include some index of effect size or strength of relationship in your Results section" (p. 25).

The APA's first highlighted exhortation is that an author "should routinely provide evidence that your study has sufficient power…(e.g., see Cohen, 1988)" (p. 24). The reference cited here by the APA is the volume *Statistical Power Analysis for the Behavioral Sciences* (2nd ed.) by the late psychometrician Jacob Cohen, who has been credited with foundational work in statistical meta-analysis (Borenstein, 1999). In his APA-cited volume, Cohen states:

---

[72] Herek (2006), p. 612.
[73] Anderssen et al. (2002), p. 348.
[74] Neuman (1997), p. 150.
[75] Herek (2006), p. 612.
[76] Further, single mothers have been repeatedly selected to represent heterosexual parents as documented in this paper's response to question 3.
[77] Herek (2006), p. 612.
[78] Stacey and Biblarz (2001, p. 168), Footnote 9.
[79] Patterson, p. 15 (from APA Brief, 2005).

Most psychologists of whatever stripe believe that samples, even small samples, mirror the characteristics of their parent populations. In effect, they operate on the unstated premise that the law of large numbers holds for small numbers as well.... [Citing Tversky and Kahneman] "The believer in the law of small numbers has incorrect intuitions about significance level, power, and confidence intervals. Significance levels are usually computed and reported, but power and confidence levels are not. Perhaps they should be".

But as we have seen, too many of our colleagues have not responded to [this] admonition.... They do so at their peril (p. xv).

Let us contextualize "the law of small numbers" with respect to the same-sex parenting studies cited in the APA Brief. The combined non-representative sample total of all 59 same-sex parenting studies in the 2005 APA Brief (pp. 23–45) is 7800[80] (see Table 1). By comparison, Table 2 lists 15 prominent studies that contrast children's outcomes in intact, single-parent, divorced, and/or step-family forms using large probability samples and comparison groups.[81] The average sample size in these studies is 9911[82]—a figure larger than all 59 same-sex parenting studies combined (7800).

We now turn to another question relating to Cohen's statements: How many of the published same-sex parenting studies with a heterosexual comparison group cited in APA's Brief (pp. 23–45) "provide[d] evidence" of statistical power, consistent with *APA's Publication Manual* and the "admonition" of Jacob Cohen who is cited in the APA manual? An examination of the studies indicates that only four of the 59 did so.[83]

In addition to Cohen's (1988) statement that statistical power is ignored at our own peril, he offered several tables in his volume for researchers to reference. Employing these tables, statistical experts Lerner and Nagai (2001) computed the sample sizes required for "a power level of .80, or a Type II error rate of .20, or one in five findings" (p. 102). At this power level, the minimum number of cases required to detect a small effect size[84] is 393 for a T-test or ANOVA, or 780-plus for Chi-Square or Pearson Correlation Coefficient tests.[85] In Table 1 of this report, the 59 published same-sex parenting studies cited in the APA Brief (pp. 23–45) are compared against these standards. A close examination indicates that not a single study, including the few that reported power, meets the standards needed to detect a small effect size. Indeed, it appears that only two of the comparison studies (Bos et al., 2003, 2004) have combined sample sizes of even half of "the minimum number of cases".[86]

In their book-length examination of same-sex parenting studies, Lerner and Nagai (2001) further indicate that 17 of the 22 same-sex parenting comparison studies they reviewed had been designed in such a way that the odds of failing to find a significant difference [between homo- and hetero-sexual groups] was 85% or higher.[87] Indeed, only one of the 22 studies they analyzed revealed a probability of Type II error below 77 percent, and that study *did* find differences.[88] These methodological concerns (and others) were raised and explained in Lerner and Nagai's monograph (see pp. 95–108), and in an 81-page report by Nock (2001) preceding the APA Brief.[89] Nock concluded:

All of the [same-sex parenting] articles I reviewed contained at least one fatal flaw of design or execution. Not a single one was conducted according to generally accepted standards of scientific research.... [I]n my opinion, the only acceptable conclusion at this point is that the literature on this topic does not constitute a solid body of scientific evidence (Nock, 2001, pp. 39, 47).

---

[80] This figure (7800) includes same-sex parents and their children, as well as heterosexual comparison samples (1404), psychologists (388), and college students' perception reports (489).

[81] Table 2 lists 15 studies that contrast children's outcomes in intact families compared with other family forms using large, probability samples and comparison groups. The focal topics of these studies are not "sexual preference, gender role behavior...[and] gender identity" (Anderssen et al., 2002, p. 343), but outcomes such as "educational attainment", "labor force attachment", and "early childbearing" (McLanahan and Sandefur, 1994, pp. 20–21), as recommended in the earlier examination of question 5. Further, all but two of the 15 studies employ longitudinal designs, as recommended in the earlier examination of question 6.

[82] This figure is the result of 148,667 divided by 15 studies.

[83] These include Chan et al. (1998b), Fulcher et al. (2002), Golombok and Tasker (1996), and Tasker and Golombok (1997).

[84] By way of context, in a 67 study meta-analysis of the average differences in outcomes between children with "divorced and continuously married parents", Amato (2001) reported an average weighted effect size of between −0.12 and −0.22 (a −0.17 average) with an advantage in all five domains considered to children of continuously married parents (p. 360). These effect sizes of about .20, although statistically robust, would be classified by Cohen (1992) as small effect sizes. Even so, based on the data, most family scholars would agree that children whose parents remain continuously married tend to fare slightly to moderately better than when parents divorce. However, large numbers were needed to determine this "small" but important effect. Indeed, most effect sizes in social science research tend to be small. Rigorous and sound social science tends to include and account for many influential factors that each has a small but meaningful effect size. In social science, detecting a novel "large effect" from a single variable (whether it is divorce, remarriage, or same-sex parenting), is a comparatively rare occurrence. If we are to examine possible effects of same-sex parenting with scientific precision and rigor, related examinations would, like Amato's work, be designed and refined to detect "small effect" sizes.

[85] Cohen (1988) proposes a "relatively high power" of .90 for cases where one is trying to "demonstrate the r [difference] is trivially small" (p. 104). If the .90 power were applied, the required sample sizes would further increase. However, because none of the studies in Table 1 of the present report approach the .80 power levels, .90 calculations are unnecessary here.

[86] The "minimum number of cases" is 393. The two Bos et al. studies both have combined samples of 200. Four other larger samples are not comparison studies Crawford et al. (1999), Johnson and O'Connor (2002), King and Black (1999), and Morris et al. (2002).

[87] Lerner and Nagai (2001, p. 103).

[88] The single exception was Cameron and Cameron (1996) with a comparatively low probability error rate of 25%. This study, like the Sarantakos (1996) study mentioned earlier, did report some significant differences between children of heterosexual and homosexual parents but, like Sarantakos (1996), was not addressed in the body of the 2005 APA brief but was instead moved to a footnote on p. 7. See Redding (2008) for additional discussion (p. 137).

[89] For similar critiques preceding the 2005 APA brief, seeNock (2001), Schumm (2004), Wardle (1997), and Williams (2000). For similar critiques post-dating the 2005 APA brief, see Byrd (2008), Schumm (2010a,b, 2011), and Redding (2008, p. 138).

More specifically, Nock identified: (a) several flaws related to sampling (including biased sampling, non-probability sampling, convenience sampling, etc.); (b) poorly operationalized definitions; (c) researcher bias; (d) lack of longitudinal studies; (e) failure to report reliability; (f) low response rates; and (g) lack of statistical power (pp. 39–40).[90] Although some of these flaws are briefly mentioned in the 2005 APA Summary of Research Findings on Lesbian and Gay Parenting, many of the significant concerns raised by Nock or Lerner and Nagai are not substantively addressed.[91] Indeed, the Lerner and Nagai volume and the Nock report are neither mentioned nor referenced.

To restate, in connection with the APA's published urging that researchers: "Take seriously the statistical power considerations" and "routinely provide evidence", the academic reader is left at a disadvantage.[92] Only a few comparison studies specifically reported statistical power at all and no comparison study approached the minimum sample size of 393 needed to find a small effect.

The author's response to question 7 has examined how comparisons have been made from a research methods standpoint. In summary, some same-sex parenting researchers have acknowledged that "miniscule samples"[93] significantly increase "the chance to conclude that no differences exist between groups when in fact the differences do exist"—thereby casting "doubt on the external validity of the studies".[94] An additional concern is that the APA Brief's claim of "repeatedly replicated" findings of no significant difference rested almost entirely on studies that were published without reports of the APA-urged effect sizes and statistical power analyses.[95] This inconsistency seems to justify scientific skepticism, as well as the effort of more closely assessing the balance, precision, and rigor behind the conclusions posed in the 2005 APA Brief.

3. Conclusion

The 2005 APA Brief, near its outset, claims that "even taking into account all the questions and/or limitations that may characterize research in this area, none of the published research suggests conclusions different from that which will be summarized" (p. 5). The concluding summary later claims, "Indeed, the evidence to date suggests that home environments provided by lesbian and gay parents are as likely as those provided by heterosexual parents to support and enable children's psychosocial growth" (p. 15).[96]

We now return to the overarching question of this paper: Are we witnessing the emergence of a new family form that provides a context for children that is equivalent to the traditional marriage-based family? Even after an extensive reading of the same-sex parenting literature, the author cannot offer a high confidence, data-based "yes" or "no" response to this question. To restate, not one of the 59 studies referenced in the 2005 APA Brief (pp. 23–45; see Table 1) compares a large, random, representative sample of lesbian or gay parents and their children with a large, random, representative sample of married parents and their children. The available data, which are drawn primarily from small convenience samples, are insufficient to support a strong generalizable claim either way. Such a statement would not be grounded in science. To make a generalizable claim, representative, large-sample studies are needed—many of them (e.g., Table 2).

Some opponents of same-sex parenting have made "egregious overstatements"[97] disparaging gay and lesbian parents. Conversely, some same-sex parenting researchers seem to have contended for an "exceptionally clear"[98] verdict of "no difference" between same-sex and heterosexual parents since 1992. However, a closer examination leads to the conclusion that strong, generalized assertions, including those made by the APA Brief, were not empirically warranted.[99] As noted by Shiller (2007) in *American Psychologist*, "the line between science and advocacy appears blurred" (p. 712).

The scientific conclusions in this domain will increase in validity as researchers: (a) move from small convenience samples to large representative samples; (b) increasingly examine critical societal and economic concerns that emerge during adolescence and adulthood; (c) include more diverse same-sex families (e.g., gay fathers, racial minorities, and those without middle-high socioeconomic status); (d) include intact, marriage-based heterosexual families as comparison groups; and (e)

---

[90] Four of these seven issues are addressed in the present paper. The exceptions include researcher bias, failure to report reliability, and low response rates.

[91] The 2005 APA Brief's Summary on Research Findings acknowledges criticisms of same-sex parenting research including: (a) non-representative sampling, (b) "poorly matched or no control groups", (c) "well-educated, middle class [lesbian] families", and (d) "relatively small samples" (p. 5). The respective responses to these criticisms in the APA brief are: (a) "contemporary research on children of lesbian and gay parents involves a wider array of sampling techniques than did earlier studies"; (b) "contemporary research on children of lesbian and gay parents involves a wider array of research designs (and hence, control groups) than did earlier studies"; (c) "contemporary research on children of lesbian and gay parents involves a greater diversity of families than did earlier studies"; and (d) "contemporary research has benefited from such criticisms" (p. 5). The APA Brief does not challenge the validity of these research criticisms but notes that improvements are being made.

[92] See Schumm (2010b) for more comprehensive, article-length treatment of these statistical issues.

[93] Stacey and Biblarz (2001, p. 168).

[94] Anderssen et al. (2002, p. 348).

[95] Schumm (2010b).

[96] The APA Brief also states that "the existing data are still limited, and any conclusions must be seen as tentative". Also, that "it should be acknowledged that research on lesbian and gay parents and their children, though no longer new, is still limited in extent" (p. 15). For some scientists, these salient points seem to be overridden by the APA Brief's conclusions.

[97] This reality has been disapprovingly documented by Shiller (2007).

[98] Patterson (1992).

[99] In 2006, the year following APA's release of the brief on Lesbian and Gay Parenting, "former APA president Nicholas Cummings argued that there has been significant erosion" of the APA's established principle (Shiller (2007), p. 712)...that "when we speak as psychologists we speak from research evidence and clinical experience and expertise" (Cummings (2006), p. 2).

constructively respond to criticisms from methodological experts.[100] Specifically, it is vital that critiques regarding sample size, sampling strategy, statistical power, and effect sizes not be disregarded. Taking these steps will help produce more methodologically rigorous and scientifically informed responses to significant questions affecting families and children.

References

Akerlof, G., 1998. Men without children. Economic Journal 108, 287–309.

Amato, P., 1991. Parental absence during childhood and depression in later life. Sociological Quarterly 32, 543–556.

Amato, P., 2001. Children of divorce in the 1990s: an update of the Amoato and Keith (1991) meta-analysis. Journal of Family Psychology 15, 355–370.

Amato, P., 2005. The impact of family formation change on the cognitive, social, and emotional well-being of the next generation. The Future of Children 15, 75–96.

Amato, P., Booth, A., 2000. A Generation at Risk: Growing Up in an Era of Family Upheaval. Harvard University Press, Cambridge, MA.

Anderssen, N., Amlie, C., Ytteroy, E.A., 2002. Outcomes for children with lesbian or gay parents: a review of studies from 1978 to 2000. Scandinavian Journal of Psychology 43, 335–351.

Publication manual of the American Psychological Association (forth ed.), 1994. APA, Washington, DC.

Publication manual of the American Psychological Association (fifth ed.), 2001. APA, Washington, DC.

Publication manual of the American Psychological Association (sixth ed.), 2010. APA, Washington, DC.

Aquilino, W.S., 1994. Impact of childhood family disruption on young adults' relationships with parents. Journal of Marriage and the Family 56, 295–313.

Bachman, J.G. et al, 1997. Smoking, Drinking and Drug Abuse in Young Adulthood. Erlbaum, Mahwah, NJ.

Bailey, J.M., Bobrow, D., Wolfe, M., Mikach, S., 1995. Sexual orientation of adult sons of gay fathers. Developmental Psychology 31, 124–129.

Barrett, H., Tasker, F., 2001. Growing up with a gay parent: views of 101 gay fathers on their sons' and daughters' experiences. Educational and Child Psychology 18, 62–77.

Battle, J., 1998. What beats having two parents?: educational outcomes for African–American students in single- versus dual-parent families. Journal of Black Studies 28, 783–801.

Bigner, J.J., Jacobsen, R.B., 1989a. The value of children to gay and heterosexual fathers. Journal of Homosexuality 19, 163–172.

Bigner, J.J., Jacobsen, R.B., 1989b. Parenting behaviors of homosexual and heterosexual fathers. Journal of Homosexuality 19, 173–186.

Blackmon, L., Clayton, O., Glenn, N., Malone-Colon, L., Roberts, A., 2005. The Consequences of Marriage for African Americans: A Comprehensive Literature Review. Institute for American Values, New York.

Borenstein, M., 1999. Jacob Cohen, PhD, 1923–1998. Archives of General Psychiatry 56, 581.

Bos, H.M.W., van Balen, F., van den Boom, D.C., 2003. Planned lesbian families: their desire and motivation to have children. Human Reproduction 10, 2216–2224.

Bos, H.M.W., van Balen, F., van den Boom, D.C., 2004. Experience of parenthood, couple relationship, social support, and child-rearing goals in planned lesbian mother families. Journal of Child Psychology and Psychiatry 45, 755–764.

Bozett, F.W., 1980. Gay fathers: how and why they disclose their homosexuality to their children. Family Relations 29, 173–179.

Brewaeys, A., Ponjaert, I., Van Hall, E.V., Golombok, S., 1997. Donor insemination: child development and family functioning in lesbian mother families. Human Reproduction 12, 1349–1359.

Brown, S.L., 2004. Family structure and child well-being: the significance of parental cohabitation. Journal of Marriage and Family 66, 351–367.

Byrd, A.D., 2008. Conjugal marriage fosters healthy human and societal development. In: Wardle, L. (Ed.), What's the Harm? Does Legalizing Same-Sex Marriage Really Harm Individuals, Families or Society? University Press, Lanham, MD, pp. 3–26.

Cameron, P., Cameron, K., 1996. Homosexual parents. Adolescence 31, 757–776.

Chan, R.W., Brooks, R.C., Raboy, B., Patterson, C.J., 1998a. Division of labor among lesbian and heterosexual parents: associations with children's adjustment. Journal of Family Psychology 12, 402–419.

Chan, R.W., Raboy, B., Patterson, C.J., 1998b. Psychosocial adjustment among children conceived via donor insemination by lesbian and heterosexual mothers. Child Development 69, 443–457.

Chase-Lansdale, P.L., Cherlin, A.J., Kiernan, K.K., 1995. The long-term effects of parental divorce on the mental health of young adults: a developmental perspective. Child Development 66, 1614–1634.

Cherlin, A.J. et al, 1995. Parental divorce in childhood and demographic outcomes in young adulthood. Demography 32, 299–318.

Cherlin, A.J., Chase-Lansdale, P.L., McRae, C., 1998. Effects of parental divorce on mental health throughout the life course. American Sociological Review 63, 239–249.

Ciano-Boyce, C., Shelley-Sireci, L., 2002. Who is mommy tonight? Lesbian parenting issues. Journal of Homosexuality 43, 1–13.

Cohen, J., 1988. Statistical Power Analysis for the Behavioral Sciences, second ed. Erlbaum, Hillsdale, NJ.

Cohen, J., 1992. A power primer. Psychological Bulletin 112, 155–159.

Crawford, I., McLeod, A., Zamboni, B.D., Jordan, M.B., 1999. Psychologists' attitudes toward gay and lesbian parenting. Professional Psychology: Research and Practice 30, 394–401.

Cummings, N.A., 2006. The APA and psychology need reform. Paper presented at the annual convention of the American Psychological Association (August 12). New Orleans, LA.

Cutler, D.M. et al., 2000. Explaining the rise in youth suicide. Working Paper 7713. National Bureau of Economic Research, Cambridge.

Demo, D.H., Cox, M.J., 2000. Families with young children: a review of research in the 1990s. Journal of Marriage and the Family 62, 876–895.

Ellis, B.J. et al, 2003. Does father absence place daughters at special risk for early sexual activity and teenage pregnancy? Child Development 74, 801–821.

Flaks, D., Fisher, I., Masterpasqua, F., Joseph, G., 1995. Lesbians choosing motherhood: a comparative study of lesbian and heterosexual parents and their children. Developmental Psychology 31, 104–114.

Flewelling, R.L., Bauman, K.E., 1990. Family structure as a predictor of initial substance use and sexual intercourse in early adolescence. Journal of Marriage and the Family 52, 171–181.

Fulcher, M., Chan, R.W., Raboy, B., Patterson, C.J., 2002. Contact with grandparents among children conceived via donor insemination by lesbian and heterosexual mothers. Parenting: Science and Practice 2, 61–76.

Gartrell, N., Hamilton, J., Banks, A., Mosbacher, D., Reed, N., Sparks, C.H., Bishop, H., 1996. The national lesbian family study: 1. Interviews with prospective mothers. American Journal of Orthopsychiatry 66, 272–281.

Gartrell, N., Banks, A., Hamilton, J., Reed, N., Bishop, H., Rodas, C., 1999. The national lesbian family study: II. Interviews with mothers of toddlers. American Journal of Orthopsychiatry 69, 362–369.

Gartrell, N., Banks, A., Reed, N., Hamilton, J., Rodas, C., Deck, A., 2000. The national lesbian family study: III. Interviews with mothers of five-year olds. American Journal of Orthopsychiatry 70, 542–548.

Gartrell, N., Deck, A., Rodas, C., Peyser, H., Banks, A., 2005. The national lesbian family study: 4. Interviews with the 10-year old children. American Journal of Orthopsychiatry 75, 518–524.

Gaudino, J.A. et al, 1999. No fathers' names: a risk factor for infant mortality in the state of Georgia. Social Science and Medicine 48, 253–265.

---

[100] At least one such study (Rosenfeld, 2010) has emerged in the years since the 2005 APA brief was issued. This study features a very large sample but has also received criticism (Schumm, 2011).

Gershon, T.D., Tschann, J.M., Jemerin, J.M., 1999. Stigmatization, self-esteem, and coping among the adolescent children of lesbian mothers. Journal of Adolescent Health 24, 437–445.

Glenn, N.D., 1989. What we know, what we say we know: discrepancies between warranted and stated conclusions in the social sciences. In: Eulau, H. (Ed.), Crossroads of Social Science. The ICPSR 25th Anniversary Volume. Agathon Press, New York, pp. 119–140.

Glenn, N.D., 1997. A reconsideration of the effect of no-fault divorce on divorce rates. Journal of Marriage and the Family 59, 1023–1025.

Golombok, S., Rust, J., 1993. The pre-school activities inventory: a standardized assessment of gender role in children. Psychological Assessment 5, 131–136.

Golombok, S., Tasker, F., 1996. Do parents influence the sexual orientation of their children? Findings from a longitudinal study of lesbian families. Developmental Psychology 32, 3–11.

Golombok, S., Spencer, A., Rutter, M., 1983. Children in lesbian and single-parent households: psychosexual and psychiatric appraisal. Journal of Child Psychology and Psychiatry 24, 551–572.

Golombok, S., Tasker, F., Murray, C., 1997. Children raised in fatherless families from infancy: family relationships and the socioemotional development of children of lesbian and single heterosexual mothers. Journal of Child Psychology and Psychiatry 38, 783–791.

Golombok, S., Perry, B., Burston, A., Murray, C., Mooney-Somers, J., Stevens, M., Golding, J., 2003. Children with lesbian parents: a community study. Developmental Psychology 39, 20–33.

Green, R., 1978. Sexual identity of 37 children raised by homosexual or transsexual parents. American Journal of Psychiatry 135, 692–697.

Green, R., Mandel, J.B., Hotvedt, M.E., Gray, J., Smith, L., 1986. Lesbian mothers and their children: a comparison with solo parent heterosexual mothers and their children. Archives of Sexual Behavior 7, 175–181.

Harper, C., McLanahan, S., 2004. Father absence and youth incarceration. Journal of Research on Adolescence 14, 369–397.

Harris, M.B., Turner, P.H., 1986. Gay and lesbian parents. Journal of Homosexuality 12, 101–113.

Heiss, J., 1996. Effects of African American family structure on school attitude and performance. Social Problems 43, 246–267.

Herek, G.M., 2006. Legal recognition of same-sex relationships in the United States: a social science perspective. American Psychologist 61, 607–621.

Hetherington, M., Kelly, J., 2002. For Better or for Worse: Divorce Reconsidered. Norton, New York.

Hoeffer, B., 1981. Children's acquisition of sex-role behavior in lesbian mother families. American Journal of Orthopsychiatry 5, 536–544.

Horwitz, A.V., White, H.R., Howell-White, S., 1996. Becoming married and mental health: a longitudinal study of a cohort of young adults. Journal of Marriage and the Family 58, 895–907.

Huggins, S.L., 1989. A comparative study of self-esteem of adolescent children of divorced lesbian mothers and divorced heterosexual mothers. Journal of Homosexuality 18, 123–135.

Jekielek, S., 1998. Parental conflict, marital disruption, and children's emotional well-being. Social Forces 76, 905–936.

Johnson, S.M., O'Connor, E., 2002. The Gay Baby Boom: The Psychology of Gay Parenthood. NYU Press, New York.

Johnson, R.A. et al, 1996. The Relationship Between Family Structure and Adolescent Substance Abuse. US Dept. of Health and Human Services, Rockville, MD.

Kamark, E.C., Galston, W.A., 1990. Putting Children First: A Progressive Family Policy for the 1990s. Progressive Policy Institute, Washington, DC.

King, B.R., Black, K.N., 1999. College students' perceptual stigmatization of the children of lesbian mothers. American Journal of Orthopsychiatry 69, 220–227.

Kirkpatrick, M., Smith, C., Roy, R., 1981. Lesbian mothers and their children: a comparative survey. American Journal of Orthopsychiatry 51, 545–551.

Koepke, L., Hare, J., Moran, P., 1992. Relationship quality in a sample of lesbian couples with children and child-free lesbian couples. Family Relations 41, 224–229.

Kuhn, T.S., 1970/1996. The Structure of Scientific Revolutions, third ed. University of Chicago Press, Chicago.

Kweskin, S.L., Cook, A.S., 1982. Heterosexual and homosexual mothers' self-described sex-role behavior and ideal sex-role behavior in children. Sex Roles 8, 967–975.

Lansford, J.E., 2009. Parental divorce and children's adjustment. Perspectives on Psychological Science 4, 140–152.

Lerner, R., Nagai, A., 2001. No Basis: What the Studies Don't Tell us About Same-Sex Parenting. Marriage Law Project, Washington, DC.

Lewis, K.G., 1980. Children of lesbians: Their point of view. Social Work, 198–203.

Lichter, D.T., Graefe, D.R., Brown, J.B., 2003. Is marriage a panacea? Union formation among economically disadvantaged unwed mothers. Social Problems 50, 60–86.

Lott-Whitehead, L., Tully, C.T., 1993. The family lives of lesbian mothers. Smith College Studies in Social Work 63, 265–280.

Lyons, T.A., 1983. Lesbian mother's custody fears. Women & Therapy 2, 231–240.

MacCallum, F., Golombok, S., 2004. Children raised in fatherless families from infancy: a follow-up of children of lesbian and single heterosexual mothers at early adolescence. Journal of Child Psychology and Psychiatry 45, 1407–1419.

Manning, W.D., Lamb, K.A., 2003. Adolescent well-being in cohabiting, married, and single-parent families. Journal of Marriage and Family 65, 876–893.

Margolin, L., 1992. Child abuse by mothers' boyfriends: why the overrepresentation? Child Abuse and Neglect 16, 541–551.

McLanahan, S., Sandefur, G., 1994. Growing Up with a Single Parent: What Hurts, What Helps. Harvard University Press, Cambridge, MA.

McLeod, A.C., Crawford, I., Zecheister, J., 1999. Heterosexual Undergraduates' Attitudes Toward Gay Fathers and their Children. Journal of Psychology and Human Sexuality 11, 43–62.

Miller, B., 1979. Gay fathers and their children. Family Coordinator 28, 544–552.

Miller, J.A., Jacobsen, R.B., Bigner, J.J., 1981. The child's home environment for lesbian versus heterosexual mothers: a neglected area of research. Journal of Homosexuality 7, 49–56.

Mitchell, K.S., Booth, A., King, V., 2009. Adolescents with nonresident fathers: are daughters more disadvantaged than sons? Journal of Marriage and Family 71, 650–662.

Moore, M.R., 2008. Gendered power relations among women: a study of household decision making in Black, lesbian step families. American Sociological Review 73, 335–356.

Moore, K.A., Jekielek, S.M., Emig, C.E., 2002. Marriage From a Child's Perspective: How Does Family Structure Affect Children, and What Can We Do About It? Child Trends Research Brief, Washington, DC.

Morris, J.F., Balsam, K.F., Rothblum, E.D., 2002. Lesbian and bisexual mothers and non-mothers: demographics and the coming out process. Journal of Family Psychology 16, 144–156.

Mucklow, B.M., Phelan, G.K., 1979. Lesbian and traditional mothers' responses to adult responses to child behavior and self concept. Psychological Reports 44, 880–882.

Neuman, W.L., 1997. Social Research Methods, third ed. Allyn & Bacon, Boston.

Nock, S.L., 1998. Marriage in Men's Lives. Oxford University Press, New York.

Nock, S., 2001. The Affidavit of Steven Nock, Halpern v. Attorney General of Canada, No. 684/00 (Ont. Sup. Ct. of Justice).

O'Connell, A., 1993. Voices from the heart: the developmental impact of a mother's lesbianism on her adolescent children. Smith College Studies in Social Work 63, 281–299.

Oliver, M.L., Shapiro, T.M., 1997. Black Wealth/White Wealth. Routledge, New York.

Page, M.E., Stevens, A.H., 2005. Understanding racial differences in the economic costs of growing up in a single-parent family. Demography 42, 75–90.

Pagelow, M.D., 1980. Heterosexual and lesbian single mothers: a comparison of problems, coping, and solutions. Journal of Homosexuality 5, 198–204.

Patterson, C.J., 1992. Children of lesbian and gay parents. Child Development 63, 1025–1042.

Patterson, C.J., 1994. Children of the lesbian baby boom: Behavioral adjustment, self-concepts, and sex-role identity. In: Greene, B., Herek, G. (Eds.), Contemporary Perspectives on Lesbian and Gay Psychology: Theory, Research, and Application. Sage, Beverly Hills, CA, pp. 156–175.

Patterson, C.J., 1995. Families of the lesbian baby boom: parents' division of labor and children's adjustment. Developmental Psychology 31, 115–123.

Patterson, C.J., 2000. Family relationships of lesbians and gay men. Journal of Marriage and the Family 62, 1052–1069.
Patterson, C.J., 2001. Families of the lesbian baby boom: maternal mental health and child adjustment. Journal of Gay and Lesbian Psychotherapy 4 (3/4), 91–107.
Patterson, C.J., 2005. Lesbian and gay parents and their children: summary of research findings. Lesbian and Gay Parenting: American Psychological Association, pp. 5–22.
Patterson, C.J., Hurst, S., Mason, C., 1998. Families of the lesbian baby boom: children's contacts with grandparents and other adults. American Journal of Orthopsychiatry 68, 390–399.
Phillips, C.P., Asbury, C.A., 1993. Parental divorce/separation and the motivational characteristics and educational aspirations of African American university students. The Journal of Negro Education 62, 204–210.
Rand, C., Graham, D.L.R., Rawlings, E.I., 1982. Psychological health and factors the court seeks to control in lesbian mother custody trials. Journal of Homosexuality 8, 27–39.
Rank, M.R., Hirschl, T.A., 1999. The economic risk of childhood in America: estimating the probability of poverty across the formative years. Journal of Marriage and the Family 61, 1058–1067.
Redding, R., 2008. It's really about sex: same-sex marriage, lesbigay parenting, and the psychology of disgust. Duke Journal of Gender Law & Policy 15, 128–193.
Roese, N.J., Olson, J.M., 2007. Better, stronger, faster self-serving judgment, affect regulation, and the optimal vigilance hypothesis. Perspectives on Psychological Science 2, 124–141.
Rosenfeld, M.J., 2010. Nontraditional families and childhood progress through school. Demography 47, 755–775.
Sarantakos, S., 1996. Children in three contexts: family, education, and social development. Children Australia 21, 23–31.
Sarantakos, S., 2000. Same-Sex Couples. Harvard Press, Sydney.
Sarantakos, S., 2005. Social Research, third ed. Palgrave Macmillan.
Sarantakos, S., 2007a. Data analysis, vol. 4. Sage, Thousand Oaks, CA.
Sarantakos, S., 2007b. Tool Kit for Quantitative Data Analysis. Palgrave Macmillan.
Schumm, W.R., 2004. What was really learned from Tasker and Golombok's (1995) study of lesbian and single parent mothers? Psychological Reports 94, 422–424.
Schumm, W.R., 2010a. Comparative relationship stability of lesbian mother and heterosexual mother families: a review of evidence. Marriage & Family Review 46, 499–509.
Schumm, W.R., 2010b. Statistical requirements for properly investigating a null hypothesis. Psychological Reports 107, 953–971.
Schumm, W.R., 2011. Child outcomes associated with lesbian parenting: Comments on Biblarz and Stacy's 2010 report. Journal of Human Sexuality 3, 35–80.
Schwandt, T., 2001. Dictionary of Qualitative Inquiry. Sage, Thousand Oaks, CA.
Shiller, V.M., 2007. Science and advocacy issues in research on children of gay and lesbian parents. American Psychologist 62, 712–713.
Siegel, C. et al, 1996. Mortality from intentional and unintentional injury among infants of young mothers in Colorado, 1982–1992. Archives of Pediatric and Adolescent Medicine 150, 1077–1083.
Siegenthaler, A.L., Bigner, J.J., 2000. The value of children to lesbian and non-lesbian mothers. Journal of Homosexuality 39, 73–91.
Simon, R.W., 2002. Revisiting the relationships among gender, marital status, and mental health. American Journal of Sociology 107, 1065–1096.
Stacey, J., Biblarz, T.J., 2001. (How) does the sexual orientation of parents matter? American Sociological Review 66, 159–183.
Steckel, A., 1985. Separation-Individuation in Children of Lesbian and Heterosexual Couples. Unpublished doctoral dissertation, The Wright Institute Graduate School, Berkeley, CA.
Steckel, A., 1987. Psychosocial development of children in lesbian mothers. In: Bozett, F.W. (Ed.), Gay and Lesbian Parents. Praeger, New York, pp. 75–85.
Strasser, M., 2008. The alleged harms of recognizing same-sex marriage. In: Wardle, L. (Ed.), What's the Harm? Does Legalizing Same-Sex Marriage Really Harm Individuals, Families or Society? University Press, Lanham, MD, pp. 27–46.
Sullivan, M., 1996. Rozzie and Harriett? Gender and family parents of lesbian coparents. Gender and Society 10, 747–767.
Tasker, F.L., Golombok, S., 1995. Adults raised as children in lesbian families. American Journal of Orthopsychiatry 65, 203–215.
Tasker, F.L., Golombok, S., 1997. Growing Up in a Lesbian Family: Effects on Child Development. Guilford, New York.
Tasker, F.L., Golombok, S., 1998. The role of co-mothers in planned lesbian-led families. Journal of Lesbian Studies 2, 49–68.
Teachman, J.R. et al, 1998. Sibling resemblance in behavioral and cognitive outcomes: the role of father presence. Journal of Marriage and the Family 60, 835–848.
Vanfraussen, K., Ponjaert-Kristoffersen, I., Brewaeys, A., 2003. Family functioning in lesbian families created by donor insemination. American Journal of Orthopsychiatry 73, 78–90.
Wainright, J.L., Russell, S.T., Patterson, C.J., 2004. Psychosocial adjustment, school outcomes, and romantic relationships of adolescents with same-sex parents. Child Development 75, 1886–1898.
Waite, L., 1995. Does marriage matter? Demography 32, 483–507.
Waite, L., Gallagher, M., 2000. The Case for Marriage: Why Married People are Happier, Healthier, and Better off Financially. Doubleday, New York.
Wallerstein, J., Lewis, J.M., Blakeslee, S., 2001. The Unexpected Legacy of Divorce. Hyperion, New York.
Wardle, L.D., 1997. The potential impact of homosexual parenting on children. University of Illinois Law Review 1997, 833–919.
Weitoft, G.R. et al, 2003. Mortality, severe morbidity, and injury in children living with single parents in Sweden: a population-based study. The Lancet 361, 289–295.
Wilcox, W.B. et al, 2005. Why Marriage Matters, second ed. Institute for American Values, New York.
Wilcox, W.B. et al, 2011. Why Marriage Matters, third ed. Institute for American Values, New York.
Williams, R.N., 2000. A critique of the research on same-sex parenting. In: Dollahite, D.C. (Ed.), Strengthening Our Families. Bookcraft, Salt Lake City, UT, pp. 325–355.
Wolfinger, N.H., 2005. Understanding the Divorce Cycle: The Children of Divorce in their Own Marriages. Cambridge University Press, New York.
Wright, J.M., 1998. Lesbian Stepfamilies: An Ethnography of Love. Harrington Park, New York.

Summary of Mark Regnerus's

"How Different Are the Adult Children of Parents Who Have Same-Sex Relationships? Findings from the New Family Structures Study"

Social Science Research 41(4) (July 2012): 752–770, http://dx.doi.org/
10.1016/j.ssresearch.2012.03.009

and

"Parental Same-Sex Relationships, Family Instability, and Subsequent Life Outcomes for Adult Children: Answering Critics of the New Family Structures Study with Additional Analyses"

Social Science Research 41(6) (November 2012): 1367–1377,
http://dx.doi.org/10.1016/j.ssresearch.2012.08.015

In "How Different," sociologist Mark Regnerus of the Population Research Center at the University of Texas at Austin, presents new and extensive empirical evidence that suggests that there are differences in outcomes between the children of parents who have had a same-sex relationship and children raised by their married, biological mother and father.

This evidence is based on data from the 2011 New Family Structures Study (NFSS), of which Regnerus was the lead investigator. It surveyed 2,988 young adults for the specific purpose of collecting nationally representative data about children from various family structures. The roster includes intact biological families, late-divorced families, stepfamilies, single-parent families, adoptive families, families with a parent who has been in a same-sex relationship,[1] and other family types (such as families with a deceased parent). The NFSS has been acknowledged by critics to be "better situated than virtually all previous studies to detect differences between these groups in the population."[2]

Strengths of the NFSS

The NFSS data and its "How Different" summary article are unique among gay-parenting research in four significant respects: First, the NFSS drew from a large, random sample of the U.S. population of young adults (ages 18–39). To date, the first generation of gay-parenting research has relied upon small, nonprobability samples for data, which are inadequate for drawing general conclusions about the population of gay parents at large.[3]

For example, one of the more famous gay-parenting data collection efforts, the National Longitudinal Lesbian Family Study (NLLFS), used what's called a convenience sample, recruiting respondents not randomly from the population but from announcements posted in lesbian newspapers, at women's bookstores, and at lesbian events in several major metropolitan areas.[4] While these types of samples are valuable for gathering information about the behaviors of specific groups (in this case, women active in a lesbian community in a major urban area—and eager to contribute to research about their parenting), they are inadequate when the goal is to grasp general trends about the larger population of lesbian parents, many of whom do not have the socioeconomic, racial, geographic, or behavioral patterns of the selected group. Any claims about a general population that are based on a group that does not represent it must be limited, because the sample will be less diverse than what a truly representative sample would reveal.[5]

A second strength of the NFSS is that it focuses on the responses of adults who were once children in these households. Normally, studies on gay parenting focus on what is going on inside the households of lesbian and gay parents at present, while the children are still under their parents' care. Moreover, these studies typically interview the *parents* for their point of view about what it is like to parent as a gay man or lesbian woman. Such research cannot tell us how the children turn out later as adults or what they experienced while growing up. Moreover, in some cases, the data is collected in an atmosphere of awareness about the possible political ramifications of the replies, so parental bias in the reporting is a concern.[6]

Third, the comparison group of the Regnerus report is the intact (married) biological family. First-generation gay-parenting research has compared gay or lesbian families to single, divorced, or stepparent families—or has compared a select and often socioeconomically privileged population of gay or lesbian parents to a broad, representative sample of the general population.[7] "How Different" compares the outcomes of children who reported having a mother who had a lesbian relationship with another woman (MLR for short) or a father who had a gay relationship with another man (FGR) with the outcomes of children who reported coming from an intact, married biological family (IBF). The rationale for this choice is that the intact biological family has long been considered to be the gold standard for children, in part because household stability (intact parental relationships) have well-documented advantages for children. So in "How Different," the bar is kept high to determine if there are differences between children from the more traditional biological family and children from these new family structures.[8]

Fourth, the NFSS gathered data about children's outcomes in forty different areas of vital interest to parenting researchers, covering the social, emotional, and relational well-being of the adult children.[9] Categories ranged from satisfaction with their adult romantic relationships to living on public assistance to ever having experienced poverty, suffered sexual assault, or pled guilty to a crime. The Rosenfeld study (see note 3), by comparison, measured one important outcome of children's well-being: educational achievement. Most first-generation gay-parenting research studies have looked at gender-related and emotional outcomes in children (such as sexual identity/orientation and self-esteem), which are of less interest to society. Below is a summary of some of the most significant findings from the NFSS:[10]

Race

Public perceptions and stereotypes of gay/lesbian households with children usually assume them to be white, upper-middle-class members of society. In response to questions about race, the NFSS found that 48 percent of FGR respondents and 43 percent of MLR respondents indicated that they were either black or Hispanic, a number much higher than previously suggested by studies based on convenience samples.[11]

Public Assistance

On economic outcomes, grown children of a mother who had been in a lesbian relationship were almost four times more likely to be currently on public assistance than were the grown children of IBFs. As young adults, they were also 3.5 times more likely to be unemployed.

Crime

On criminal outcomes, the children of fathers who had been in a gay relationship showed the greatest propensity to be involved in crime. They were, on average, more frequently arrested, and they pled guilty to more non-minor offenses than did the young-adult children in any other category. The children of mothers who had had a lesbian relationship reported the second-highest average frequency of involvement in crimes and arrests, and in both categories, the young-adult children of IBFs reported the lowest average frequency of involvement in crimes or arrests.

Sexual Victimization

Contrary to recent and widely circulated conclusions[12] that there is no sexual victimization in lesbian households, the NFSS found that, when asked if they were ever touched sexually as children by a parent or another adult, the children of mothers who had had a lesbian relationship were eleven times more likely to say "yes" than were the children from an IBF, and the children of fathers who had had a gay relationship were three times more likely to say "yes." The children of IBFs were the least likely of all family types to have ever been touched sexually in this way: Only 2 percent reported affirmatively (compared to 23 percent of children of MLRs). When asked if they were ever forced to have sex against their will, the children of mothers who had had a lesbian relationship were the worst off again, four times more likely to say "yes" than were the children of IBFs. The children of FGRs were three times more likely to have been forced to have sex than were the children of IBFs.

In percentages, 31 percent of MLRs said they had been forced to have sex, compared with 25 percent of FGRs and 8 percent of IBFs. These results are generally consistent with research on heterosexual families; for instance, a recent federal report showed that children are least likely to be sexually, physically, or emotionally abused in an intact, biological, married family.[13]

Sexually Transmitted Infections

When asked if they had ever had a sexually transmitted infection (STI), the young-adult children of FGRs were three times more likely to say "yes" than were those of IBFs. Children of MLRs were two-and-a-half times more likely to say "yes," followed by the children of stepfamilies, who were two times more likely. Children of IBFs and children from "other" family types were the least likely of all to have had an STI.

Marijuana/Smoking

When asked to report upon frequency of marijuana use, the young-adult children of divorced parents were the worst off, reporting to use marijuana on average one-and-a-half times more frequently than the children of IBFs. Next came the children of MLRs, followed by the children of single parents, and the children of FGRs. The children adopted by people unrelated to them and the children of IBFs reported least-frequent marijuana use as young adults. When asked about frequency of smoking, the young-adult children of mothers who had had a lesbian relationship reported highest frequency, followed by the children of fathers who had had a gay relationship. The children of IBFs ranked lowest in smoking frequency for all family-of-origin types.

Perceived Safety

Respondents were asked to report their sentiment about their family experiences while growing up. The children of MLRs reported the lowest levels of perceived safety in their childhood homes, followed by children of FGRs, with the children of IBFs reporting the highest levels of perceived safety.

Mental Health

When asked if they were recently or currently in therapy "for a problem connected with anxiety, depression, relationships, etc.," the children adopted by nonrelatives reported receiving such therapy the most, followed by the children of MLRs. The children from IBFs were least likely of all family types to report receiving this therapy.

On the CES-D depression index—an eight-measure survey of respondents' happy-to-depressed thoughts over the previous seven days—the young-adult children of MLRs and FGRs reported statistically significant higher levels of depression than did young-adult children from IBFs. Specifically, the young-adult children of FGRs were two times more likely to have thought about suicide in the previous twelve months than were the children of MLRs (the second highest percentage), and almost five times more likely than the children from IBFs.

Romantic Relationships

When asked to rate their own current romantic-relationship quality, the adult children of FGRs reported the lowest quality, followed by children adopted by nonrelatives, the children of stepfamilies, and then the children of MLRs. The children from IBFs reported the highest levels of relationship quality.

When asked about the number of times they had thought that their current relationship was in trouble, the children of FGRs reported the highest numbers again, followed by the children of divorced parents. The children from IBFs reported that they had deemed their relationship to be in trouble the least number of times.

When asked about infidelity, children of MLRs were three times more likely to say they had had an affair while married/cohabiting than were children from IBFs, followed by children from stepfamilies (who were two-and-a-half times more likely to have had an affair than were IBFs) and children of FGRs (who were twice as likely).

Sexual Orientation and Behavior

The NFSS asked respondents to identify their sexual orientation and found that children of MLRs were more likely to report same-sex romantic relationships and bisexuality than were any other group. They were least likely, then, to identify as entirely heterosexual. Children of FGRs were the next least likely, and children from IBFs were most likely of all to identify as fully heterosexual.

Daughters of MLRs reported an average of just over one female sex partner and four male sex partners in their lifetimes, in contrast to daughters from IBFs, who reported an average of only 0.22 female sex partners and 2.79 male sex partners in their lifetimes. Daughters of MLRs were also most likely to self-report asexuality, "not sexually attracted to either males or females" (4.1 percent of females of MLRs, compared to 0.5 percent of females from IBFs).

An Overall Finding of Differences

Taken together, "How Different" found that there are differences between children raised by a parent who had a same sex relationship and children raised in an intact, married biological family in a variety of social, emotional, and relational outcomes.

On twenty-five out of forty outcomes evaluated, there were statistically significant differences between children from IBFs and those of MLRs in many areas that are unambiguously suboptimal, such as receiving welfare, a need for therapy, a history of infidelity, STIs, sexual victimization, lower educational attainment, lower sense of safety within the family of origin, depression, attachments and dependencies, marijuana use, frequency of smoking, and criminal behavior.

On eleven out of forty outcomes, there were statistically significant differences between children from IBFs and those who reported having an FGR in areas such as thoughts of suicide, STIs, being forced to have sex against their will, lower sense of safety within the family of origin, depression, poor relationship quality, frequency of smoking, and criminal behavior.

There were important differences in both comparisons, but the young-adult children of MLRs exhibited the least favorable outcomes in a wider array of categories when compared to children from IBFs and fared worse in more categories than did the children of FGRs.

Reply to Critics: Addressing Same-Sex Parent Instability

In "Answering Critics" Regnerus offers a detailed reply addressing six different areas of concern that critics raised, including new analyses of data not found in the original essay. Of all of these concerns, the most significant criticism of the study involved the issue of how to handle the instability found within same-sex parental relationships. This summary focuses upon how Regnerus addresses this particular criticism, what methods he suggests for future research to address the instability factor, and the possible underlying causes of instability in same-sex relationships.

In his original article, "How Different," Regnerus alerts readers that the type of household that the young adults experienced while they were young was rarely a "planned" same-sex-parent household. The study found that the young adults surveyed (born 1973–1994) who had a parent who had a gay or lesbian relationship were usually conceived within a heterosexual marriage that then experienced divorce or separation, leaving the child with a single parent. Before, during, or after the divorce or separation, that parent had at least one same-sex romantic relationship.[14]

To be more specific, among the respondents who said their mother had a same-sex romantic relationship, 91 percent reported living with their mother while she was in the relationship, but fewer (57 percent) said they had lived with *both* their mother and her partner for at least four months at some point prior to age eighteen. An even smaller share (23 percent) said that they had spent at least three years living in the same household with their mother's romantic partner. This is to say that out of 2,988 respondents, only forty children reported living with two women (i.e., their mother and her partner) for three years or more. Only two out of the 15,000 screened had spent a span of eighteen years with the same two women. Among those who said that their father had had a same-sex relationship, there was even less longevity. Forty-two percent reported living with him while he was in the relationship, and only 24 percent reported living with him and his partner for at least four months. Only 1.1 percent of children whose father had had a same-sex relationship spent at least three years in the same household with both men.[15] No children lived with two men in a gay relationship for their entire childhood. These results strongly suggest that the parents' same-sex relationships were often short-lived, a finding consistent with the broader research on elevated levels of instability among same-sex romantic partners.[16]

Critics accused Regnerus of bad methodology and even ill will for not comparing children from the intact biological family to children from intact lesbian families and intact gay families. This was the so-called "apples to oranges" criticism of the NFSS.

In anticipation of this concern, Regnerus had stressed that despite the study drawing from a large, representative sample of the U.S. population and despite using screening tactics designed to boost the number of respondents who reported having had a parent who had had a same-sex relationship, a very small segment reported to have been parented by the same two gay or lesbian parents for three years or more. It was an insufficient number to make reliable comparisons between these groups and intact biological families.[17]

Nevertheless, criticism focused on this aspect—that Regnerus did not compare children from stable same-sex families to children from stable opposite-sex families. Critics further alleged that the NFSS represented an "outdated" data set, looking at parents' sexual behavior patterns in the 1970s–1990s, which were obsolete for making up-to-date judgments about children's outcomes in different family structures. Critics further alleged that today, there are many more stable same-sex households in the U.S. population (and that any remaining patterns of instability would decrease to the extent that same-sex couples could marry). Therefore, critics argued, the study was to be regarded as irrelevant to modern debates.

In "Answering Critics," Regnerus suggests that readers may have unrealistic expectations about same-sex families, partly because the popular media has given most attention to the well-educated, wealthy, white lesbian and gay families who use artificial reproductive technology (ART) to have children and who plan to raise them in a long-term household. The popular mind seems to have assumed these families to represent a general trend in the population and so have found it objectionable when these families were not found in the study's sample.

However, Regnerus points out that *no studies* based upon a large, random national sample of the population have confirmed the stable same-sex couple to be the norm. On the contrary, he cites a number of scholars who have found evidence for comparatively higher break-up rates among same-sex couples in the general population, even in countries where the social stigma is much less and same-sex marriage is legal and accepted. For instance, he cites Andersson and colleagues, whose 2006 study of same-sex marriages in Norway and Sweden found that "divorce risk levels are considerably higher in same-sex marriages,"[18] such that Swedish lesbian couples are more than three times as likely to divorce as are Swedish heterosexual couples, and Swedish gay couples are 1.35 times more likely to divorce (after controls). He refers to Timothy Biblarz and Judith Stacey, two outspoken advocates for same-sex marriage in the U.S. academy, who nevertheless acknowledge that lesbian parents face "a somewhat greater risk of splitting up," due in part, they suggest, to their "high standards of equality." And he cites Rosenfeld, who found higher patterns of instability among lesbian couples using a nationally representative data set of American relationships.[19]

Further, Regnerus challenges readers to consider whether they might have a race and class bias in favor of white, upper-middle-class portrayals of same-sex families, neglecting to consider the presence of black and Hispanic, as well as less-educated or less-economically-privileged parents in same-sex relationships (with a greater risk of household instability). He agrees with Rosenfeld: "The literature on same-sex couple parenting has tended to feature studies of the kind of women who can afford ART: white, upper-middle-class women. Nationally representative data tend to paint a different picture . . . same-sex couple parents tend to be more working class and are much more likely to be nonwhite compared with heterosexual married couples."[20]

Therefore, in order to be fair, Regnerus suggests that research on children's outcomes in the *general population* should include children from diverse families. He also proposes that the issue of household instability be one that scholars wrestle with, not explain away through methodological choices or ignore by using datasets of relatively more stable same-sex couples, as his critics have pressed him to do. To that end, Regnerus makes recommendations about how to deal with the issue of instability in future research.

Dealing with Channels or Pathways of Instability

Regnerus explains that family instability may be the very channel, or pathway, through which suboptimal child outcomes arise within same-sex parenting households. To explain what pathways are, he uses an example: measuring whether women or men are more likely to develop lung cancer.[21]

It is known that lung cancer is associated with smoking. Smoking is a common pathway, or channel, through which lung cancer arises. So "if, for example, most men smoked, but very few women ever did so, it is entirely unhelpful to declare that—controlling for smoking—there is no effect of gender on lung cancer."[22] Such an analysis would suggest that there are "no differences" between men and women when it comes to developing lung cancer, when that would not be the case in reality. Additionally, a real cause (that many men are smoking) would be masked, when in fact it ought to be of major concern.

Similarly, Regnerus notes, family instability is likely to be a pathway for suboptimal child outcomes. To "control for" instability (as past gay-parenting scholars have tended to do) would be to overlook the pathway and result in "a model that is unhelpful for understanding social reality."[23] In short, Regnerus encourages future research to study the possible link between same-sex-parent families, family instability, and negative outcomes for children.

Finally, Regnerus proposes a thesis for the observed instability among same-sex couples based on a sexual-economics approach to romantic relationships: "This perspective places no blame for instability on sexual orientation per se, but rather on stable gender differences and preferences in relationships."[24] Basically, the thesis is that women are more likely to set the bar high (in romantic relationships) for the meeting of their emotional needs and are more likely to be dissatisfied in relationships, making them more likely to separate. Gay men, by contrast, appear to be more stable in their relationships than are lesbian women, but the male sex drive has a greater tendency toward multiple partners, and so the men are less likely to remain monogamous, presenting a different kind of instability in households, the effects of which on children are unknown.[25]

Conclusion

In "How Different," Dr. Mark Regnerus presents new and compelling evidence for the view that young-adult children of parents who have same-sex relationships suffer significant and problematic outcomes when compared to young-adult children from IBFs. This conclusion contrasts strongly with the first generation of gay-parenting research, which claimed that there were "no differences" (and some benefits) to being raised by same-sex parents, a claim made despite a lack of empirical evidence for significant numbers of stable, two-parent gay/lesbian households in the U.S. population.[26]

Regnerus's conclusion better accords with the established body of social science over the last twenty-five years, which found children to do best when they are raised by their married, biological mother and father.[27] At the turn of the millennium, social scientists widely agreed that children raised by unmarried mothers, divorced parents, cohabiting parents, and stepparents fared worse than did children raised by their still-married, biological parents.[28] Although data on gay and lesbian parenting was not yet available (it was too rare to study adequately), it was difficult to imagine that gay and lesbian parents would be able to accomplish what heterosexuals in stepparenting, adoptive, single-parenting, and cohabiting contexts had not been able to do: namely, replicate the optimal child-rearing environment of an IBF.

By challenging these claims, Regnerus's "How Different" is consistent with the consensus that existed at the turn of the millennium. He concludes with a reminder of the social costs of family breakdown: "Insofar as the number of intact, biological mother/father families continues to shrink in the United States, as it has, this portends growing challenges within families, but also heightened dependence on public health organizations, federal and state public assistance, psychotherapeutic resources, substance use programs, and the criminal justice system."[29]

Notes

1. In "How Different," Regnerus uses the terms "lesbian mother" and "gay father." In "Answering Critics," he changes these two admittedly generalized descriptions to "respondents who report a maternal (or mother's) lesbian relationship, and respondents who report a paternal (or father's) gay relationship" (1368).

2. Paul R. Amato, "The Well-Being of Children with Gay and Lesbian Parents," *Social Science Research* 41 (2012): 771–774, p. 772. David Eggebeen, who, like Amato is critical of Regnerus's "How Different," nevertheless argues that the real importance of the paper is "the description of a new data set that offers significant advantages. Whether the New Family Structures Study has the possibility of unsettling previously settled questions depends in equal parts on the richness of the information collected, as well as the willingness of scholars to make use of these data" (David J. Eggebeen, "What Can We Learn from Studies of Children Raised by Gay or Lesbian Parents?" *Social Science Research* 41 (2012): 775–778, p. 777).

3. See Regnerus, "How Different," 753, 755 (citing Nock 2001; Perrin and Committee on Psychosocial Aspects of Child and Family Health 2002; Redding 2008). At the time of publication, there was only one other same-sex-parenting study that relied upon a large, random sample: that of Michael Rosenfeld of Stanford University, who used 2000 U.S. Census data (Michael J. Rosenfeld, "Nontraditional Families and Childhood Progress through School," *Demography* 47 [August 2010]: 755–775). "How Different" was the second-known same-sex parenting study to rely upon a large, random national sample. Douglas Allen, Catherine Pakaluk, and Joseph Price (2013) offered a third study, a re-examination of Rosenfeld's research. Douglas Allen (2013) offered another study based upon the large, random national sample of the 2006 Canada Census. All of these papers are summarized in this book.

4. See Regnerus, "How Different," 753.

5. This problem is compounded when these studies compare data from a small convenience sample of gay or lesbian parents with data on heterosexual parenting from a large, population-level sample. Although researchers usually mention this limitation of their studies in their analysis, the media almost always fail to transmit that limitation to the public at large, so the overall portrayal of same-sex parents is privileged. By contrast, the NFSS drew a large, random sample from the general U.S. population so that comparisons would be representative of the general population.

6. Fiona Tasker (2010: 36) warns against this: "Parental self-report, of course, may be biased. It is plausible to argue that, in a prejudiced social climate, lesbian and gay parents may have more at stake in presenting a positive picture. . . . Future studies need to consider using additional sophisticated measures to rule out potential biases" (cited in Regnerus, "How Different," 3 [also citing Bos and Sandfort 2010; Brewaeys et al. 1997]).

7. "Rosenfeld (2010: 757) notes that of the forty-five studies listed in Tasker's (2005) review article, only two included 'a more traditional family control group built into the study.'" (Regnerus, "Answering Critics," 1368–1369).

8. "If stability is a key asset for households with children, then it is sensible to use intact biological families in any comparative assessment" (Regnerus, "Answering Critics," 1368).

9. Interactive visual representations of the findings are available at FamilyStructureStudies.com.

10. An important qualification that Regnerus stresses is that the study does not claim to establish *causality* between parenting styles and child outcomes. In other words, the results are not a "report card" on gay parenting but a report on the average condition of grown children from households of parents who had a same-sex relationship versus those from IBFs. So, for instance, when the study finds that children who had a parent who had been in a same-sex romantic relationship are much more likely to suffer from depression as young adults than are the children who came from intact biological families, the study does not claim that the gay parent was the *cause* of the depression in his or her child but simply that such children on average had more depression, for reasons unidentified by the study. The goal was simply to identify average differences among the groups of children and to test just how strong the groups' differences were. That said, the study did control for many other variables, such as age, gender, race or ethnicity, level of mother's education, perceived household income while growing up, the degree of legislative gay-friendliness of the respondent's home state, and the experience of being bullied as a youth. Controls help sociologists eliminate alternative explanations for a given outcome, making the causal link between parenting structure and children's outcomes more likely (though still not for certain) when the results remain statistically significant after controls are applied.

11. See Regnerus, "How Different," 757. These figures generally agree with those of Rosenfeld's (2010) analysis of American Community Survey data, "which reported that 37% and 42% of children from female and male same-sex households are Black and Hispanic, respectively" (Regnerus, "Answering Critics," 1371).

12. For example, see *Huffington Post*, "Child Abuse Rate at Zero Percent in Lesbian Households, New Report Finds," November 17, 2011, available at huffingtonpost.com.

13. See Andrea J. Sedlak, Jane Mettenburg, Monica Basena, Ian Petta, Karla McPherson, Angela Greene, and Spencer Li, "Fourth National Incidence Study of Child Abuse and Neglect (NIS-4): Report to Congress, Executive Summary," U.S. Department of Health and Human Services, Administration for Children and Families, available at acf.hhs.gov.

14. Regnerus reports that "just under half of [MLR and FGR] respondents reported that their biological parents were once married. This distinguishes NFSS from numerous studies that have been entirely concerned with 'planned' gay and lesbian families, such as the NLLFS" ("How Different," 757). The claim that today's gay and lesbian couples are *more* likely to plan for children using IVF, surrogacy, or adoption than to have children through a prior heterosexual union has not been confirmed yet with data. Moreover, because IVF is expensive, it is usually restricted to persons from the upper-middle class. The NFSS suggests that children who were raised by a parent who had a same-sex relationship often came from economically disadvantaged backgrounds. (See Regnerus, "How Different," table 2 scores on "Family received welfare growing up.")

15. See Regnerus, "How Different," 757.

16. See Charles Q. Strohm, "The Stability of Same-Sex Cohabitation, Different-Sex Cohabitation, and Marriage," California Center for Population Research, UCLA (February 1, 2012); Gunnar Andersson, Turid Noack, Ane Seierstad, and Harald Weedon-Fekjaer, "The Demographics of Same-Sex Marriages in Norway and Sweden," *Demography* 43 (February 2006): 79–98.

17. "Perhaps in social reality there really are two 'gold standards' of family stability and context for children's flourishing—a heterosexual stably coupled household and the same among gay/lesbian households—but no population-based sample analysis is yet able to *consistently confirm wide evidence* of the latter" (Regnerus, "Answering Critics," 1377).

18. Andersson et al., "Demographics of Same-Sex Marriages," 95: "We found that divorce risks are higher in same-sex partnerships than opposite-sex marriages and that unions of lesbians are considerably less stable, or more dynamic, than unions of gay men. . . . In Norway, 13% of partnerships of men and 21% of female partnerships are likely to end in divorce within six years from partnership registration. In Sweden, 20% of male partnerships and 30% of female marriages are likely to end in divorce within five years of partnership formation. These levels are higher than the corresponding 13% of heterosexual marriages that end in divorce within five years in Sweden."

19. Regnerus, "Answering Critics," 1370.

20. Ibid.

21. The example wasn't based on data but was just used to demonstrate his point.

22. Regnerus, "Answering Critics," 1369.

23. Ibid.

24. Ibid., 1370. Regnerus cites here Baumeister, 2010.

25. Regnerus, "Answering Critics," 1370.

26. For examples, see Judith Stacey and Timothy Biblarz, "(How) Does the Sexual Orientation of Parents Matter?" *American Sociological Review* 66 (April 2001): 159–183; Fiona Tasker, "Lesbian Mothers, Gay Fathers, and Their Children: A Review," *Journal of Developmental and Behavioral Pediatrics* (June 2005): 224–240; Jennifer L. Wainright and Charlotte J. Patterson, "Delinquency, Victimization, and Substance Use Among Adolescents with Female Same-Sex Parents," *Journal of Family Psychology* 20 (September 2006): 526–530; Rosenfeld, "Nontraditional Families."

27. For examples, see Sara McLanahan and Gary Sandefur, *Growing Up with a Single Parent* (Cambridge, MA: Harvard University Press, 1994); Sara McLanahan, "Parent Absence or Poverty: Which Matters More?" pp. 35–48 in Greg Duncan and Jeanne Brooks-Gunn, eds., *Consequences of Growing Up Poor* (New York: Russell Sage Foundation, 1997); Elizabeth Marquardt and David Popenoe, *Life Without Father* (Cambridge, MA: Harvard University Press, 1996); Bruce J. Ellis, John E. Bates, Kenneth A. Dodge, David M. Fergusson, L. John Horwood, Gregory S. Pettit, and Lianne Woodward, "Does Father Absence Place Daughters at Special Risk for Early Sexual Activity and Teenage Pregnancy?" *Child Development* 74 (May–June 2003): 801–821; Sara McLanahan, Elisabeth Donahue, and Ron Haskins, "Introducing the Issue," *Future of Children* 15 (Autumn 2005): 3–12; Mary Parke, "Are Married Parents Really Better for Children?" Center for Law and Social Policy, Washington, DC (May 2003); Elizabeth Marquardt, "Family Structure and Children's Educational Outcomes" (New York: Institute for American Values, 2005); Elizabeth Marquardt, *Between Two Worlds: The Inner Lives of Children of Divorce* (New York: Crown, 2005); W. Bradford Wilcox et al., *Why Marriage Matters, Second Edition: Twenty-Six Conclusions from the Social Sciences* (New York: Institute for American Values, 2005).

28. Child Trends, a nonpartisan research organization, summarized the scholarly consensus: "Research clearly demonstrates that family structure matters for children, and the family structure that helps children the most is the family headed by two biological parents in a low-conflict marriage" (Kristin Anderson Moore, Susan M. Jekielek, and Carol Emig, "Marriage from a Child's Perspective: How Does Family Structure Affect Children, and What Can Be Done about It?" Research Brief, Child Trends, Washington, D.C. [June 2002]). Likewise, Sara McLanahan, of Princeton Univesity, and Gary Sandefur, of the University of Wisconsin–Madison, wrote, "If we were asked to design a system for making sure that children's basic needs were met, we would probably come up with something quite similar to the two-parent ideal. Such a design, in theory, would not only ensure that children had access to the time and money of two adults, it also would provide a system of checks and balances that promoted quality parenting. The fact that both parents have a biological connection to the child would increase the likelihood that the parents would identify with the child and be willing to sacrifice for that child, and it would reduce the likelihood that either parent would abuse the child" (Sara McLanahan and Gary Sandefur, *Growing Up With a Single Parent: What Hurts, What Helps* [Cambridge, MA: Harvard University Press, 1994], 38).

29. Regnerus, "How Different," 766.

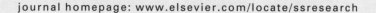

Contents lists available at SciVerse ScienceDirect

Social Science Research

journal homepage: www.elsevier.com/locate/ssresearch

How different are the adult children of parents who have same-sex relationships? Findings from the New Family Structures Study

Mark Regnerus

Department of Sociology and Population Research Center, University of Texas at Austin, 1 University Station A1700, Austin, TX 78712-0118, United States

ARTICLE INFO

Article history:
Received 1 February 2012
Revised 29 February 2012
Accepted 12 March 2012

Keywords:
Same-sex parenting
Family structure
Young adulthood
Sampling concerns

ABSTRACT

The New Family Structures Study (NFSS) is a social-science data-collection project that fielded a survey to a large, random sample of American young adults (ages 18–39) who were raised in different types of family arrangements. In this debut article of the NFSS, I compare how the young-adult children of a parent who has had a same-sex romantic relationship fare on 40 different social, emotional, and relational outcome variables when compared with six other family-of-origin types. The results reveal numerous, consistent differences, especially between the children of women who have had a lesbian relationship and those with still-married (heterosexual) biological parents. The results are typically robust in multivariate contexts as well, suggesting far greater diversity in lesbian-parent household experiences than convenience-sample studies of lesbian families have revealed. The NFSS proves to be an illuminating, versatile dataset that can assist family scholars in understanding the long reach of family structure and transitions.

© 2012 Elsevier Inc. All rights reserved.

1. Introduction

The well-being of children has long been in the center of public policy debates about marriage and family matters in the United States. That trend continues as state legislatures, voters, and the judiciary considers the legal boundaries of marriage. Social science data remains one of the few sources of information useful in legal debates surrounding marriage and adoption rights, and has been valued both by same-sex marriage supporters and opponents. Underneath the politics about marriage and child development are concerns about family structures' possible effects on children: the number of parents present and active in children's lives, their genetic relationship to the children, parents' marital status, their gender distinctions or similarities, and the number of transitions in household composition. In this introduction to the New Family Structures Study (NFSS), I compare how young adults from a variety of different family backgrounds fare on 40 different social, emotional, and relational outcomes. In particular, I focus on how respondents who said their mother had a same-sex relationship with another woman—or their father did so with another man—compare with still-intact, two-parent heterosexual married families using nationally-representative data collected from a large probability sample of American young adults.

Social scientists of family transitions have until recently commonly noted the elevated stability and social benefits of the two-parent (heterosexual) married household, when contrasted to single mothers, cohabiting couples, adoptive parents, and ex-spouses sharing custody (Brown, 2004; Manning et al., 2004; McLanahan and Sandefur, 1994). In 2002, Child Trends—a well-regarded nonpartisan research organization—detailed the importance for children's development of growing up in "the presence of *two biological parents*" (their emphasis; Moore et al., 2002, p. 2). Unmarried motherhood, divorce, cohabitation, and step-parenting were widely perceived to fall short in significant developmental domains (like education, behavior problems, and emotional well-being), due in no small part to the comparative fragility and instability of such relationships.

E-mail address: regnerus@prc.utexas.edu

In their 2001 *American Sociological Review* article reviewing findings on sexual orientation and parenting, however, sociologists Judith Stacey and Tim Biblarz began noting that while there are some differences in outcomes between children in same-sex and heterosexual unions, there were not as many as family sociologists might expect, and differences need not necessarily be perceived as *deficits*. Since that time the conventional wisdom emerging from comparative studies of same-sex parenting is that there are very few differences of note in the child outcomes of gay and lesbian parents (Tasker, 2005; Wainright and Patterson, 2006; Rosenfeld, 2010). Moreover, a variety of possible advantages of having a lesbian couple as parents have emerged in recent studies (Crowl et al., 2008; Biblarz and Stacey, 2010; Gartrell and Bos, 2010; MacCallum and Golombok, 2004). The scholarly discourse concerning gay and lesbian parenting, then, has increasingly posed a challenge to previous assumptions about the supposed benefits of being raised in biologically-intact, two-parent heterosexual households.

1.1. Sampling concerns in previous surveys

Concern has arisen, however, about the methodological quality of many studies focusing on same-sex parents. In particular, most are based on non-random, non-representative data often employing small samples that do not allow for generalization to the larger population of gay and lesbian families (Nock, 2001; Perrin and Committee on Psychosocial Aspects of Child and Family Health, 2002; Redding, 2008). For instance, many published studies on the children of same-sex parents collect data from "snowball" or convenience samples (e.g., Bos et al., 2007; Brewaeys et al., 1997; Fulcher et al., 2008; Sirota, 2009; Vanfraussen et al., 2003). One notable example of this is the National Longitudinal Lesbian Family Study, analyses of which were prominently featured in the media in 2011 (e.g., *Huffington Post, 2011*). The NLLFS employs a convenience sample, recruited entirely by self-selection from announcements posted "at lesbian events, in women's bookstores, and in lesbian newspapers" in Boston, Washington, and San Francisco. While I do not wish to downplay the significance of such a longitudinal study—it is itself quite a feat—this sampling approach is a problem when the goal (or in this case, the practical result and conventional use of its findings) is to generalize to a population. All such samples are biased, often in unknown ways. As a formal sampling method, "snowball sampling is known to have some serious problems," one expert asserts (Snijders, 1992, p. 59). Indeed, such samples are likely biased toward "inclusion of those who have many interrelationships with, or are coupled to, a large number of other individuals" (Berg, 1988, p. 531). But apart from the knowledge of individuals' inclusion probability, unbiased estimation is not possible.

Further, as Nock (2001) entreated, consider the convenience sample recruited from within organizations devoted to seeking rights for gays and lesbians, like the NLLFS sampling strategy. Suppose, for example, that the respondents have higher levels of education than comparable lesbians who do not frequent such events or bookstores, or who live elsewhere. If such a sample is used for research purposes, then anything that is correlated with educational attainment—like better health, more deliberative parenting, and greater access to social capital and educational opportunities for children—will be biased. Any claims about a population based on a group that does not represent it will be distorted, since its sample of lesbian parents is less diverse (given what is known about it) than a representative sample would reveal (Baumle et al., 2009).

To compound the problem, results from nonprobability samples—from which meaningful statistics cannot be generated—are regularly compared with population-level samples of heterosexual parents, which no doubt are comprised of a blend of higher and lower quality parents. For example, Gartrell et al. (2011a,b) inquired about the sexual orientation and behavior of adolescents by comparing data from the National Survey of Family Growth (NSFG) with those in the snowball sample of youth in the NLLFS. Comparing a population-based sample (the NSFG) to a select sample of youth from same-sex parents does not provide the statistical confidence demanded of good social science. Until now, this has been a primary way in which scholars have collected and evaluated data on same-sex parents. This is not to suggest that snowball samples are *inherently* problematic as data-collection techniques, only that they are not adequate for making useful comparisons with samples that are entirely different with regard to selection characteristics. Snowball and various other types of convenience sampling are simply not widely generalizable or comparable to the population of interest as a whole. While researchers themselves commonly note this important limitation, it is often entirely lost in the translation and transmission of findings by the media to the public.

1.2. Are there notable differences?

The "no differences" paradigm suggests that children from same-sex families display no notable disadvantages when compared to children from other family forms. This suggestion has increasingly come to include even comparisons with intact biological, two-parent families, the form most associated with stability and developmental benefits for children (McLanahan and Sandefur, 1994; Moore et al., 2002).

Answering questions about notable between-group differences has nevertheless typically depended on with whom comparisons are being made, what outcomes the researchers explored, and whether the outcomes evaluated are considered substantial or superficial, or portents of future risk. Some outcomes—like sexual behavior, gender roles, and democratic parenting, for example—have come to be valued differently in American society over time.

For the sake of brevity—and to give ample space here to describing the NFSS—I will avoid spending too much time describing previous studies, many of whose methodological challenges are addressed by the NFSS. Several review articles, and at least one book, have sought to provide a more thorough assessment of the literature (Anderssen et al., 2002; Biblarz and Stacey, 2010; Goldberg, 2010; Patterson, 2000; Stacey and Biblarz, 2001a). Suffice it to say that versions of the phrase "no differences" have been employed in a wide variety of studies, reports, depositions, books, and articles since 2000 (e.g., Crowl et al., 2008; Movement Advancement Project, 2011; Rosenfeld, 2010; Tasker, 2005; Stacey and Biblarz, 2001a,b; Veldorale-Brogan and Cooley, 2011; Wainright et al., 2004).

Much early research on gay parents typically compared the child development outcomes of divorced lesbian mothers with those of divorced heterosexual mothers (Patterson, 1997). This was also the strategy employed by psychologist Fiona Tasker (2005), who compared lesbian mothers with single, divorced heterosexual mothers and found "no systematic differences between the quality of family relationships" therein. Wainright et al. (2004), using 44 cases in the nationally-representative Add Health data, reported that teenagers living with female same-sex parents displayed comparable self-esteem, psychological adjustment, academic achievement, delinquency, substance use, and family relationship quality to 44 demographically "matched" cases of adolescents with opposite-sex parents, suggesting that here too the comparisons were not likely made with respondents from stable, biologically-intact, married families.

However, small sample sizes can contribute to "no differences" conclusions. It is not surprising that statistically-significant differences would *not* emerge in studies employing as few as 18 or 33 or 44 cases of respondents with same-sex parents, respectively (Fulcher et al., 2008; Golombok et al., 2003; Wainright and Patterson, 2006). Even analyzing matched samples, as a variety of studies have done, fails to mitigate the challenge of locating statistically-significant differences when the sample size is small. This is a concern in all of social science, but one that is doubly important when there may be motivation to confirm the null hypothesis (that is, that there are in fact no statistically-significant differences between groups). Therefore, one important issue in such studies is the simple matter of if there is enough statistical power to detect meaningful differences should they exist. Rosenfeld (2010) is the first scholar to employ a large, random sample of the population in order to compare outcomes among children of same-sex parents with those of heterosexual married parents. He concluded—after controlling for parents' education and income and electing to limit the sample to households exhibiting at least 5 years of co-residential stability—that there were no statistically-significant differences between the two groups in a pair of measures assessing children's progress through primary school.

Sex-related outcomes have more consistently revealed distinctions, although the tone of concern about them has diminished over time. For example, while the daughters of lesbian mothers are now widely understood to be more apt to explore same-sex sexual identity and behavior, concern about this finding has faded as scholars and the general public have become more accepting of GLB identities (Goldberg, 2010). Tasker and Golombok (1997) noted that girls raised by lesbian mothers reported a higher number of sexual partners in young adulthood than daughters of heterosexual mothers. Boys with lesbian mothers, on the other hand, appear to display the opposite trend—fewer partners than the sons of heterosexual mothers.

More recently, however, the tone about "no differences" has shifted some toward the assertion of differences, and that same-sex parents appear to be *more* competent than heterosexual parents (Biblarz and Stacey, 2010; Crowl et al., 2008). Even their romantic relationships may be better: a comparative study of Vermont gay civil unions and heterosexual marriages revealed that same-sex couples report higher relationship quality, compatibility, and intimacy, and less conflict than did married heterosexual couples (Balsam et al., 2008). Biblarz and Stacey's (2010) review article on gender and parenting asserts that,

> based strictly on the published science, one could argue that two women parent better on average than a woman and a man, or at least than a woman and man with a traditional division of labor. Lesbian coparents seem to outperform comparable married heterosexual, biological parents on several measures, even while being denied the substantial privileges of marriage (p. 17).

Even here, however, the authors note that lesbian parents face a "somewhat greater risk of splitting up," due, they suggest, to their "asymmetrical biological and legal statuses and their high standards of equality" (2010, p. 17).

Another meta-analysis asserts that non-heterosexual parents, on average, enjoy significantly better relationships with their children than do heterosexual parents, together with no differences in the domains of cognitive development, psychological adjustment, gender identity, and sexual partner preference (Crowl et al., 2008).

However, the meta-analysis reinforces the profound importance of *who* is doing the reporting—nearly always volunteers for small studies on a group whose claims about documentable parenting successes are very relevant in recent legislative and judicial debates over rights and legal statuses. Tasker (2010, p. 36) suggests caution:

> Parental self-report, of course, may be biased. It is plausible to argue that, in a prejudiced social climate, lesbian and gay parents may have more at stake in presenting a positive picture….Future studies need to consider using additional sophisticated measures to rule out potential biases…

Suffice it to say that the pace at which the overall academic discourse surrounding gay and lesbian parents' comparative competence has shifted—from slightly-less adept to virtually identical to more adept—is notable, and rapid. By comparison, studies of adoption—a common method by which many same-sex couples (but more heterosexual ones) become parents—have repeatedly and consistently revealed important and wide-ranging differences, on average, between adopted children and biological ones. In fact, these differences have been so pervasive and consistent that adoption experts now emphasize that "acknowledgement of difference" is critical for both parents and clinicians when working with adopted children and teens (Miller et al., 2000). This ought to give social scientists studying gay parenting outcomes pause, especially in light of concerns noted above about small sample sizes and the absence of a comparable recent, documented improvement in outcomes from youth in adopted families and stepfamilies.

Far more, too, is known about the children of lesbian mothers than about those of gay fathers (Biblarz and Stacey, 2010; Patterson, 2006; Veldorale-Brogan and Cooley, 2011). Biblarz and Stacey (2010, p. 17) note that while gay-male families remain understudied, "their daunting routes to parenthood seem likely to select more for strengths than limitations." Others are not so optimistic. One veteran of a study of the daughters of gay fathers warns scholars to avoid overlooking the family dynamics of "emergent" gay parents, who likely outnumber planned ones: "Children born into heterosexually organized marriages where fathers come out as gay or bisexual also face having to deal with maternal bitterness, marital conflict, possible divorce, custody issues, and father's absence" (Sirota, 2009, p. 291).

Regardless of sampling strategy, scholars also know much less about the lives of *young-adult* children of gay and lesbian parents, or how their experiences and accomplishments as adults compare with others who experienced different sorts of household arrangements during their youth. Most contemporary studies of gay parenting processes have focused on the present—what is going on inside the household when children are still under parental care (Tasker, 2005; Bos and Sandfort, 2010; Brewaeys et al., 1997). Moreover, such research tends to emphasize *parent-reported* outcomes like parental divisions of labor, parent–child closeness, daily interaction patterns, gender roles, and disciplinary habits. While such information is important to learn, it means we know far more about the *current* experience of *parents* in households with children than we do about young adults who have already moved through their childhood and now speak for themselves. Studies on family structure, however, serve scholars and family practitioners best when they span into adulthood. Do the children of gay and lesbian parents look comparable to those of their heterosexual counterparts? The NFSS is poised to address this question about the lives of young adults between the ages of 18 and 39, but not about children or adolescents. While the NFSS is not the answer to all of this domain's methodological challenges, it is a notable contribution in important ways.

1.3. The New Family Structures Study

Besides being brand-new data, several other aspects about the NFSS are novel and noteworthy. First, it is a study of young adults rather than children or adolescents, with particular attention paid to reaching ample numbers of respondents who were raised by parents that had a same-sex relationship. Second, it is a much larger study than nearly all of its peers. The NFSS interviewed just under 3000 respondents, including 175 who reported their mother having had a same-sex romantic relationship and 73 who said the same about their father. Third, it is a weighted probability sample, from which meaningful statistical inferences and interpretations can be drawn. While the 2000 (and presumably, the 2010) US Census Integrated Public Use Microdata Series (IPUMS) offers the largest nationally-representative sample-based information about youth in same-sex households, the Census collects much less outcome information of interest. The NFSS, however, asked numerous questions about respondents' social behaviors, health behaviors, and relationships. This manuscript provides the first glimpse into those outcomes by offering statistical comparisons of them among eight different family structures/experiences of origin. Accordingly, there is much that the NFSS offers, and not just about the particular research questions of this study.

There are several things the NFSS is not. The NFSS is not a longitudinal study, and therefore cannot attempt to broach questions of causation. It is a cross-sectional study, and collected data from respondents at only one point in time, when they were between the ages of 18 and 39. It does not evaluate the offspring of gay marriages, since the vast majority of its respondents came of age prior to the legalization of gay marriage in several states. This study cannot answer political questions about same-sex relationships and their legal legitimacy. Nevertheless, social science is a resource that offers insight to political and legal decision-makers, and there have been enough competing claims about "what the data says" about the children of same-sex parents—including legal depositions of social scientists in important cases—that a study with the methodological strengths of this one deserves scholarly attention and scrutiny.

2. Data collection, measures, and analytic approach

The NFSS data collection project is based at the University of Texas at Austin's Population Research Center. A survey design team consisting of several leading family researchers in sociology, demography, and human development—from Penn State University, Brigham Young University, San Diego State University, the University of Virginia, and several from the University of Texas at Austin—met over 2 days in January 2011 to discuss the project's sampling strategy and scope, and continued to offer advice as questions arose over the course of the data collection process. The team was designed to merge scholars across disciplines and ideological lines in a spirit of civility and reasoned inquiry. Several additional external consultants also gave close scrutiny to the survey instrument, and advised on how best to measure diverse topics. Both the study protocol and the questionnaire were approved by the University of Texas at Austin's Institutional Review Board. The NFSS data is intended to be publicly accessible and will thus be made so with minimal requirements by mid-late 2012. The NFSS was supported in part by grants from the Witherspoon Institute and the Bradley Foundation. While both of these are commonly known for their support of conservative causes—just as other private foundations are known for supporting more liberal causes—the funding sources played no role at all in the design or conduct of the study, the analyses, the interpretations of the data, or in the preparation of this manuscript.

2.1. The data collection process

The data collection was conducted by Knowledge Networks (or KN), a research firm with a very strong record of generating high-quality data for academic projects. Knowledge Networks recruited the first online research panel, dubbed the KnowledgePanel®, that is representative of the US population. Members of the KnowledgePanel® are randomly recruited by telephone and mail surveys, and households are provided with access to the Internet and computer hardware if needed. Unlike other Internet research panels sampling only individuals with Internet access who volunteer for research, the KnowledgePanel® is based on a sampling frame which includes both listed and unlisted numbers, those without a landline telephone and is not limited to current Internet users or computer owners, and does not accept self-selected volunteers. As a result, it is a random, nationally-representative sample of the American population. At last count, over 350 working papers, conference presentations, published articles, and books have used Knowledge Networks' panels, including the 2009 National Survey of Sexual Health and Behavior, whose extensive results were featured in an entire volume of the *Journal of Sexual Medicine*—and prominently in the media—in 2010 (Herbenick et al., 2010). More information about KN and the KnowledgePanel®, including panel recruitment, connection, retention, completion, and total response rates, are available from KN. The typical within survey response rate for a KnowledgePanel® survey is 65%. Appendix A presents a comparison of age-appropriate summary statistics from a variety of socio-demographic variables in the NFSS, alongside the most recent iterations of the Current Population Survey, the National Longitudinal Study of Adolescent Health (Add Health), the National Survey of Family Growth, and the National Study of Youth and Religion—all recent nationally-representative survey efforts. The estimates reported there suggest the NFSS compares very favorably with other nationally-representative datasets.

2.2. The screening process

Particularly relevant for the NFSS is the fact that key populations—gay and lesbian parents, as well as heterosexual adoptive parents—can be challenging to identify and locate. The National Center for Marriage and Family Research (2010) estimates that there are approximately 580,000 same-sex households in the United States. Among them, about 17%—or 98,600—are thought to have children present. While that may seem like a substantial number, in population-based sampling strategies it is not. Locating minority populations requires a search for a probability sample of the general population, typically by way of screening the general population to identify members of rarer groups. Thus in order to boost the number of respondents who reported being adopted or whose parent had a same-sex romantic relationship, the screener survey (which distinguished such respondents) was left in the field for several months between July 2011 and February 2012, enabling existing panelists more time to be screened and new panelists to be added. Additionally, in late Fall 2011, former members of the KnowledgePanel® were re-contacted by mail, phone, and email to encourage their screening. A total of 15,058 current and former members of KN's KnowledgePanel® were screened and asked, among several other questions, "From when you were born until age 18 (or until you left home to be on your own), did either of your parents <u>ever</u> have a romantic relationship with someone of the same sex?" Response choices were "Yes, my mother had a romantic relationship with another woman," "Yes, my father had a romantic relationship with another man," or "no." (Respondents were also able to select both of the first two choices.) If they selected either of the first two, they were asked about whether they had ever lived with that parent while they were in a same-sex romantic relationship. The NFSS completed full surveys with 2988 Americans between the ages of 18 and 39. The screener and full survey instrument is available at the NFSS homepage, located at: www.prc.utexas.edu/nfss.

2.3. What does a representative sample of gay and lesbian parents (of young adults) look like?

The weighted screener data—a nationally-representative sample—reveal that 1.7% of all Americans between the ages of 18 and 39 report that their father or mother has had a same-sex relationship, a figure comparable to other estimates of children in gay and lesbian households (e.g., Stacey and Biblarz (2001a,b) report a plausible range from 1% to 12%). Over twice as many respondents report that their mother has had a lesbian relationship as report that their fathers have had a gay relationship. (A total of 58% of the 15,058 persons screened report spending their entire youth—up until they turned 18 or left the house—with their biological mother and father.)

While gay and lesbian Americans typically become parents today in four ways—through one partner's previous participation in a heterosexual union, through adoption, in-vitro fertilization, or by a surrogate—the NFSS is more likely to be comprised of respondents from the first two of these arrangements than from the last two. Today's children of gay men and lesbian women are more apt to be "planned" (that is, by using adoption, IVF, or surrogacy) than as little as 15–20 years ago, when such children were more typically the products of heterosexual unions. The youngest NFSS respondents turned 18 in 2011, while the oldest did so in 1990. Given that unintended pregnancy is impossible among gay men and a rarity among lesbian couples, it stands to reason that gay and lesbian parents today are far more selective about parenting than the heterosexual population, among whom unintended pregnancies remain very common, around 50% of total (Finer and Henshaw, 2006). The share of all same-sex parenting arrangements that is planned, however, remains unknown. Although the NFSS did not directly ask those respondents whose parent has had a same-sex romantic relationship about the manner of their own birth, a failed heterosexual union is clearly the modal method: just under half of such respondents reported that their biological parents were once married. This distinguishes the NFSS from numerous studies that have been entirely concerned with "planned" gay and lesbian families, like the NLLFS.

Among those who said their mother had a same-sex relationship, 91% reported living with their mother while she was in the romantic relationship, and 57% said they had lived with their mother and her partner for at least 4 months at some point prior to age 18. A smaller share (23%) said they had spent at least 3 years living in the same household with a romantic partner of their mother's.

Among those who said their father had a same-sex relationship, however, 42% reported living with him while he was in a same-sex romantic relationship, and 23% reported living with him and his partner for at least 4 months (but less than 2% said they had spent at least 3 years together in the same household), a trend similarly noted in Tasker's (2005) review article on gay and lesbian parenting.

Fifty-eight (58) percent of those whose biological mothers had a same-sex relationship also reported that their biological mother exited the respondent's household at some point during their youth, and just under 14% of them reported spending time in the foster care system, indicating greater-than-average household instability. Ancillary analyses of the NFSS suggests a likely "planned" lesbian origin of between 17% and 26% of such respondents, a range estimated from the share of such respondents who claimed that (1) their biological parents were never married or lived together, and that (2) they never lived with a parental opposite-sex partner or with their biological father. The share of respondents (whose fathers had a same-sex relationship) that likely came from "planned" gay families in the NFSS is under 1%.

These distinctions between the NFSS—a population-based sample—and small studies of planned gay and lesbian families nevertheless raise again the question of just how unrepresentative convenience samples of gay and lesbian parents actually are. The use of a probability sample reveals that the young-adult children of parents who have had same-sex relationships (in the NFSS) look less like the children of today's stereotypic gay and lesbian couples—white, upper–middle class, well-educated, employed, and prosperous—than many studies have tacitly or explicitly portrayed. Goldberg (2010, pp. 12–13) aptly notes that existing studies of lesbian and gay couples and their families have largely included "white, middle-class persons who are relatively 'out' in the gay community and who are living in urban areas," while "working-class sexual minorities, racial or ethnic sexual minorities, sexual minorities who live in rural or isolated geographical areas" have been overlooked, understudied, and difficult to reach. Rosenfeld's (2010) analysis of Census data suggests that 37% of children in lesbian cohabiting households are Black or Hispanic. Among respondents in the NFSS who said their mother had a same-sex relationship, 43% are Black or Hispanic. In the NLLFS, by contrast, only 6% are Black or Hispanic.

This is an important oversight: demographic indicators of where gay *parents* live today point less toward stereotypic places like New York and San Francisco and increasingly toward locales where families are more numerous and overall fertility is higher, like San Antonio and Memphis. In their comprehensive demographic look at the American gay and lesbian population, Gates and Ost (2004, p. 47) report, "States and large metropolitan areas with relatively low concentrations of gay and lesbian couples in the population tend to be areas where same-sex couples are more likely to have children in the household." A recent updated brief by Gates (2011, p. F3) reinforces this: "Geographically, same-sex couples are most likely to have children in many of the most socially conservative parts of the country." Moreover, Gates notes that racial minorities are disproportionately more likely (among same-sex households) to report having children; whites, on the other hand, are disproportionately less likely to have children. The NFSS sample reveals the same. Gates' Census-based assessments further raise questions about the sampling strategies of—and the popular use of conclusions from—studies based entirely on convenience samples derived from parents living in progressive metropolitan locales.

2.4. The structure and experience of respondents' families of origin

The NFSS sought to provide as clear a vision as possible of the respondents' household composition during their childhood and adolescence. The survey asked respondents about the marital status of their biological parents both in the past and present. The NFSS also collected "calendar" data from each respondent about their relationship to people who lived with them in their household (for more than 4 months) from birth to age 18, as well as who has lived with them from age 18—after they have left home—to the present. While the calendar data is utilized only sparingly in this study, such rich data enables researchers to document who else has lived with the respondent for virtually their entire life up to the present.

For this particular study, I compare outcomes across eight different types of family-of-origin structure and/or experience. They were constructed from the answers to several questions both in the screener survey and the full survey. It should be noted, however, that their construction reflects an unusual combination of interests—the same-sex romantic behavior of parents, and the experience of household stability or disruption. The eight groups or household settings (with an acronym or short descriptive title) evaluated here, followed by their maximum unweighted analytic sample size, are:

1. IBF: Lived in intact biological family (with mother and father) from 0 to 18, and parents are still married at present (*N* = 919).
2. LM: R reported R's mother had a same-sex romantic (lesbian) relationship with a woman, regardless of any other household transitions (*N* = 163).
3. GF: R reported R's father had a same-sex romantic (gay) relationship with a man, regardless of any other household transitions (*N* = 73).

4. Adopted: R was adopted by one or two strangers at birth or before age 2 (N = 101).
5. Divorced later or had joint custody: R reported living with biological mother and father from birth to age 18, but parents are not married at present (N = 116).
6. Stepfamily: Biological parents were either never married or else divorced, and R's primary custodial parent *was* married to someone else before R turned 18 (N = 394).
7. Single parent: Biological parents were either never married or else divorced, and R's primary custodial parent did *not* marry (or remarry) before R turned 18 (N = 816).
8. All others: Includes all other family structure/event combinations, such as respondents with a deceased parent (N = 406).

Together these eight groups account for the entire NFSS sample. These eight groups are largely, but not entirely, mutually exclusive in reality. That is, a small minority of respondents might fit more than one group. I have, however, forced their mutual exclusivity here for analytic purposes. For example, a respondent whose mother had a same-sex relationship might also qualify in Group 5 or Group 7, but in this case my analytical interest is in maximizing the sample size of Groups 2 and 3 so the respondent would be placed in Group 2 (LMs). Since Group 3 (GFs) is the smallest and most difficult to locate randomly in the population, its composition trumped that of others, even LMs. (There were 12 cases of respondents who reported both a mother and a father having a same-sex relationship; all are analyzed here as GFs, after ancillary analyses revealed comparable exposure to both their mother and father).

Obviously, different grouping decisions may affect the results. The NFSS, which sought to learn a great deal of information about respondents' families of origin, is well-poised to accommodate alternative grouping strategies, including distinguishing those respondents who lived with their lesbian mother's partner for several years (vs. sparingly or not at all), or early in their childhood (compared to later). Small sample sizes (and thus reduced statistical power) may nevertheless hinder some strategies.

In the results section, for maximal ease, I often make use of the acronyms IBF (child of a still-intact biological family), LM (child of a lesbian mother), and GF (child of a gay father). It is, however, very possible that the same-sex romantic relationships about which the respondents report were *not* framed by those respondents as indicating their own (or their parent's own) understanding of their parent as gay or lesbian or bisexual in sexual *orientation*. Indeed, this is more a study of the children of parents who have had (and in some cases, are still in) same-sex relationships than it is one of children whose parents have self-identified or are "out" as gay or lesbian or bisexual. The particular parental relationships the respondents were queried about are, however, gay or lesbian in content. For the sake of brevity and to avoid entanglement in interminable debates about fixed or fluid orientations, I will regularly refer to these groups as respondents with a gay father or lesbian mother.

2.5. Outcomes of interest

This study presents an overview of 40 outcome measures available in the NFSS. Table 1 presents summary statistics for all variables. Why *these* outcomes? While the survey questionnaire (available online) contains several dozen outcome questions of interest, I elected to report here an overview of those outcomes, seeking to include common and oft-studied variables of interest from a variety of different domains. I include all of the particular indexes we sought to evaluate, and a broad list of outcomes from the emotional, relational, and social domains. Subsequent analyses of the NFSS will no doubt examine other outcomes, as well as examine the same outcomes in different ways.

The dichotomous outcome variables summarized in Table 1 are the following: relationship status, employment status, whether they voted in the last presidential election, and use of public assistance (both currently and while growing up), the latter of which was asked as "Before you were 18 years old, did anyone in your immediate family (that is, in your household) ever receive public assistance (such as welfare payments, food stamps, Medicaid, WIC, or free lunch)?" Respondents were also asked about whether they had ever seriously thought about committing suicide in the past 12 months, and about their utilization of counseling or psychotherapy for treatment of "any problem connected with anxiety, depression, relationships, etc."

The Kinsey scale of sexual behavior was employed, but modified to allow respondents to select the best description of their sexual orientation (rather than behavior). Respondents were asked to choose the description that best fits how they think about themselves: 100% heterosexual, mostly heterosexual but somewhat attracted to people of your own sex, bisexual (that is, attracted to men and women equally), mostly homosexual but somewhat attracted to people of the opposite sex, 100% homosexual, or not sexually attracted to either males or females. For simplicity of presentation, I create a dichotomous measure indicating 100% heterosexual (vs. anything else). Additionally, unmarried respondents who are currently in a relationship were asked if their romantic partner is a man or a woman, allowing construction of a measure of "currently in a same-sex romantic relationship."

All respondents were asked if "a parent or other adult caregiver ever touched you in a sexual way, forced you to touch him or her in a sexual way, or forced you to have sexual relations?" Possible answers were: no, never; yes, once; yes, more than once; or not sure. A broader measure about forced sex was asked before it, and read as follows: "Have you ever been physically forced to have any type of sexual activity against your will?" It employs identical possible answers; both have been dichotomized for the analyses (respondents who were "not sure" were not included). Respondents were also asked if they

Table 1
Weighted summary statistics of measures, NFSS.

NFSS variables	Range	Mean	SD	N
Currently married	0,1	0.41	0.49	2988
Currently cohabiting	0,1	0.15	0.36	2988
Family received welfare growing up	0,1	0.34	0.47	2669
Currently on public assistance	0,1	0.21	0.41	2952
Currently employed full-time	0,1	0.45	0.50	2988
Currently unemployed	0,1	0.12	0.32	2988
Voted in last presidential election	0,1	0.55	0.50	2960
Bullied while growing up	0,1	0.36	0.48	2961
Ever suicidal during past year	0,1	0.07	0.25	2953
Recently or currently in therapy	0,1	0.11	0.32	2934
Identifies as entirely heterosexual	0,1	0.85	0.36	2946
Is in a same-sex romantic relationship	0,1	0.06	0.23	1056
Had affair while married/cohabiting	0,1	0.19	0.39	1869
Has ever had an STI	0,1	0.11	0.32	2911
Ever touched sexually by parent/adult	0,1	0.07	0.26	2877
Ever forced to have sex against will	0,1	0.13	0.33	2874
Educational attainment	1–5	2.86	1.11	2988
Family-of-origin safety/security	1–5	3.81	0.97	2917
Family-of-origin negative impact	1–5	2.58	0.98	2919
Closeness to biological mother	1–5	4.05	0.87	2249
Closeness to biological father	1–5	3.74	0.98	1346
Self-reported physical health	1–5	3.57	0.94	2964
Self-reported overall happiness	1–5	4.00	1.05	2957
CES-D depression index	1–4	1.89	0.62	2815
Attachment scale (depend)	1–5	2.97	0.84	2848
Attachment scale (anxiety)	1–5	2.51	0.77	2830
Impulsivity scale	1–4	1.88	0.59	2861
Level of household income	1–13	7.42	3.17	2635
Current relationship quality index	1–5	3.98	0.98	2218
Current relationship is in trouble	1–4	2.19	0.96	2274
Frequency of marijuana use	1–6	1.50	1.23	2918
Frequency of alcohol use	1–6	2.61	1.36	2922
Frequency of drinking to get drunk	1–6	1.70	1.09	2922
Frequency of smoking	1–6	2.03	1.85	2922
Frequency of watching TV	1–6	3.15	1.60	2919
Frequency of having been arrested	1–4	1.29	0.63	2951
Frequency pled guilty to non-minor offense	1–4	1.16	0.46	2947
N of female sex partners (among women)	0–11	0.40	1.10	1975
N of female sex partners (among men)	0–11	3.16	2.68	937
N of male sex partners (among women)	0–11	3.50	2.52	1951
N of male sex partners (among men)	0–11	0.40	1.60	944
Age	18–39	28.21	6.37	2988
Female	0,1	0.51	0.50	2988
White	0,1	0.57	0.49	2988
Gay-friendliness of state of residence	1–5	2.58	1.78	2988
Family-of-origin structure groups				
Intact biological family (IBF)	0,1	0.40	0.49	2988
Mother had same-sex relationship (LM)	0,1	0.01	0.10	2988
Father had same-sex relationship (GF)	0,1	0.01	0.75	2988
Adopted age 0–2	0,1	0.01	0.75	2988
Divorced later/joint custody	0,1	0.06	0.23	2988
Stepfamily	0,1	0.17	0.38	2988
Single parent	0,1	0.19	0.40	2988
All others	0,1	0.15	0.36	2988
Mother's education				
Less than high school	0,1	0.15	0.35	2988
Received high school diploma	0,1	0.28	0.45	2988
Some college/associate's degree	0,1	0.26	0.44	2988
Bachelor's degrees	0,1	0.15	0.36	2988
More than bachelor's	0,1	0.08	0.28	2988
Do not know/missing	0,1	0.08	0.28	2988
Family-of-origin income				
$0–20,000	0,1	0.13	0.34	2988
$20,001–40,000	0,1	0.19	0.39	2988
$40,001–75,000	0,1	0.25	0.43	2988
$75,001–100,000	0,1	0.14	0.34	2988
$100,001–150,000	0,1	0.05	0.22	2988

(continued on next page)

Table 1 (*continued*)

NFSS variables	Range	Mean	SD	N
$150,001–200,000	0,1	0.01	0.11	2988
Above $200,000	0,1	0.01	0.10	2988
Do not know/missing	0,1	0.22	0.42	2988

had ever had a sexually-transmitted infection, and if they had ever had a sexual relationship with someone else while they (the respondent) were married or cohabiting.

Among continuous variables, I included a five-category educational achievement measure, a standard five-point self-reported measure of general physical health, a five-point measure of overall happiness, a 13-category measure of total household income before taxes and deductions last year, and a four-point (frequency) measure of how often the respondent thought their current relationship "might be in trouble" (never once, once or twice, several times, or numerous times). Several continuous variables were constructed from multiple measures, including an eight-measure modified version of the CES-D depression scale, an index of the respondent's reported current (romantic) relationship quality, closeness to the respondent's biological mother and father, and a pair of attachment scales—one assessing dependability and the other anxiety. Finally, a pair of indexes captures (1) the overall safety and security in their family while growing up, and (2) respondents' impressions of negative family-of-origin experiences that continue to affect them. These are part of a multidimensional relationship assessment instrument (dubbed RELATE) designed with the perspective that aspects of family life, such as the quality of the parent's relationship with their children, create a family tone that can be mapped on a continuum from safe/predictable/rewarding to unsafe/chaotic/punishing (Busby et al., 2001). Each of the scales and their component measures are detailed in Appendix B.

Finally, I evaluate nine count outcomes, seven of which are frequency measures, and the other two counts of gender-specific sexual partners. Respondents were asked, "During the past year, how often did you..." watch more than 3 h of television in a row, use marijuana, smoke, drink alcohol, and drink with the intent to get drunk. Responses (0–5) ranged from "never" to "every day or almost every day." Respondents were also asked if they have ever been arrested, and if they had ever been convicted of or pled guilty to any charges other than a minor traffic violation. Answers to these two ranged from 0 (no, never) to 3 (yes, numerous times). Two questions about respondents' number of sex partners were asked (of both men and women) in this way: "How many different women have you ever had a sexual relationship with? This includes any female you had sex with, even if it was only once or if you did not know her well." The same question was asked about sexual relationships with men. Twelve responses were possible: 0, 1, 2, 3, 4–6, 7–9, 10–15, 16–20, 21–30, 31–50, 51–99, and 100+.

2.6. Analytic approach

My analytic strategy is to highlight distinctions between the eight family structure/experience groups on the 40 outcome variables, both in a bivariate manner (using a simple *T*-test) and in a multivariate manner using appropriate variable-specific regression techniques—logistic, OLS, Poisson, or negative binomial—and employing controls for respondent's age, race/ethnicity, gender, mother's education, and perceived family-of-origin income, an approach comparable to Rosenfeld's (2010) analysis of differences in children making normal progress through school and the overview article highlighting the findings of the first wave of the Add Health study (Resnick et al., 1997). Additionally, I controlled for having been bullied, the measure for which was asked as follows: "While growing up, children and teenagers typically experience negative interactions with others. We say that someone is bullied when someone else, or a group, says or does nasty and unpleasant things to him or her. We do not consider it bullying when two people quarrel or fight, however. Do you recall ever being bullied by someone else, or by a group, such that you still have vivid, negative memories of it?"

Finally, survey respondents' current state of residence was coded on a scale (1–5) according to how expansive or restrictive its laws are concerning gay marriage and the legal rights of same-sex couples (as of November 2011). Emerging research suggests state-level political realities about gay rights may discernibly shape the lives of GLB residents (Hatzenbuehler et al., 2009; Rostosky et al., 2009). This coding scheme was borrowed from a *Los Angeles Times* effort to map the timeline of state-level rights secured for gay unions. I modified it from a 10-point to a 5-point scale (Times Research Reporting, 2012). I classify the respondent's current state in one of the following five ways:

- 1 = Constitutional amendment banning gay marriage and/or other legal rights.
- 2 = Legal ban on gay marriage and/or other legal rights.
- 3 = No specific laws/bans and/or domestic partnerships are legal.
- 4 = Domestic partnerships with comprehensive protections are legal and/or gay marriages performed elsewhere are recognized.
- 5 = Civil unions are legal and/or gay marriage is legal.

Each case in the NFSS sample was assigned a weight based on the sampling design and their probability of being selected, ensuring a sample that is nationally representative of American adults aged 18–39. These sample weights were used in every statistical procedure displayed herein unless otherwise noted. The regression models exhibited few (N < 15) missing values on the covariates.

This broad overview approach, appropriate for introducing a new dataset, provides a foundation for future, more focused analyses of the outcomes I explore here. There are, after all, far more ways to delineate family structure and experiences—and changes therein—than I have undertaken here. Others will evaluate such groupings differently, and will construct alternative approaches of testing for group differences in what is admittedly a wide diversity of outcome measures.

I would be remiss to claim causation here, since to document that having particular family-of-origin experiences—or the sexual relationships of one's parents—causes outcomes for adult children, I would need to not only document that there is a correlation between such family-of-origin experiences, but that no other plausible factors could be the common cause of any suboptimal outcomes. Rather, my analytic intention is far more modest than that: to evaluate the presence of simple group differences, and—with the addition of several control variables—to assess just how robust such group differences are.

3. Results

3.1. Comparisons with still-intact, biological families (IBFs)

Table 2 displays mean scores on 15 dichotomous outcome variables which can be read as simple percentages, sorted by the eight different family structure/experience groups described earlier. As in Tables 3 and 4, numbers that appear in bold indicate that the group's estimate is statistically different from the young-adult children of IBFs, as discerned by a basic T-test (p < 0.05). Numbers that appear with an asterisk (*) beside it indicate that the group's dichotomous variable estimate from a logistic regression model (not shown) is statistically-significantly different from IBFs, after controlling for respondent's age, gender, race/ethnicity, level of mother's education, perceived family-of-origin's income, experience with having been bullied as a youth, and the "gay friendliness" of the respondent's current state of residence.

At a glance, the number of statistically-significant differences between respondents from IBFs and respondents from the other seven types of family structures/experiences is considerable, and in the vast majority of cases the optimal outcome—where one can be readily discerned—favors IBFs. Table 2 reveals 10 (out of 15 possible) statistically-significant differences in simple *t*-tests between IBFs and LMs (the pool of respondents who reported that their mother has had a lesbian relationship), one higher than the number of simple differences (9) between IBFs and respondents from both single-parent and stepfamilies. All but one of those associations is significant in logistic regression analyses contrasting LMs and IBFs (the omitted category).

Beginning at the top of Table 2, the marriage rates of LMs and GFs (those who reported that their father had a gay relationship) are statistically comparable to IBFs, while LMs' cohabitation rate is notable higher than IBFs' (24% vs. 9%, respectively). Sixty-nine (69) percent of LMs and 57% of GFs reported that their family received public assistance at some point while growing up, compared with 17% of IBFs; 38% of LMs said they are currently receiving some form of public assistance, compared with 10% of IBFs. Just under half of all IBFs reported being employed full-time at present, compared with 26% of

Table 2
Mean scores on select dichotomous outcome variables, NFSS (can read as percentage: as in, 0.42 = 42%).

	IBF (intact bio family)	LM (lesbian mother)	GF (gay father)	Adopted by strangers	Divorced late (>18)	Stepfamily	Single-parent	All other
Currently married	0.43	0.36	0.35	0.41	0.36*	0.41	0.37	0.39
Currently cohabiting	0.09	**0.24***	0.21	0.07^	**0.31***	**0.19***	**0.19***	0.13
Family received welfare growing up	0.17	**0.69***	0.57*	0.12^	**0.47***^	**0.53***^	**0.48***^	**0.35**^
Currently on public assistance	0.10	**0.38***	0.23	**0.27***	**0.31***	**0.30***	**0.30***	**0.23***
Currently employed full-time	0.49	**0.26***	0.34	0.41	0.42	0.47^	0.43^	**0.39**
Currently unemployed	0.08	**0.28***	0.20	0.22*	0.15	0.14	**0.13**^	**0.15**
Voted in last presidential election	0.57	**0.41**	0.73*^	0.58	0.63^	0.57^	0.51	0.48
Thought recently about suicide	0.05	0.12	0.24*	0.07	0.08	0.10	0.05	0.09
Recently or currently in therapy	0.08	**0.19***	0.19	**0.22***	0.12	**0.17***	**0.13***	0.09
Identifies as entirely heterosexual	0.90	**0.61***	0.71*	0.82^	0.83^	**0.81***^	**0.83***^	**0.82***^
Is in a same-sex romantic relationship	0.04	0.07	0.12	0.23	0.05	**0.13***	0.03	0.02
Had affair while married/cohabiting	0.13	**0.40***	0.25	0.20	0.12^	**0.32***	0.19^	0.16^
Has ever had an STI	0.08	0.20*	0.25*	0.16	0.12	**0.16***	**0.14***	0.08
Ever touched sexually by parent/adult	0.02	**0.23***	0.06^	0.03^	0.10*	**0.12***	**0.10***	**0.08***^
Ever forced to have sex against will	0.08	**0.31***	0.25*	0.23*	0.24*	**0.16***	**0.16***^	0.11^

Bold indicates the mean scores displayed are statistically-significantly different from IBFs (currently intact, bio mother/father household, column 1), without additional controls.

An asterisk (*) next to the estimate indicates a statistically-significant difference (p < 0.05) between the group's coefficient and that of IBF's, controlling for respondent's age, gender, race/ethnicity, level of mother's education, perceived household income while growing up, experience being bullied as a youth, and state's legislative gay-friendliness, derived from logistic regression models (not shown).

A caret (^) next to the estimate indicates a statistically-significant difference (p < 0.05) between the group's mean and the mean of LM (column 2), without additional controls.

Table 3
Mean scores on select continuous outcome variables, NFSS.

	IBF (intact bio family)	LM (lesbian mother)	GF (gay father)	Adopted by strangers	Divorced late (>18)	Stepfamily	Single- parent	All other
Educational attainment	3.19	**2.39**[*]	**2.64**[*]	3.21[^]	**2.88**[*^]	**2.64**[*]	**2.66**[*]	**2.54**[*]
Family-of-origin safety/security	4.13	**3.12**[*]	**3.25**[*]	**3.77**[*^]	**3.52**[*]	**3.52**[*^]	**3.58**[*^]	**3.77**[*^]
Family-of-origin negative impact	2.30	**3.13**[*]	**2.90**[*]	**2.83**[*]	**2.96**[*]	**2.76**[*]	**2.78**[*]	**2.64**[*^]
Closeness to biological mother	4.17	4.05	**3.71**[*]	3.58	3.95	4.03	**3.85**[*]	**3.97**
Closeness to biological father	3.87	3.16	3.43	–	**3.29**[*]	3.65	**3.24**[*]	3.61
Self-reported physical health	3.75	**3.38**	3.58	3.53	**3.46**	3.49	**3.43**[*]	**3.41**
Self-reported overall happiness	4.16	3.89	3.72	3.92	4.02	**3.87**[*]	3.93	3.83
CES-D depression index	1.83	**2.20**[*]	**2.18**[*]	1.95	2.01	1.91[^]	1.89[^]	1.94[^]
Attachment scale (depend)	2.82	**3.43**[*]	3.14	**3.12**[*]	**3.08**[^]	**3.10**[*^]	**3.05**[^]	**3.02**[^]
Attachment scale (anxiety)	2.46	2.67	2.66	2.66	2.71	2.53	2.51	2.56
Impulsivity scale	1.90	2.03	2.02	1.85	1.94	1.86[^]	1.82[^]	1.89
Level of household income	8.27	**6.08**	7.15	7.93[^]	7.42[^]	**7.04**	6.96	**6.19**[*]
Current relationship quality index	4.11	3.83	**3.63**[*]	3.79	3.95	**3.80**[*]	3.95	3.94
Current relationship is in trouble	2.04	**2.35**	**2.55**[*]	2.35	**2.43**	**2.35**[*]	**2.26**[*]	2.15

Bold indicates the mean scores displayed are statistically-significantly different from IBFs (currently intact, bio mother/father household, column 1), without additional controls.

An asterisk ([*]) next to the estimate indicates a statistically-significant difference ($p < 0.05$) between the group's coefficient and that of IBF's, controlling for respondent's age, gender, race/ethnicity, level of mother's education, perceived household income while growing up, experience being bullied as a youth, and state's legislative gay-friendliness, derived from OLS regression models (not shown).

A caret ([^]) next to the estimate indicates a statistically-significant difference ($p < 0.05$) between the group's mean and the mean of LM (column 2), without additional controls.

Table 4
Mean scores on select event-count outcome variables, NFSS.

	IBF (intact bio family)	LM (lesbian mother)	GF (gay father)	Adopted by strangers	Divorced late (>18)	Stepfamily	Single- parent	All other
Frequency of marijuana use	1.32	**1.84**[*]	1.61	1.33[^]	**2.00**[*]	1.47	**1.73**[*]	1.49
Frequency of alcohol use	2.70	2.37	2.70	2.74	2.55	2.50	2.66	2.44
Frequency of drinking to get drunk	1.68	1.77	2.14	1.73	1.90	1.68	1.74	1.64
Frequency of smoking	1.79	**2.76**[*]	**2.61**[*]	**2.34**[*]	**2.44**[*]	**2.31**[*]	**2.18**[*]	1.91[^]
Frequency of watching TV	3.01	**3.70**[*]	3.49	3.31	3.33	**3.43**[*]	3.25	2.95[^]
Frequency of having been arrested	1.18	**1.68**[*]	**1.75**[*]	1.31[^]	1.38	**1.38**[*^]	**1.35**[*^]	**1.34**[*^]
Frequency pled guilty to non-minor offense	1.10	**1.36**[*]	**1.41**[*]	1.19	1.30	**1.21**[*]	**1.17**[*^]	1.17[^]
N of female sex partners (among women)	0.22	**1.04**[*]	**1.47**[*]	0.47[^]	**0.96**[*]	0.47[*^]	**0.52**[*^]	0.33[^]
N of female sex partners (among men)	2.70	3.46	4.17	3.24	3.66	**3.85**[*]	3.23	3.37
N of male sex partners (among women)	2.79	**4.02**[*]	**5.92**[*]	3.49	**3.97**[*]	**4.57**[*]	**4.04**[*]	2.91[^]
N of male sex partners (among men)	0.20	**1.48**[*]	**1.47**[*]	0.27	**0.98**[*]	0.55	0.42	0.44

Bold indicates the mean scores displayed are statistically-significantly different from IBFs (currently intact, bio mother/father household, column 1), without additional controls.

An asterisk ([*]) next to the estimate indicates a statistically-significant difference ($p < 0.05$) between the group's coefficient and that of IBF's, controlling for respondent's age, gender, race/ethnicity, level of mother's education, perceived household income while growing up, experience being bullied as a youth, and state's legislative gay-friendliness, derived from Poisson or negative binomial regression models (not shown).

A caret ([^]) next to the estimate indicates a statistically-significant difference ($p < 0.05$) between the group's mean and the mean of LM (column 2), without additional controls.

LMs. While only 8% of IBF respondents said they were currently unemployed, 28% of LM respondents said the same. LMs were statistically less likely than IBFs to have voted in the 2008 presidential election (41% vs. 57%), and more than twice as likely—19% vs. 8%—to report being currently (or within the past year) in counseling or therapy "for a problem connected with anxiety, depression, relationships, etc.," an outcome that was significantly different after including control variables.

In concurrence with several studies of late, the NFSS reveals that the children of lesbian mothers seem more open to same-sex relationships (Biblarz and Stacey, 2010; Gartrell et al., 2011a,b; Golombok et al., 1997). Although they are not statistically different from most other groups in having a same-sex relationship *at present*, they are much less apt to identify entirely as heterosexual (61% vs. 90% of respondents from IBFs). The same was true of GF respondents—those young adults who said their father had a relationship with another man: 71% of them identified entirely as heterosexual. Other sexual differences are notable among LMs, too: a greater share of daughters of lesbian mothers report being "not sexually attracted to either males or females" than among any other family-structure groups evaluated here (4.1% of female LMs, compared to 0.5% of female IBFs, not shown in Table 2). Exactly why the young-adult children of lesbian mothers are more apt to experience same-sex attraction and behaviors, as well as self-report asexuality, is not clear, but the fact that they do seems consistent across studies. Given that lower rates of heterosexuality characterize other family structure/experience types in the

NFSS, as Table 2 clearly documents, the answer is likely located not simply in parental sexual orientation but in successful cross-sex relationship role modeling, or its absence or scarcity.

Sexual conduct within their romantic relationships is also distinctive: while 13% of IBFs reported having had a sexual relationship with someone else while they were either married or cohabiting, 40% of LMs said the same. In contrast to Gartrell et al.'s (2011a,b) recent, widely-disseminated conclusions about the absence of sexual victimization in the NLLFS data, 23% of LMs said yes when asked whether "a parent or other adult caregiver ever touched you in a sexual way, forced you to touch him or her in a sexual way, or forced you to have sexual relations," while only 2% of IBFs responded affirmatively. Since such reports are more common among women than men, I split the analyses by gender (not shown). Among female respondents, 3% of IBFs reported parental (or adult caregiver) sexual contact/victimization, dramatically below the 31% of LMs who reported the same. Just under 10% of female GFs responded affirmatively to the question, an estimate not significantly different from the IBFs.

It is entirely plausible, however, that sexual victimization could have been at the hands of the LM respondents' biological father, prompting the mother to leave the union and—at some point in the future—commence a same-sex relationship. Ancillary (unweighted) analyses of the NFSS, which asked respondents how old they were when the first incident occurred (and can be compared to the household structure calendar, which documents who lived in their household each year up until age 18) reveal this possibility, up to a point: 33% of those LM respondents who said they had been sexually victimized by a parent or adult caregiver reported that they were also living with their biological father in the year that the first incident occurred. Another 29% of victimized LMs reported never having lived with their biological father at all. Just under 34% of LM respondents who said they had at some point lived with their mother's same-sex partner reported a first-time incident at an age that was equal to or higher than when they first lived with their mother's partner. Approximately 13% of victimized LMs reported living with a foster parent the year when the first incident occurred. In other words, there is no obvious trend to the timing of first victimization and when the respondent may have lived with their biological father or their mother's same-sex partner, nor are we suggesting by whom the respondent was most likely victimized. Future exploration of the NFSS's detailed household structure calendar offers some possibility for clarification.

The elevated LM estimate of sexual victimization is not the only estimate of increased victimization. Another more general question about forced sex, "Have you ever been physically forced to have any type of sexual activity against your will" also displays significant differences between IBFs and LMs (and GFs). The question about forced sex was asked *before* the question about sexual contact with a parent or other adult and may include incidents of it but, by the numbers, clearly includes additional circumstances. Thirty-one percent of LMs indicated they had, at some point in their life, been forced to have sex against their will, compared with 8% of IBFs and 25% of GFs. Among female respondents, 14% of IBFs reported forced sex, compared with 46% of LMs and 52% of GFs (both of the latter estimates are statistically-significantly different from that reported by IBFs).

While I have so far noted several distinctions between IBFs and GFs—respondents who said their father had a gay relationship—there are simply fewer statistically-significant distinctions to note between IBFs and GFs than between IBFs and LMs, which may or may not be due in part to the smaller sample of respondents with gay fathers in the NFSS, and the much smaller likelihood of having lived with their gay father while he was in a same-sex relationship. Only six of 15 measures in Table 2 reveal statistically-significant differences in the regression models (but only one in a bivariate environment). After including controls, the children of a gay father were statistically more apt (than IBFs) to receive public assistance while growing up, to have voted in the last election, to have thought recently about committing suicide, to ever report a sexually-transmitted infection, have experienced forced sex, and were less likely to self-identify as entirely heterosexual. While other outcomes reported by GFs often differed from IBFs, statistically-significant differences were not as regularly detected.

Although my attention has been primarily directed at the inter-group differences between IBFs, LMs, and GFs, it is worth noting that LMs are hardly alone in displaying numerous differences with IBFs. Respondents who lived in stepfamilies or single-parent families displayed nine simple differences in Table 2. Besides GFs, adopted respondents displayed the fewest simple differences (three).

Table 3 displays mean scores on 14 continuous outcomes. As in Table 2, bold indicates simple statistically-significant outcome differences with young-adult respondents from still-intact, biological families (IBFs) and an asterisk indicates a regression coefficient (models not shown) that is significantly different from IBFs after a series of controls. Consistent with Table 2, eight of the estimates for LMs are statistically different from IBFs. Five of the eight differences are significant as regression estimates. The young-adult children of women who have had a lesbian relationship fare worse on educational attainment, family-of-origin safety/security, negative impact of family-of-origin, the CES-D (depression) index, one of two attachment scales, report worse physical health, smaller household incomes than do respondents from still-intact biological families, and think that their current romantic relationship is in trouble more frequently.

The young-adult GF respondents were likewise statistically distinct from IBF respondents on seven of 14 continuous outcomes, all of which were significantly different when evaluated in regression models. When contrasted with IBFs, GFs reported more modest educational attainment, worse scores on the family-of-origin safety/security and negative impact indexes, less closeness to their biological mother, greater depression, a lower score on the current (romantic) relationship quality index, and think their current romantic relationship is in trouble more frequently.

As in Table 2, respondents who reported living in stepfamilies or in single-parent households also exhibit numerous simple statistical differences from IBFs—on nine and 10 out of 14 outcomes, respectively—most of which remain significant in the regression models. On only four of 14 outcomes do adopted respondents appear distinctive (three of which remain significant after introducing controls).

Table 4 displays mean scores on nine event counts, sorted by the eight family structure/experience groups. The NFSS asked all respondents about experience with male and female sexual partners, but I report them here separately by gender. LM respondents report statistically greater marijuana use, more frequent smoking, watch television more often, have been arrested more, pled guilty to non-minor offenses more, and—among women—report greater numbers of both female and male sex partners than do IBF respondents. Female LMs reported an average of just over one female sex partner in their lifetimes, as well as four male sex partners, in contrast to female IBFs (0.22 and 2.79, respectively). Male LMs report an average of 3.46 female sex partners and 1.48 male partners, compared with 2.70 and 0.20, respectively, among male IBFs. Only the number of male partners among men, however, displays significant differences (after controls are included).

Among GFs, only three bivariate distinctions appear. However, six distinctions emerge after regression controls: they are more apt than IBFs to smoke, have been arrested, pled guilty to non-minor offenses, and report more numerous sex partners (except for the number of female sex partners among male GFs). Adopted respondents display no simple differences from IBFs, while the children of stepfamilies and single parents each display six significant differences with young adults from still-intact, biological mother/father families.

Although I have paid much less attention to most of the other groups whose estimates also appear in Tables 2–4, it is worth noting how seldom the estimates of young-adult children who were adopted by strangers (before age 2) differ statistically from the children of still-intact biological families. They display the fewest simple significant differences—seven—across the 40 outcomes evaluated here. Given that such adoptions are typically the result of considerable self-selection, it should not surprise that they display fewer differences with IBFs.

To summarize, then, in 25 of 40 outcomes, there are simple statistically-significant differences between IBFs and LMs, those whose mothers had a same-sex relationship. After controls, there are 24 such differences. There are 24 simple differences between IBFs and stepfamilies, and 24 statistically-significant differences after controls. Among single (heterosexual) parents, there are 25 simple differences before controls and 21 after controls. Between GFs and IBFs, there are 11 and 19 such differences, respectively.

3.2. Summary of differences between LMs and other family structures/experiences

Researchers sometimes elect to evaluate the outcomes of children of gay and lesbian parents by comparing them not directly to stable heterosexual marriages but to other types of households, since it is often the case—and it is certainly true of the NFSS—that a gay or lesbian parent first formed a heterosexual union prior to "coming out of the closet," and witnessing the dissolution of that union (Tasker, 2005). So comparing the children of such parents with those who experienced no union dissolution is arguably unfair. The NFSS, however, enables researchers to compare outcomes across a variety of other types of family-structural history. While I will not explore in-depth here all the statistically-significant differences between LMs, GFs, and other groups *besides* IBFs, a few overall observations are merited.

Of the 239 possible between-group differences here—not counting those differences with Group 1 (IBFs) already described earlier—the young-adult children of lesbian mothers display 57 (or 24% of total possible) that are significant at the $p < 0.05$ level (indicated in Tables 2–4 with a caret), and 44 (or 18% of total) that are significant after controls (not shown). The majority of these differences are in suboptimal directions, meaning that LMs display worse outcomes. The young-adult children of gay men, on the other hand, display only 11 (or 5% of total possible) between-group differences that are statistically significant at the $p < 0.05$ level, and yet 24 (or 10% of total) that are significant after controls (not shown).

In the NFSS, then, the young-adult children of a mother who has had a lesbian relationship display more significant distinctions with other respondents than do the children of a gay father. This may be the result of genuinely different experiences of their family transitions, the smaller sample size of children of gay men, or the comparatively-rarer experience of living with a gay father (only 42% of such respondents reported ever living with their father while he was in a same-sex relationship, compared with 91% who reported living with their mother while she was in a same-sex relationship).

4. Discussion

Just how different are the adult children of men and women who pursue same-sex romantic (i.e., gay and lesbian) relationships, when evaluated using population-based estimates from a random sample? The answer, as might be expected, depends on to whom you compare them. When compared with children who grew up in biologically (still) intact, mother–father families, the children of women who reported a same-sex relationship look markedly different on numerous outcomes, including many that are obviously suboptimal (such as education, depression, employment status, or marijuana use). On 25 of 40 outcomes (or 63%) evaluated here, there are bivariate statistically-significant ($p < 0.05$) differences between children from still-intact, mother/father families and those whose mother reported a lesbian relationship. On 11 of 40 outcomes (or 28%) evaluated here, there are bivariate statistically-significant ($p < 0.05$) differences between children from still-intact, mother/father families and those whose father reported a gay relationship. Hence, there are differences in both comparisons, but there are many more differences by any method of analysis in comparisons between young-adult children of IBFs and LMs than between IBFs and GFs.

While the NFSS may best capture what might be called an "earlier generation" of children of same-sex parents, and includes among them many who witnessed a failed heterosexual union, the basic statistical comparisons between this group and those of others, especially biologically-intact, mother/father families, suggests that notable differences on many outcomes do in fact exist. This is inconsistent with claims of "no differences" generated by studies that have commonly employed far more narrow samples than this one.

Goldberg (2010) aptly asserts that many existing studies were conducted primarily comparing children of heterosexual divorced and lesbian divorced mothers, potentially leading observers to erroneously attribute to parental sexual orientation the corrosive effects of enduring parental divorce. Her warning is well-taken, and it is one that the NFSS cannot entirely mitigate. Yet when compared with other young adults who experienced household transitions and who witnessed parents forming new romantic relationships—for example, stepfamilies—the children of lesbian mothers looked (statistically) significantly different just under 25% of the time (and typically in suboptimal directions). Nevertheless, the children of mothers who have had same-sex relationships are far less apt to differ from stepfamilies and single parents than they are from still-intact biological families.

Why the divergence between the findings in this study and those from so many previous ones? The answer lies in part with the small or nonprobability samples so often relied upon in nearly all previous studies—they have very likely underestimated the number and magnitude of real differences between the children of lesbian mothers (and to a lesser extent, gay fathers) and those raised in other types of households. While the architects of such studies have commonly and appropriately acknowledged their limitations, practically—since they are often the only studies being conducted—their results are treated as providing information about gay and lesbian household experiences *in general*. But this study, based on a rare large probability sample, reveals far greater diversity in the experience of lesbian motherhood (and to a lesser extent, gay fatherhood) than has been acknowledged or understood.

Given that the characteristics of the NFSS's sample of children of LMs and GFs are close to estimates of the same offered by demographers using the American Community Study, one conclusion from the analyses herein is merited: the sample-selection bias problem in very many studies of gay and lesbian parenting is not incidental, but likely profound, rendering the ability of much past research to offer valid interpretations of *average* household experiences of children with a lesbian or gay parent suspect at best. Most snowball-sample-based research has, instead, shed light on *above-average* household experiences.

While studies of family structure often locate at least modest benefits that accrue to the children of married biological parents, some scholars attribute much of the benefit to socioeconomic-status differences between married parents and those parents in other types of relationships (Biblarz and Raftery, 1999). While this is likely true of the NFSS as well, the results presented herein controlled not only for socioeconomic status differences between families of origin, but also political-geographic distinctions, age, gender, race/ethnicity, and the experience of having been bullied (which was reported by 53% of LMs but only 35% of IBFs).

To be sure, those NFSS respondents who reported that a parent of theirs had had a romantic relationship with a member of the same sex are a very diverse group: some experienced numerous household transitions, and some did not. Some of their parents may have remained in a same-sex relationship, while others did not. Some may self-identify as lesbian or gay, while others may not. I did not explore in detail the diversity of household experiences here, given the overview nature of this study. But the richness of the NFSS—which has annual calendar data for household transitions from birth to age 18 *and* from age 18 to the present—allows for closer examination of many of these questions.

Nevertheless, to claim that there are few meaningful statistical differences between the different groups evaluated here would be to state something that is empirically inaccurate. Minimally, the population-based estimates presented here suggest that a good deal more attention must be paid to the real diversity among gay and lesbian parent experiences in America, just as it long has been among heterosexual households. Child outcomes in stable, "planned" GLB families and those that are the product of previous heterosexual unions are quite likely distinctive, as previous studies' conclusions would suggest. Yet as demographers of gay and lesbian America continue to note—and as the NFSS reinforces—planned GLB households only comprise a portion (and an unknown one at that) of all GLB households with children.

Even if the children in planned GLB families exhibit better outcomes than those from failed heterosexual unions, the former still exhibits a diminished context of kin altruism (like adoption, step-parenting, or nonmarital childbirth), which have typically proven to be a risk setting, on average, for raising children when compared with married, biological parenting (Miller et al., 2000). In short, if same-sex parents are able to raise children with no differences, despite the kin distinctions, it would mean that same-sex couples are able to do something that heterosexual couples in step-parenting, adoptive, and cohabiting contexts have themselves not been able to do—replicate the optimal childrearing environment of married, biological-parent homes (Moore et al., 2002). And studies focusing on parental roles or household divisions of labor in planned GLB families will fail to reveal—because they have not measured it—how their children fare as adults.

The between-group comparisons described above also suggest that those respondents with a lesbian mother and those with a gay father do not always exhibit comparable outcomes in young adulthood. While the sample size of gay fathers in the NFSS was modest, any monolithic ideas about same-sex parenting experiences in general are not supported by these analyses.

Although the NFSS offers strong support for the notion that there are significant differences among young adults that correspond closely to the parental behavior, family structures, and household experiences during their youth, I have not and will not speculate here on causality, in part because the data are not optimally designed to do so, and because the causal reckoning for so many different types of outcomes is well beyond what an overview manuscript like this one could ever purport to accomplish. Focused (and more complex) analyses of unique outcomes, drawing upon idiosyncratic, domain-specific conceptual models, is recommended for scholars who wish to more closely assess the functions that the number, gender, and sexual decision-making of parents may play in young adults' lives. I am thus not suggesting that growing up with a lesbian mother or gay father causes suboptimal outcomes *because of* the sexual orientation or sexual behavior of the parent; rather, my point is more modest: the groups display numerous, notable distinctions, especially when compared with young adults whose biological mother and father remain married.

There is more that this article does not accomplish, including closer examinations of subpopulations, consideration of more outcomes and comparisons between other groups, and stronger tests of statistical significance—such as multiple regression with more numerous independent variables, or propensity score matching. That is what the NFSS is designed to foster. This article serves as a call for such study, as well as an introduction to the data and to its sampling and measurement strengths and abilities. Future studies would optimally include a more significant share of children from planned gay families, although their relative scarcity in the NFSS suggests that their appearance in even much larger probability samples will remain infrequent for the foreseeable future. The NFSS, despite significant efforts to randomly over-sample such populations, nevertheless was more apt to survey children whose parents exhibited gay and lesbian relationship behavior *after* being in a heterosexual union. This pattern may remain more common today than many scholars suppose.

5. Conclusion

As scholars of same-sex parenting aptly note, same-sex couples have and will continue to raise children. American courts are finding arguments against gay marriage decreasingly persuasive (Rosenfeld, 2007). This study is intended to neither undermine nor affirm any legal rights concerning such. The tenor of the last 10 years of academic discourse about gay and lesbian parents suggests that there is little to nothing about them that might be negatively associated with child development, and a variety of things that might be uniquely positive. The results of analyzing a rare large probability sample reported herein, however, document numerous, consistent differences among young adults who reported maternal lesbian behavior (and to a lesser extent, paternal gay behavior) prior to age 18. While previous studies suggest that children in planned GLB families seem to fare comparatively well, their actual representativeness among all GLB families in the US may be more modest than research based on convenience samples has presumed.

Although the findings reported herein may be explicable in part by a variety of forces uniquely problematic for child development in lesbian and gay families—including a lack of social support for parents, stress exposure resulting from persistent stigma, and modest or absent legal security for their parental and romantic relationship statuses—the empirical claim that no notable differences exist must go. While it is certainly accurate to affirm that sexual orientation or parental sexual behavior need have nothing to do with the *ability* to be a good, effective parent, the data evaluated herein using population-based estimates drawn from a large, nationally-representative sample of young Americans suggest that it may affect the *reality* of family experiences among a significant number.

Do children need a married mother and father to turn out well as adults? No, if we observe the many anecdotal accounts with which all Americans are familiar. Moreover, there are many cases in the NFSS where respondents have proven resilient and prevailed as adults in spite of numerous transitions, be they death, divorce, additional or diverse romantic partners, or remarriage. But the NFSS also clearly reveals that children appear most apt to succeed well as adults—on multiple counts and across a variety of domains—when they spend their entire childhood with their married mother and father, and especially when the parents remain married to the present day. Insofar as the share of intact, biological mother/father families continues to shrink in the United States, as it has, this portends growing challenges within families, but also heightened dependence on public health organizations, federal and state public assistance, psychotherapeutic resources, substance use programs, and the criminal justice system.

Appendix A. Comparison of weighted NFSS results with parallel national survey results on selected demographic and lifestyle variables, US adults (in percentages)

	NFSS 2011, N = 941 (18–23)	NSYR 2007–2008, N = 2520 (18–23)	NFSS 2011, N = 1123 (24–32)	Add Health 2007–2008, N = 15,701 (24–32)	NFSS 2011, N = 2988 (18–39)	NSFG 2006–2010, N = 16,851 (18–39)	CPS ASEC 2011, N = 58,788 (18–39)
Gender							
Male	52.6	48.3	47.3	50.6	49.4	49.8	50.4
Female	47.4	51.7	52.8	49.4	50.6	50.2	49.6

Appendix A (*continued*)

	NFSS 2011, N = 941 (18–23)	NSYR 2007–2008, N = 2520 (18–23)	**NFSS** 2011, N = 1123 (24–32)	**Add Health** 2007–2008, N = 15,701 (24–32)	**NFSS** 2011, N = 2988 (18–39)	**NSFG** 2006–2010, N = 16,851 (18–39)	**CPS ASEC** 2011, N = 58,788 (18–39)
Age							
18–23					28.9	28.6	28.2
24–32					41.2	40.6	42.1
33–39					29.9	30.9	29.8
Race/ethnicity							
White, NH	54.2	68.3	60.2	69.2	57.7	61.6	59.6
Black, NH	11.0	15.0	13.0	15.9	12.6	13.3	13.2
Hispanic	24.9	11.2	20.7	10.8	20.8	18.6	19.5
Other (or multiple), NH	10.0	5.5	6.2	4.2	8.9	6.5	7.8
Region							
Northeast	18.9	11.8	16.5		17.6		17.5
Midwest	18.7	25.6	23.3		21.1		21.2
South	34.3	39.1	39.6		36.7		37.0
West	28.2	23.5	20.6		24.6		24.4
Mother's education (BA or above)	28.4	33.3	24.6	21.9	25.3	22.2	
Respondent's education (BA or above)	5.3	3.8	33.7	30.0	26.5	24.2	
Household income (current)							
Under $10,000	21.0		9.7	5.6	11.9	9.5	5.7
$10,000–19,999	13.3		9.1	6.9	9.2	13.1	7.4
$20,000–29,999	11.6		10.3	10.1	10.5	13.5	9.5
$30,000–39,999	8.0		11.0	11.1	9.6	13.4	9.4
$40,000–49,999	6.5		12.8	11.8	9.9	8.5	9.1
$50,000–74,999	14.9		22.3	24.3	19.2	19.5	20.3
$75,000 or more	24.7		24.9	30.2	29.8	22.7	38.6
Ever had sex	66.5	75.6	90.6	93.9	85.6	91.2	
Never been married	89.3	92.8	45.7	50.0	51.7	52.3	54.4
Currently married	8.0	6.9	44.9	44.6	40.6	39.2	37.9
Church attendance							
Once a week or more	18.4	20.2	22.1	16.0	22.3	26.2	
Never	32.3	35.6	31.2	32.1	31.7	25.8	
Not religious	21.1	24.7	22.5	20.2	22.0	21.7	
Self-reported health							
Poor	1.8	1.5	1.0	1.2	1.5	0.7	
Fair	8.4	9.2	11.0	7.9	10.7	5.3	
Good	28.7	26.7	37.6	33.5	33.9	24.9	
Very Good	39.6	37.5	35.7	38.2	37.3	40.9	
Excellent	21.5	25.2	14.8	19.1	16.7	28.3	
Never drinks alcohol	30.5	21.9	22.4	26.1	25.4	18.7	

Appendix B. Construction of outcome indexes

B.1. CES-D (depression) index (8 items, α = 0.87)

Respondents were asked to think about the past 7 days, and assess how often each of the following things were true about them. Answer categories ranged from "never or rarely" (0) to "most of the time or all of the time" (3). Some items were reverse-coded for the index variable (e.g., "You felt happy."):

1. You were bothered by things that usually do not bother you.
2. You could not shake off the blues, even with help from your family and your friends.
3. You felt you were just as good as other people.
4. You had trouble keeping your mind on what you were doing.
5. You felt depressed.
6. You felt happy.
7. You enjoyed life.
8. You felt sad.

B.2. Current romantic relationship quality (6 items, α = 0.96)

Respondents were asked to assess their current romantic relationship. Answer categories ranged from strongly disagree (1) to strongly agree (5):

1. We have a good relationship.
2. My relationship with my partner is very healthy.
3. Our relationship is strong.
4. My relationship with my partner makes me happy.
5. I really feel like part of a team with my partner.
6. Our relationship is pretty much perfect.

B.3. Family-of-origin relationship safety/security (4 items, α = 0.90)

Respondents were asked to evaluate the overall atmosphere in their family while growing up by responding to four statements whose answer categories ranged from strongly disagree (1) to strongly agree (5):

1. My family relationships were safe, secure, and a source of comfort.
2. We had a loving atmosphere in our family.
3. All things considered, my childhood years were happy.
4. My family relationships were confusing, inconsistent, and unpredictable.

B.4. Family-of-origin negative impact (3 items, α = 0.74)

Respondents were asked to evaluate the present-day impact of their family-of-origin experiences by responding to three statements whose answer categories ranged from strongly disagree (1) to strongly agree (5):

1. There are matters from my family experience that I am still having trouble dealing with or coming to terms with.
2. There are matters from my family experience that negatively affect my ability to form close relationships.
3. I feel at peace about anything negative that happened to me in the family in which I grew up.

B.5. Impulsivity (4 items, α = 0.76)

Respondents were asked to respond to four statements about their decision-making, especially as it concerns risk-taking and new experiences. Answer categories ranged from 1 (never or rarely) to 4 (most or all of the time):

1. When making a decision, I go with my 'gut feeling' and do not think much about the consequences of each alternative.
2. I like new and exciting experiences, even if I have to break the rules.
3. I am an impulsive person.
4. I like to take risks.

B.6. Closeness to biological mother and father (6 items, α = 0.89 and 0.92)

Respondents were asked to evaluate their current relationship with up to four parent figures—who they reported living with for at least 3 years when they were 0–18 years old—by reporting the frequency of six parent–child interactions. For each parent figure, these six items were coded and summed into a parental closeness index. From these, I derived indices of closeness to the respondent's biological mother and biological father. Response categories ranged from never (1) to always (5):

1. How often do you talk openly with your parent about things that are important to you?
2. How often does your parent really listen to you when you want to talk?
3. How often does your parent explicitly express affection or love for you?
4. Would your parent help you if you had a problem?
5. If you needed money, would you ask your parent for it?
6. How often is your parent interested in the things you do?

B.7. Attachment (depend, 6 items, α = 0.80; anxiety, 6 items, α = 0.82)

For a pair of attachment measures, respondents were asked to rate their general feelings about romantic relationships, both past and present, in response to 12 items. Response categories ranged from "not at all characteristic of me" (1) to "very characteristic of me" (5). Items 1–6 were coded and summed into a "depend" scale, with higher scores denoting greater comfort with depending upon others. Items 7–12 were coded and summed into an anxiety scale, with higher scores denoting greater anxiety in close relationships, in keeping with the original Adult Attachment Scale developed by Collins and Read (1990). The measures employed were:

1. I find it difficult to allow myself to depend on others.
2. I am comfortable depending on others.
3. I find that people are never there when you need them.
4. I know that people will be there when I need them.
5. I find it difficult to trust others completely.
6. I am not sure that I can always depend on others to be there when I need them.
7. I do <u>not</u> worry about being abandoned.
8. In relationships, I often worry that my partner does not really love me.
9. I find that others are reluctant to get as close as I would like.
10. In relationships, I often worry that my partner will not want to stay with me.
11. I want to merge completely with another person.
12. My desire to merge sometimes scares people away.

References

Anderssen, Norman, Amlie, Christine, Erling, Ytteroy A., 2002. Outcomes for children with lesbian or gay parents. A review of studies from 1978 to 2000. Scandinavian Journal of Psychology 43 (4), 335–351.

Balsam, Kimberly F., Beauchaine, Theodore P., Rothblum, Esther D., Solomon, Sondra E., 2008. Three-year follow-up of same-sex couples who had civil unions in Vermont, same-sex couples not in civil unions, and heterosexual married couples. Developmental Psychology 44, 102–116.

Baumle, Amanda K., Compton, D'Lane R., Poston Jr., Dudley L., 2009. Same-Sex Partners: The Demography of Sexual Orientation. SUNY Press, Albany, NY.

Berg, Sven, 1988. Snowball sampling. In: Kotz, Samuel, Johnson, Norman L. (Eds.), Encyclopedia of Statistical Sciences, vol. 8. Wiley-Interscience, New York.

Biblarz, Timothy J., Raftery, Adrian E., 1999. Family structure, educational attainment, and socioeconomic success: rethinking the 'pathology of matriarchy'. American Journal of Sociology 105, 321–365.

Biblarz, Timothy J., Stacey, Judith, 2010. How does the gender of parents matter? Journal of Marriage and Family 72 (1), 3–22.

Bos, Henny M.W., Sandfort, Theo G.M., 2010. Children's gender identity in lesbian and heterosexual two-parent families. Sex Roles 62, 114–126.

Bos, Henny M.W., van Balen, Frank, van den Boom, Dymphna C., 2007. Child adjustment and parenting in planned lesbian parent families. American Journal of Orthopsychiatry 77, 38–48.

Brewaeys, Anne, Ponjaert, Ingrid, Van Hall, Eylard V., Golombok, Susan, 1997. Donor insemination: child development and family functioning in lesbian mother families. Human Reproduction 12, 1349–1359.

Brown, Susan L., 2004. Family structure and child well-being: the significance of parental cohabitation. Journal of Marriage and Family 66 (2), 351–367.

Busby, Dean M., Holman, Thomas B., Taniguchi, Narumi, 2001. RELATE: relationship evaluation of the individual, family, cultural, and couple contexts. Family Relations 50, 308–316.

Collins, Nancy L., Read, Stephen J., 1990. Adult attachment, working models, and relationship quality in dating couples. Journal of Personality and Social Psychology 58, 644–663.

Crowl, Alicia L., Ahn, Soyeon, Baker, Jean, 2008. A meta-analysis of developmental outcomes of same-sex and heterosexual parents. Journal of GLBT Family Sciences 4 (3), 385–407.

Finer, Lawrence B., Henshaw, Stanley K., 2006. Disparities in rates of unintended pregnancy in the United States, 1994 and 2001. Perspectives on Sexual and Reproductive Health 38, 90–96.

Fulcher, Megan, Sutfin, Erin L., Patterson, Charlotte J., 2008. Individual differences in gender development: associations with parental sexual orientation, attitudes, and division of labor. Sex Roles 57, 330–341.

Gartrell, Nanette K., Bos, Henny M.W., 2010. US national longitudinal lesbian family study: psychological adjustment of 17-year-old adolescents. Pediatrics 126 (1), 1–11.

Gartrell, Nanette K., Bos, Henny M.W., Goldberg, Naomi G., 2011a. Adolescents of the U.S. national longitudinal lesbian family study: sexual orientation, sexual behavior, and sexual risk exposure. Archives of Sexual Behavior 40, 1199–1209.

Gartrell, Nanette K., Bos, Henny M.W., Goldberg, Naomi G., 2011b. New trends in same-sex sexual contact for American adolescents? Archives of Sexual Behavior. http://dx.doi.org/10.1007/s10508-011-9883-5.

Gates, Gary J., 2011. Family formation and raising children among same-sex couples. NCFR Report 56 (4), F1–F3.

Gates, Gary J., Ost, Jason, 2004. The Gay and Lesbian Atlas. The Urban Institute Press, Washington, DC.

Goldberg, Abbie E., 2010. Lesbian and Gay parents and Their Children: Research on the Family Life Cycle. APA Books, Washington, DC.

Golombok, Susan, Perry, Beth, Burston, Amanda, Murray, Clare, Mooney-Somers, Julie, Stevens, Madeleine, Golding, Jean, 2003. Children with lesbian parents: a community study. Developmental Psychology 39, 20–33.

Golombok, Susan., Tasker, Fiona., Murray, Clare., 1997. Children raised in fatherless families from infancy: family relationships and the socioemotional development of children of lesbian and single heterosexual mothers. Journal of Child Psychology and Psychiatry 38, 783–792.

Hatzenbuehler, Mark L., Keyes, Katherine M., Hasin, Deborah S., 2009. State-level policies and psychiatric morbidity in lesbian, gay, and bisexual populations. American Journal of Public Health 99 (12), 2275–2281.

Herbenick, Debby, Reece, Michael, Schick, Vanessa, Sanders, Stephanie A., Dodge, Brian, Fortenberry, J.Dennis, 2010. Sexual behavior in the United States: results from a national probability sample of men and women ages 14–94. Journal of Sexual Medicine 7 (Suppl. 5), 255–265.

Huffington Post: Healthy Living, 2011. Child Abuse Rate at Zero Percent in Lesbian Households, New Report Finds. The Huffington Post. <http://www.huffingtonpost.com/2010/11/10/lesbians-child-abuse-0-percent_n_781624.html> (accessed 01.13.12).

Times Research Reporting, 2012. Interactive: Gay Marriage Chronology. Los Angeles Times. <http://www.latimes.com/news/local/la-gmtimeline-fl,0,5345296.htmlstory> (accessed 01.03.12).

MacCallum, Fiona, Golombok, Susan, 2004. Children raised in fatherless families from infancy: a follow-up of children of lesbian and single heterosexual mothers at early adolescence. Journal of Psychology and Psychiatry 45, 1407–1419.

Manning, Wendy D., Smock, Pamela J., Majumdar, Debarun, 2004. The relative stability of cohabiting and marital unions for children. Population Research and Policy Review 23, 135–159.

McLanahan, Sara, Sandefur, Gary, 1994. Growing Up with a Single Parent: What Hurts, What Helps. Harvard University Press, Cambridge.

Miller, Brent C., Fan, Xitao, Christensen, Matthew, Grotevant, Harold, van Dulmen, Manfred, 2000. Comparisons of adopted and nonadopted adolescents in a large, nationally representative sample. Child Development 71 (5), 1458–1473.

Moore, Kristin Anderson, Jekielek, Susan M., Emig, Carol, 2002. Marriage from a Child's Perspective: How Does Family Structure Affect Children, and What Can We Do About It? Child Trends Research Brief, Child Trends, Washington, DC.

Movement Advancement Project, Family Equality Council and Center for American Progress, 2011. All Children Matter: How Legal and Social Inequalities Hurt LGBT Families, Full Report.

National Center for Family and Marriage Research, 2010. Same-Sex Couple Households in the US, 2009. Family Profiles, FP-10-08.

Nock, Steven L., 2001. Affidavit of Steven Nock. Halpern et al. v. Canada and MCCT v. Canada. ON S.C.D.C. <http://marriagelaw.cua.edu/Law/cases/Canada/ontario/halpern/aff_nock.pdf> (accessed 12.20.11).

Patterson, Charlotte J., 1997. Children of lesbian and gay parents. In: Ollendick, Thomas H., Prinz, Ronald J. (Eds.), Advances in Clinical Child Psychology, vol. 19. Plenum, New York.

Patterson, Charlotte J., 2000. Family relationships of lesbians and gay men. Journal of Marriage and the Family 62, 1052–1069.

Patterson, Charlotte J., 2006. Children of lesbian and gay parents. Current Directions in Psychological Science 15 (5), 241–244.

Perrin, Ellen C., Committee on Psychosocial Aspects of Child and Family Health, 2002. Technical report: coparent or second-parent adoption by same-sex partners. Pediatrics 109, 341–344.

Redding, Richard R., 2008. It's really about sex: same-sex marriage, lesbigay parenting, and the psychology of disgust. Duke Journal of Gender Law and Policy 16, 127–193.

Resnick, Michael D., Bearman, Peter S., Blum, Robert W., Bauman, Karl E., Harris, Kathleen M., Jones, Jo, Tabor, Joyce, Beuhring, Trish, Sieving, Renee E., Shew, Marcia, Ireland, Marjorie, Bearinger, Linda H., Udry, J.R., 1997. Protecting adolescents from harm: findings from the national longitudinal study on adolescent health. Journal of the American Medical Association 278 (10), 823–832.

Rosenfeld, Michael, 2007. The Age of Independence: Interracial Unions, Same-Sex Unions and the Changing American Family. Harvard University Press, Cambridge, MA.

Rosenfeld, Michael J., 2010. Nontraditional families and childhood progress through school. Demography 47, 755–775.

Rostosky, Sharon Scales, Riggle, Ellen D.B., Horne, Sharon G., Miller, Angela D., 2009. Marriage amendments and psychological distress in lesbian, gay, and bisexual (LGB) adults. Journal of Counseling Psychology 56 (1), 56–66.

Sirota, Theodora, 2009. Adult attachment style dimensions in women who have gay or bisexual fathers. Archives of Psychiatric Nursing 23 (4), 289–297.

Snijders, Tom A.B., 1992. Estimation on the basis of snowball samples: how to weight? Bulletin de Méthodologie Sociologique 36, 59–70.

Stacey, Judith, Biblarz, Timothy J., 2001a. (How) does the sexual orientation of parents matter? American Sociological Review 66 (2), 159–183.

Stacey, Judith, Biblarz, Timothy, 2001b. Affidavit of Judith Stacey and Timothy Biblarz. Halpern et al. v. Canada and MCCT v. Canada. ON S.C.D.C. <http://www.samesexmarriage.ca/docs/stacey_biblarz.pdf> (accessed 12.20.11).

Tasker, Fiona, 2005. Lesbian mothers, gay fathers, and their children: a review. Developmental and Behavioral Pediatrics 26 (3), 224–240.

Tasker, Fiona, 2010. Same-sex parenting and child development: reviewing the contribution of parental gender. Journal of Marriage and Family 72, 35–40.

Tasker, Fiona L., Golombok, Susan, 1997. Growing Up in a Lesbian Family. Guilford, New York.

Vanfraussen, Katrien, Ponjaert-Kristoffersen, Ingrid, Brewaeys, Anne, 2003. Family functioning in lesbian families created by donor insemination. American Journal of Orthopsychiatry 73 (1), 78–90.

Veldorale-Brogan, Amanda, Cooley, Morgan, 2011. Child outcomes for children with LGBT parents. NCFR Report 56 (4), F15–F16.

Wainright, Jennifer L., Patterson, Charlotte J., 2006. Delinquency, victimization, and substance use among adolescents with female same-sex parents. Journal of Family Psychology 20 (3), 526–530.

Wainright, Jennifer L., Russell, Stephen T., Patterson, Charlotte J., 2004. Psychosocial adjustment, school outcomes, and romantic relationships of adolescents with same-sex parents. Child Development 75 (6), 1886–1898.

Social Science Research 41 (2012) 1367–1377

Contents lists available at SciVerse ScienceDirect

Social Science Research

journal homepage: www.elsevier.com/locate/ssresearch

Parental same-sex relationships, family instability, and subsequent life outcomes for adult children: Answering critics of the new family structures study with additional analyses

Mark Regnerus

Population Research Center, University of Texas at Austin, 1 University Station A1700, Austin, TX 78712-0118, United States

ARTICLE INFO	ABSTRACT
Article history: Available online 28 August 2012 Keywords: Same-sex households Family structure Young adulthood	The July 2012 publication of my study on the outcomes of young adults who report parental same-sex relationship behavior raised a variety of questions about the New Family Structures Study and my analyses and interpretations of it. This follow-up article seeks to address a variety of the more common criticisms that have been raised, to offer new commentary and analyses, and to pose questions for future analysts of the NFSS and other datasets that are poised to consider how household dynamics are associated with youth and young-adult outcomes. The new analyses I present here still reveal numerous differences between adult children who report maternal same-sex behavior (and residence with her partner) and those with still-married (heterosexual) biological parents. Far fewer differences appear between the former and several other groups, most notably never-married single mothers.

1. Introduction

The July 2012 publication in this journal of my study on the young-adult children of parents who have had a same-sex relationship created more criticism and scrutiny than have most sociological studies. The intensity of the response can be attributed largely to the fact that the results of this study—based on a large population-based sample—differed markedly from earlier research based largely on small, nonrandom samples of same-sex families. Others would no doubt disagree. Apart from criticisms about measurement or sampling issues, concern has been expressed about all manner of minutiae, as well as details about the publication process, the funding agencies, and even the data collection firm.[1] Some perceive it as a tool for this or that political project, a role it was never designed to fill. It cannot answer political or legal questions, and is by definition a retrospective look at household composition and dynamics. The controversy surrounding its publication and reception has also aptly generated concern about freedom of inquiry in general. But in this manuscript I wish to get back to the basic task at hand—addressing concerns, describing the data in greater detail, and pursuing additional analyses of them.

E-mail address: regnerus@prc.utexas.edu

[1] The audit of the publication process of the original study—a rather uncommon and disturbing experience in social science research—appears elsewhere in this issue. While its author has long harbored negative sentiment about me, the audit nevertheless ought to dispel suspicions of malfeasance in the review process. It concluded that an ideologically-balanced pool of reviewers recommended publication. Concern has been also raised about the relationship of the author to the pair of funding agencies. As noted in the study, I have always operated without strings from either organization. No funding agency representatives were consulted about research design, survey contents, analyses, or conclusions. Any allegations that the funders might have improperly influenced me are simply false. Finally, Knowledge Networks is a premier online research organization, and their data collection efforts are featured in hundreds of published articles in the social sciences, public opinion, health, and other journals—including the August 2012 issue of the *American Sociological Review* (see Rosenfeld and Thomas, 2012)—and are utilized by the American National Election Studies. Simply put, the KnowledgePanel® is a high-quality data source.

0049-089X/$ - see front matter © 2012 Elsevier Inc. All rights reserved.
http://dx.doi.org/10.1016/j.ssresearch.2012.08.015

While sample size issues—as well as concerns about representativeness—have long hampered the general line of inquiry into same-sex parents and child outcomes, prior to the NFSS most suppositions about possible problems with studies based on nonrandom samples were intellectual rather than data based. That is, it was easy for scholars to admit the limitations of their study samples. What was more difficult, however, was to grasp just how nonrandom they were and how that might affect their results (Marks, 2012). Even while family scholars have long acknowledged the likelihood of demographic diversity among same-sex households, most have been unable to document the extent of this diversity in a statistically-meaningful way. National probability surveys have typically been constrained by the relatively small number of same-sex households in the general population, resulting in small sample sizes and limited statistical power to detect between-group differences. Most research has instead relied on snowball and convenience samples, which often minimize genuine racial, socioeconomic, and geographic heterogeneity (Tasker, 2005). Others have turned to the Census and the American Community Survey for more representative demographic characteristics of same-sex couples with children (Rosenfeld, 2010; Gates and Ost, 2004). However, these population-based resources are not able to tell us about gay or lesbian single parents or non-residential parents. In addition, Census data provide very little detail about the diversity of family structures experienced by children of same-sex parents over time.

Thus the original NFSS study, while subject to its own documented limitations, suggested the possibility that previous nonrandom studies were painting a rosier picture of child outcomes than would be the case were a more random sample to be employed or if the outcomes were based on the reports of young adults themselves rather than relying on parental self-reports. In other words, the original study muddied what had largely been, up to that time, a relatively consistent, positive portrait of child outcomes in gay and lesbian households (however defined).

In this article, I address six areas of concern with the original study, including an extended discussion of the challenges of dealing with household and relational instability in analyses, before briefly reporting the results of alternative approaches to presenting overview data. Throughout the article I make greater use of the NFSS's detailed family history calendar data to look at the variety of family structure experiences in the households in which young adults reported maternal same-sex relationship behavior.

2. Responses to criticisms

2.1. What constitutes an LM or GF respondent?

Concern about the use of the acronyms LM (lesbian mother) and GF (gay father) in the original study is arguably the most reasonable criticism. In hindsight, I wish I would have labeled LMs and GFs as MLRs and FGRs, that is, respondents who report a maternal (or mother's) lesbian relationship, and respondents who report a paternal (or father's) gay relationship. While in the original study's description of the LM and GF categories I carefully and accurately detailed what respondents fit the LM and GF categories, I recognize that the acronyms LM and GF are prone to conflate sexual orientation, which the NFSS did not measure, with same-sex relationship behavior, which it did measure. The original study, indeed the entire data collection effort, was always focused on the respondents' awareness of parental same-sex relationship behavior rather than their own assessment of parental sexual orientation, which may have differed from how their parent would describe it. Therefore, I will use the (albeit awkward) dual acronyms of LM/MLR and GF/FGR to provide orienting reference to the original study's acronym while capitalizing on the more appropriate acronym, which I begin using exclusively in the section on new analyses.

Some critics have correctly noted that the LM/MLR measure includes respondents who appear to have lived both with their mother and her romantic partner for many years, as well as respondents who never lived with their mother's romantic partner. The relationship(s) may or may not have been brief—the NFSS survey did not directly inquire about their number or duration. While it is possible that a one-night stand might have sufficed as a definition here, it stretches the imagination to hold that many respondents would have (a) been aware of such solitary experiences, (b) classify it/them as a "romantic relationship", and (c) list it when queried. In my own studies of heterosexual behavior, romantic relationships are typically perceived as enduring for far longer than an evening. In Wave III of the National Longitudinal Study of Adolescent Health, less than three percent of all young adults' sexual relationships that were identified by respondents as "romantic" in content (rather than nonromantic) lasted for only a day (Regnerus and Uecker, 2011). However, it is a fair request to assess those LM/MLR respondents who lived with their mother and her romantic partner separately from those that did not. I do so below.

2.2. Comparing apples to oranges?

The most consistent criticism is that the original study's analyses "compare apples to oranges". That is, the primary comparison is between LM/MLRs, GF/FGRs, and intact biological families (IBFs), and that given prevalent instability in the NFSS sample of the former pair's households, that to compare them to IBFs is to cause the former pair to look poorly. However, if stability is a key asset for households with children, then it is sensible to use intact biological families in any comparative assessment. But this has rarely been the approach employed in past research: Rosenfeld (2010: 757) notes that of the 45 studies listed in Tasker's (2005) review article, only two included "a more traditional family control group built into the study".

Moreover, it is inaccurate to imply that the original study did not evaluate distinctions between LM/MLRs and other categories that displayed some degree of instability. Tables 2–4 in the original study (not shown) displayed indicators of statistically-significant differences between LM/MLRs and all other groups, and I briefly describe on page 13 (Section 3.2) of the original study text the number of (and percent of possible) statistically-significant differences both before and after controls between both LM/MLR and GF/FGR categories and all non-IBF groups.

The primary concern here, I presume, is that the LM/MLR and GF/FGR categories are comprised of households that have experienced *varying* degrees of instability, and that similar experiences of instability in the one ought to be compared with similar experiences in the other. In an ideal data world, that makes sense. But this is not as simple as it might seem, since there is likewise varying degrees of instability in the groups denoted as "stepfamily" and "single parent" in the original study. The household rosters, assessed over the course of 18 years, reveal quite diverse degrees of instability in stepfamilies and single-parent households. For example, some respondents in the "single parent" category certainly witnessed their never-married mother enter and exit multiple relationships, and yet I combined them with respondents whose mother never entered another relationship after divorcing the respondent's father. Some respondents entered a stepfamily as young children, while others later in adolescence. Thus the "apples versus oranges" criticism is, upon closer inspection, not a very realistic one in social reality. Americans' households, traced over the course of respondents' first 18 years of life, reveal considerable family diversity that requires challenging—and subjective—measurement decisions from researchers, as I noted in the original text.

Many critics have focused on the small number of stably-coupled lesbian families in the NFSS data, and some have taken this as a sign of a suspect dataset. It could be an undercount, but it may not be. A closer look at the respondents who stated that their mother had a same-sex romantic relationship and that they lived with both her and her partner at some point further reveals the short-term nature of many of the relationships. Of the 85 respondents who claimed such, 31 reported living with their mother's partner for up to 1 year only.[2] An additional 20 reported this relationship for up to 2 years, five for 3 years, and eight for 4 years.

2.2.1. Relationship Instability: Control variable or pathway in analyses of child outcomes?

What should social scientists do about household (and by inference, parental relationship) instability that is nearly coterminous with a key independent variable, in this case the LM/MLR and GF/FGR categories? It is not a simple decision. Control for instability?[3] But what does it mean to "control for" instability in this scenario? It is quite possible that household instability—via parental romantic-relationship fragility—was a key pathway or mechanism linking the LM/MLRs with the comparatively higher emotional and social challenges they report. This tendency to overlook pathways in favor of control variables more broadly reflects a typical misguided tendency in social science research to always search for "independent" effects of variables, often missing the pathways explaining how social phenomena actually operate. In this case, parental same-sex relationships, family instability, and more problematic young-adult life outcomes are quite possibly linked. In assessing young-adult outcomes, controlling for the effect of a parent's same-sex relationship with a "family instability" variable and concluding—presumably—that there is no association could well be the wrong thing to do. This is "controlling for the pathways", a model that is unhelpful for understanding social reality. If, for example, most men smoked, but very few women ever did so, it is entirely unhelpful to declare that—controlling for smoking—there is no effect of gender on lung cancer. In that case, men's predilection for smoking would merit close scrutiny and concern. Indeed, a key purpose of social science is "to identify and understand the various underlying causal mechanisms that produce identifiable outcomes and events of interest" (Smith, 2010: 293).

2.2.2. Gay and lesbian relationship instability: An artifact of the past?

Since the NFSS did not select by design a group of unstable gay or lesbian parents, a key issue is whether or not the LM/MLR and GF/FGR households are more unstable than those of heterosexual couples. If stability was comparatively rarer in the lives of MLRs and FGRs growing up some decades ago when stigma was more pronounced and social support for lesbian and gay parents far more modest than today, is it a safe assumption that the NFSS study is a "dated" one by definition and that if the study could be replicated in the future that the associations here would very likely disappear? Perhaps, but hardly certain: assumptions about comparative relationship stability among gay and lesbian couples—including parents—can and have been empirically tested using other data on current relationships.

---

[2] As I note below in greater detail, I have included in the LM/MLR group the 12 cases in which the respondent indicated that both parents had had a same-sex relationship. In the previous study, I analyzed them only as GF/FGRs, given sample-size concerns.

[3] One option is to utilize the NFSS calendars and create a measure of the number of household transitions rather than the experience of one or more transitions (Potter, 2012). But the household calendars could well miss the exact number of transitions, since the NFSS only asked respondents to denote when someone else lived with them for at least 4 months. This also overlooks parental romantic relationships which were either brief or else not residential (yet potentially still influential). And in cases of excessive household instability, respondents may experience survey fatigue and may underreport transitions when filling out what amounts to be for them a rather complicated household calendar. Moreover, to suggest that all romantic partner dissolution creates problems for respondents is short-sighted. Indeed, some dissolutions solve problems (Amato, 2000). Such is the messy business of documenting and assessing household histories.

A study of Norwegian and Swedish same-sex marriages notes that divorce risk is higher in same-sex marriages and that the "risk of divorce for female partnerships actually is more than twice that for male unions" (Andersson et al., 2006: 89). Moreover, early same-sex marriages—those occurring shortly after a shift in marriage law—exhibited a similar risk of divorce as did more recent marriages, suggesting no notable variation in instability over time as a function of new law or pent-up demand among more stable, longstanding relationships. The study authors estimate that in Sweden, 30% of female marriages are likely to end in divorce within 6 years of formation, compared with 20% for male marriages and 13% for heterosexual ones. Moreover, they found lesbian couples to be more "sociodemographically homogamous" than other couples, and speculate that "this situation may be conducive to a high level of dynamism in the relationship, but perhaps not to the kind of inertia that is related to marital stability" (Andersson et al., 2006: 96). Biblarz and Stacey (2010: 17) similarly note this phenomenon in their review of research on lesbian parents, asserting that they face a "somewhat greater risk of splitting up", due in part, they suggest, to their "their high standards of equality". A follow-up assessment of more recent Norwegian statistics, presented at the 2012 annual meeting of the Population Association of America (PAA), found no evidence that the gender gap in same-sex divorce has closed (Noack et al., 2012).

Michael Rosenfeld detects the same pattern in a study of nationally-representative data on American relationships presented at the 2012 annual meeting of the American Sociological Association. He finds that lesbian couples report higher relationship satisfaction *alongside* higher break-up rates. The highest stability rates appear among heterosexual married couples, while notably better stability is located among married gay and lesbian couples than among those in civil unions (as would be expected). Yet his analysis too detects greater instability among lesbian couples in general, a finding that persists even after a lengthy series of control variables are included. While lesbian couples in the study are more apt to be raising children, the presence of children does not appear to be a factor in the diminished relationship stability evident among them.

That few LM/MLR respondents reported stability in their mother and her partner's relationship (in the domicile in which the respondent lived) ought not be simply chalked up to greater stigma or insufficient social support as factors that account for the entirety of the association. In light of evidence of the same pattern among current lesbian couples in the US and Scandinavia, it remains an open question.

While the cited study authors tend to find the difference in divorce behavior between lesbians and gay men intriguing, this "lesbian effect" is anticipated in a sexual economics approach to romantic relationships (e.g., Baumeister, 2010). This perspective places no blame for instability on sexual orientation per se, but rather on stable gender differences and preferences in relationships (e.g., for women, a significantly higher bar for the relationship's quality and emotional satisfaction). Gay men's relationships thus appear predictably more stable than lesbian relationships, but are less likely to be sexually monogamous when compared with lesbian or heterosexual relationships (Hoff and Beougher, 2010). Here again, this is believed to be due not to sexual orientation but stable gender differences in relationship preferences and sex drive (Baumeister and Vohs, 2004). While the effect of relationship stability on child health and development is well-documented and apparent in the original NFSS study's findings—as well as this follow-up exploration—the effect on children of parental nonmonogamy is not well understood.

2.3. Is the NFSS a representative sample?

As an extension of the second concern, many critics have focused on the small number of stably-coupled lesbian families in the NFSS data. Indeed, only two cases of LM/MLRs reported living with their mother and her partner uninterrupted from age 1 to 18. Of the 85 cases (out of 175 total LM/MLRs) wherein the respondent indicated living in residence for a time with both their mother and her female partner, only 19 spent at least five consecutive years together, and six cases spent 10 or more consecutive years together. Some have taken this as a sign of a suspect and non-representative dataset. It could be an undercount, but it may well not be. Rather, readers would do well to keep in mind anachronistic expectations concerning an era in which enduring same-sex relationships *with children* were simply less common, and those that existed certainly subject to greater social scrutiny and stigma. And, as noted above, there may be stability distinctions that foster unreasonable expectations, especially following upon decades of research conclusions based on nonrandom samples.

Moreover, such expectations also tend to reveal a class bias that may hamper studies in this domain, given that families wherein same-sex couples pursue the complicated—and potentially quite expensive—process of deciding just how and when they will have a child tend to be more educated, wealthy, and white than the families of many NFSS LM/MLRs. Rosenfeld (2010: 757) notes:

> …the literature on same-sex couple parenting has tended to feature studies of the kind of women who can afford ART: white, upper-middle-class women. Nationally representative data tend to paint a different picture: in the US census, same-sex couple parents tend to be more working class and are much more likely to be nonwhite compared with heterosexual married couples.

The children of such a selective group—those who conceive by ART, or assisted reproductive technology—would be expected to witness greater stability and to fare better, enjoying advantages that tend to benefit children regardless of their parents' race, age, or sexual orientation. While this selective group is hardly the only face of same-sex parents in America, they are the ones who receive the majority of popular and scholarly attention.

In his assessment of group differences in academic progress, moreover, Rosenfeld (2010) restricted his Census-based sample to the children of same-sex couples "who had been living with both parents for at least 5 years", thus raising the like-

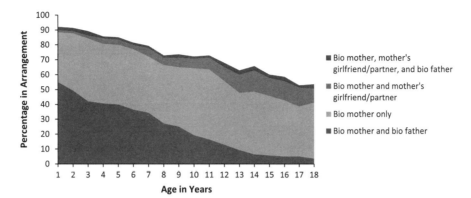

Fig. 1. Frequency of four living arrangements of young adults who reported maternal same-sex romantic relationship behavior, by age, NFSS (unweighted).

lihood that his sample was more residentially and relationally stable than a sample that included the children of same-sex couples who had not met this threshold of inclusion. I did not restrict my sample in the same manner, though such a measurement decision is potentially quite influential on respondents' outcomes. His "no differences" conclusion may be a result of dropping more unstable households from his analytic sample.

2.3.1. Differences and similarities between the NFSS and the census

While no sampling strategy can compete with a genuine census in scope, it is important to note that the Census does *not* ask respondents about their sexual orientation or any sort of sexual behavior. It can only identify couples of the same sex who are co-residing at the time of the survey. Gay or lesbian parents who are raising children as single parents or who do not live with their children are not enumerated as such in the Census.

The NFSS, which relied on asking respondents about their parents' same-sex relationship activity, includes numerous single-parent households among its LM/MLR and GF/FGR categories, as Fig. 1 details. Given greater instability among lesbian couples, failing to account for lesbian single-parent households seems a notable limitation. The original NFSS study's sample may actually be more representative than Rosenfeld's *Demography* article, since I did not impose stability limitations and could measure single-parent gay- and lesbian-headed households.

The Census also only takes a snapshot of a household, meaning it offers few insights into the family-structure dynamics of same-sex households. Thus the Census and the NFSS may reveal quite different household arrangements. The Census has an unparalleled ability to measure the fraction of households with children that are headed by same-sex couples.[4] The NFSS, looking retrospectively, can document parental same-sex relationships as reported by young adults who did not spend their entire childhood living with their biological parents, and can describe the stability of household arrangements over time. What results are simply different strengths and weaknesses. And yet both exhibit comparable race and class diversity. Rosenfeld's (2010) analysis of ACS data reported that 37% and 42% of children from female and male same-sex households are Black and Hispanic, respectively. He also noted that same-sex couples with children have, on average, less education and lower household incomes than both heterosexual couples with children and same-sex couples without children.

2.4. Mixed-orientation marriages?

There seems to be no scholarly consensus—as may well be the case in social reality—about what exactly makes a mother a *lesbian* mother, and what makes a father a *gay* father. Some critics seem to have largely presumed that the NFSS's LM/MLR or GF/FGR parent is in fact lesbian or gay, respectively, in their sexual orientation, despite my caution against doing so in the original study. (Others appear to question whether any of them are gay or lesbian.) Some speculate that what I have largely captured in the original study's findings are the challenges facing "mixed-orientation marriages" wherein a respondent's parent elects "against their orientation" to marry someone of the opposite sex, only to witness the subsequent dissolution of their union followed by the commencement of a same-sex relationship. As I noted in the original study text, there appear to be plenty of failed heterosexual unions in the data. Fig. 1 displays the unweighted frequencies of four of the most common living arrangements among LM/MLR respondents beginning at age 1 up through age 18.[5] As already noted, a slight majority spend their early years with their biological mother and father, a figure that diminishes to about 5% by age 18.[6] A consistently large segment of LM/MLRs (~35%) reports living exclusively with their biological mother, while a much smaller segment reports

---

[4] This ability is tempered, as is the case in many data collection efforts, by other challenges. In the case of the Census, the prevalence of gender miscoding may create notable over-counts of the number of same-sex households in the US (Black et al., 2007).

[5] Tables 1–3, however, employ weighted estimates, in consonance with the original study.

[6] An unknown (though likely sizable) number of the respondents who report living with both their "biological mother and father" do not share the same residence with them, but rather spend time in each one's household.

Table 1
Mean scores on select dichotomous outcome variables, NFSS (can read as percentage: as in, 0.43 = 43%).

	1-IBF	2-MLR no partner	3-MLR + partner	4-FGR	5	6	7	8	9	10	11	12	13	14	15
Currently married	0.43	0.31	0.38	0.38	**0.36***	0.49	0.37	0.41	**0.27**	**0.21***	**0.17***	0.47	0.63	0.41	0.45
Currently cohabiting	0.09	0.18	**0.27***	0.23	**0.31***	0.11	**0.20***	0.10	**0.25***	**0.18***	**0.31***	**0.22***	**0.28***	**0.07^**	**0.32***
Family received welfare growing up	0.17	**0.72***	**0.70***	**0.51***	**0.47***	**0.41*,^**	**0.49***	**0.37^**	**0.70***	**0.75***	**0.56**	**0.58***	**0.13^**	**0.12^**	**0.47***
Currently on public assistance	0.10	0.32	**0.49***	**0.14^**	**0.31***	**0.21^**	**0.22*,^**	**0.27***	**0.52***	**0.44***	**0.49***	0.28	**0.11^**	**0.27***	**0.25**
Currently employed full-time	0.49	0.36	**0.17***	0.36	**0.42*,^**	**0.48^**	0.44	**0.55^**	**0.42^**	**0.31**	**0.09***	**0.52***	**0.75***	**0.41^**	**0.42^**
Currently unemployed	0.08	**0.10^**	**0.40***	0.23	**0.15^**	**0.13^**	**0.15^**	**0.06^**	0.18	**0.19**	**0.34***	**0.03***	**0.00***	0.22	**0.12^**
Voted in last presidential election	0.57	0.46	0.43	**0.71*,^**	0.63	0.53	0.58	0.52	0.58	**0.43***	0.37	**0.70*,^**	0.44	0.58	0.59
Thought recently about suicide	0.05	**0.23***	0.09	0.17	0.12	0.10	0.06	0.02	0.11	0.09	0.03	0.04	**0.01**	0.07	0.11
Recently or currently in therapy	0.08	**0.30***	0.17	0.10	0.12	**0.17***	**0.20***	0.11	**0.24***	0.13	0.09	0.13	**0.01*,^**	**0.22***	0.09
Identifies as entirely heterosexual	0.90	**0.45***	**0.68***	**0.80***	0.83	**0.82***	**0.82***	**0.89^**	0.80	**0.77***	0.83	**0.91***	**0.96***	0.82	**0.72^**
Is in a same-sex romantic relationship	0.04	0.12	0.02	0.14	0.05	**0.15^**	0.01	**0.00***	0.05	0.01	0.04	**0.13***	-	0.23	0.21
Had an affair while married/cohabiting	0.13	**0.42***	**0.38***	0.26	**0.12^**	**0.28***	0.17	**0.09^**	**0.48***	0.23	0.18	0.23	0.18	0.20	0.30
Has ever had an STI	0.08	0.21	**0.26***	**0.18***	0.12	0.12	**0.17***	**0.06^**	**0.25***	**0.19***	**0.26***	0.17	0.08	0.16	0.12
Ever touched sexually by an adult	0.02	**0.16***	**0.26***	0.07	**0.10***	**0.09***	**0.10***	**0.10***	**0.20***	**0.15***	0.11	**0.05***	**0.02^**	**0.03^**	0.09
Ever forced to have sex against will	0.08	**0.42***	**0.27***	**0.17***	**0.24***	**0.18***	**0.20***	0.13	0.17	0.17	0.11	0.12	0.10	**0.23***	0.17

*1 = Lived with both bio mother and father from 0 to 18 or until left home (*N* = 919).
*2 = MLR, but never lived with mother's same-sex romantic partner (*N* = 90).
*3 = MLR, spent time in residence with mother's same-sex romantic partner (*N* = 85).
*4 = FGR (*N* = 61).
*5 = Lived with both bio mom and dad until 18, but subsequently they've gotten a divorce (*N* = 116).
*6 = Parents were married, but got a divorce, R lived with mother, and R reported subsequent relationship(s) and remarriage (*N* = 223).
*7 = Parents were married, but got a divorce, R lived with mother, and R reported subsequent relationship(s) but no remarriage (*N* = 278).
*8 = Parents were married, but got a divorce, R lived with mother, and R reported NO subsequent relationship before 18 (*N* = 108).
*9 = Parents never married, R lived with mother, and R reported subsequent relationship(s) and marriage (*N* = 104).
*10 = Parents never married, R lived with mother, and R reported subsequent relationship(s) but no marriage (*N* = 221).
*11 = Parents never married, R lived with mother, and R reported NO subsequent relationship (*N* = 48).
*12 = Parents were married, but one parent died, and R reported subsequent relationship(s), possibly including remarriage (*N* = 117).
*13 = Parents were married, but one parent died, and R reported NO subsequent relationship (*N* = 28).
*14 = Adopted by strangers at birth or 1 year (at some point, either one or two adopted parents) (*N* = 101).
*15 = Parents were married, but got a divorce, R lived with father (84% of the time, R said father had another relationship) (*N* = 95).

Bold indicates the mean scores displayed are statistically-significantly different from IBFs (currently intact, bio mother/father household, column 1), without additional controls.
An asterisk (*) next to the estimate indicates a statistically-significant difference (*p* < 0.05) between the group's coefficient and that of IBF's, controlling for respondent's age, gender, race/ethnicity, level of mother's education, perceived household income while growing up, experience being bullied as a youth, and state's legislative gay-friendliness, derived from logistic regression models (not shown).
A caret (^) next to the estimate indicates a statistically-significant difference (*p* < 0.05) between the group's mean and the mean of Group 3 (MLR + partner), without additional controls.

Table 2
Mean scores on select continuous outcome variables, NFSS.

	1-IBF	2-MLR no partner	3-MLR + partner	4-FGR	5	6	7	8	9	10	11	12	13	14	15
Educational attainment	3.19	**2.34***	**2.41***	2.70	**2.88*^**	**2.72***	**2.82*^**	**3.06^**	**2.41***	**2.18***	**2.01***	**2.78**	2.92	**3.21^**	**2.79***
Family-of-origin safety/security	4.13	**3.23***	**2.97***	**3.35***	**3.52*^**	**3.70*^**	**3.45*^**	**3.71*^**	**3.35***	**3.44*^**	**3.59*^**	**3.63*^**	4.02^	**3.77*^**	**3.12***
Family-of-origin negative impact	2.30	**3.30***	**2.97***	**2.89***	**2.96***	**2.67***	**2.97***	2.55	**3.04***	**2.74***	**3.02***	**2.72***	2.62	**2.83***	2.67
Closeness to biological mother	4.17	4.07	4.03	**3.71***	3.95	**4.26***	**3.88**	3.90	**3.63**	**3.50***	4.20	3.87	4.17	3.58	**3.79**
Closeness to biological father	3.87	3.16	3.18	3.44	**3.29***	3.53	3.29	**2.77***	-	**1.57*^**	**3.01**	3.28	3.27	-	3.89
Self-reported physical health	3.75	3.50	**3.24**	3.67	**3.46**	**3.51**	**3.58^**	**3.42**	**3.40**	**3.28***	**3.09***	3.54	3.66	3.53	3.54
Self-reported overall happiness	4.16	3.63	4.04	3.79	4.02	3.94	3.93	3.83	3.88	3.70	3.64	4.03	**4.58*^**	3.92	3.80
CES-D depression index	1.83	**2.37***	**2.12**	**2.07**	2.01	1.88	1.92	1.84	**2.02**	2.08	1.99	1.76^	**1.48*^**	1.95	1.90
Attachment scale (depend)	2.82	**3.63***	**3.27**	3.10	**3.08**	3.00	**3.12***	2.84	**3.26**	**3.22***	**3.40***	**3.16**	2.52^	**3.12***	3.10
Attachment scale (anxiety)	2.46	2.77	2.63	2.60	2.71	2.47	2.54	2.41	2.66	2.65	2.77	2.51	2.03	**2.66***	2.49
Impulsivity scale	1.90	2.03	2.06	1.95	1.94	1.79^	1.93	1.84^	1.98	1.79^	1.81	1.86	**1.66*^**	1.85	1.76^
Level of household income	8.27	**6.45***	**5.96**	7.08	7.42	7.46^	7.67^	7.34	**5.72***	**5.38***	**3.67*^**	7.68^	**9.03*^**	7.93^	7.73^
Current relationship quality index	4.11	3.80	**3.76**	**3.73***	3.95	3.88	3.94	3.92	**3.65**	**3.66***	3.92	3.77	4.36^	3.79	4.02
Current relationship is in trouble	2.04	**2.60***	2.21	2.47	2.43	2.15	**2.32***	2.19	**2.77*^**	**2.45***	2.60	2.31	1.85	2.35	2.31

Bold indicates the mean scores displayed are statistically-significantly different from IBFs (currently intact, bio mother/father household, column 1), without additional controls.
An asterisk (*) next to the estimate indicates a statistically-significant difference ($p < 0.05$) between the group's coefficient and that of IBFs, controlling for respondent's age, gender, race/ethnicity, level of mother's education, perceived household income while growing up, experience being bullied as a youth, and state's legislative gay-friendliness, derived from OLS regression models (not shown).
A caret (^) next to the estimate indicates a statistically-significant difference ($p < 0.05$) between the group's mean and the mean of Group 3 (MLR + partner), without additional controls.

Table 3
Mean scores on select event-count outcome variables, NFSS.

	1-IBF	2-MLR no partner	3-MLR + partner	4-FGR	5	6	7	8	9	10	11	12	13	14	15
Frequency of marijuana use	1.32	1.78	1.85*	1.62	2.00*	1.32	**1.71***	1.61	1.86*	**1.99***	1.70	1.50	1.62	1.33	1.50
Frequency of alcohol use	2.70	2.58	2.41	2.42	2.55	**2.35**	2.64	2.87	2.84*	2.63	**1.89**	2.55	2.59	2.74	2.84
Frequency of drinking to get drunk	1.68	1.89	1.88	1.89	1.90	1.58	1.75	1.91	1.96*	1.78	1.37	1.73	**1.32**	1.73	1.68
Frequency of smoking	1.79	**2.95***	**2.84***	2.22	2.44	**2.25***	2.03	2.31	2.38	**2.27**	2.14	1.90	2.59	2.34*	2.44
Frequency of watching TV	3.01	**4.21***	3.46	3.17	3.33	3.21	3.24	3.47	**3.98***	**3.50**	3.51	3.37	**2.27***	3.31	2.77
Frequency of having been arrested	1.18	**1.82***	**1.76***	1.52	1.38	**1.39*^**	**1.37*^**	1.17*	1.34*	**1.43***	1.47*	1.27*	1.37	1.31^	**1.53***
Freq pled guilty to non-minor offense	1.10	**1.43***	**1.35***	1.36	1.30	1.20	1.21*	1.10^	1.22	1.15	1.18	1.20	1.23	1.19	1.24
N of female sex partners (among women)	0.22	**1.66*^**	**0.70***	**0.74***	**0.96***	**0.52***	0.41	0.14*	0.51	**0.64***	0.94	0.52	0.36	0.47	0.47*
N of female sex partners (among men)	2.70	2.37^	3.97	4.16	3.66	3.79	3.30	2.03*	3.91*	4.38*	2.06	4.52*	3.43	3.24	5.60
N of male sex partners (among women)	2.79	**5.73*^**	2.98	**4.51***	**3.97***	**4.55*^**	**4.05*^**	3.70	**4.90*^**	**4.42*^**	4.13	3.38	3.36	3.49	**4.53*^**
N of male sex partners (among men)	0.20	2.13*	1.18*	1.47*	0.98	0.37	0.10^	0.72	0.20	0.35*	0.62*	0.21	0.47*	0.27	1.76

Bold indicates the mean scores displayed are statistically-significantly different from IBFs (currently intact, bio mother/father household, column 1), without additional controls.
An asterisk (*) next to the estimate indicates a statistically-significant difference ($p < 0.05$) between the group's coefficient and that of IBFs, controlling for respondent's age, gender, race/ethnicity, level of mother's education, perceived household income while growing up, experience being bullied as a youth, and state's legislative gay-friendliness, derived from Poisson or negative binomial regression models (not shown).
A caret (^) next to the estimate indicates a statistically-significant difference ($p < 0.05$) between the group's mean and the mean of Group 3 (MLR + partner), without additional controls.

their early years were spent with both their biological mother and her same-sex partner. The household presence of a same-sex partner begins emerging slowly but steadily through the course of childhood. In numerous cases LM/MLR respondents indicated first living with their mother's girlfriend/partner at a comparatively older age (for example, 54 began at or after age 10, 40 at or after age 13, and 18 at or after age 16).

Whether these were in fact mixed-orientation marriages or relationships is of course impossible to discern with confidence, since the study did not ask the respondents to identify their parents' sexual orientation, a decision I remain comfortable with given the era the data are describing. Many LM/MLR and GF/FGR respondents may well have witnessed their parents' mixed-orientation marriage. On the other hand, given the documented fluidity of women's sexuality, I would hesitate to assert that a same-sex relationship—especially if relatively brief—is indicative of a fixed sexual orientation (Diamond, 2008).

While the etiology of homosexuality is not under study here, the matter seems tacitly embedded in criticisms about classification. As such, the original study should be understood in the manner in which it is explicitly titled—about the adult children of parents who have same-sex relationships. If for whatever reason that is an unsatisfying anchor—parental sexual behavior rather than orientation—it is beyond the scope of an academic study to be something it is not. Nevertheless, it suggests the importance of consistently employing the acronyms MLR and FGR.

2.5. Bisexuality in the NFSS?

As an extension of this, a few critics have raised the possibility that plenty of the NFSS LM/MLRs and GF/FGRs may in reality be bisexual in orientation. In an unpublished study of the most recent two series of data from the National Survey of Family Growth—presented at the 2012 PAA conference—Danielle Wondra reports that self-identified bisexual men and women are notably more likely to desire a (or another) child than self-identified gay or lesbian respondents. Suffice it to say that more research needs to be conducted on bisexual parents outside of a simplistic "mixed-orientation" rubric that may not reflect the reality of many couples' history of sexual experiences or preferences. Moreover, claims about "mixed orientation marriages" unnecessarily problematize bisexuality by prioritizing a dualistic (either/or) essentialism about sexual orientation that may not fit social reality (Diamond, 2008).

If the complex calendar histories are any clue, bisexuality is probable among some NFSS respondents' parents. Such frequencies of opposite-sex relationship behavior or opposite-sex attraction are not out of step with other studies of same-sex partnerships (Andersson et al., 2006; Potter, 2012; Rosenfeld, 2012). Nevertheless, only four LM/MLRs reported an opposite-sex parent figure—a stepfather—living in the household *after* having reported a same-sex parent figure (i.e., a mother's girlfriend/partner). In sum, the B in LGBT parenting deserves more attention than it has been given, and may constitute a more significant share of such households-with-children than has often been recognized.

2.6. Foster care experiences

A few critics have raised the suggestion that in the era represented by the NFSS respondents, gay and lesbian parents were more apt to either adopt foster children, or—at the other extreme—faced the forcible placement of their own children in foster care. Either scenario raises concern about the original study's claim that LM/MLR respondents were the most apt to report experience with the foster care system. This concern prompted a detailed exploration of the calendar data for the 21 LM/MLR respondents who reported such an experience, in order to discern the timing of their foster system experience. As with the original study's discussion about the timing of sexual victimization, here too the story is muddied. Three of the 21 LM/MLRs who spent time in foster care did so immediately prior to reporting living in a household with their mother and her female partner—one of the two scenarios anticipated by critics. Four of the 21 spent some time in foster care following their report of living in a household with their mother and her partner—the other scenario that concerned critics. Whether any of these seven cases actually match those scenarios in reality is impossible to know from the data. The remaining 14 cases display calendar data less apt to suggest either of these two scenarios as a likely fit. Just under half of the 21 respondents reported their foster care experience beginning before age 10.

3. Alternative analyses

Tables 1–3 display results in a manner similar to Tables 2–4 in the original study (not shown), with several changes made in response to criticisms:

1. I split the LM/MLRs (hereafter, MLRs) between those who never lived with their mother's same-sex romantic partner and those that have.

Why this particular division? Of the 85 cases wherein the respondent indicated living in residence with both their mother and her female partner, only 19 spent five consecutive years together, and six cases spent 10 consecutive years together. While this is not quite the comparison some critics seek, the statistical power is simply not present for a direct comparison of the most stable MLRs, given uncommon relationship longevity in their households-of-origin. It is true, though, that greater longevity of such in residence relationships tended to reveal better outcomes at face value.

2. I shifted the 12 cases wherein a respondent reported that both parents had had a same-sex relationship from FGR to MLR.

As noted in the original study, analyses of the household calendar data for these 12 cases revealed comparable exposure to both their mother and father. As a result, there are now 90 MLR cases who never reported living with their mother's partner/girlfriend, 85 MLRs who did, and 63 FGRs. As reported in the original study, the latter group very infrequently reported living with their father and his partner/boyfriend, so this group remains unaltered in its structure.

3. I expanded the total number of groups to 15 in order to better reflect the different experiences of stability and partnering in American households. I did not include an "others" catch-all group in this set of analyses. As a result, the final tables reflect just under 400 fewer cases than in the original study.

Given the outcome measures are the same as employed in the original study, I do not describe their operationalization here. That can be located in the original study's text and its Appendix B. The analytic strategy—an overview featuring both simple between-group means tests as well as an indicator of statistical significance after controlling for several independent variables via outcome-appropriate forms of regression analyses—remains the same as well, for comparability.

As was the case in the original analyses, Tables 1–3 reveal that those adult children who report a maternal same-sex relationship—regardless of whether their mother ever resided with her same-sex partner—look far more similar to adult children of other types of households than they do to those from stably-intact biological families. There are 20 simple statistically-significant differences between group 2 (MLRs who never lived with their mother's same-sex partner) and IBFs, and an identical number between group 3 (MLRs who did live with their mother's same-sex partner for a time) and IBFs. After controls—via regression analysis—there are 21 and 19 statistically-significant differences between groups 2 and 3, respectively, and IBFs. These numbers are a dip from those reported in the original study.

Most of the distinctions between IBFs and groups 2 and 3 are consistent with those reported in the original study. On 16 different outcomes, *both* groups 2 and 3 appear statistically different from IBFs prior to controls (i.e., regression models); the same is true of 13 outcomes after controls. There are nine simple differences between FGRs and IBFs prior to controls, and 12 after them. As in the original study, distinctions between the two MLR groups and IBFs appear in the domains of sexuality, sexual behavior, sexual victimization, household economics and work, educational attainment, smoking, arrests, and retrospective sentiment about family life while growing up.[7]

Carets denote a simple statistically-significant difference between group 3 (MLRs who spent time living with their mother's partner) and all non-IBF groups. Of the 517 possible between-group differences, 89% (or 17%) appear significant at the bivariate level, a decline from the 24% figure when assessing all MLRs together in the original study. Several groups compare similarly to group 3 in terms of very few simple differences:

- Group 4 (FGRs): two differences.
- Group 11 (never-married single mothers with no subsequent relationships): two differences.
- Group 9 (single mothers who subsequently remarried): four differences.
- Group 10 (never-married single mothers with relationships but no marriage): four differences.
- Group 2 (MLRs who did not live with their same-sex partner): four differences.

Group 10 displays by far the most pre- and post-regression statistically-significant differences with IBFs (31 and 23, respectively), and tends to fare consistently poorly across most outcomes which are agreeably suboptimal. Group 3 (MLRs who lived with their mother's partner) compare less favorably with:

- Group 8 (divorced, lived with mother, no subsequent relationships): 12 differences.
- Group 13 (parents married until one died, no subsequent relationships): 15 differences.

In general, groups 8 and 13 fared rather well on many outcomes, shedding light on the likely importance of avoiding further household transitions. Where outcomes are clearly discernible as optimal or suboptimal—for example, educational attainment or STI, respectively—group 8 fares better than groups 6–7, whose only distinction is subsequent maternal romantic relationships and, in group 6's case, remarriage. Additional parental romantic partners, even remarriages, seem to make a (negative) difference. As in the original study, there is much that these analyses cannot document, including causation as well as any effects of sexual orientation. Selectivity is very likely at work on multiple outcomes.

Analyses comparing younger versus older NFSS respondents may prove a fertile avenue of exploration. Initial ancillary analyses suggest that older young adult MLRs seem to have struggled more than younger ones. Whether this is a function

---

[7] As noted in the original study text, the NFSS data is insufficiently capable of discerning much information about the context surrounding respondents' sexual victimization. No simplistic conclusions about it ought to be discerned from the analyses.

of time exposure, or more pronounced social stigma further in the past than among the "newest" young adult MLRs, is difficult to say, given the interpretive limitations of this data. Alternately, some challenges may cumulate over time; it may be that the older respondents have simply had more time to experience particular outcomes.

4. Conclusion

This follow-up study has sought to address six common criticisms that have arisen following the July 2012 publication in this journal of the original study entitled, "How different are the adult children of parents who have same-sex relationships?" One in particular, about comparing stable heterosexual couples to stable same-sex couples, is particularly challenging to accomplish with all but the very largest datasets (which, in turn, tend to have fewer interesting outcome measures). It also raises important conceptual and analytic questions about how to navigate persistent instability in the NFSS's MLR and FGR cases. This is complicated by contemporary evidence in the US and Scandinavia suggesting that lesbian relationships in particular—including legally married couples—continue to exhibit instability in excess of heterosexual relationships and even gay male relationships.

Perhaps in social reality there really are two "gold standards" of family stability and context for children's flourishing—a heterosexual stably-coupled household and the same among gay/lesbian households—but no population-based sample analyses is yet able to *consistently confirm wide evidence* of the latter. Moreover, a stronger burden of proof than has been employed to date ought to characterize studies which conclude "no differences", especially in light of longstanding reliance on nonrandom samples of unknown bias and the high risk of making Type II errors in small-sample studies (Marks, 2012; Nock, 2001). In other words, the science here remains young. Until much larger random samples can be drawn and evaluated, the probability-based evidence that exists—including additional NFSS analyses herein—suggests that the biologically-intact two-parent household remains an optimal setting for the long-term flourishing of children.

Of course the flourishing of children involves many other factors besides parental relationship structure and decision-making, as analyses of the NFSS and numerous other datasets confirm. Indeed, most young-adult respondents in the NFSS report ample success and largely avoid problematic physical and emotional difficulties, regardless of their parents' experiences, decisions, and actions.

References

Amato, Paul R., 2000. The consequences of divorce for adults and children. Journal of Marriage and Family 62, 1269–1287.

Andersson, Gunnar, Noack, Turid, Seierstad, Ane, Weedon-Fekjaer, Harald, 2006. The demographics of same-sex marriages in Norway and Sweden. Demography 43, 79–98.

Baumeister, Roy F., 2010. Is There Anything Good About Men? How Cultures Flourish by Exploiting Men. Oxford University Press, New York.

Baumeister, Roy F., Vohs, Kathleen D., 2004. Sexual economics: sex as female resource for social exchange in heterosexual interactions. Personality and Social Psychology Review 8 (4), 339–363.

Biblarz, Timothy J., Stacey, Judith, 2010. How does the gender of parents matter? Journal of Marriage and Family 72 (1), 3–22.

Black Dan, Gates Gary, Sanders Seth, Taylor Lowell. 2007. The Measurement of Same-Sex Unmarried Partner Couples in the 2000 US Census. California Center for Population Research, Los Angeles.

Diamond, Lisa M., 2008. Sexual Fluidity: Understanding Women's Love and Desire. Harvard University Press, Cambridge, MA.

Gates, Gary J., Ost, Jason, 2004. The Gay & Lesbian Atlas. The Urban Institute Press, Washington, DC.

Hoff, Colleen C., Beougher, Sean C., 2010. Sexual agreements among gay male couples. Archives of Sexual Behavior 39, 774–787.

Marks, Loren., 2012. Same-sex parenting and children's outcomes: a closer examination of the American Psychological Association's brief on lesbian and gay parenting. Social Science Research 41, 735–751.

Nock, Steven L., 2001. Affidavit of Steven Nock. Halpern et al. v. Canada and MCCT v. Canada. ON S.C.D.C. <http://marriagelaw.cua.edu/Law/cases/Canada/ontario/halpern/aff_nock.pdf> (accessed 12.20.11).

Potter, Daniel, 2012. Same-sex parent families and children's academic achievement. Journal of Marriage and Family 74, 556–571.

Regnerus, Mark, Uecker, Jeremy, 2011. Premarital Sex in America: How Young Americans Meet, Mate, and Think about Marrying. Oxford University Press, New York.

Rosenfeld, Michael J., 2010. Nontraditional families and childhood progress through school. Demography 47, 755–775.

Rosenfeld, Michael J., Thomas, Reuben J., 2012. Searching for a mate: the rise of the internet as a social intermediary. American Sociological Review 77 (4), 523–547.

Smith, Christian, 2010. What is a Person? Rethinking Humanity, Social Life, and the Moral Good from the Person Up. The University of Chicago Press, Chicago.

Tasker, Fiona, 2005. Lesbian mothers, gay fathers, and their children: a review. Developmental and Behavioral Pediatrics 26 (3), 224–240.

Summary of Walter R. Schumm's

"Methodological Decisions and the Evaluation of Possible Effects of Different Family Structures on Children: The New Family Structures Survey (NFSS)"

Social Science Research 41 (November 2012): 1357–1366,
http://dx.doi.org/10.1016/j.ssresearch.2012.08.011

The publication of Mark Regnerus's "How Different" met with immediate responses from the public. Regnerus faced criticisms, including accusations of bias and poor science, from groups opposed to his methods and findings. Others responded to these attacks by defending Regnerus's methods and championing the rights of researchers to publish their findings without fear of political reprisal. Defenders of the article insisted that Regnerus had gathered some of the best data available and that his interpretations of the findings were well within standard social-scientific practice.

Four months later, in the same peer-reviewed journal, Walter Schumm (a researcher unrelated to the NFSS) published this article, which serves as an overview of the challenges faced by social scientists studying family structure and child outcomes. Schumm first lists and describes some important considerations when gathering and evaluating social-scientific data. He then takes the NFSS as a case study, evaluating it along the lines of the considerations he outlined.

Challenges Faced by Scholars Studying Parenting

Sampling

Schumm first addresses the challenge of gathering samples for a social-scientific study, whether in the form of survey respondents or interview participants. He points out the merits of a random sample over a nonrandom ("convenience") sample,[1] explaining that a random sample is more reliable, more useful for interpretation, but also much more expensive and less-efficiently collected than a nonrandom sample.

In addition to randomness, researchers must consider sample size. The greater the number of respondents, the greater power that the statistical tests wield in the interpretation of the results. If a group is too small, or too nonrandom—or if too many people decline to participate, even in a random sample—then results could lose so much power as to be completely useless when estimating for the nation as a whole. (Schumm points out that unfortunately, this doesn't stop some social scientists from using low-powered statistics to draw conclusions.)

Defining the Study Group

Schumm then moves to addressing the specific challenges of family scholars: How does one define a family? And what types of families are there? Family structures change over time (through divorce, marriage, cohabitation, death, separation), and good social science must account for these changes in the life of a child: "To have a more complete understanding of family structure, one may ask 'at what age?', 'for how long?' and 'with whom?' "[2]

Added to this task is a somewhat newer one faced by scientists: defining and measuring sexual orientation. The three main measurements—sexual attraction (To whom are you attracted?), sexual behavior (With whom do you engage in sexual activity?), and sexual identity (What orientation do you consider yourself?)—don't always match up with one another; two people living identical lives might report very different measurements in any of these three areas. In addition, some people view their sexual orientation as more fluid, susceptible to changes and choices throughout their lives. Others view it as a fixed reality. Different perspectives in the minds of study participants will lead them to give different responses, especially over the course of their lifetime.

Interpreting the Data

Next, Schumm discusses the researcher's undertaking of interpreting the data once they are collected. He points out the folly of a simple *causality* interpretation. In other words, usually only *associations* can be identified (such that one thing X is associated with another thing Y) rather than stronger claims of causality (that this thing X causes that thing Y to happen). The question of which thing might cause which (X or Y) is a more complicated matter. And it might be that a third variable (Z) is actually causing *both* X and Y to occur.

Further, there might be a middleman of sorts, an entirely other variable (let's say, Q) by which the association occurs, so that if Q were absent, X might not result in Y at all. Variables such as Q are considered to be "mediating" the whole thing, and they ought to be taken into account whenever possible. For instance, consider an example (not in Schumm's essay) such as the association that exists between growing up in poverty and getting poor grades in school. We cannot assume that the poverty is causing the failing grades any more than that the failing grades are making the child poor. A *mediating variable* might be that many of the poor children are *hungry* when they are at school, and that this hunger is leading to poor grades. If hunger is indeed a mediating variable, then children who are poor and hungry and children who are poor but *not* hungry might perform differently from one another.

There are also variables that might be "moderating" the effect that X is having on Y—making X more (or less) influential over Y. Continuing the above example, whether or not a child is receiving charitable assistance could be a moderating variable, because it might turn out that poor children who are getting food from a church pantry, for instance, are able to bring up their grades somewhat so that the poverty is having less of an effect on their school performance.

Taking all these mediating and moderating variables into account requires experience and a very careful consideration of the entire field of view when interpreting data.

Funding Concerns

Schumm raises the question of how the research is funded. Research cannot start without funding, and funding is hard to come by. Also, funding agents might try to manipulate researchers in order to produce certain findings. He evaluates the NFSS's funding sources below.

Comparison to Previous Research

Finally, research must compare itself to a previous body of research. Do the current results seem in line with what has been produced by good science already? If not, then that raises questions as to how well the research was conducted.

Evaluating the NFSS

So how did Regnerus's research pass through the gauntlet of these challenges—sampling responsibly, defining family forms and sexual orientation, analyzing scientifically and thoroughly, interpreting soberly, gathering sufficient funding from nonintrusive sources, and corroborating results with previous research?

Schumm has no criticism for Regnerus on his sampling plan: "Despite the challenges involved, . . . Regnerus chose to use a random sample rather than a convenience sample, for all family types, not just the more common types."[3] Schumm points out that some researchers use comparatively smaller groups of convenience samples (such as for studying lesbian parenting couples), even when they use random samples for the more common family types. But he denounces this practice: "Combining a random sample with a convenience sample largely defeats the purpose of using a random sample in the first place."[4] Schumm also endorses the research firm that Regnerus hired to obtain his random sample, pointing out that it has been used by many other researchers studying the lives of gay, lesbian, and bisexual persons as well as other important topics.

Schumm then begins to address specific accusations that had been issued against Regnerus's research. One such charge was that his sample sizes for the same-sex family types were too small to make any inferences at all—or perhaps they would have been larger if he had defined the families correctly. Specifically, critics accused him of not surveying enough *stable* same-sex couples (couples who had remained together for their child's entire childhood).

Schumm replies that previous studies that had been accepted by the scientific community had even smaller such samples. He references several published studies, including Danielle Julien and colleagues' 2008 study[5] of lesbian women, which found only ten lesbian mothers out of the 8,875 sexually active women surveyed. Of these, not one household seemed to have remained stable for a child's entire eighteen years (or perhaps weren't far enough along in their parenting to predict that they would). Regnerus's study at least located two such stable lesbian-parenting couples.

In the same vein, "several attempts to study gay father families have ended in failure," Schumm points out, "because too few such families were located to permit meaningful statistical analysis."[6] Regnerus, in comparison, sampled 2,988 randomly chosen respondents, discovering 175 adult children of women who had had a same-sex relationship and 73 adult children of men who reported the same. "Some have claimed that Regnerus's sample was too small," Schumm states, "but his sample is clearly larger than most other previous studies."[7]

Other concerns when dealing with social-science research regard missing data (for instance, if someone fills out a survey but leaves some questions blank) and response rates (whether or not the person chosen to survey agrees to participate). After reviewing the response rates and missing-data measurements of at least nine studies similar to Regnerus's, Schumm concludes, "Clearly, if there is a missing data concern with the NFSS, it is not alone among other studies."[8]

Defining the Study Group

Schumm points out that "Regnerus analyzed as many as eight types of families, at least keeping pace with other similar studies."[9] Then he addresses what he called one of Regnerus's "most controversial decisions": "expanding the 'net' for possible GLBT families by including any family for which an adult child reported that one or both parents had been in a same-sex romantic relationship at some point between the child's birth and age 18."[10]

This is the point around which much of the opposition against Regnerus had revolved. Critics argued that this was not a fair way to describe GLBT families and accused Regnerus of trying to malign stable same-sex couples by conflating them with those who had merely had same-sex encounters. Schumm responds, however, that multiple studies have used similar study techniques to try to create a larger sample size of GLBT families since they are relatively rare in the general population.[11] And at least six of these studies included children who had been raised in heterosexual families before one or both parents began homosexual relationships,[12] including one "study published within the past decade in the well-known APA journal, *Developmental Psychology*, [where] children who had spent most of their life in heterosexual families were, in fact, included within the operational definition of children from lesbian families."[13] Yet this study (and the others) suffered none of the critical backlash that the NFSS has endured.

Reflecting on the challenges he mentions in the first part of the article about how to define a homosexual family, Schumm reminds readers of the substantially higher rates of instability among homosexual relationships: "It may be very rare (and difficult) to find stable same-sex parent couples, especially those with no prior heterosexual sexual experience, who have raised a child full-time, continuously with no separations, from birth to age 18."[14] Again, he calls on the publications of several researchers to support his point. One article in particular that did not receive the backlash that Regnerus's did fell well short of his practice; it utilized a convenience sample of thirty-two adult children (of lesbian parenting couples) over the internet and did not gather any demographic information (such as gender or age of those responding) or ask how long the respondents had been in a same-sex parented home.[15] "If Regnerus can be criticized for expanding or 'tweaking' his definition of 'lesbian' and 'gay' parents in order to enlarge his sample," Schumm concludes, "he has not been alone among other scholars in so doing. At least he was clear about his definitions, even if one begs to differ with them."[16]

Interpreting the Data

At this point, Schumm reminds his reader of the importance of always taking into consideration variables that might be affecting the research results. For instance, how much money a family has, and how much education, would make a difference in how successfully a child from that family met certain goals in life. That success might have little to do with the sexual orientation of his or her parents. However, not all researchers are scrupulous in accounting for these variables: "What often occurs in research," he explains, "is that older, high-income, well-educated same-sex parents with one or two children are compared to younger, moderate-income, less-well-educated heterosexual parents with several children, without statistical controls."[17]

By "statistical controls," Schumm means the practice of taking these differences into account when analyzing data. Controls help sociologists eliminate alternative explanations for a given outcome. If an association (such as between parenting structure and children's happiness) continues to show up in results after controls are applied, it means that the likelihood of the structure causing the outcome is greater. And when controls aren't applied, results can be wholly unreliable. When the income of the parents, for instance, isn't accounted for, "even a negligent parent could purchase high quality child care services, which might easily mask the parent's actual ineffectiveness."[18]

In addition to the obvious differences such as family income, number of children, and how far parents went in school, there is a common challenge called "social desirability." This means that a respondent will often give a report to a researcher that depicts what the respondent believes to be attractive to the public. This is especially a challenge when studying same-sex parenting. People on both sides of the debate would be tempted to lean toward reporting what they *want* to be true—or at least what they want to be reported. This is a tricky problem.

Schumm points out that most studies of same-sex parenting either disregard the challenge of social desirability entirely or measure it but don't take it into account when interpreting their results. Regnerus, he points out, tried to reduce the social desirability bias to some extent through the design of his study: He surveyed the children rather than the parents. Like most researchers, Regnerus did not try to measure social desirability directly in his survey.

As for taking into account mediating and moderating variables (explained earlier), Schumm reiterates his concerns with the current practice of social scientists in general. He would have liked to have seen Regnerus consider more deeply the variables that come into play with his conclusions, but he concedes that such a practice is currently not standard procedure: "While I would prefer more attention to mediating variables, it is not uncommon for contemporary researchers to merely predict child outcomes from a variable capturing family structure and a series of control variables, as Regnerus did."[19]

In other words, other social scientists follow the same procedure Regnerus followed: predicting outcomes for children based on a definition of their family structure while growing up—while taking into account and controlling for important variables that could affect the results. In the case of the NFSS, these variables included a wide range of things such as age, gender, race or ethnicity, level of mother's education, perceived household income while growing up, the degree of legislative gay-friendliness of the respondent's home state, and experience of being bullied as a youth.

Next, Schumm touches on the complex topic of "effect sizes," which is a measurement of how big a difference a variable really makes in an outcome. A larger effect size for a variable would mean that it made a big difference; a smaller one would mean that a variable made a difference but not a very influential one. "Since at least 1994," Schumm informs the reader, "the American Psychological Association . . . has called for the reporting of effect sizes in social science research."[20]

He points out again that many social scientists fall far short of perfection on this mark, referencing one review where more than 92 percent of the studies did not report effect sizes at all:[21] "It is remarkable that the APA will commend studies of same-sex parents when those very studies routinely ignore or violate official APA research guidelines."[22] While Regnerus did not report effect sizes, in most cases, he reported the statistics necessary to calculate them. Specifically, he provided the standard deviation for some of his tables (but not for all). But, he "has agreed to provide the missing ones upon request, which will permit the calculation of effect sizes."[23]

Funding Concerns

Schumm notes that "Regnerus has been criticized for accepting funding from conservative agencies" but clarifies that "it is not readily apparent how that differs from situations where other scholars have accepted funding from progressive agencies; both types of agencies may have had vested interests in the outcomes of the research."[24] He points out that, like the NFSS, the National Longitudinal Lesbian Family Study (NLLFS) had to receive funding from somewhere, and those funds came from five institutions and foundations that desired to see certain national trends come to light. However, proof of funding from a particular source does not suffice to condemn the research as being biased or unfair.

Comparison to Previous Research

At this point, Schumm addresses the question of whether or not Regnerus's research results are in line with what has already been produced by good science. First, he addresses the question of whether same-sex relationships are less stable (tend to break up more) than heterosexual relationships. He indicates that this question has been "a matter of controversy." Some scholars have found that there is no difference in stability between the two groups. However, other scholars have found dramatic differences. Schumm lists multiple studies, some summarized in chapter seven of this book, investigating a full range of findings. These studies indicate a great deal of difference over time: "Lau . . . using British longitudinal data over an 8-year period, found significant differences in relationship stability."[25] Referencing his own earlier research, he points out that "over 10 years, about 15–20% of heterosexual parent couples separated compared to about 40–45% of lesbian parent couples."[26] He also points out a more recent study that measured "family transitions," or changes in family structure (such as separation of parents):

> Most recently, Potter (2012) found that between birth and fifth grade, almost 95% of married biological parent families experienced no family transitions whereas 100% of same-sex parent families did experience at least one family transition; between kindergarten and eight grade, the corresponding percentages were almost 96% no transitions and almost 70% at least one transition for lesbian mother families and 100% at least one transition for gay father families.[27]

Next, Schumm compares Regnerus's finding that children of parents in a same-sex relationship were much less likely to identify as heterosexual.[28] He references "several studies . . . as well as other reports . . . which concur in observing significantly higher rates of same-sex behavior or identity among children of same-sex versus heterosexual parents."[29]

Then Schumm turns to illicit drug use, one of the outcomes measured for the adult children in the NFSS study. After citing a number of previous studies, Schumm argues that Regnerus's findings either paralleled or did not substantially deviate from them. He points readers to additional investigations before summarizing,[30] "Finding similar results from a variety of other samples and methods does not validate Regnerus's methods necessarily, but it does suggest that his methods were not so skewed as to override patterns also seen elsewhere."[31]

Schumm begins to conclude his article with a judgment of Regnerus's research methods. Admitting that "many would differ with some of Regnerus's many methodological decisions," he points out that, for the NFSS, they are "within the ball park of what other credible and distinguished researchers have been doing within the past decade."[32]

Schumm calls for more and better methods to be pursued, despite the challenges: "Further work can help answer questions with respect to how to better define lesbian mother and gay father families, although the combined effect of changes in sexual orientation and changes in relationship status may make finding even a minimally adequate size . . . *random* sample . . . nearly impossible."[33] Finally, Schumm reminds the reader that Regnerus's main conclusion is a refutation of the idea that there are no differences in outcomes for children from same-sex verses intact biological families, and he quotes John M. Hoenig and Dennis M. Heisey: "In matters of public health and regulation, it is often more important to be protected against erroneously concluding no difference exists when one does."[34]

Notes

1. A random sample is one where respondents are chosen randomly by some method and then pursued for their responses. A convenience sample is one where data is gathered only from people who volunteer information or for whom it is convenient to do so. Nonrandom collection reduces the costs and complications of a study but often introduces bias and can result in skewed findings, as often, those motivated to participate also have a vested interest in the results of the study.
2. Schumm, "Methodological Decisions," 1358.
3. Schumm, "Methodological Decisions," 1359.
4. Ibid.
5. Schumm references Danielle Julien et al., "Adjustment Among Mothers Reporting Same-Gender Sexual Partners: A Study of a Representative Population Sample from Quebec Province (Canada)," *Archives of Sexual Behavior* 37 (December 2008): 864–876.
6. Schumm, "Methodological Decisions," 1359.
7. Ibid., 1360.
8. Ibid.
9. Ibid.
10. Ibid.
11. Schumm says, "Using a specific point in the family life cycle to study the effect of a variable is not uncommon." (In this case, the specific point would be a parent engaging in a homosexual relationship. The variable would be having experienced gay parenting.) He specifically references Henny Bos et al., "Adolescents of the U.S. National Longitudinal Lesbian Family Study: Male Role Models, Gender Role Traits, and Psychological Adjustment," *Gender & Society* 26 (August 2012): 603–638.
12. Here, Schumm references Theodora Sirota, "Adult Attachment Style Dimensions in Women Who Have Gay or Bisexual Fathers," *Archives of Psychiatric Nursing* 23 (August 2009): 289–297; Liz Short, "Lesbian Mothers Living Well in the Context of Heterosexism and Discrimination: Resources, Strategies and Legislative Change," *Feminism & Psychology* 17 (February 2007): 57–74; Susan Golombok, Ann Spencer, and Michael Rutter, "Children in Lesbian and Single-parent Households: Psychosexual and Psychiatric Appraisal," *Journal of Child Psychology & Psychiatry* 24 (October 1983): 551–572; Susan Golombok et al., "Children with Lesbian Parents: A Community Study," *Developmental Psychology* 39 (January 2003): 20–33; Marjorie G. Welsh, "Growing Up in a Same-Sex Parented Family: the Adolescent Voice of Experience," *Journal of GLBT Family Studies* 7 (2011): 49–71; Amy Hequembourg, "Unscripted Motherhood: Lesbian Mothers Negotiating Incompletely Institutionalized Family Relationships," *Journal of Social and Personal Relationships* 21 (December 2004): 739–762.
13. Schumm, "Methodological Decisions," 1360.
14. Ibid., 1361.
15. Schumm refers to Anna Leddy, Nanette Gartrell, and Henny Bos, "Growing Up in a Lesbian Family: The Life Experiences of the Adult Daughters and Sons of Lesbian Mothers," *Journal of GLBT Family Studies* 8 (2012): 243–257.
16. Schumm, "Methodological Decisions," 1361.
17. Ibid.

18. Ibid. Here, Schumm references two articles by Rachel H. Farr, Stephen L. Forssell, and Charlotte J. Patterson: "Gay, Lesbian, and Heterosexual Adoptive Parents: Couple and Relationship Issues," *Journal of GLBT Family Studies* 6 (2010): 199–213; "Parenting and Child Development in Adoptive Families: Does Parental Sexual Orientation Matter?" *Applied Developmental Science* 14 (July–September 2010): 164–178.

19. Schumm, "Methodological Decisions," 1361.

20. Ibid., 1362.

21. Here, Schumm references his own "Statistical Requirements for Properly Investigating a Null Hypothesis," *Psychological Reports* 107 (December 2010): 953–971.

22. Schumm, "Methodological Decisions," 1362.

23. Ibid.

24. Ibid.

25. Ibid. Here, Schumm references p. 981 of Charles Q. Lau, "The Stability of Same-Sex Cohabitation, Different-sex Cohabitation, and Marriage," *Journal of Marriage and Family* 74 (October 2012): 973–988.

26. Schumm, "Methodological Decisions," 1362. Schumm is referencing his "Comparative Relationship Stability of Lesbian Mother and Heterosexual Mother Families: A Review of Evidence," *Marriage & Family Review* 46 (2010): 499–509.

27. This data was provided to Schumm by the researcher (Daniel Potter) in May and June of 2012.

28. Schumm, "Methodological Decisions," 1363.

29. Ibid.

30. Ibid. Here, Schumm refers the reader to his "Child Outcomes Associated with Lesbian Parenting: Comments on Biblarz and Stacey's 2010 Report," *Journal of Human Sexuality* 3 (2011): 35–80; "Are Two Lesbian Parents Better Than a Mom and a Dad? Logical and Methodological Flaws in Recent Studies Affirming the Superiority of Lesbian Parenthood," *Ave Maria Law Review* 10 (Fall 2011): 79–118; "Lessons for the 'Devilish Statistical Obfuscator,' *or* How to Argue for a Null Hypothesis: A Guide for Students, Attorneys, and Other Professionals," *Innovative Teaching* 1 (April 2012): 1–13.

31. Schumm, "Methodological Decisions," 1363.

32. Ibid., 1364.

33. Ibid.

34. Ibid. Schumm's quote of Hoenig and Heisey comes from their "The Abuse of Power: The Pervasive Fallacy of Power Calculations for Data Analysis," *The American Statistician* 55 (February 2001): 19–24.

Social Science Research 41 (2012) 1357–1366

Contents lists available at SciVerse ScienceDirect

Social Science Research

journal homepage: www.elsevier.com/locate/ssresearch

Methodological decisions and the evaluation of possible effects of different family structures on children: The new family structures survey (NFSS)

Walter R. Schumm

School of Family Studies and Human Services, Kansas State University, 1700 Anderson Avenue, Manhattan, KS 66506-1403, United States

ARTICLE INFO	ABSTRACT
Article history: Available online 21 August 2012 *Keywords:* Same-sex parenting Gay Lesbian Methodology New Family Structures Survey Family structures	Every social science researcher must make a number of methodological decisions when planning and implementing research projects. Each such decision carries with it both advantages and limitations. The decisions faced and made by Regnerus (2012) are discussed here in the wider context of social science literature regarding same-sex parenting. Even though the apparent outcomes of Regnerus's study were unpopular, the methodological decisions he made in the design and implementation of the New Family Structures Survey were not uncommon among social scientists, including many progressive, gay and lesbian scholars. These decisions and the research they produced deserve considerable and continued discussion, but criticisms of the underlying ethics and professionalism are misplaced because nearly every methodological decision that was made has ample precedents in research published by many other credible and distinguished scholars. © 2012 Elsevier Inc. All rights reserved.

1. Introduction

Evaluating the long-term effects of different family structures upon children is not an easy task. In designing and implementing such research, numerous methodological decisions must be made, each with its own strengths and weaknesses. Ideally, such research should be designed so outcomes are clear and meaningful. While methods and measures can be planned in advance, one thing that should *not* be planned in advance is the outcome, because one essential aspect of science is that you are not sure what the outcome will be – otherwise, why conduct the research? Some might point to instances where a commercial enterprise funded academic research to prove that its commercial products had more value than others, but researchers should maintain their independence and academic integrity. For instance, I was once hired by lawyers who wanted me to find a certain outcome that was not, in fact, true; when I refused to twist the data to support the desired conclusion, I was summarily fired – which was OK by me, since twisting data to support a false conclusion is not how science should be done (Schumm, 2010c).

If one wants to investigate the effect of family structure (e.g., having parents of one or another sexual persuasion) on child outcomes, there are several methodological choices one must make, as detailed below. While seasoned researchers are no doubt familiar with these issues, some readers may be less so.

1.1. Sample

The participants in the study can be selected randomly or non-randomly. Random samples can be generalized more accurately to the population from which they were drawn and support the application of inferential statistics. However, random

E-mail address: schumm@k-state.edu

samples are more expensive to obtain than convenience samples. Convenience samples entail a risk of not being representative of any population and may reflect a host of selection biases. Technically, inferential statistics should not be used with non-random samples, although that rule is routinely ignored by many social scientists. At the same time, hard-to-find groups may at times most easily be located through non-random methods. Some scholars might combine participants from both random and non-random samples.

1.2. Size of sample

Sample size determines much of the relative power of statistical tests (some tests have more power than others given different assumptions; more reliable measures can also provide greater power). Without a large enough sample, one may not be able to detect small or medium effect sizes with adequate statistical power, as noted by Marks (2012). For example, Wainright et al. (2004) compared sons and daughters of 44 same-sex and 44 opposite-sex parents; their results featured effect sizes as large as 0.78 (anxiety scores, sons) in favor of the children of heterosexual parents, but yet, because of the small sample size, none of those outcomes were statistically significant. If a non-random sample is chosen, higher statistical power may mean nothing since selection bias may overwhelm the results. Just targeting a larger sample is not enough, as a high response rate is also important for reducing bias associated with nonresponse as well as methods for inducing low levels of missing data from participants who do respond.

1.3. Definition of family forms

Family structure is not a static phenomenon. From children's birth to their adulthood, their family structures can and often do change. To have a more complete understanding of family structure, one may ask "at what age?", "for how long?" and "with whom?" Even if the structure (two-parents at home) remained the same, the "with whom" might change over time (one parent might be replaced by another person). In considering gay or lesbian parenting as a family form, a new question occurs – how to measure sexual orientation. A related decision concerns how many other types of family forms to measure as comparison groups.

1.4. Measurement of sexual orientation

Typically, sexual orientation is measured in terms of sexual attraction, sexual behavior, and sexual orientation identity (Sell, 2007). Measuring sexual orientation in multiple ways is more expensive and almost always yields results where attraction, behavior, and identity do not always match exactly. Furthermore, at least some persons view sexual orientation as a choice they made at a specific time or age while for others, there is at least some modulation over time around their primary orientation. For example, Herek et al. (2010) obtained a sample of 241 gay men, 152 lesbians, and 269 bisexuals (110 men, 159 women) with a response rate of 30% (p. 180). Overall, they found that 25% of their sample reported they had a "fair amount/great deal" of choice about their sexual orientation with another 14% having a "small amount" of choice. Thus, Herek et al.'s research confirmed Sarantakos's (2000) findings that some GLB persons have reported their sexual orientation as a choice (i.e., as "fluid," subject to change). Furthermore, the concept of sexual orientation as "fluid" rather than fixed at birth has received support from many studies (Baumeister, 2000; Diamond, 2000, 2006, 2008a,b; Diamond and Butterworth, 2008; Diamond and Savin-Williams, 2000; Diamond and Wallen, 2011; Dickson et al., 2003; Gartrell, Banks, Reed, Hamilton, Rodas, and Deck, 2000; Kinnish et al., 2005; Mock and Eibach, 2012; Rosario et al., 1996, 2006; Savin-Williams and Diamond, 2000; Savin-Williams et al., 2012; Savin-Williams and Ream, 2007). Stein (2007) concluded that "the empirical premises of the 'born that way' argument – that lesbians, gay men, and bisexuals are born with their sexual orientations or that sexual orientations are immutable – are at best dubious" (p. 133). These matters are important because individuals who view their sexual orientation as a choice may be more likely to self-identify as LGB later in life, even after having a child within a previous heterosexual relationship.

1.5. Statistical analyses

There are numerous possibilities for statistically analyzing data. A standard, though potentially misleading, approach is to predict child outcomes from several independent variables, one or more of which represent different family structures. A variety of possible control variables, including social desirability, may also be included in any statistical model; if such variables are measured, they should be included when testing models statistically. In addition to significance levels, effect sizes should be reported to indicate the relative magnitude of the apparent impact of the independent variables. Advances have been made recently in terms of demonstrating evidence for causality in social science research (Gangl, 2010; Ho and Rubin, 2011; Rothstein, 2007), but most research suggests associations rather than proving causality. In order to develop models for testing that might reflect reality more closely, it is helpful to consider the use of mediating and moderating variables (Warner, 2013).

1.6. Who will pay for the research?

Research is expensive. Either the researcher pays the costs or the researchers may obtain funds from others. If "others" are willing to fund the research, they often have an agenda such that they would rather see certain findings come from what they funded than other findings. Researchers are human, not perfect, and can be swayed by the values of their funding sources.

1.7. Are results consistent with other research?

Different methodologies can yield similar results. If a particular methodology seems to lead to unique results, it may be possible that the unusual findings are an artifact of the methodology. However, if a methodology leads to results similar to those found by a variety of other methodologies, that outcome would tend to confirm the validity of the findings more strongly.

2. Assessing the new family structures study as a case example

2.1. Random sample

Despite the challenges involved (Binson et al., 2007), Regnerus (2012) chose to use a random sample rather than a convenience sample, for all family types, not just the more common types. Regnerus devoted several paragraphs in his report to the development and characteristics of his sample, making it unlikely that reviewers of his manuscript would have missed how it was obtained and described. Other researchers have made different choices, often utilizing non-random samples (Schumm, 2005, 2008, 2010a, 2011; Marks, 2012). A few researchers have used random samples. For example, Golombok et al. (2003) began with a random sample but found very few (0.22%) lesbian couples with children; to achieve a larger sample of lesbian parents with children, they then adopted a methodology of obtaining a supplemental convenience sample of lesbian parents. Combining a random sample with a convenience sample largely defeats the purpose of using a random sample in the first place. As Julien et al. (2008) noted with respect to Golombok et al., "This strategy raised statistical power, but it also led to comparing a group of heterosexual mothers free of selection bias to a group of lesbian mothers not entirely free of selection bias" (p. 865). Other recent uses of random samples have included Potter (2012) and Rosenfeld (2010).

Regnerus obtained his random sample using "Knowledge Networks (or KN), a research firm with a very strong record of generating high-quality panel data for academic projects" (2012, p. 756). Some have criticized the use of KN, but my brief search of the academic literature found KN having been used for data collection in many research studies with GLB persons (Egan et al., 2008; Gilbert et al., 2011; Herek, 2009; Herek et al., 2010; Reiter et al., 2010), social science research (Barabas and Jerit, 2010; Bleakley et al., 2010; Brooks, 2010; Feld and Felson, 2008; Kahan et al., 2010; Levendusky, 2010; Mollborn, 2009; Winneg and Jamieson, 2010; Wirth and Bodenhausen, 2009), medical research (Condit and Shen, 2011; Harris et al., 2009a,b; Kumar et al., 2012; Manne et al., 2012; Song and Ling, 2011), and psychiatric research (Krueger et al., 2012; Sanders et al., 2010). Smith (2003) has compared the KN and General Social Surveys, finding that they agreed closely on many comparisons but did yield some systematic differences (especially differing on "don't know" responses and percentage of extreme answers on agree/disagree scales).

2.2. Size of sample

Regnerus (2012) identified, in his sample of 2988 respondents, 175 adult children who reported that their mother had once been in a same-sex romantic relationship along with 73 who said that of their father. Leaving aside the issue of how to define same-sex parents for the moment, much smaller samples of both homosexual and heterosexual families have often been used (Marks, 2012; Schumm, 2010a,b, 2011). Potter (2012) analyzed data from 19,107 (p. 562) families of whom only 72 (0.38%) were same-sex parent families at the time the focal child was in kindergarten. Julien et al. (2008), after accounting for missing data, found 179 sexual minority (lesbian or bisexual) women of a total sample of 8875 sexually active women; of those 179, only 38 were mothers. Of the 38 mothers, ten were lesbians. Some of the 38 sexual minority mothers had been in previous heterosexual partnerships (28.9%) and some were not currently living with a partner (40.8%). Thus, it is likely that fewer than ten of the participants reflected lesbian parent couples who were living together but had never consorted with a man in a previous heterosexual relationship (<0.11%). Moreover, since most of the sexual minority mothers sampled were under the age of 30 (28.9%) or 40 (36.8%), it is unlikely that many of them had raised any children to the age of 18 or older. In sum, it is not clear that Julien et al. (2008) found any lesbian couple families who had been stable for the entire 18 years of raising a child, even though they sampled nearly 9000 sexually active women. Regnerus found only two such families in the NFSS, which is not as much of an anomaly as some have suggested, given Julien et al.'s (2008) similar findings.

Several attempts to study gay father families have ended in failure because too few such families were located to permit meaningful statistical analysis (Schumm, 2011, p. 114). Patterson (2009) compared 18 lesbian families and 18 heterosexual families in one of her published reports. Leddy et al. (2012) reported results from an internet survey of 32 adult children of lesbian mothers. Reczek et al. (2009) reported an analysis based on only ten gay and ten lesbian couples, though later they reported research that added five more gay and five more lesbian couples (Reczek and Umberson, 2012), along with 20 heterosexual couples. Some have claimed that Regnerus's sample was too small, but his sample is clearly larger than most other previous studies.

2.3. Response rates and missing data

Regnerus (2012, p. 756) estimated the response rate for Knowledge Network surveys at about 65% without reporting the precise rate for the NFSS. It is not clear how response rates might have differed within the NFSS for adult children from different types of families. Farr et al. (2010a,b) found different response rates for gay and lesbian parents (75%) than for their heterosexual parents (41%). Herek et al. (2010) estimated the response rate in his survey at only 30% (p. 180). Kurdek (2008) surveyed 610 couples who had applied for civil unions in Vermont; of the 598 eligible, 199 (33.3%) returned surveys from both partners with a higher response rate from lesbian couples than from gay couples.

Some variables measured by Regnerus (2012) appeared to have no missing data at all while other variables appeared to have some (p. 759). Missing data in a study by Julien et al. (2008) reduced the number of lesbian and bisexual women participants from 220 to 179 (18.6% loss). When Wainright et al. (2004, p. 1892) compared 44 children of same-sex and 44 children of heterosexual parents, missing data reduced the sample size from 88 to as low as 64 (27.3% loss). Many other recent studies concerning LGBT issues have not reported missing data, while those that did featured ranges between 9% and 17% (Schumm, 2011, pp. 88–89). Leddy et al. (2012) lost 8.6% of their data because of incomplete surveys. Potter (2012, p. 563) reported as much as 14% missing data for his first wave of participants. When Erich et al. (2009) conducted a web survey of over 200 parents and children, they lost (because of missing information) as much as 55% of their data from parents and as much as nearly 70% of their data from children. Clearly, if there is a missing data concern with the NFSS, it is not alone among other studies.

2.4. How many family types?

Most studies that have compared GLBT families with other families have limited their selection of other families, often to single parent heterosexual families (Schumm, 2010a). However, Golombok et al. (2003) studied both single parent and dual parent heterosexual and lesbian families. Both Potter (2012) and Rosenfeld (2010) considered a wide variety of family types in their studies. Regnerus (2012) analyzed as many as eight types of families, at least keeping pace with other similar studies.

2.5. Measuring family types (including GLBT status)

It appears to be difficult to find an adequate number of same-sex parents from even large random samples. Regnerus, in one of his most controversial decisions, expanded the "net" for possible GLBT families by including any family for which an adult child reported that one or both parents had been in a same-sex romantic relationship at some point between the child's birth and age 18. Using a specific point in the family life cycle to study the effect of a variable is not uncommon. Bos et al. (2012) used age 17 as their "some point" to assess the impact of having a male role model on children from lesbian families, using no information on how long the children had that male role model or if they had known a variety of male role models over the years, from time to time.

Moreover, many children from eventual gay or lesbian families have been born into heterosexual families (Sirota, 2009). Short (2007) studied 68 lesbian women with 52 children in Australia, with 21% of those children having been born in a previous heterosexual relationship. Golombok et al. (1983, p. 569) compared lesbian and single-parent heterosexual families where 92% of the lesbian mothers' children had lived in a heterosexual home for some time, with 65% having lived as such for over 2 years, and 32% for over 5 years (Schumm, 2005, p. 443). Golombok et al. (2003) reported that 72% (28/39) of their children had been born into a heterosexual family; furthermore, those children were an average of over 4 years old when their mother entered into a lesbian relationship. Even though the initial criteria was to study children of age 7, Golombok et al. (2003) expanded the criteria for children of lesbian parents to as low as age 5, in order to increase sample size. Thus, in this study published within the past decade in the well-known APA journal, *Developmental Psychology*, children who had spent most of their life in heterosexual families were, in fact, included within the operational definition of children from lesbian families. Welsh (2011) recruited 14 adolescents between the ages of 13 and 18, requiring only that they have lived with a gay or lesbian parent for the previous five years, regardless of whether that parent currently had a partner or had the child in a previous heterosexual relationship. Hequembourg (2004) studied 40 lesbian mothers, finding that 20 of them had been heterosexually married before coming out and 19 had given birth to their children during a previous heterosexual marriage; four had conceived through alternative insemination and four had adopted children (one had engaged in a one-night-stand to get pregnant, another had been raped by a family member, others were foster parents).

Likewise, even though Patterson (2009) used only 18 lesbian families in one study, in other studies (Wainright and Patterson, 2006) using the same source of data, she expanded the definition of "lesbian" – or at least "same sex" – to increase the sample size to 44 (a 144% increase). Even if you start with lesbian couples using donor insemination to have their own child, some of the lesbian mothers may leave their partner and re-partner with a male, as two of the 78 couples did by age five of their child (Gartrell et al., 2000, p. 543) or they may change their gender to male, creating an apparent heterosexual couple, as did one of the 78 couples by age five of their child (Gartrell et al., 2000). When Gartrell and her colleagues compare stable and unstable lesbian families, the unstable group may be contaminated by the presence of a few heterosexual families rather than consisting of "pure" new lesbian parent couples or lesbian single parents. Because lesbian parents appear to have substantially higher rates of relationship instability than do heterosexual parents (Schumm, 2010d), it may be very rare (and difficult) to find stable same-sex parent couples, especially those with no prior heterosexual sexual experience, who have raised a child full-time, continuously with no separations, from birth to age 18.

Furthermore, given the apparent fluidity of sexual orientation in general, but especially for women, it may even be rare for parents to maintain a same-sex orientation for 18 years, much less remaining with the same partner for that time. If Regnerus can be criticized for expanding or "tweaking" his definition of "lesbian" and "gay" parents in order to enlarge his sample, he has not been alone among other scholars in so doing. At least he was clear about his definitions, even if one begs to differ with them. In contrast, Leddy et al. (2012) conducted an internet convenience sample of 32 adult offspring (no demographic information, such as gender or age of adult offspring, reported) of lesbians, delimiting the family background requirement only as "raised in a lesbian family" where the duration of same-sex parenting or number or types of partner changes (if any) was never specified.

2.6. Control variables (including social desirability)

What often occurs in research with same-sex parents is that older, high-income, well educated same-sex parents with one or two children are compared to younger, moderate-income, less well educated heterosexual parents with several children, without statistical controls for the demographic differences between the groups (Schumm, 2005, 2010b). If one wants to assess the effect of parental sexual orientation on child outcomes, factors such as parental age, income, education, and number of children should be taken into account; otherwise, any conclusions about the role of sexual orientation may be confounded with socioeconomic effects, particularly *per capita* household income. Some convenience samples (Farr et al., 2010a,b) have used same-sex couples with annual household incomes of upwards of $200,000, easily within the top 5% of all US households. At such high incomes, regardless of a parent's sexual orientation, even a negligent parent could purchase high quality child care services, which might easily mask the parent's actual ineffectiveness in raising children.

Social desirability has been acknowledged as an important issue for same-sex parents, who might well have logical reasons for presenting their parenting skills and children's outcomes in the best possible light (Gartrell et al., 1996, p. 279). Most studies have not measured social desirability at all, while some have measured it but not used it as a control variable (Erich et al., 2005). Regnerus (2012, p. 754) mentioned social desirability and controlled for it in part by his design of surveying adult children of various family types rather than surveying the parents. Like most others researching same-sex parenting, Regnerus (2012) does not appear to have assessed social desirability directly in his survey instrument.

2.7. Multivariate analyses: mediating or moderating variables?

Hair et al. (2006, pp. 249–268) spent a great deal of time in their text discussing multicollinearity in multiple regression analyses because of the dramatic impact that high multicollinearity can have on regression results, even leading researchers to draw inappropriate conclusions. Regardless of the explanation, simply predicting a dependent variable from a host of predictor variables by itself does little to "prove" causality or even to explain the mere correlational role of mediating factors. As was observed over 30 years ago, multiple regression – applied inexpertly – can be as much of a stumbling block as a stepping stone (Schumm et al., 1980). Rucker et al. (2011) proposed that "overemphasizing the X → Y relationship before or after controlling for a mediator can lead to misleading, or even false, conclusions in theory testing" (p. 360) and that "significant indirect effects can occur in the absence of significant total or direct effects" (p. 362). They concluded that "researchers should explore these [indirect or mediating] effects regardless of the significance of the total or direct effect" (p. 368). Similarly, Gangl (2010) has argued that merely "including a series of observed variables in a regression specification is woefully inadequate and is eventually unlikely to identify any causal effect of interest" (p. 27) especially if indirect effects are not considered. Nevertheless, Gangl argues that much sociological practice appears to ignore such precautions (p. 37). I would concur with Gangl's observation. Ho and Rubin (2011) have noted that "When groups differ sharply, regression may not credibly 'control' for confounding factors" (p. 26) with an implication that research design is more important than merely using multivariate statistics for predicting one variable (without much theoretical basis) from a host of other variables. Numerous recent reports have adopted a methodology of predicting an outcome variable from a host of independent variables, one of the latter being a measure of family structure. While I would prefer more attention to mediating variables, it is not uncommon for contemporary researchers to merely predict child outcomes from a variable capturing family structure and a series of control variables, as Regnerus (2012) did. Wainright and Patterson (2006) predicted several adolescent risk behaviors from family structure, gender of adolescent, parental education, quality of family relationships, care from adults and peers, and family income. Rosenfeld (2010) predicted one child outcome from a host (>70) of independent variables, without mediation. Potter (2012) did likewise, except for using more than one outcome variable and fewer independent variables. As discussed later, Potter found that same-sex families were very unstable compared to married biological parent families. When he controlled for family transitions in his model, the math and reading scores evened out between the children of married biological parent families and same-sex families, but such statistical controls are risky because it is not clear what those controls mean when almost all of one group has no transitions while almost all of the other group has some transitions. When and if

Regnerus incorporates mediating variables into his analyses, he will need to be careful to consider the potential effects of such unusual patterns.

2.8. Effect sizes

Since at least 1994, the American Psychological Association (1994, p. 18, 2001, p. 25; 2010, pp. 33-34) has called for the reporting of effect sizes in social science research. In my review (Schumm, 2010a) of 13 recently published reports concerning LGBT issues, most (>92%) violated APA standards by not reporting effect sizes; some of the reports did not even report standard deviations or degrees of freedom for their statistical tests. It is remarkable that the APA will commend studies of same-sex parents when those very studies routinely ignore or violate official APA research guidelines. Regnerus (2012) did not report standard deviations in all of his tables but has agreed to provide the missing ones upon request, which will permit the calculation of effect sizes.

2.9. Funding concerns

Regnerus (2012) acknowledged his sources of funding as being recognized for their "support of conservative causes" (p. 755) but noted that "the funding sources played no role at all in the design or conduct of the study, the analyses, the interpretations of the data, or in the preparation of the manuscript" (p. 755). The obligation of the scholar is to acknowledge all sources of funding and to keep all research activity independent of that funding. For example, Bos, Goldberg, van Gelderen, and Gartrell (2012) stated that "The NLLFS [National Longitudinal Lesbian Family Study] has been supported in part by small grants from the Gill Foundation, the Lesbian Health Fund of the Gay Lesbian Medical Association, the Horizons Foundation, the Roy Scrivner Fund of the American Psychological Association, and the Williams Institute at UCLA School of Law. The Williams Institute has also provided personnel support to the NLLFS. Funding sources played no role in the design or conduct of the study; the management, analysis, or interpretation of the data; or the preparation, review, or approval of the manuscript" (p. 603). Numerous publications have been derived from NLLFS data. Although Regnerus has been criticized for accepting funding from conservative agencies, it is not readily apparent how that differs from situations where other scholars have accepted funding from progressive agencies; both types of agencies may have had vested interests in the outcomes of the research.

2.10. Similar results

2.10.1. Stability

Whether same-sex relationships are more or less stable than heterosexual relationships has been a matter of controversy, with some scholars concluding that there were no differences (Goldberg, 2010, p. 27; Redding, 2008, p. 164). However, Kurdek (2004, p. 894; 2005, p. 253) reported that over 11–12 years, 3.1% of his heterosexual parent couples and 18.7% of his heterosexual nonparents ended their relationships (14.5%, 70/483, all heterosexual couples) compared to 19.0% (24/126) of his nonparent gay couples and 23.8% (24/101) of his nonparent lesbian couples; he concluded that "gay and lesbian couples dissolve their relationships more frequently than heterosexual couples, especially heterosexual couples with children" (p. 896). Kurdek (2005, p. 253) cited Scandinavian data involving nearly 3000 same-sex unions and over 200,000 heterosexual unions (Andersson et al., 2006) in which lesbian couples with legal unions in Norway and Sweden were more likely to break up (11.3%, 20.0%) than were gay couples with legal unions (7.9%, 14.3%), compared to 8% for heterosexual marriages in Sweden. Using a 10 year panel study from the Netherlands, Kalmijn et al. found dissolution rates of 21.6%, 30.1%, and 74.4%, respectively, for married heterosexual couples, cohabiting heterosexual couples, and same-sex couples (p. 165), with female same-sex couples being more stable than male same-sex couples (p. 175). Strohm (2010, p. 169); Lau (2012, p. 981), using British longitudinal data over an 8 year period, found significant differences in relationship stability for married heterosexuals ($N = 8174$, 18% dissolved), heterosexual cohabiting couples ($N = 17,219$, 40% dissolved), lesbian couples ($N = 125$, 69% dissolved), and gay male couples ($N = 138$, 79% dissolved). Strohm's (2010) data for heterosexual married couples parallels results found by Wilson and Smallwood (2008) for England and Wales (20% dissolved by 8 years).

After acknowledging that "Perhaps the most important "bottom-line" question asked about gay and lesbian couples is whether their relationships last" (p. 252), Kurdek (2005) reiterated that "The limited data available indicate that gay and lesbian couples may be less stable than married heterosexual couples" (p. 251). Biblarz and Stacey (2010) concluded that lesbian mothers had less stable relationships than heterosexual mothers, citing MacCallum and Golombok, 2004. After comparing relationship duration for 15 lesbian couples, 15 gay couples, and 20 heterosexual couples from a convenience sample, and considering Andersson et al. (2006), Reczek and Umberson concluded that "lesbian relationships are of shorter average duration than gay and straight relationships" (p. 1785). Reviewing a much larger number of studies, Schumm (2010d) found that over 10 years, about 15–20% of heterosexual parent couples separated compared to about 40–45% of lesbian parent couples. Sarantakos (2000) also found greater instability among Australian same-sex couples. Hequembourg (2004) found that only 35% of her 40 lesbian mothers had been with their current partner for more than ten years. Others have concluded that same-sex relationships are less stable (Byrd, 2011, pp. 23–24; Gartrell et al., 2011; Whitton and Buzzella, 2012). Most recently, Potter (2012) found that between birth and fifth grade, almost 95% of married biological parent families experienced no family transitions whereas 100% of same-sex parent families did experience at least one family transition; between kindergarten and eighth grade, the corresponding percentages were almost 96% no transitions and almost 70% at least one transition for lesbian mother families and 100% at least one transition for gay father families.[1]

What difference would instability make for children? Gartrell et al. (2006) indicated that among the nearly half of their lesbian mothers who had separated, some children has been exposed to as many as six of their mother's new sexual partners in less than 10 years. Tasker and Golombok (1997) appeared to find that 24% of their lesbian mothers had five or more sexual partners over the 15 years of their longitudinal study. There appears to be some degree of scientific consensus (Popenoe, 2009, Strohschein, 2010, Whitton and Buzzella, 2012) that multiple primary caregiver transitions, presumably regardless of the sexual orientation of parents, are stressful for children and increase the risk of poor child outcomes.

2.11. Child sexual orientation

Regnerus (2012) reported that adult children of lesbian mothers and of gay fathers were significantly less likely to identify as entirely heterosexual, with estimated effect sizes of 0.81 and 0.53, respectively, using $SD = 0.36$ for all comparisons. Women with lesbian mothers or gay fathers were both significantly more likely to report more female sex partners, with estimated effect sizes of 0.75 and 1.14, respectively, using $SD = 1.10$ for both comparisons. Men with lesbian mothers or gay fathers were both significantly more likely to report more male sex partners, with estimated effect sizes of 0.80 and 0.79, respectively, using $SD = 1.60$ for both comparisons. Does other research support this finding? Indeed, there are several studies, cited in Schumm (2008, 2011), as well as other reports (Gartrell et al., 2011; Goldberg and Kuvalanka, 2012; Lick et al., 2011; Murray and McClintock, 2005; Sarantakos, 2000, p. 133) which concur in observing significantly higher rates of same-sex behavior or identity among children of same-sex versus heterosexual parents (using a comparison rate of 10% for heterosexual parents if no comparison group was provided).

2.12. Drug Abuse

Regnerus (2012) reported significantly higher levels of marijuana use and smoking among adult children of lesbian mothers (p. 762). Sirota (1997) reported a substantially higher rate of drug use by daughters of gay fathers (44.1%, 30/68) compared to daughters of heterosexual fathers (14.7%, 10/68) ($p < 0.001$). It could be argued that her finding cannot be generalized to gay or lesbian parents who use surrogates or artificial insemination; however, Goldberg, Bos, and Gartrell (2011) reported that among the children of lesbian mothers, children born after the lesbian couples had formed (i.e., not from a previous heterosexual relationship), alcohol use and marijuana/hashish use were both higher for both sons and daughters of lesbian parents compared to a matched group of children of heterosexual parents. Use of hallucinogens was also significantly higher for the sons of lesbians. No significant differences were found for cocaine, tranquilizer, or barbiturates use. Sarantakos (2000, p. 131) reported that the adult children of homosexual parents reported higher proportions of drug use than children from married or cohabiting heterosexual couples.

While Goldberg et al. (2011) cited Wainright and Patterson (2006) for evidence of no differences in drug use between children of same-sex female couples and heterosexual couples, a closer inspection of Table 1 (p. 528) in Wainright and Patterson (2006) revealed effect sizes for nine measures of tobacco, alcohol, marijuana, and other drug use (and a measure of delinquency) from 0.00 to 0.27, none favoring the children of same-sex couples, even though the same-sex parents rated their parent–child relationships better and their children reported lower levels of victimization. Schumm and Crow (2010) argued that the chances of someone conducting ten statistical tests and finding none of them favoring one side of the null hypothesis was very unlikely ($p < 0.05$) unless the correlations among the ten tests averaged 0.50 or higher (then $p \leqslant 0.10$, a criterion used by Wainright and Patterson themselves on p. 529). Subsequently, Schumm and Canfield (2011) demonstrated that it was possible to have data in which one set of statistical tests would yield almost no significant results and yet almost any other type of such tests would yield significant results. Wainright and Patterson (2006) did not report the correlations among their measures and used only one type of statistical test – nor did they report results on the basis of children's gender. As noted by O'Leary (2010, p. 421), Marquardt et al. (2010) found a trend for donor-insemination children of lesbian parents to report substance abuse problems more often (21.1%, 8/38) than biological children of heterosexual parents (11.0%, 62/563) (two-sided Fisher's Exact Test, $p < 0.07$). Julien et al. (2008) detected a trend ($p < 0.06$, one-sided Fisher's Exact Test) for her lesbian mothers (26.3%) to be more likely to use illegal drugs than matched heterosexual mothers (10.5%). Trocki et al. (2009), using data from a large national random sample, the 2000 National Alcohol Survey, reported higher marijuana use, bar patronage, and sensation seeking among lesbian women compared to exclusively heterosexual women. Byrd (2011, p. 16) and Rosario (2008) both cited studies in which lesbians had higher rates of lifetime substance abuse, leaving open the possibility that higher rates of substance abuse among their children might reflect imitation of parental modeling.

Space precludes further discussion of similarities with Regnerus's (2012) results, but more information can be found elsewhere (Schumm, 2010b, 2011, 2012). Finding similar results from a variety of other samples and methods does not validate Regnerus's methods necessarily, but it does suggest that his methods were not so skewed as to override patterns also seen elsewhere.

---

[1] Data provided by Daniel Potter on 30 May and 20 June 2012 by email.

2.13. Conclusions

Like all researchers, Regnerus (2012) made a number of methodological decisions in planning and implementing his research. While other researchers might not have made exactly the same set of methodological decisions, that does not mean that his decisions were improper or notably different than those of many other scholars. Other scholars, including well-known progressive scholars, have defined same-sex families using parents who had previously been in mixed orientation relationships or marriages. The NFSS data set is one of the few that can specify exactly how the family patterns of adult children changed over the life of the child. Further work can help answer questions with respect to how to better define lesbian mother and gay father families, although the combined effect of changes in sexual orientation and changes in relationship status may make finding even a minimally adequate size ($N > 30$) *random* sample of adult children from stable lesbian mothers or gay fathers nearly impossible. While many would differ with some of Regnerus's many methodological decisions, his decisions are within the ball park of what other credible and distinguished researchers have been doing within the past decade. We would do well to remember Hoenig and Heisey's (2001) argument that "In matters of public health and regulation, it is often more important to be protected against erroneously concluding no difference exists when one does" (p. 23). Regardless of his particular methodological decisions, Regnerus's apparent results caution us about making such types of erroneous conclusions, no matter what pressures may exist to do otherwise.

References

American Psychological Association, 1994. Publication Manual of the American Psychological Association, fourth ed. American Psychological Association, Washington, DC.

American Psychological Association, 2001. Publication Manual of the American Psychological Association, fifth ed. American Psychological Association, Washington, DC.

American Psychological Association, 2010. Publication Manual of the American Psychological Association, sixth ed. American Psychological Association, Washington, DC.

Andersson, G., Noack, T., Seierstad, A., Weedon-Fekjaer, H., 2006. The demographics of same-sex marriages in Norway and Sweden. Demography 43, 79–98.

Barabas, J., Jerit, J., 2010. Are survey experiments externally valid? American Political Science Review 104, 226–242.

Baumeister, R.F., 2000. Gender differences in erotic plasticity: the female sex drive as socially flexible and responsive. Psychological Bulletin 126, 347–374.

Biblarz, T., Stacey, J., 2010. How does the gender of parents matter? Journal of Marriage and Family 72, 3–22.

Binson, D., Blair, J., Huebner, D.M., Woods, W.J., 2007. Sampling in surveys of lesbian, gay, and bisexual people. In: Meyer, I.H., Northridge, M.E. (Eds.), The Health of Sexual Minorities. Springer, New York, pp. 375–418.

Bleakley, A., Hennessy, M., Fishbein, M., 2010. Predicting preferences for types of sex education in US schools. Sexuality Research & Social Policy 7, 50–57.

Bos, H., Goldberg, N., van Gelderen, L., Gartrell, N., 2012. Adolescents of the US national longitudinal lesbian family study: male role models, gender role traits, and psychological adjustment. Gender & Society 26, 603–638.

Brooks, D.J., 2010. A negativity gap? Voter gender, attack politics, and participation in American elections. Politics & Gender 6, 319–341.

Byrd, A.D., 2011. Homosexual couples and parenting: what science can and cannot say. Journal of Human Sexuality 3, 4–34.

Condit, C.M., Shen, L., 2011. Public understanding of risks from gene–environment interaction in common diseases: implications for public communication. Public Health Genomics 14, 115–124.

Diamond, L., 2000. Sexual identity, attractions, and behavior among young sexual-minority women over a 2-year period. Developmental Psychology 36, 241–250.

Diamond, L.M., 2006. What we got wrong about sexual identity development: unexpected findings from a longitudinal study of young women. In: Omoto, A.M., Kurtzman, H.S. (Eds.), Sexual Orientation and Mental Health. American Psychological Association, Washington, DC, pp. 73–94.

Diamond, L.M., 2008a. Female bisexuality from adolescence to adulthood: results from a 10-year longitudinal study. Developmental Psychology 44, 5–14.

Diamond, L.M., 2008b. Sexual Fluidity: Understanding Women's Love and Desire. Harvard University Press, Cambridge, MA.

Diamond, L.M., Butterworth, M., 2008. Questioning gender and sexual identity: dynamics links over time. Sex Roles 59, 365–376.

Diamond, L.M., Savin-Williams, R.C., 2000. Explaining diversity in the development of same-sex sexuality among young women. Journal of Social Issues 56, 297–313.

Diamond, L.M., Wallen, K., 2011. Sexual minority women's sexual motivation around the time of ovulation. Archives of Sexual Behavior 40, 237–246.

Dickson, N., Paul, C., Herbison, P., 2003. Same-sex attraction in a birth cohort: prevalence and persistence in early adulthood. Social Science & Medicine 56, 1607–1615.

Egan, P.J., Edelman, M.S., Sherrill, K., 2008. Findings from the Hunter College Poll of Lesbians, Gays, and Bisexuals. Hunter College, New York.

Erich, S., Kanenberg, H., Case, K., Allen, T., Bogdanos, T., 2009. An empirical analysis of factors affecting adolescent attachment in adoptive families with homosexual and straight parents. Children and Youth Services Review 31, 398–404.

Erich, S., Leung, P., Kindle, P., 2005. A comparative analysis of adoptive family functioning with gay, lesbian, and heterosexual parents and their children. Journal of GLBT Family Studies 1, 43–60.

Farr, R.H., Forssell, S.L., Patterson, C.J., 2010a. Gay, lesbian, and heterosexual adoptive parents: couple and relationship issues. Journal of GLBT Family Studies 6, 199–213.

Farr, R.H., Forssell, S.L., Patterson, C.J., 2010b. Parenting and child development in adoptive families: does parental sexual orientation matter? Applied Developmental Science 14, 164–178.

Feld, S.L., Felson, R.B., 2008. Gender norms and retaliatory violence against spouses and acquaintances. Journal of Family Issues 29, 692–703.

Gangl, M., 2010. Causal inference in sociological research. Annual Review of Sociology 36, 21–47.

Gartrell, N., Banks, A., Reed, N., Hamilton, J., Rodas, C., Deck, A., 2000. The national lesbian family study: 3. Interviews with mothers of five-year-olds. American Journal of Orthopsychiatry 70, 542–548.

Gartrell, N., Bos, H.M.W., Goldberg, N.G., 2011. Adolescents of the US national longitudinal lesbian family study: sexual orientation, sexual behavior, and sexual risk exposure. Archives of Sexual Behavior 40, 1199–1209.

Gartrell, N., Hamilton, J., Banks, A., Mosbacher, D., Reed, N., Sparks, C.H., Bishop, H., 1996. The national family lesbian study: 1. Interviews with prospective mothers. American Journal of Orthopsychiatry 66, 272–281.

Gartrell, N., Rodas, C., Deck, A., Peyser, H., Banks, A., 2006. The USA national lesbian family study: interviews with mothers of 10-year olds. Feminism & Psychology 16, 175–192.

Gilbert, P., Brewer, N.T., Reiter, P.L., Ng, T.W., Smith, J.S., 2011. HPV vaccine acceptability in heterosexual, gay, and bisexual men. American Journal of Men's Health 5, 297–305.

Goldberg, A.E., 2010. Lesbian and Gay Parents and their Children: Research on the Family Life Cycle. American Psychological Association, Washington, DC.

Goldberg, N.G., Bos, H.M.W., Gartrell, N.K., 2011. Substance use by adolescents of the USA National Longitudinal Lesbian Family Study. Journal of Health Psychology 16, 1231–1240.

Goldberg, A.E., Kuvalanka, K.A., 2012. Marriage (In)equality: the perspectives of adolescents and emerging adults with lesbian, gay, and bisexual parents. Journal of Marriage and Family 74, 34–52.

Golombok, S., Perry, B., Burston, A., Murray, C., Mooney-Somers, J., Stevens, M., Golding, J., 2003. Children with lesbian parents: a community study. Developmental Psychology 39, 20–33.

Golombok, S., Spencer, A., Rutter, M., 1983. Children in lesbian and single-parent households: psychosexual and psychiatric appraisal. Journal of Child Psychology & Psychiatry 24, 551–572.

Hair Jr., J.F., Black, W.C., Babin, B.J., Anderson, R.E., Tatham, R.L., 2006. Multivariate Data Analysis, sixth ed. Pearson/Prentice Hall, Upper Saddle River, NJ.

Harris, K.M., Maurer, J., Lurie, N., 2009a. Do people who intend to get a flu shot actually get one? Journal of General Internal Medicine 24, 1311–1313.

Harris, K.M., Schonlau, M., Lurie, N., 2009b. Surveying a nationally representative Internet-based panel to obtain timely estimates of influenza vaccination rates. Vaccine 27, 815–818.

Hequembourg, A., 2004. Unscripted motherhood: lesbian mothers negotiating incompletely institutionalized family relationships. Journal of Social and Personal Relationships 21, 739–762.

Herek, G.M., 2009. Hate crimes and stigma-related experiences among sexual minority adults in the United States: prevalence estimates from a national probability sample. Journal of Interpersonal Violence 24, 54–74.

Herek, G.M., Norton, A.T., Allen, T.J., Sims, C.L., 2010. Demographic, psychological, and social characteristics of self-identified lesbian, gay, and bisexual adults in a US probability sample. Sexuality Research and Social Policy 7, 176–200.

Ho, D.E., Rubin, D.B., 2011. Credible causal inference for empirical legal studies. Annual Review of Law and Social Science 7, 17–40.

Hoenig, J., Heisey, D.M., 2001. The abuse of power: the pervasive fallacy of power calculations for data analysis. The American Statistician 55, 19–24.

Julien, D., Jouvin, E., Jodoin, E., l'Archeveque, Chartrand, E., 2008. Adjustment among mothers reporting same-gender sexual partners: a study of a representative population sample from Quebec province (Canada). Archives of Sexual Behavior 37, 864–876.

Kahan, D.M., Braman, D., Cohen, G.L., Gastil, J., Slovic, P., 2010. Who fears the HPV vaccine, who doesn't, and why? An experimental study of the mechanisms of cultural cognition. Law and Human Behavior 34, 501–516.

Kalmijn, M., Loeve, A., Manting, D., 2007. Income dynamics in couples and the dissolution of marriage and cohabitation. Demography 44, 159–179.

Kinnish, K.K., Strassberg, D.S., Turner, C.W., 2005. Sex differences in the flexibility of sexual orientation: a multidimensional retrospective assessment. Archives of Sexual Behavior 34, 173–183.

Krueger, R.F., Derringer, J., Markon, K.E., Watson, D., Skodol, A.E., 2012. Initial construction of a maladaptive personality trait model and inventory for DSM-5. Psychological Medicine 42, 1879–1890.

Kumar, S., Quinn, S.C., Kim, K.H., Daniel, L.H., Freimuth, V.S., 2012. The impact of workplace policies and other social factors on self-reported influenza-like illness incidence during the 2009 H1N1 pandemic. American Journal of Public Health 102, 134–140.

Kurdek, L.A., 2004. Are gay and lesbian cohabiting couples *really* different from heterosexual married couples? Journal of Marriage and Family 66, 880–900.

Kurdek, L.A., 2005. What do we know about gay and lesbian couples? Current Directions in Psychological Science 14, 251–254.

Kurdek, L.A., 2008. A general model of relationship commitment: evidence from same-sex partners. Personal Relationships 15, 391–405.

Lau, C.Q., 2012. The stability of same-sex cohabitation, different-sex cohabitation, and marriage. Jounal of Marriage and Family 74, 973–988.

Leddy, A., Gartrell, N., Bos, H., 2012. Growing up in a lesbian family: the life experiences of the adult daughters and sons of lesbian mothers. Journal of GLBT Family Studies 8, 243–257.

Levendusky, M.S., 2010. Clearer cues, more consistent voters: a benefit of elite polarization. Political Behavior 32, 111–131.

Lick, D.J., Schmidt, K.M., Patterson, C.J., 2011. The rainbow families scale (RFS): a measure of experiences among individuals with lesbian and gay parents. Journal of Applied Measurement 12, 222–241.

MacCallum, F., Golombok, S., 2004. Children raised in fatherless families from infancy: a follow-up of children of lesbian and single heterosexual mothers at early adolescence. Journal of Child Psychology and Psychiatry 45, 1407–1419.

Manne, S., Kashy, D., Weinberg, D.S., Boscarino, J.A., Bowen, D.J., 2012. Using the interdependence model to understand spousal influence on colorectal cancer screening intentions: a structural equation model. Annals of Behavioral Medicine 43, 320–329.

Marquardt, E., Glenn, N., Clark, K., 2010. My Daddy's Name Is Donor. Institute for American Values, New York.

Marks, L., 2012. Same-sex parenting and children's outcomes: a closer examination of the American Psychological Association's brief on lesbian and gay parenting. Social Science Research 41, 735–751.

Mock, S.E., Eibach, R.P., 2012. Stability and change in sexual orientation identity over a 10-year period in adulthood. Archives of Sexual Behavior 41, 641–648.

Mollborn, S., 2009. Norms about nonmarital pregnancy and willingness to provide resources to unwed parents. Journal of Marriage and Family 71, 122–134.

Murray, P.D., McClintock, K., 2005. Children of the closet: a measurement of the anxiety and self-esteem of children raised by a non-disclosed homosexual or bisexual parent. Journal of Homosexuality 49, 77–95.

O'Leary, D., 2010. Is the psychological adjustment of donor-conceived children of lesbians higher than that of other children? The Linacre Quarterly 77, 415–425.

Patterson, C.J., 2009. Lesbian and gay parents and their children: a social science perspective. In: Hope, D.A. (Ed.), Contemporary Perspectives on Lesbian, Gay, and Bisexual Identities: Nebraska Symposium on Motivation. Springer Science and Business Media, New York, pp. 141–182.

Popenoe, D., 2009. Cohabitation, marriage, and child wellbeing: a cross-national perspective. Sociology 46, 429–436.

Potter, D., 2012. Same-sex families and children's academic achievement. Journal of Marriage and Family 74, 556–571.

Reczek, C., Elliott, S., Umberson, D., 2009. Commitment without marriage: union formation among long-term same-sex couples. Journal of Family Issues 30, 738–756.

Reczek, C., Umberson, D., 2012. Gender, health behavior, and intimate relationships: lesbian, gay, and straight contexts. Social Science & Medicine 74, 1783–1790.

Redding, R.E., 2008. It's really about sex: same-sex marriage, lesbigay parenting, and the psychology of disgust. Duke Journal of Gender Law & Policy 15, 127–193.

Regnerus, M., 2012. How different are the adult children of parents who have same-sex relationships? Findings from the new family structures study. Social Science Research 41, 752–770.

Reiter, P.L., Brewer, N.T., McRee, A., Gilbert, P., Smith, J.S., 2010. Acceptability of HPV vaccine among a national sample of gay and bisexual men. Sexually Transmitted Diseases 37, 197–203.

Rosario, M., 2008. Elevated substance use among lesbian and bisexual women: possible explanations and intervention implications for an urgent public health concern. Substance Use & Misuse 43, 1268–1270.

Rosario, M., Meyer-Bahlburg, H.F.L., Hunter, J., Exner, T.M., Gwadz, M., Keller, M., 1996. The psychosexual development of urban lesbian, gay, and bisexual youths. Journal of Sex Research 33, 113–126.

Rosario, M., Schrimshaw, E.W., Hunter, J., Braun, L., 2006. Sexual identity development among lesbian, gay, and bisexual youths: consistency and change over time. Journal of Sex Research 43, 46–58.

Rosenfeld, M.J., 2010. Nontraditional families and childhood progress through school. Demography 47, 755–775.

Rothstein, B., 2007. How to get at causality in the social sciences: multiple regressions versus case studies. Comparative Social Research 24, 351–360.

Rucker, D.D., Preacher, K.J., Tormala, Z.L., Petty, R.E., 2011. Mediation analysis in social psychology: current practices and new recommendations. Social and Personality Psychology Compass 5 (6), 359–371.

Sanders, A.R., Levinson, D.F., Duan, J., Dennis, J.M., Li, R., Kendler, K.S., Rice, J.P., Shi, J., Mowry, B.J., Amin, F., Silverman, J.M., Buccola, N.G., Byerley, W.F., Black, D.W., Freedman, R., Cloninger, C.R., Gejman, P.V., 2010. The internet-based MGS2 control sample: self report of mental illness. The American Journal of Psychiatry 167, 854–865.

Sarantakos, S., 2000. Same-sex Couples. Harvard Press, Sydney, Australia.

Savin-Williams, R.C., Diamond, L.M., 2000. Sexual identity trajectories among sexual minority youths: gender comparisons. Archives of Sexual Behavior 29, 607–627.

Savin-Williams, R.C., Joyner, K., Rieger, G., 2012. Prevalence and stability of self-reported sexual orientation identity during young adulthood. Archives of Sexual Behavior 41, 103–110.

Savin-Williams, R.C., Ream, G.L., 2007. Prevalence and stability of sexual orientation components during adolescence and young adulthood. Archives of Sexual Behavior 36, 385–394.

Schumm, W.R., 2005. Empirical and theoretical perspectives from social science on gay marriage and child custody issues. St. Thomas Law Review 18, 425–471.

Schumm, W.R., 2008. Re-evaluation of the no differences' hypothesis concerning gay and lesbian parenting as assessed in eight early (1979–1986) and four later (1997–1998) dissertations. Psychological Reports 103, 275–304.

Schumm, W.R., 2010a. Statistical requirements for properly investigating a null hypothesis. Psychological Reports 107 (3), 953–971.

Schumm, W.R., 2010b. Child outcomes associated with lesbian parenting: comments on Biblarz and Stacey's 2010 report. Journal of Human Sexuality 3, 35–80.

Schumm, W.R., 2010c. How science is done. Marriage and Family Review 46, 323–326.

Schumm, W.R., 2010d. Comparative relationship stability of lesbian mother and heterosexual mother families: a review of evidence. Marriage and Family Review 46, 499–509.

Schumm, W.R., 2011. Are two lesbian parents better than a mom and a dad? Logical and methodological flaws in recent studies affirming the superiority of lesbian parenthood. Ave Maria Law Review 10, 79–120.

Schumm, W.R., 2012. Lessons for the "devilish statistical obfuscator", or how to argue for a null hypothesis: a guide for students, attorneys, and other professionals. Innovative Teaching 1 (2), 1–13.

Schumm, W.R., Canfield, K.R., 2011. Statistically evaluating multiple comparisons among correlated measures: a practical example. Psychology and Education 48 (3/4), 51–55.

Schumm, W.R., Crow, J.R., 2010. Statistically evaluating multiple comparisons among correlated measures. Psychology and Education 47 (3/4), 27–30.

Schumm, W.R., Southerly, W.T., Figley, C.R., 1980. Stumbling block or stepping stone: path analysis in family studies. Journal of Marriage and the Family 42, 251–262.

Sell, R.L., 2007. Defining and measuring sexual orientation for research. In: Meyer, I.H., Northridge, M.E. (Eds.), The Health of Sexual Minorities. Springer, New York, pp. 355–374.

Short, L., 2007. Lesbian mothers living well in the context of heterosexism and discrimination: resources, strategies, and legislative change. Feminism & Psychology 17, 57–74.

Sirota, T.H., 1997. A Comparison of Adult Attachment Style Dimensions between Women who have Gay or Bisexual Fathers and Women who have Heterosexual Fathers. Unpublished doctoral dissertation, New York University, Garden City, NY.

Sirota, T., 2009. Adult attachment style dimensions in women who have gay or bisexual fathers. Archives of Psychiatric Nursing 23, 289–297.

Smith, T.W., 2003. An experimental comparison of knowledge networks and the GSS. International Journal of Public Opinion Research 15, 167–179.

Song, A.V., Ling, P.M., 2011. Social smoking among young adults: investigation of intentions and attempts to quit. American Journal of Public Health 101, 1291–1296.

Stein, E., 2007. Ethical, legal, social, and political implications of scientific research on sexual orientation. In: Meyer, I.H., Northridge, M.E. (Eds.), The Health of Sexual Minorities. Springer, New York, pp. 130–148.

Strohschein, L., 2010. Generating heat or light? The challenge of social address variables. Journal of Marriage and Family 72, 23–28.

Strohm, C.Q., 2010. The Formation and Stability of Same-sex and Different-sex Relationships. Unpublished dissertation, University of California, Los Angeles.

Tasker, F.L., Golombok, S., 1997. Growing Up in a Lesbian Family: Effects on Child Development. Guilford Press, New York.

Trocki, K.F., Drabble, L.A., Midanik, L.T., 2009. Tobacco, marijuana, and sensation seeking: comparisons across gay, lesbian, bisexual, and heterosexual groups. Psychology of Addictive Behaviors 23, 620–631.

Wainright, J.L., Patterson, C.J., 2006. Delinquency, victimization, and substance use among adolescents with female same-sex parents. Journal of Family Psychology 20, 526–530.

Wainright, J.L., Russell, S.T., Patterson, C.J., 2004. Psychosocial adjustment, school outcomes, and romantic relationships of adolescents with same-sex parents. Child Development 75, 1886–1898.

Warner, R.M., 2013. Applied Statistics: From Bivariate through Multivariate Techniques, second ed. Sage, Los Angeles.

Welsh, M.G., 2011. Growing up in a same-sex parented family: the adolescent voice of experience. Journal of GLBT Family Studies 7, 49–71.

Whitton, S.W., Buzzella, B.A., 2012. Using relationship education programs with same-sex couples: a preliminary evaluation of program utility and needed modifications. Marriage and Family Review 48, 669–690.

Wilson, B., Smallwood, S., 2008. The proportion of marriages ending in divorce. Population Trends 131, 28–36.

Winneg, K., Jamieson, K.H., 2010. Party identification in the 2008 presidential election. Presidential Studies Quarterly 40, 247–263.

Wirth, J.H., Bodenhausen, G.V., 2009. The role of gender in mental-illness stigma. Psychological Science 20, 169–173.

Summary of Douglas W. Allen, Catherine R. Pakaluk, and Joseph Price's

"Nontraditional Families and Childhood Progress through School: A Comment on Rosenfeld"

Demography 50 (June 2013): 955–961,
http://dx.doi.org/10.1007/s13524-012-0169-x

and

"Normal Progress through School: Further Results"

white paper (June 2, 2014)

The authors begin by noting the great challenge it is to study same-sex-parented families and child outcomes. At the time of the article's publication, there was only one applicable nationally representative data set available in the United States: the 2000 Census 5-Percent Public Use Microdata Sample.[1] Dr. Michael Rosenfeld used this data set to study children's progress through school and concluded that there were no differences among the children: "Children of same-sex couples cannot be distinguished with statistical certainty from children of heterosexual married couples."[2]

After a careful examination of his study, the authors argue that Rosenfeld made a series of methodological decisions that led to his conclusion of "no differences."[3] First, he omitted from study two major groups of children: those who had experienced a residential move in the previous five years, and those not biologically related to the *head* of the household. By omitting these groups of children, he significantly reduced his sample size, creating a situation in which the outcomes of the children of same-sex parents appeared indistinguishable from those of any other children. Second, he failed to reduce the measurement error in his child-outcome measure, which resulted in another bias toward statistical insignificance.

Progress through school is an important signal of child welfare, because children who are held back in school are at much higher risk of dropping out of high school, which is correlated with lower financial earnings, higher unemployment rates, lower self-esteem, and higher mortality rates.[4] Moreover, studies have found that effective parenting plays an important role in school performance.[5] Therefore, it matters for children whether different parenting structures are correlated with normal or suboptimal progress through school.[6]

In the first of these two papers, the authors explain why Rosenfeld's decisions to reduce the sample led to a finding of statistical insignificance. They then replicate his procedures while correcting his sample restrictions and discover statistically significant differences between children of same-sex parents and children raised by a married mother and father.

In the second paper, they take their research a step further and distinguish between the gender distributions of the same-sex households (i.e., boys and girls in lesbian- versus gay-parented homes). They find that not only are there significant differences between the children of different family structures, but there are differences in child outcomes among the same-sex families themselves. Finally, they show that simply eliminating the measurement error in the "normal progress" outcome measure also leads to statistically significant differences across the different households.

Critique of Rosenfeld

The initial Allen, Pakaluk, and Price critique of Rosenfeld has two parts. The first is to show that the means Rosenfeld chose (dropping groups of children from the sample) to meet his intended ends undermined his intention. The second challenges Rosenfeld's intention of studying only children that meet the criteria of having family stability and biological relatedness to a parent.

Rosenfeld's intent behind dropping the first group of children, the children who had moved within the previous five years, was to study only children from relatively stable families. Rosenfeld reasoned that children with instability at home would have causes that affect their performance at school and, since same-sex households are likely more unstable, it would be unfair to compare these children to children from more stable, opposite-sex homes.

However, Allen, Pakaluk, and Price argue that dropping these children from the sample was an inadequate method to select for family stability, because a change in *residence* does not necessarily betoken a change in *family structure*. Families often move for reasons unrelated to a change in family structure (such as moving for a new job, for school, or to be closer to extended family). Indeed, when Allen et al. looked at the data, they discovered that 47.6 percent of the children dropped from the sample were from families headed by a married mother and father, the family form that experiences higher levels of stability. This is to say that Rosenfeld greatly reduced his sample size (which meant a loss in precision and a greater chance of finding no statistical differences when there might truly be some) while likely excluding a great many stable families (defeating his goal of comparing children from stable families). Allen et al. argue that it would have been more reasonable to include these children in the sample but to *control* for whether or not they had changed residences in the previous five years. This method has the benefit of accounting for family movement while still maintaining a large sample.

The second group of children Rosenfeld omitted were those not biologically related to the household head, because he reasoned it was unfair to compare children who were biologically related to their parents (such as children from a married-mother-and-father family) to children who were not biologically related (such as adopted children or those in foster care). Again, Allen and colleagues note that by dropping these children, Rosenfeld reduced his sample size.

The problem with this second sample restriction, the authors point out, is that in the case of same-sex families, the designation "household head" is arbitrary with respect to the biological connection with the children.[7] Indeed, when they look at Rosenfeld's data, the authors find that 17.7 percent of the children raised by same-sex couples were dropped from the sample, even though 75.1 percent of these *were* biologically related to the *second* partner, the one not considered the household head.[8] Although this large group of children had biological relatedness to one of their parents—meeting the criteria of biological relatedness Rosenfeld sought—Rosenfeld dropped these children from study. Allen and colleagues argue that it would have been more prudent to include all of these children in the sample and to *control for* whether the children were biologically related to one or more of their parents.[9]

The Allen, Pakaluk, and Price paper further argues that it is important to include all children. It is not simply that Rosenfeld's methods failed to meet his stated ends; his goal of studying only certain children from relatively more stable and biologically related households was off the mark as well. The researchers point out that it is important to include these children in the sample for the very reason that family instability and loss of a biological parent are likely to be the very channels, or mechanisms, by which the negative effects of new family structures are often caused.[10]

To look at the issue of channels by an analogy, imagine that a group of doctors would like to study whether adults in urban areas have better or worse sleep quality than adults in rural areas. The doctors take a very large, random sample of citizens, distinguish them according to urban or rural residence, and look at the responses related to quality of sleep. However, the doctors decide to exclude from the sample any adults who drink coffee after 3:00 p.m. or are exposed to bright light before bedtime, as they feel it's unfair to compare residents with this handicap to those without it. As it happens, this decision causes them to drop from the sample half of the adults from urban areas. Then, the doctors run the numbers and find no statistical differences in quality of sleep between those who live in urban areas and those in rural areas.

We would rightly question whether these doctors have removed from the sample the very channels by which poor sleep is caused. Urban life tends to revolve around densely populated areas where drinking coffee is a frequent occurrence and bright light is the norm at night. We might even say that the researchers are misrepresenting the very experience of urban living by removing these adults from the sample.

Likewise, Allen, Pakaluk, and Price point out that scholars have identified channels by which children's outcomes are influenced—two of these channels being family instability and the loss of one or more biological parents.[11] Same-sex families are—by definition—families where a child has experienced a separation from one or both biological parents. Moreover, same-sex couples have demonstrated greater levels of instability and shorter duration of cohabitation than have opposite-sex couples.

So when Rosenfeld decides to drop from the sample the children who are not biologically related to a household head or who have experienced a residential move in the previous five years, he takes measures to remove the children who experience the channels by which negative child outcomes often arise. One might say that he misrepresents the very experience of same-sex parenting for children. Allen, Pakaluk, and Price therefore challenge Rosenfeld and other scholars to include these children in the sample to gain a more complete understanding of what children from new family structures experience.

Doing It Right: Including All the Children

Allen and colleagues restore the omitted groups of children one group at a time, first by including the children who had changed residences in the previous five years. By returning these children, the sample size increases by more than 80 percent, and the researchers find that the children of married heterosexual parents are 26.1 percent more likely to make normal progress through school than are the children of same-sex parents, a statistically significant difference.[12]

Odds Ratios of Children's Normal Progress through School, Including Children Who Moved in Previous Five Years
(with Controls)

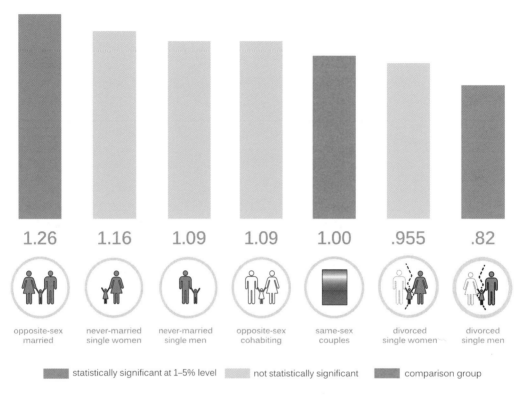

1.26	1.16	1.09	1.09	1.00	.955	.82
opposite-sex married	never-married single women	never-married single men	opposite-sex cohabiting	same-sex couples	divorced single women	divorced single men

statistically significant at 1–5% level   not statistically significant   comparison group

Source: Allen, Pakaluk, and Price, "Nontraditional Families," table 3, column 2.

Next, the authors return the children who were not biologically related to the household head to the sample and drop the first omitted group of children. In this scenario, the sample size increases a bit, and the researchers find that the children of heterosexual married families have 29-percent-better odds of making normal progress through school than do children from same-sex homes, again a statistically significant difference.

Odds Ratios of Children's Normal Progress through School, Including Children Not Biologically Related to Head of Household
(with Controls)

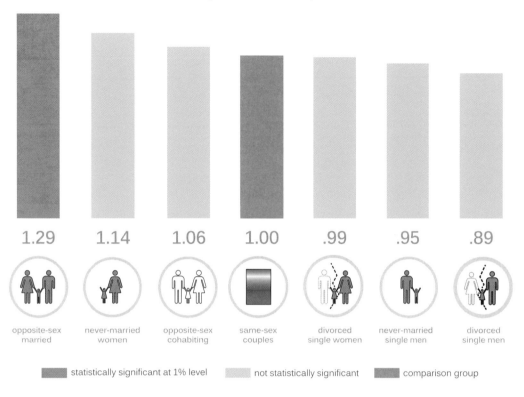

Source: Allen, Pakaluk, and Price, "Nontraditional Families," table 3, column 3.

Finally, the researchers return both groups of children to the sample, restoring the original sample of 1.6 million children, and add controls. In this scenario, shown in the graph on the following page, the children of heterosexual married couples are 35 percent more likely to make normal progress through school than are children in same-sex families, again a statistically significant difference.

Odds Ratios of Children's Normal Progress through School, Unrestricted Model Including All Children
(with Controls)

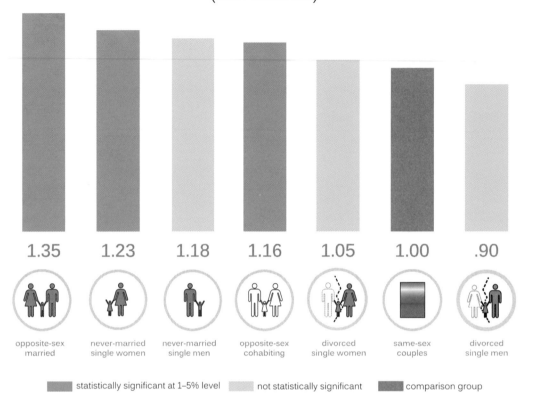

1.35	1.23	1.18	1.16	1.05	1.00	.90
opposite-sex married	never-married single women	never-married single men	opposite-sex cohabiting	divorced single women	same-sex couples	divorced single men

■ statistically significant at 1–5% level ▢ not statistically significant ■ comparison group

Source: Allen, Pakaluk, and Price, "Nontraditional Families," table 3, column 4.

The conclusion of Allen, Pakaluk, and Price's first paper is that Rosenfeld made a series of questionable decisions about what children to include in the sample for study, decisions which yielded a conclusion of "no statistical differences" among the households. By increasing the sample size and controlling for Rosenfeld's concerns, the authors find noteworthy and statistically significant differences.

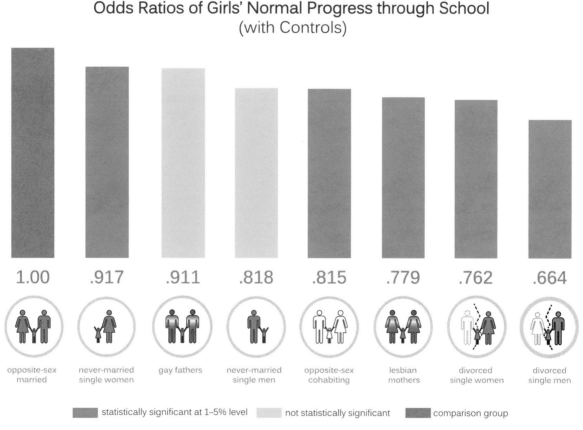

Further Results: Making Gender Distinctions

In their second paper, "Further Results," the researchers begin with the full, unrestricted sample of children and ask whether the gender of the children in same-sex families might make a difference in progress through school. They discover that girls in same-sex-parented homes have better odds of making normal progress through school than do boys in same-sex-parented homes.[13]

Then the researchers separate the lesbian households from the gay households, while keeping the groups of children segregated by gender, and discover additional differences between the boys' and the girls' outcomes. They find that while the girls are more likely to make normal progress in school than are the boys, the boys have the lowest of *all* odds of making normal progress through school when they are from gay-parented homes.

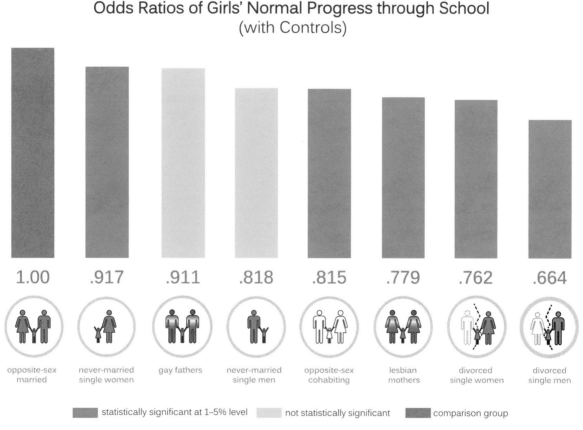

Odds Ratios of Girls' Normal Progress through School
(with Controls)

1.00	.917	.911	.818	.815	.779	.762	.664
opposite-sex married	never-married single women	gay fathers	never-married single men	opposite-sex cohabiting	lesbian mothers	divorced single women	divorced single men

statistically significant at 1–5% level   not statistically significant   comparison group

Source: Allen, Pakaluk, and Price, "Nontraditional Families," table 2, column 2.

Odds Ratios of Boys' Normal Progress through School
(with Controls)

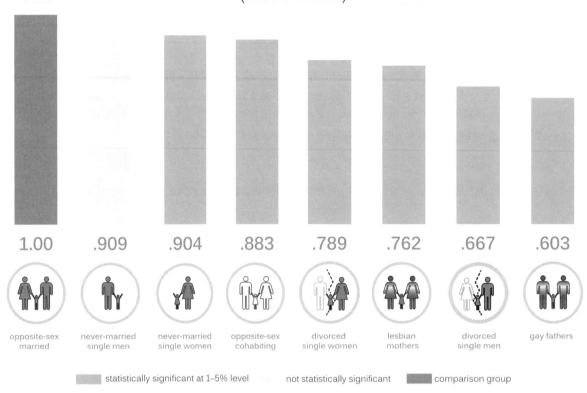

Source: Allen, Pakaluk, and Price, "Nontraditional Families," table 2, column 3.

In the case of both genders, then, children are more likely to make normal progress through school in the home of a single mother or with cohabiting parents than in the home of two same-sex parents, with boys performing less well than girls in same-sex homes, and especially poorly in gay-parented homes.

Interestingly, this latter result is the opposite of what Allen found in 2013 with the Canada Census data, where girls raised by gay fathers showed the poorest school performance of all other children.[14] Allen notes that this difference in findings is probably due to a number of factors, including the rarity of children in same-sex homes and measurement errors in the U.S. Census. "The reasonable conclusion to draw is that gender matters. Prudence would suggest less confidence in how much and in what direction."[15]

Conclusion

Allen, Pakaluk, and Price critique Rosenfeld's decision to exclude certain children from the U.S. Census sample on the grounds that his decisions failed to adequately accomplish his intended goal of studying children from more stable families and with a biological relationship to a parent. They further challenge Rosenfeld (and other scholars) to not overlook children in these more challenging situations, suggesting that the link between same-sex parenting, biological-parent loss, and family instability is more relevant to children's outcomes than researchers let on. The authors also conclude that gender *matters*. Scholarship should study the link between gender distribution in each family type and children's outcomes, and not group all same-sex families or all children into one category.

When Allen, Pakaluk, and Price include all the children in the sample and add controls, they find notable and statistically significant differences in child outcomes: the odds of children from married-mother-and-father families making normal progress through school are 35-percent higher than those of children from same-sex-parent families. The odds of girls in lesbian-parent homes making normal progress are only 78 percent as high as those of girls in married-mother-and-father homes. For boys, the odds are 76 percent as high when in a lesbian home and 60 percent as high when in a gay-parented home, compared to married-mother-and-father homes. All of these are statistically significant differences between the groups of children. Given the ripple effects of falling behind in school, these are differences to notice.

Notes

1. Rosenfeld wrote his article prior to the release of the *New Family Structures Study*, the only other U.S. nationally representative data set available that includes same-sex-parented children.

2. See Appendix: Michael J. Rosenfeld, "Nontraditional Families and Childhood Progress through School," *Demography* 47 (August 2010): 755–775, p. 770.

3. Allen, Pakaluk, and Price also point out that Rosenfeld confuses "no differences" with "statistical insignificance." He actually found the latter but claimed to find the former.

4. See Rosenfeld, 758 (citing Alexander, Entwisle, and Horsey, 1997; Guo, Brooks-Gunn, and Harris, 1996; Moller et al., 2006; Roderick, 1994; Rumberger, 1987; Tillman, Guo, and Harris, 2006; McLanahan, 1985).

5. See Rosenfeld, 758 (citing Brooks-Gunn and Markman, 2005).

6. Allen, Pakaluk, and Price explain that the 2000 U.S. Census is a limited tool for measuring "normal progress through school" because of measurement errors. See their "Further Results," this volume, 8–10.

7. "The exact question on the census form asks whether the child is the 'natural-born son/daughter' of the household head. Of course, in a same-sex household, only one parent, at most, can be biologically related to the child and there is no reason why this parent must be the household head for census purposes" (Allen, Pakaluk, and Price, "Further Results," 3).

8. Allen, Pakaluk, and Price, "Further Results," 3.

9. Still, even when the children who are not biologically related to either parent are kept out of the sample but all of the children biologically related to *either* parent are placed back in, the authors find a statistical difference in child outcomes across the different households.

10. Allen, Pakaluk, and Price, "Further Results," 4.

11. "Necessarily, all of the children of same-sex couples will experience some degree of loss of relation to a parent: either they will be related to only one parent in the home (and stepchild to the other parent) or unrelated to both parents (adopted or foster). Such experiences could plausibly be the very channel through which negative effects might operate" (Allen, Pakaluk, and Price, "Further Results," 4). "There is also evidence that same-sex partnerships are less stable than heterosexual partnerships (both cohabiting and married) and this finding has a high degree of robustness (see Kurdek, 1998; Lau, 2012; Andersson et al., 2006; Kalmijn et al., 2007). One might surmise that stability is an important channel through which the child outcomes are produced. It is important that this channel be recognized in the data" (Ibid., 5).

12. Allen, Pakaluk, and Price, "Nontraditional Families," 955.

13. See Allen, Pakaluk, and Price, "Further Results," 6 (table 1, columns 2 and 3).

14. See Douglas W. Allen, "High School Graduation Rates Among Children of Same-Sex Households," *Review of Economics of the Household* 11 (December 2013): 635–658, included in this volume.

15. Allen, Pakaluk, and Price, "Further Results," 11.

Demography (2013) 50:955–961
DOI 10.1007/s13524-012-0169-x

Nontraditional Families and Childhood Progress Through School: A Comment on Rosenfeld

Douglas W. Allen · Catherine Pakaluk · Joseph Price

Published online: 18 November 2012
© Population Association of America 2012

Abstract We reexamine Rosenfeld's (2010) study on the association between child outcomes and same-sex family structure. Using the same data set, we replicate and generalize Rosenfeld's findings and show that the implications of his study are different when using either alternative comparison groups or alternative sample restrictions. Compared with traditional married households, we find that children being raised by same-sex couples are 35 % less likely to make normal progress through school; this difference is statistically significant at the 1 % level.

Keywords School progress · Gay and lesbian families

Introduction

Although there has been considerable research on the effect of family structure on child outcomes, almost none of the research using nationally representative samples has included same-sex parents as part of the analysis. The main barrier is the lack of a nationally representative data set with enough children being raised by same-sex couples to provide a basis for meaningful statistical inference. The one U.S. data set that currently provides enough data to conduct this analysis is the U.S. Public-Use Microdata Sample of the decennial census.

D. W. Allen (✉)
Department of Economics, Simon Fraser University, 8888 University Drive, Burnaby, BC V5A 1S6, Canada
e-mail: allen@sfu.ca

C. Pakaluk
Department of Economics, Ave Maria University, Ave Maria, FL, USA

J. Price
Department of Economics, Brigham Young University, Provo, UT, USA

🖄 Springer

Rosenfeld (2010) used data from the 2000 census 5 % Public-Use Microdata Sample to examine the association between same-sex parenting and child outcomes (as measured by normal school progress). His study concluded that the outcomes of children raised by same-sex couples "cannot be distinguished with statistical certainty from children of heterosexual married couples" (p. 770). However, our findings suggest a reevaluation of this conclusion. We present an alternative approach that updates the original study with important estimates of the magnitude of the effect sizes and their corresponding confidence intervals. We also provide a model that allows for robustness checks to the sample restrictions employed in the original study.

Our analysis proceeds in two parts. First, we show that the omitted group chosen for the regression itself informs the interpretation of the data because statistical precision is low. An alternative omitted variable leads to the finding that the outcomes of children raised by same-sex couples cannot be distinguished with statistical certainty from almost any other family structure, including well-documented disadvantaged groups, such as children being raised by a never-married mother. We also update the original study by providing standard errors and odds ratios for each of the coefficients. These two additions to the original study provide insight into the magnitude of the differences between groups and the size of the confidence intervals around these differences.

Second, we present an unrestricted model as a robustness check on the original findings by incorporating controls for the subgroups that Rosenfeld identifies as potential confounders. These subgroups are those in which the children in the sample are not biologically related to the household head (e.g., adopted children and stepchildren) and those in which the children and parents have not lived in the same residence for the previous five years. However, while we share Rosenfeld's concern that these groups are potential confounders, the use of a restricted model both eliminates two of the channels through which family structure might actually affect child outcomes and reduces the sample by 55 %, thus making the standard errors sufficiently imprecise to detect a statistically significant difference. We present an alternative approach that accommodates the various concerns by incorporating controls for the subgroups into an unrestricted model. With this approach, we recreate the original results on the restricted sample and compare them to the more precise results from the unrestricted model with controls.

Alternative Comparisons and the Magnitude of the Effect Sizes

Table 1 provides descriptive statistics for the children in the sample by family structure type. The outcome variable is whether the child is making normal progress through school and is based on a comparison of the child's age and current grade in school. This measure has been used in past studies because it is the only measure of child outcomes in the U.S. census data (Cáceres-Delpiano 2006; Conley and Glauber 2006) and it is correlated with other outcomes later in life, such as dropping out of high school (Eide and Showalter 2001). The fraction of children who are not making normal progress in schools varies from 1.83 % to 3.08 % across the different family structure types.

 Springer

Table 1 provides the sample means for each of the control variables used in the regressions for each of the family structure types. The variables for "own child" (R_1) and "same location for 5 or more years" (R_2) are used to model the effects of the subset restrictions of interest.

Table 2, column 1, merely replicates the findings from the original study when the omitted group is children being raised by heterosexual married couples. Thus, all coefficients in column 1 provide inferences about the difference in outcomes between children being raised by heterosexual married couples and those in the other six family types. These results provide the basis for the original study's conclusion that children being raised by homosexual partners cannot be distinguished with statistical certainty from children of heterosexual married couples. However, there are good reasons to reevaluate this finding.

First, the magnitude of the coefficient for children raised in same-sex households is similar to that of never-married women, a family structure type which is documented to have worse child outcomes relative to married heterosexual couples. These alternative comparisons are difficult using the results of the original study because the main regression tables do not include the standard errors on the regression coefficients. One way to make these comparisons more transparent is to have the main group of interest (children of same-sex couples) be the omitted group in the regression, which is what we do in the second column of Table 2. The first coefficient is the same in column 1 and 2, since this particular comparison is the same when we switch which of the two is the omitted group. However, the rest of the coefficients now provide inferences about the difference between the reported group and same-sex households. These results highlight that an equally valid interpretation of the original study is that the outcomes of children in same-sex households cannot be determined with statistical certainty from those of children in almost any other family type (except divorced men).

Table 1 Summary statistics for households with children (2000 census)

	Heterosexual Married	Same-Sex Couples	Heterosexual Cohabiting	Divorced Women	Never-Married Women	Divorced Men	Never-Married Men
Median Income ($)	58,000	48,820	40,250	24,000	15,900	35,800	29,000
% of Children Who Are:							
"Own" children (R_1)	85.7	82.3	83.1	91.7	97.8	87.8	90.9
Stepchildren	7.27	8.32	12.37	0.26	0.22	2.08	5.41
Foster children	0.32	0.81	0.97	0.76	0	0.35	0
Adopted	2.73	3.58	1.45	2.25	1.96	2.47	3.70
Other relation to head	4.03	4.95	2.14	5.02	0	7.32	0
Same location 5+ years (R_2)	52.4	42.2	21.3	39.5	35.3	47.0	37.2
Hispanic	15.8	23.9	23.2	16.7	16.4	12.4	21.2
Non-Hispanic black	8.21	16.6	22.0	24.1	61.8	13.0	34.5
Held back in school	1.83	2.81	2.56	2.76	2.80	3.08	2.59
N	1,189,833	8,632	66,642	215,021	77,879	46,654	6,153

Notes: The unit of observation in this table is the child. All of the results are weighted using the census sampling weights.

 Springer

Table 2 Association between family type and making normal progress through school (alternative comparison groups)

	Logistic Regression Coefficients		Odds Ratios	
	(1)	(2)	(3)	(4)
Same-Sex Couples	−0.142	—	0.867	—
	[0.125]		[0.108]	
Heterosexual Married	—	0.142	—	1.153
		[0.125]		[0.144]
Heterosexual, Cohabiting	−0.237**	−0.094	0.789**	0.910
	[0.057]	[0.136]	[0.045]	[0.124]
Separated/Divorced/Widowed Women	−0.315**	−0.173	0.730**	0.841
	[0.026]	[0.127]	[0.019]	[0.107]
Never-Married Women	−0.151**	−0.008	0.860**	0.992
	[0.041]	[0.130]	[0.035]	[0.129]
Separated, Divorced, Widowed Men	−0.399**	−0.257†	0.671**	0.773†
	[0.046]	[0.132]	[0.031]	[0.102]
Never-Married Men	−0.357*	−0.215	0.700*	0.807
	[0.123]	[0.175]	[0.087]	[0.141]
Unweighted N	716,740	716,740	716,740	716,740

Notes: Each regression includes controls for disability, race, logged income, highest education in household, birthplace, metropolitan status, private school attendance, and state fixed effects. Standard errors are provided in brackets.

$^\dagger p < .10$; $^* p < .05$; $^{**} p < .01$

The second reason to reevaluate the conclusions of the original study is that the effect sizes are quite large in magnitude despite falling short of statistical significance. The final two columns of Table 2 report the odds ratios that correspond to each of the coefficients from the first two columns. These odds ratios measure the percent difference in likelihood of a child making normal progress in school between children in the omitted group and each of the other groups. For example, column 4 of Table 2 indicates that children in traditional homes are 15 % more likely to make normal progress than children raised in same-sex households. Although this estimate is not statistically significant, the corresponding 95 % confidence interval for the difference ranges from −10 % to +47 %. Thus, while we are unable to reject the hypothesis that there is no difference, this approach also makes it impossible to rule out even very large differences (nearly 50 %).

Robustness Checks and the Unrestricted Model

The original study used a sample in which the children are biologically related to the household head (R_1) and in which the children and parents have been living at the same address for the past five years (R_2). Table 1 provides the fraction of children who are affected by each of these restrictions for each family structure type.

 Springer

The motivation for the restrictions is to avoid a measurement error that would occur if a child's family structure is based on a current household composition that is different from what the child had experienced when his or her progress in school was being affected. However, these sample restrictions also cut off two of the channels through which family structure can influence child outcomes: biological relatedness and household instability. The sample restrictions also reduce the sample size by more than one-half, decreasing the precision of the estimates and making detection of a true difference in outcomes more difficult. In the alternative approach adopted here, we test an unrestricted model with the full sample of children but include controls for the important subgroups R_1 and R_2.

To provide a baseline, column 1 of Table 3 presents the same restricted model used in column 4 of Table 2. In this model (as in the original study), both restrictions R_1 and R_2 are in place, but we present the coefficients as odds ratios for ease of interpretation. Column 2 presents a model in which R_1 is left in place while R_2 is relaxed to allow for children to be included who have not been in the same location for five years, though an indicator variable for the subgroup is included in the regression. By relaxing R_2 alone, the sample size increases by more than 80 %, from 716,719 to 1,397,144. The differential for children in heterosexual married households is +25.8 %, which lies squarely within the 95 % confidence interval from the

Table 3 Association between family type and making normal progress through school (varying the sample restrictions)

	(1)	(2)	(3)	(4)
Married Heterosexual	1.153	1.258**	1.295*	1.354**
	[0.144]	[0.097]	[0.137]	[0.089]
Heterosexual, Cohabiting	0.910	1.086	1.057	1.156[†]
	[0.124]	[0.088]	[0.123]	[0.081]
Divorced Women	0.841	0.955	0.993	1.053
	[0.107]	[0.074]	[0.107]	[0.070]
Never-Married Women	0.992	1.161[†]	1.140	1.232**
	[0.129]	[0.093]	[0.127]	[0.085]
Divorced Men	0.773[†]	0.821*	0.895	0.900
	[0.102]	[0.067]	[0.101]	[0.064]
Never-Married Men	0.807	1.096	0.952	1.183
	[0.141]	[0.124]	[0.152]	[0.122]
Sample Restriction				
Own child (R_1)	X	X		
Five-year resident (R_2)	X		X	
Unweighted N	716,719	1,397,199	792,794	1,610,880

Notes: Each cell reports the odds ratio from a logit regression with the omitted group being children being raised by same-sex couples. Each regression includes controls for disability, race, logged income, highest education in household, birthplace, metropolitan status, private school attendance, and state fixed effects. In column 2 we also control for whether the household moved; in column 3 we control for whether a child is the parent's own child; and in column 4 we control for both. Standard errors are provided in brackets.

[†]$p < .10$; *$p < .05$; **$p < .01$

 Springer

restricted model (column 1), but the point estimate is larger in magnitude and is statistically significant at the 1 % level.

Column 3 presents a symmetric model in which we reinstitute the five-year location restriction (R_2) but relax the "own-child" restriction (R_1). This restriction removes not only adopted and foster children but any child who is not biologically related to the household head (the majority of which are biologically related to the spouse or partner of the household head). Relaxing R_1 increases the sample size more modestly, from 716,719 to 792,260. In this model, there is a differential of +29 % for children in heterosexual married homes as compared with those in same-sex households. This estimate is statistically significant at the 1 % level.

One potential concern with this specification is that children who are adopted by heterosexual married couples may have a different profile than children who are adopted by same-sex couples. When we exclude adopted children from the regression in column 3, the sample size drops to 770,325 with an estimated differential of +24 %, which is statistically significant at the 5 % level.

The final column of Table 3 presents the unrestricted model in which both sample restrictions are relaxed. This provides estimates utilizing the full sample of 1.6 million children.[1] In this specification, we include controls for the important subgroups, as in the previous two regressions. Here, the differential in the likelihood of making normal school progress is +35 % for children in heterosexual married households, which is statistically significant at the 1 % level.

Two alternative comparisons in this final specification are also illuminating. First, some have suggested that the appropriate comparison for children being raised in same-sex households would be heterosexual cohabiting partners because, at the time of the 2000 census, same-sex couples were unable to obtain a civil marriage. Under this comparison, children who are being raised by a heterosexual cohabiting couple are about 15 % more likely to be making normal progress in school than children being raised by same-sex couples, and this difference is statistically significant at the 5 % level. Second, the three family types that cannot be distinguished with "statistical certainty" from same-sex households—even with the full sample—are divorced men, divorced women, and never-married men.

Conclusion

Together, these findings are strikingly different from those of the original study—and the differences are large enough to be noteworthy. With respect to normal school progress, children residing in same-sex households can be distinguished statistically from those in traditional married homes and in heterosexual cohabiting households. The magnitude of the differences is large enough to be relevant for current and future policy debates, as well as to indicate a real need for more research into the channels through which family structure affects child development and educational outcomes.

---

[1] A careful reader might notice that the sum of the increase in the sample size in columns 2 and 3 (680,448 and 75,554) is less than the increase when we relax both restrictions (894,140). The additional 138,138 children are those for whom both restrictions apply.

 Springer

References

Cáceres-Delpiano, J. (2006). The impacts of family size on investment in child quality. *Journal of Human Resources, 41,* 738–754.

Conley, D., & Glauber, R. (2006). Parental educational investment and children's academic risk estimates of the impact of sibship size and birth order from exogenous variation in fertility. *Journal of Human Resources, 46,* 722–737.

Eide, E., & Showalter, M. (2001). The effect of grade retention on educational and labor market outcomes. *Economics of Education Review, 20,* 563–576.

Rosenfeld, M. (2010). Nontraditional families and childhood progress through school. *Demography, 47,* 755–775.

 Springer

Normal Progress Through School: Further Results

Douglas W. Allen

Catherine R. Pakaluk

Joseph Price

2 June 2014

I.   Introduction

We are grateful to the editors of Demography for publishing our comment on Rosenfeld's 2010 watershed paper. At the time of that publication, we were limited to comments and estimations directly germane to the original paper. Here we examine several empirical issues stemming from the 2000 census which show how tenuous the "no-difference" conclusion is. The first is to exploit the gender composition of households, that is, to account for whether boys or girls are residing with lesbian or gay couples. The second is to examine more carefully the outcome measure of "normal progress" in order to remove measurement error caused by the nature of the census question.

In Rosenfeld's original paper, the category for 'children residing with same sex couples' includes all boys and girls living with lesbian and gay couples. But lumping everyone together was unnecessary. The 2000 U.S. census contains information on the gender composition of households, and this extra information can be used to address the question of "no-difference" in child outcomes across household types.

Variation across gender composition is important for two reasons. First, it provides a type of "natural experiment" in the testing of differences. For the most part, child gender is a random variable, and we can think of boys and girls as being randomly assigned to family types.[1] Therefore, systematic differences in gendered child outcomes across different family types can reasonably be attributed to effects of family type. Second, understanding effects by gender can help provide insight into the nature of "same-sex" households. Gay households have two male parents and lesbian households have two female parents. In a profound way, they are opposites

---

[1] There is some evidence that lesbian couples who are inseminated artificially are more likely to have boys than girls. However, the difference is small, and the fraction of children arriving into lesbian families through this channel even smaller.

of one another, and categorizing them together as "same-sex" is likely to mask important and divergent outcomes.

Here we show that there are differences in our outcome measure, normal progress through school, depending on the gender composition of same-sex households. Not only do differences exist between gay and lesbian homes, but the gender of the child matters as well. We also show that the gender of the child does not matter for other household types.

A second aspect of Rosenfeld's analysis that also requires a reexamination has to do with the way the outcome measure "normal progress" is constructed. Normal progress in school is implied when a child's age is appropriate to that child's grade. Had the 2000 census provided information on each child's age and grade, all would be well. Unfortunately, the 2000 census only measures age and grade for two age brackets. This means that for most of the children in the sample, there is no information on their progress through school. Hence a measurement error is introduced into the analysis, and this biases the results downwards and reduces the precision of the estimates.

Here we show that, when examining only those cases where we know for certain whether normal progress has been made or not, there is a large and significant "difference" effect. This difference exists even when we maintain all of the other questionable Rosenfeld sample restrictions.

Although we may speculate on these differences, our goal here is merely to document two important findings: first, based on school performance, a claim of "no-difference" is not currently supported by representative datasets; and second, children perform best when raised by two opposite sex married parents. Any variation on this norm results in poorer performance, the level of which depends on family type and gender composition.

II. Data and Methods

This paper is an extension of our earlier comment, and therefore, we continue to use the same full sample of children from the 2000 census 5% public-use microdata sample to examine the association between same-sex parenting and child outcomes as measured by normal school progress.

In our original comment, we showed the dramatic effect of removing Rosenfeld's two sample restrictions: examining only "own" children, and only those with residential stability. In his reply to our comment, Rosenfeld essentially reasserted his claim that these restrictions are necessary for correct inference. Hence, before we examine the new results, let us briefly defend the use of the full sample.

A. *Who are the "own" children of the household?*

Rosenfeld argues that it is misleading to compare the outcome of an adopted or foster child to one who is biologically related to either parent. Adopted or foster children may have a number of unobservable traits that handicap their school performance and make grade failure more likely.

To address this problem, Rosenfeld opts for removing all children from the sample who are not reported as "own" children, instead of using a regression control variable for these children—a more standard approach in the literature. However, it is worth asking: which children are actually removed from the sample via this process?

The exact question on the census form asks whether the child is the "natural-born son/daughter" of the *household head*. Of course, in a same-sex household, only one parent, at most, can be biologically related to the child, and there is no reason why *this* parent must be the household head for census purposes. Thus, for same-sex couples, many of the children who are not biologically related to the household head — and therefore declared not "own" children — are, in fact, biologically related to the partner of the household head. In other words, many children who are not categorized as "own" children by the census — and who are therefore dropped from Rosenfeld's analysis — have exactly the same step-child status as others categorized as "own" children. Restricting the sample to "own" children actually means keeping only one type of "own" child, those related to the household head. The children of a partner are removed from the sample on misleading grounds.

This distinction turns out to be important. Restricting the sample to include only "own" children means that 17.7% of children being raised by same-sex couples are dropped from the sample. Some of these children are adopted or from foster homes, and an argument might be made for exclusion rather than control. But the data reveal that 75.1% of the excluded children are the biological children of the second partner! The total number of adopted and foster children is so small, it turns out that including or excluding them makes little change in the reported result. Thus, Rosenfeld's restriction is unjustified and accomplishes little but a crucial loss in precision. The correct procedure is to include all children related to at least one of the parents. In our analysis we include—and control for—adopted and foster children, though the actual procedure used to deal with them is inconsequential since there are so few relative to the overall sample size.

B. *Household Stability*

Rosenfeld also restricts his sample to children who had lived in the same home with the same parents for at least five years. He did this under the assumption that the family structure at the time of survey would then be the same as that when the child was held back in school.[2] This restriction eliminates 57.8% of children being raised by same-sex couples.

---

[2] The benefits of matching current family structure with past family structure are less than might be expected. If the current family structure of the child differs from that of the past then this introduces measurement error in the main variables of interest. This attenuates the coefficient on these variables towards zero and makes it more difficult to detect a true difference between the groups. This attenuation bias is likely to be a much smaller concern for correct statistical inference than the problems introduced by employing this sample restriction.

4

As noted in the original comment, the cost of this sample restriction is that it cuts the available sample size in half. While Rosenfeld's original sample size of over 700,000 children seems large, there are factors that reduce the statistical power in this context. First, there are only a small fraction of children being raised by same-sex couples. Second, there is a fair amount of measurement error in the outcome measure (more on this below). Third, the outcome variable is a binary variable that is relatively uncommon. In these situations, the overall sample size can be a misleading indicator of the statistical power of the analysis. As we showed in the original comment, removing these children from the sample makes a statistically significant difference in the power of the test.

Like the restriction on "own" children, one must ask whether it accomplishes what Rosenfeld intended it to do. The intent was to exclude from the analysis children who had experienced a change in family structure between the time of the survey and the prior failure to make normal progress in school. In other words, the restriction aims to restrict the sample to only those with stable family types for five years. The restriction, however, is a blunt tool for that purpose, since it only succeeds in eliminating children who have experienced a *residential move*—not children whose *family structure* has changed. The best way to see this is to consider that the restriction removes 47.6% of children being raised by heterosexual married parents, even though many of these children are likely to be biologically related to both parents before and after the residential move. So the restriction ends up removing from the analysis a great many children whose family structure has indeed been stable, but who have simply experienced change in residence. Once again, the prudent approach is to include all the children and employ standard regression controls for whether or not they changed residences over a recent period of time.

C. *Channels*

A fundamental problem with restricting sample size and discarding observations is the forfeiture of channels, or mechanisms, through which effects of family type might operate. For example, it is not possible for a child being raised by a same-sex couple to be biologically related to *both* parents. Necessarily, all of the children of same-sex couples will experience some degree of loss of relation to a parent: either they will be related to only one parent in the home (and step-child to the other parent), or unrelated to both parents (adopted or foster). Such experiences could plausibly be the very channel though which negative effects might operate.

Studies on the effect of non-biological parenting indicate that outcomes for children of step-parents and/or cohabiting partners of biological parents tend to be significantly worse than for those of children who are raised in homes where they are the shared offspring of both parents (see for instance Dawson, 1991; Fergusson, Lynskey and Horwood, 1995; Ginther and Pollak, 2004). For example, Ginther and Pollak (2004) find that variation in socio-economic factors may account for some or all of the differences in biological and non-biological family arrangements. To get a proper estimate of the true effect of being raised in a same-sex home requires all of the channels to be included. Therefore, it is important that all children be included with proper controls for the particular channels through which they may be affected.

Likewise, a similar problem arises when restricting the analysis to families who have experienced no residential changes for the previous five years. Family stability is likely to be an important channel by which normal progress through school operates. There is strong evidence that relationship instability is negatively associated with child outcomes, and there is reason to think at least part of this association is causal (see Osborne and McLanahan, 2007; Cavanaugh and Huston, 2006; Fomby and Cherlin, 2007). There is also evidence that same-sex partnerships are less stable than heterosexual partnerships (both cohabiting and married), and this finding has a high degree of robustness (see Kurdek, 1998; Lau, 2012; Andersson et al, 2006; Kalmijn et al., 2007). One might surmise therefore that stability is an important channel through which the child outcomes are produced. It is important that this channel be recognized in the data.

For all of these reasons we believe it is more reasonable to include all children and control for "own" child and stability, rather than removing these children from the sample altogether.

III.   Estimation

Table 1 reports the odds ratios for three separate logit regressions, where the dependent variable is 1 if the child makes normal progress through school. This means that at two specific ages, the child is in the age-appropriate grade. The first column replicates the results that were reported in column (4) of Table 3 of our original article (Allen et al., 2013, p. 959). This was our preferred specification.

The results here look different from what was reported in the original paper because we have changed the omitted category. Rather than using same-sex couples as the baseline, we have switched to using married, opposite-sex couples. We do this because we want to break the same-sex couples into different categories to examine a greater variety of gendered outcomes.

The results from Table 1, column (1), show that children are less likely to make normal progress in school for all household types compared to married heterosexual families. The odds of a child in a same-sex household making normal progress are just 73.8% of those for a similar child in a traditional home.

In Table 1, columns (2) and (3), we continue to combine gay and lesbian parented homes in the single category of "same-sex," but we separate the outcomes for girls and boys respectively. Once again, child performance is reduced for all family types compared to traditional homes – both girls and boys do better with married opposite-sex parents. However, one interesting difference is quite apparent. With the exception of same-sex households, the odds ratio for boys and girls are very similar for all other types of households, and are statistically indistinguishable. The similarity across boys and girls is most striking when there is a single mother or father – cases where opposite-sex parents are missing. On the other hand, the odds ratios for boys is statistically different from girls when living with same-sex parents, and the magnitude of this difference is quite large (0.824 vs 0.683). Thus, not only is there a difference in child outcomes across different family structures, there is a difference in the difference.

Table 1: Association between family type and making normal progress through school

Family Type	(1) Full sample	(2) Girls	(3) Boys
Same-Sex	0.738	0.824	0.683
	(0.048)**	(0.086)†	(0.057)**
Opposite Sex Cohabitating	0.854	0.815	0.883
	(0.022)**	(0.032)**	(0.030)**
Divorced Single Women	0.778	0.762	0.789
	(0.012)**	(0.018)**	(0.016)**
Never Married Single Women	0.910	0.917	0.904
	(0.022)**	(0.035)**	(0.029)**
Divorced Single Men	0.664	0.664	0.667
	(0.018)**	(0.030)**	(0.024)**
Never Married Single Men	0.873	0.818	0.909
	(0.070)†	(0.103)	(0.095)
Unweighted N	1,610,804	783,424	827,380

Notes: Each cell reports the odds ratio from a logit regression with the omitted group being children raised by married, heterosexual couples. Each regression includes controls for disability, race, logged income, highest education in household, birthplace, metropolitan status, private school attendance, and state fixed effects. In all columns we include controls for whether the household moved and whether a child is the own child of the household head. Standard errors are provided in brackets. †p< .10; *p < .05; **p < .01

Table 2 provides a further breakdown of results by splitting same-sex households into gay and lesbian households. We include the same three columns for outcomes: full sample, girls, and boys. Looking at column (1) of Table 2 shows that children are more likely to make normal progress through school within lesbian families compared to gay families, but the *difference* is not statistically significant. What is more notable is the difference between boys and girls sorted by the two types of same-sex families. Girls are more likely to make normal progress and there is no statistical difference between the gay and lesbian households. However, for boys the odds of making normal progress are considerably lower when they are in gay-parented homes. Indeed, the odds of making normal progress are just 60% of similar boys in traditional homes, and these odds are the lowest of all family types. Furthermore, the results for boys in gay homes are statistically different from girls in gay homes, and from boys in lesbian homes.

Table 2: Association between family type and making normal progress through school

Family Type	(1) Full sample	(2) Girls	(3) Boys
Gay	0.698	0.911	0.603
	(0.069)**	(0.163)	(0.072)**
Lesbian	0.769	0.779	0.762
	(0.066)**	(0.100)*	(0.089)**
Opposite Sex Cohabitating	0.854	0.815	0.883
	(0.022)**	(0.032)**	(0.030)**
Divorced Single Women	0.778	0.762	0.789
	(0.012)**	(0.018)**	(0.016)**
Never Married Single Women	0.910	0.917	0.904
	(0.022)**	(0.035)**	(0.029)**
Divorced Single Men	0.664	0.664	0.667
	(0.018)**	(0.030)**	(0.024)**
Never Married Single Men	0.873	0.818	0.909
	(0.070)†	(0.103)	(0.095)
Unweighted N	1,610,804	783,424	827,380

Notes: Each cell reports the odds ratio from a logit regression with the omitted group being children raised by married, heterosexual couples. Each regression includes controls for disability, race, logged income, highest education in household, birthplace, metropolitan status, private school attendance, and state fixed effects. In all columns we include controls for whether the household moved and whether a child is the own child of the household head. Standard errors are provided in brackets. †p< .10; *p < .05; **p < .01

IV. Measurement Error In "Normal Progress"

A crucial feature of the 2000 Census data that limits the statistical power of the estimation is the way in which the outcome variable is constructed. As noted above, the outcome variable is a marker of whether the child has been held back in school, and is based on a comparison between the child's age and their grade. However, the 2000 Census groups students in the lower grade levels into two separate groups with grades 1-4 in one category and grades 5-8 in the other category. Rosenfeld notes that "students attending grades 1-4 can be identified as over-age only if they are too old to be in the 4th grade (i.e. at least age 11), and students attending grades 5-8 can be identified as over-age only if they are too old for 8th grade (i.e. at least age 15)." This means that for many of the ages included in Rosenfeld's sample, there is either no or very weak information about whether the child has been held back in school.

Table 3 provides information on the ages of the children in the Rosenfeld sample who are recorded as being held back. The first two columns indicate the grade reported for the child with

8

the two options being grades 1-4 or grades 5-8. The final column indicates the total number of children of each age included in the sample. The first thing to note in this table is that for more than half of the children in the sample (374,800 children ages 10 and less) there is no valid information about whether they have been held back. In addition, there is very little information about this measure for children ages 13-14. A child aged 13 or 14 who has been held back to grades 1, 2, 3, or 4 would be much too old for his or her grade. Likely, many more 13 and 14 year olds have actually been held back to grades 5, 6, 7, and perhaps even 8. Since, however, we do not know the exact grade that any of the 13-or 14-year olds in the sample are in, we will have a large amount of measurement error for this group as well.

Table 3: The Number of Children Not Making Normal Progress

Age of Child	(1) Grades 1-4	(2) Grades 5-8	(3) Total Number of students
5	0	0	2,283
6	0	0	35,147
7	0	0	74,767
8	0	0	81,981
9	0	0	88,908
10	0	0	91,714
11	4,943	0	91,844
12	587	0	92,534
13	6	0	92,548
14	7	0	56,657
15	0	6,726	6,726
16	0	1,090	1,090
17	0	541	541
Total	5,543	8,357	716,740

A natural approach in this situation is to restrict the sample to just those ages for which the outcome variable is likely to be measured with a higher degree of precision. This approach dramatically reduces the sample size but does so by removing observations that were not providing any informative insight to begin with. Hence, since ages 11-12 and 15-16 provide the most precise information about whether the child has actually been held back in school, we re-estimate Rosenfeld's original empirical specification using both of his sample restrictions, but compare the estimates using the full age range (5-17) to the estimates using the restricted age range (11-12, 15-16). In other words, we compare the results of Rosenfeld's full sample with results from a sample where the measurement error is eliminated.

Table 4, row (1), provides results based on the full Rosenfeld sample that includes children aged 5-17, and row (2) provides results based on the restricted sample. Thus, the first coefficient in column (1) (1.153), is the original result found by Rosenfeld. For clarity we report only the coefficients for the comparison between children raised by a married heterosexual couple and children raised by a same-sex couple, the latter being the baseline group.

The results in column (1) of Table 4 show that even if we use the exact empirical specification and sample restrictions used by Rosenfeld, but narrow them to the age with the most precisely measured outcome measures, we find large and statistically significant differences. In fact, the magnitude of the coefficients indicate that the odds of children raised by married heterosexual couples to be making normal progress in school are about 35% higher than the odds for children raised by same-sex couples (and this difference is statistically significant at the 10% level). In columns (2-4), we provide the same results, but relax the own-child and residential stability restrictions. We find that the estimated differences are even larger in magnitude and are statistically significant at the 1% level. In every case, the estimated differences are larger when we use the more precisely measured outcome variables. This shows that including information on the ages for which no children are recorded as being held back biases the estimated differences between the groups towards zero.

Table 4: Association between family type and making normal progress through school (varying the sample restrictions)

	(1)	(2)	(3)	(4)
Ages 5-17	1.153	1.258***	1.295***	1.353***
	[0.144]	[0.097]	[0.137]	[0.089]
Ages 11-12, 15-16	1.345*	1.357***	1.531***	1.455***
	[0.225]	[0.145]	[0.217]	[0.134]
Sample Restriction				
Own Child	X	X		
5 Year Resident	X		X	

Notes: Each cell reports the odds ratio from a logit regression for the comparison between children being raised by a same-sex couple and children being raised by a married heterosexual couple, where children of same-sex couples are the omitted group. Each regression includes controls for disability, race, logged income, highest education in household, birthplace, metropolitan status and private school attendance and state fixed effects. In column (2) we also control for whether the household moved, in column (3) we control for whether a child is the parent's own child, and in column (4) we control for both. Standard errors are provided in brackets. *** p<0.01, ** p<0.05, * p<0.1

V.   Conclusion

We have extended the results of our 2013 comment on Rosenfeld's (2010) paper in two ways. We have examined the effects of breaking the same sex households into their more fundamental gender compositions, and of removing those observations where there is measurement error in the outcome marker.

In the case of gender composition, we have shown that a child's gender matters when living with same-sex parents, and the actual gender combination between parents and children is important. This is a significant finding because gender is randomly assigned to households, and so effects can be plausibly attributed to family type. The findings in this paper suggest that gay and lesbian family types create disparate outcomes in boys and girls. There is no systematic difference in the channel by which boys or girls arrive in these homes, and therefore, having two parents of the same gender makes a difference. This is a subtle form of "difference" that is hidden when gay and lesbian parented families are pooled together as "same-sex" families, and where boys and girls are pooled together as "children."

The gender results found here are related to those of Allen (2013). Allen (2013) replicated the Rosenfeld experiment using the 2006 Canada census and examined graduation rates rather than normal progress through school. He found results similar to those found here. Namely, the gender composition of the parents and the children matter for child outcomes in same-sex homes, but do not matter for other family structure types.[3]

In the case of outcome measurement error, we have shown that the lack of precision found by Rosenfeld is directly the result of including children in the sample for whom there is no measure of normal progress. When only those children for whom we know progress are examined, then a difference is found regardless of which sample restrictions are performed, and this difference is estimated with precision.

The Rosenfeld study was important because it was the first large random sample study of an objective performance measure that supported the long string of small biased sample studies claiming that same-sex family structure made no difference for child outcomes. Our reexamination has shown that his finding was based on a series of questionable assumptions, and that his result is extremely sensitive to the assumptions made. Our results demonstrate, once again, an important lesson in empirical work: that no single study should be taken at face value. Robustness and replication are critical in approaching the truth of any empirical situation.

---

[3] Interestingly, the gender effects found by Allen (2013) were the opposite of those found here. In that study, there were statistically significant negative effects for girls rather than boys, and this was especially pronounced in gay homes. Our view is that the differences are a result of the rarity of children in same-sex homes, the measurement error in the outcome variable, and the rarity of the outcome measure. All of these factors mean that even with hundreds of observations of children in same-sex homes, the results will be sensitive to outliers and sampling error. The reasonable conclusion to draw is that gender matters. Prudence would suggest less confidence in how much and in what direction.

11

We are only just beginning to understand same sex households, and all of the recent large random sample studies are just entering through the front door. These studies indicate that differences exist and they are likely complicated. Although a rejection of the "no-difference" claim is warranted, much more research is necessary to understand the shape and contour of specific differences, and why they occur.

12

VI. Works Cited

Allen, D.W. (2013). High school graduation rates among children of same-sex households. *Review of Economics of the Household, 11(4)*, 635-658.

Allen, D. W., Pakaluk, C., & Price, J. (2013). Nontraditional Families and Childhood Progress Through School: A Comment on Rosenfeld. *Demography , 50* (3), 955-961.

Andersson, G., Noack, T., Seierstad, A., & Weedon-Fekjær, H. (2006). The Demographics of Same-Sex Marriages in Norway and Sweden. *Demography , 43* (1), 79-98.

Cavanagh, S. E., & Huston, A. C. (2006). Family Instability and Children's Early Problem Behavior. *Social Forces , 85* (1), 551-581.

Dawson, D. A. (1991). Family Structure and Children's Health and Well-Being: Data from the 1988 National Health Interview Survey on Child Health. *Journal of Marriage and the Family , 53* (3), 573-584.

Fergusson, D. M., Lynskey, M., & Horwood, L. J. (1995). The Adolescent Outcomes of Adoption: A 16-Year Longitudinal Study. *Journal of Child Psychology and Psychiatry , 36* (4), 597–615.

Fomby, P., & Cherlin, A. J. (2007). Family Instability and Child Well-Being. *American Sociological Review , 72* (2), 181-204.

Ginther, D. K., & Pollak, R. A. (2004). Family Structure and Children's Educational Outcomes: Blended Families, Stylized Facts, and Descriptive Regressions. *Demography , 41* (4), 671-696.

Kalmijn, M., Loeve, A., & Manting, D. (2007). Income Dynamics in Couples and the Dissolution of Marriage and Cohabitation. *Demography , 44* (1), 159-179.

Kurdek, L. A. (1998). Relationship Outcomes and Their Predictors: Longitudinal Evidence from Heterosexual Married, Gay Cohabiting, and Lesbian Cohabiting Couples. *Journal of Marriage and Family , 60* (3), 553-568.

Lau, C. Q. (2012). The Stability of Same-Sex Cohabitation, Different-Sex Cohabitation, and Marriage. *Journal of Marriage and Family , 74* (5), 973–988.

Osborne, C., & McLanahan, S. (2007). Partnership Instability and Child Well-Being. *Journal of Marriage and Family , 69* (4), 1065–1083.

Rosenfeld, M. J. (2010). Nontraditional Families and Progress Through School. *Demography , 47*, 755-775.

Rosenfeld, M. J. (2013). Reply to Allen et al. *Demography , 50* (3), 963-969.

Summary of Douglas W. Allen's

"High School Graduation Rates Among Children of Same-Sex Households"

Review of Economics of the Household 11 (December 2013): 635–658,
http://dx.doi.org/10.1007/s11150-013-9220-y

Allen opens with a review of the same-sex-parenting literature. Out of fifty-three studies on same-sex parenting and child outcomes, fifty are unsuitable as sources of general information about children's welfare. These studies are (1) politicized, suggesting broad policy recommendations unwarranted by the evidence provided in the study, (2) focused on soft measures of child performance (such as subjective perceptions of self-esteem or stigma) rather than hard measures that can be replicated by third parties (such as visits to the hospital), and/or (3) based on small samples (averaging thirty to sixty respondents), nonrandom convenience samples, and/or low-powered statistical tests. Allen concludes, "A review of the same-sex parenting literature inevitably leads to the conclusion that it is a collection of exploratory studies."[1]

Only three studies (Rosenfeld, 2010; Regnerus, 2012; Allen et al., 2013) employ large, random national data sets, placing them in a category apart from the others. Of these studies, one (Rosenfeld) defends the thesis that there are "no differences" among children of same-sex and opposite-sex households. Dr. Michael Rosenfeld used the 2000 U.S. Census to study the progress through school of children in the United States from different family forms. Rosenfeld concluded that children of same-sex families make normal progress through school and that there are no corresponding differences in outcomes between them and children from opposite-sex families.[2] In this paper, Allen offers analyses of high-school graduation rates in Canada, and his results ultimately challenge Rosenfeld's methodology and findings.

Allen relies upon the 2006 Canada Census for a large, random national probability sample of nearly two million children from six different kinds of families:

1. **Single-mother families** include both straight and lesbian mothers, because the Canada Census does not distinguish the sexual orientation of single moms.

2. **Single-father families** include both straight and gay fathers.

 3. **Married heterosexual families** include opposite-sex couples in their original or a subsequent marriage. The Canada Census only records "current marital status" and does not ask whether the family includes a stepparent.

 4. **Common-law households** include opposite-sex cohabiting couples who are not legally married. In Canada, common-law cohabitants enjoy the same legal rights and bear the same obligations as do married couples.

 5. **Gay-father families** include married or unmarried cohabiting gay men. Canada has offered tax and government benefits to same-sex partners since 1997 and legal same-sex marriage since 2005. It does not include two men living together in a nongay relationship.

 6. **Lesbian-mother families** include married or unmarried cohabiting lesbian women. Again, they do not include two women cohabiting in a different capacity.

The Children

Allen restricts the sample to children from seventeen to twenty-two (around high-school age) and looks at two measures of child performance: school attendance and graduation probabilities. In the end, he finds that while gay and lesbian parents are as likely to send their children to high school as are opposite-sex parents, their children are significantly *less* likely to graduate. Specifically, the odds of children from gay-father families graduating are 69 percent as high as those of children from married heterosexual families, and the odds for children of lesbian-mother families are 60 percent as high.

In order to demonstrate just how robust the differences are among family structures, Allen guides the reader through a progression of scenarios in which the data is analyzed under different conditions. He begins with the unconditional, full-sample averages:

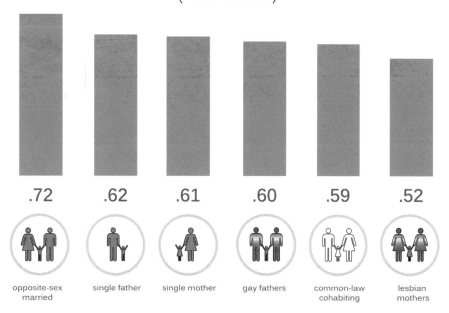

High-school Graduation Rates
(No Controls)

| .72 | .62 | .61 | .60 | .59 | .52 |
| opposite-sex married | single father | single mother | gay fathers | common-law cohabiting | lesbian mothers |

This graph presents graduation rates in their most rudimentary form, without controlling for any characteristics other than type of household. Already, these results show differences in graduation rates, with children from opposite-sex married homes coming out on top. The children of lesbian parents have the lowest graduation rates, and the children from the other family forms lie in-between these. However, these results do not account for alternative possible explanations that may be causing the children of same-sex parents to have lower graduation rates, along with children from single-parent or common-law-parent homes. For instance, children of same-sex couples could come from homes with a lower income, which could contribute to their lower graduation rates. Therefore, it is premature to conclude from this graph that family structure is strongly correlated with this outcome in the children. So, Allen plumbs deeper for alternative explanations.

In the next graph, Allen recreates one of Rosenfeld's analyses, this time with the Canadian data. Since Rosenfeld saw that same-sex households were strongly correlated with mobility, he decided to eliminate from the sample any families that had moved homes in the previous five years. His reasoning was that family disruption (such as divorce) could lead to a move, which would affect school performance for the child. By removing those families, Rosenfeld created a sample of children from relatively more stable homes. Allen tries this measure and finds the following results:

High-School Graduation Rates with a Restricted Sample
(Restriction: Families that Never Moved in Previous Five Years)

In this scenario, the findings are similar to before. Children from opposite-sex married homes come out on top, with children from lesbian-mother homes having the worst scores and all other families falling in-between these two. Additionally, in this scenario, the children from gay-father homes register lower graduation rates than in the previous scenario.

Allen then offers a different approach. He restores the full sample (i.e., includes the families that had moved within the past five years) but this time adds controls for child characteristics, parent education, and household marital status. Among the child characteristics, being disabled or having moved within the past year lowers the odds of a child graduating from high school, whereas being female, coming from an urban area, or coming from a family where everyone is the same race increases the odds of graduating. Children with parents who graduated from high school are twice as likely to graduate from high school as are children of parents who did not graduate. And children who come from a home where the parents have separated have poorer odds of graduating from high school. Allen controls for all of these child and parent characteristics so that none can be said to be the cause of the differences in outcomes.

The following graph shows the results when Allen controls for the above-mentioned factors:

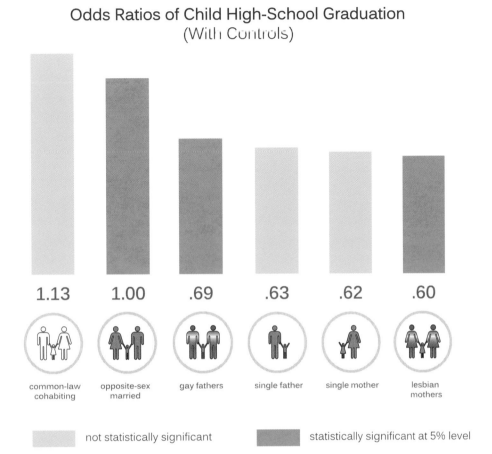

Odds Ratios of Child High-School Graduation
(With Controls)

1.13	1.00	.69	.63	.62	.60
common-law cohabiting	opposite-sex married	gay fathers	single father	single mother	lesbian mothers

not statistically significant   statistically significant at 5% level

An "odds ratio" is a way to report the odds of something occurring, compared to something else occurring. In this case, Allen holds the control group (the children from opposite-sex married families) at 1.0, and he quantifies just how strongly having a different family structure is associated with having graduated from high school, when compared to the control group. The lower the odds ratio, the lower the association with graduating from high school. In the above graph, the bars shaded in pale orange are not statistically significant and so cannot be taken as dependable figures. The bars in bold orange represent the statistically significant results, robust enough to rely on. Looking at those numbers, the children from opposite-sex married homes come out on top, with the children from lesbian-mother homes reporting the lowest scores and the children from gay-father homes again lying in-between these two.

Note that in all three graphed scenarios, the relative rankings remain. While the numerical outcomes change, the relationship between the children from opposite-sex married families and the children from same-sex families does not.

Allen then asks a different question. Does it make a difference whether the child is a girl or a boy? The Canada Census allows him to identify the gender of the children in each particular same-sex household, so he restricts the sample to either boys or girls. The following graphs the odds ratios for the girls, with controls for child and parent characteristics, as before.

Odds Ratios of Child High-School Graduation
(Girls Only, with Controls)

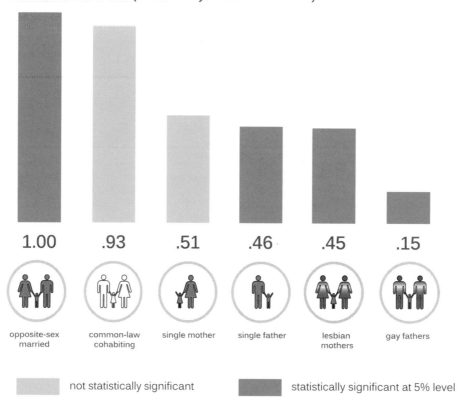

1.00	.93	.51	.46	.45	.15
opposite-sex married	common-law cohabiting	single mother	single father	lesbian mothers	gay fathers

not statistically significant   statistically significant at 5% level

Here, the girls living with two gay fathers perform the poorest of all possible combinations, with an odds of graduating only 15 percent as high as that of children living with opposite-sex married parents. Girls living with two lesbian mothers perform better, with an odds of graduating 45 percent as high as those of children living with opposite-sex married parents. However, the girls living with a single father perform better than the girls living with two gay fathers, and girls living with two lesbian mothers perform about as well as girls with a single father. So the gender makeup of the parents makes a dramatic difference for the girls, and as far as high-school graduation is concerned, having a single parent turns out to be better for them than having two parents of the same sex.

As for the boys, Allen was not able to provide statistically significant estimates, given the sample constraints:

Odds Ratios of Child High-School Graduation
(Boys Only, with Controls)

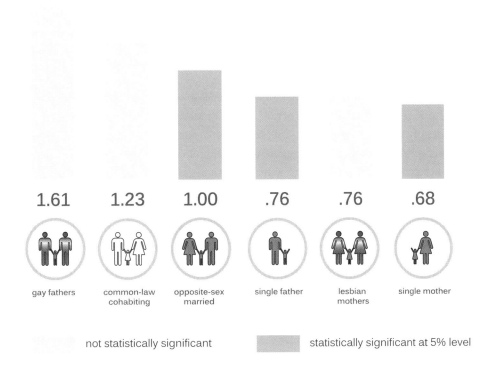

1.61	1.23	1.00	.76	.76	.68
gay fathers	common-law cohabiting	opposite-sex married	single father	lesbian mothers	single mother

not statistically significant   statistically significant at 5% level

The only findings that were statistically significant were those for boys in single-father and single-mother homes. The results for boys in same-sex households were not robust enough to be reliable. However, it is interesting to see that even here, gender appears to make a difference. Allen proposes the thesis that "sons do better with fathers, and daughters do better with mothers."[3] He notes that greater investigation would be necessary to confirm this trend in the data but that the concept is not a novel one: "Within the child development literature and pop culture, there is the belief that mothers and fathers provide different parenting inputs that are not perfectly substitutable. These results would be consistent with this notion, but further research is necessary to show any causality."[4]

As a result of these scenarios, Allen concludes that it is important to consider the gender makeup of the parents as well as the children. Lesbian parenting should be distinguished from gay parenting—not assuming that all "same-sex parenting" is the same. And the gender of the child should be noted—not assuming that boys and girls will respond in the same way to lesbian or gay parenting.

Because Allen's conclusions are so different from those of Rosenfeld, Allen takes the time to discuss three reasons why he believes he came to such different findings.

First, Rosenfeld decided to exclude from the sample any same-sex couples who had changed dwellings within the five years previous to the survey. He excluded those families because same-sex couples are highly associated with mobility. In his words, "Most of the children being raised by same-sex couples at the time of the 2000 census had previously lived through divorce or parental break-up, which research has shown to be traumatic for some children."[5] Rosenfeld thought it was unfair to include in the sample children who had experienced this kind of transition.[6]

However, Allen points out that the percentage of same-sex families associated with mobility was so high that when Rosenfeld excluded them from the sample, he created two bigger problems: first a statistical inability to distinguish the children from same-sex households from any other children, leading to a likely false null hypothesis (of "no differences" between children).[7] Second, when he removed these mobile families from the sample, he removed the very factor that could be responsible for the poor graduation rates—family instability due to marital breakup: "The increased chance of failing a grade—especially when the correlation magnitude is so close to that of single parents—could likely be the result of a previous divorce or separation since many children in same-sex households were initially born into opposite-sex families that later broke apart."[8] By contrast, Allen does not exclude these families from his sample but rather includes them and then controls for marital history.

A second reason why Allen comes to a different conclusion is because of measurement errors associated with the 2000 U.S. Census, upon which Rosenfeld relied. Because of the Defense of Marriage Amendment (DOMA), the U.S. Census was not permitted to identify same-sex couples. So Rosenfeld had to make educated guesses about who was a same-sex couple, based upon more general answers to questions about gender and who was the head of the household. Rosenfeld made the best guesses he could, given the constraints, but this was a major limitation of his study. By contrast, because same-sex marriage was legal in Canada during the time of its census, Allen is able to rely on direct self-identification of same-sex couples, which yielded greater precision in identifying family structure.

Finally, Allen distinguishes between gay and lesbian households, whereas Rosenfeld groups them together in one category. This allows for greater precision in Allen's findings.

For all of these reasons, Allen's study of Canadian same-sex parents and child high-school graduation rates is more accurate than the Rosenfeld study, and it lends credibility to the claim that at present, the strongest empirical data on the academic market supports the conclusion that there *are differences* in child outcomes across family types and that children from opposite-sex married homes *outperform* their peers living in all other family structures, including same-sex-parented households, of which lesbian households tend to perform the poorest.

Conclusion

Allen concludes that the "no differences" thesis of the vast majority of the literature on same-sex parenting is not warranted, based on the scientific merits of the research. After Allen analyses a new large, random sample from the 2005 Canada Census, he finds that children of gay and lesbian households demonstrate significantly lower odds of high-school graduation than do children from opposite-sex married parents. Moreover, Allen points out that these findings probably present a *rosier* picture for the children of same-sex families than exists in reality, because the Canada Census includes in the category of opposite-sex married parents, those who are married after a previous divorce. If Allen had been able to compare children of same-sex parents to a control group of children from *intact* (never previously divorced) opposite-sex married parents—what sociologists have called the "gold standard" for children—the graduation-rate estimates for children from these intact families probably would have been even higher, making the gap between the groups even more significant and worrying.

Allen ends by calling on the academic community to acknowledge the differences in child outcomes across family groups and investigate more carefully why these differences exist, by using more rigorous methodological designs and higher-quality statistical tests. He makes a clarion call for an "exceptional data set" that is very large, national, and random; relies upon self-reports of sexual orientation by parents; and has a retrospective design, with a timeline of each family's transitions so that researchers can look more carefully into marital history and marital instability across family structures.[9]

Notes

1. Allen, 642.

2. See Appendix: Michael Rosenfeld, "Nontraditional Families and Childhood Progress through School," *Demography* 47 (August 2010): 755–775.

3. Allen, 649.

4. Ibid., 651–652.

5. Rosenfeld, 758.

6. Ibid., 760.

7. Allen, 641.

8. Ibid., 642.

9. Ibid., 655.

Rev Econ Household
DOI 10.1007/s11150-013-9220-y

High school graduation rates among children of same-sex households

Douglas W. Allen

Received: 7 November 2012 / Accepted: 23 August 2013
© Springer Science+Business Media New York 2013

Abstract Almost all studies of same-sex parenting have concluded there is "no difference" in a range of outcome measures for children who live in a household with same-sex parents compared to children living with married opposite-sex parents. Recently, some work based on the US census has suggested otherwise, but those studies have considerable drawbacks. Here, a 20 % sample of the 2006 Canada census is used to identify self-reported children living with same-sex parents, and to examine the association of household type with children's high school graduation rates. This large random sample allows for control of parental marital status, distinguishes between gay and lesbian families, and is large enough to evaluate differences in gender between parents and children. Children living with gay and lesbian families in 2006 were about 65 % as likely to graduate compared to children living in opposite sex marriage families. Daughters of same-sex parents do considerably worse than sons.

Keywords Same sex households · Same sex parents · High school graduation

JEL Classification I21 · J12 · J16

> Children raised by gay or lesbian parents are as likely as children raised by heterosexual parents to be healthy, successful and well-adjusted. The research supporting this conclusion is accepted beyond serious debate in the field of developmental psychology.
> [Justice Vaughn Walker, section 70, Perry v. Schwarzenegger]

D. W. Allen (✉)
Department of Economics, Simon Fraser University, Burnaby, BC V5A 1S6, Canada
e-mail: allen@sfu.ca

Published online: 26 September 2013

 Springer

1 Introduction

The matter of same-sex marriage is perhaps the most significant policy issue in family law since the introduction of no-fault divorce in the late 1960s and 1970s. Much of the debate is focused on the question of equality, although issues of relationship stability, consequences for opposite sex marriages, and marriage culture are often brought up. One aspect that is seldom argued is the effect a same-sex union might have on the children within that union. The absence of any discussion on children no doubt reflects the unanimous consensus in the child development literature on this question—it makes no difference.

Within the last 15 years there have been over fifty empirical studies considering the effects on children of growing up within a same-sex household.[1] Despite the various differences in each study, all but a couple have the same conclusion: children of same-sex parents perform at least as well as children from heterosexual families. This conclusion, that there is no difference in child outcomes based on family structure, has played a major role in legal cases, legislation, popular culture, and professional opinions on gay family rights—including rights to adoption and marriage.[2] As Justice Walker claimed, to suggest otherwise is to risk not being taken seriously.

Unfortunately, the literature on child development in same-sex households is lacking on several grounds.[3] First, the research is characterized by levels of advocacy, policy endorsement, and awareness of political consequences, that is disproportionate with the strength and substance of the preliminary empirical findings. Second, the literature generally utilizes measures of child and family performance that are not easily verifiable by third party replication, which vary from one study to another in ways that make comparisons difficult, and which differ substantially from measures standardly used in other family studies.[4] But most important, almost all of the literature on same-sex parenting (which almost always

---

[1] Table 1 lists the studies. See Allen (2012) or Marks (2012) for surveys of this literature. Throughout the paper the term "same-sex household" is used to mean gay or lesbian headed households.

[2] For example, it forms the basis for the American Psychological Association's position supporting gay marriage.

[3] Economists have written a considerable amount on gay and lesbian issues *outside* of child development, and generally find differences in behavior. For example, Negrusa and Oreffice (2011) on savings rates, Oreffice (2010) on labor supply, Black et al. (2007) on labor markets, Jepsen and Jepsen (2009) on home ownership, and Carpenter and Gates (2008) on family formation. Indeed, The *Review of Economics of the Household* devoted its 2008 December issue to gay and lesbian households. Those papers examined wage differentials [Zavodny (2008), Booth and Frank (2008)], household formation [Badgett et al. (2008)], and bank deposits [Klawitter (2008)]. This is the first paper in economics to examine differences in child performance.

[4] This is often a characteristic of a nascent field. These measures include self reports on attitudes, awareness, and adjustments [e.g., McNeill and Rienzi (1998)]; self reports on parenting quality and socio-emotional child development [e.g., Golombok et al. (1997)]; self reports on psychological well-being, identity, and relationships [e.g., Tasker et al. (1995)]; self reports on family closeness, parental legitimacy, child bonding [e.g., Gartrell et al. (1999)]; and self reports on stigma and self-esteem [e.g., Gershon et al. (1999)].

✑ Springer

Table 1 Summaries of gay parenting studies

Study	Random sample	Gay sample size	Content[a]	Comparison group size	Time series data	Gay or lesbian study
Bailey et al. (1995)	No	55	Hard	None	No	G
Flaks et al. (1995)	No	30	Soft	30	No	L
Patterson (1995)	No	26	Soft	None	No	L
Tasker et al. (1995)	No	25	Soft	21	No	L
Golombok et al. (1996)	No	25	Hard	21	No	L
Sarantakos (1996)	No	58	Soft	116	Yes	G & L
Brewaeys et al. (1997)	No	30	Soft	68	No	L
Golombok et al. (1997)	No	30	Soft	83	Yes	L
Chan et al. (1998a)	No	30	Soft	16	No	L
Chan et al. (1998b)	No	55	Soft	25	No	L
McNeill and Rienzi (1998)	No	24	Soft	35	No	L
Patterson et al. (1998)	No	37	Soft	None	No	L
Gershon et al. (1999)	No	76	Soft	None	No	L
Gartrell et al. (1999)	No	84	Soft	None	Yes	L
Dundas et al. (2000)	No	27	Soft	None	No	L
Gartrell et al. (2000)	No	84	Soft	None	Yes	L
Barrett et al. (2001)	No	101	Soft	None	No	G
Chrisp (2001)	No	8	Soft	None	No	L
Patterson (2001)	No	37	Soft	None	No	L
Fulcher et al. 2002)	No	55	Soft	25	No	L
Vanfraussen et al. (2002)	No	24	Soft	24	No	L
Golombok et al. (2003)	No	39	Soft	134	No	L
Bos et al. (2004)	No	100	Soft	None	No	L
Patterson et al. (2004)	No	33	Hard	33	No	L
Stacey (2004)	No	50	Soft	None	No	G
MacCallum and Golombok (2004)	No	25	Soft	76	No	L
Wainright et al. (2004)	Yes	44	Hard	44	No	L
Gartrell et al. (2005)	No	84	Soft	None	Yes	L
Leung et al. (2005)	No	47	Soft	111	No	G & L
Scheib et al. (2005)	No	12	Soft	17	No	L
Stacey (2005)	No	50	Soft	None	No	G
Wainright et al. (2006)	Yes	44	Hard	44	No	L
Wright et al. (2006)	No	156	Soft	None	No	G
Bos et al. (2007)	No	99	Soft	100	No	L
Goldberg (2007)	No	46	Soft	None	No	G & L
Balsam et al. (2008)	No	281	Soft	55	No	G & L
Bos et al. (2008)	No	63	Soft	None	No	L
Bos et al. (2008)	No	152	Soft	None	No	L
Fairlough (2008)	No	67	Soft	None	No	G & L

 Springer

Table 1 continued

Study	Random sample	Gay sample size	Content[a]	Comparison group size	Time series data	Gay or lesbian study
Fulcher et al. (2008)	No	33	Soft	33	No	L
Goldberg et al. (2008)	No	30	Soft	None	No	L
Oswald et al. (2008)	No	190	Hard	None	No	G & L
Rothblum et al. (2008)	Pop.	475	Hard	None	No	G, L & T
Rivers et al. (2008)	Yes	18	Soft	18	No	L
Sutfin et al. (2008)	No	29	Soft	28	No	L
Wainright and Patterson (2008)	Yes	44	Soft	44	No	L
Bos (2010)	No	36	Soft	36	No	G
Gartrell and Bos (2010)	No	84	Hard	93	Yes	L
Lehmiller (2010)	No	68	Soft	86	No	G
Power et al. (2010)	No	455	Hard	None	No	G & L
Rosenfeld (2010)	Yes	3,502	Hard	>700,000	No	G & L
Regnerus (2012)	Yes	248	Hard	2,988	No	G & L
Allen et al. (2013)	Yes	8,632	Hard	1,189,833	No	G & L

G gay, *L* lesbian, and *T* transgendered

[a] Hard implies the questions asked were potentially verifiable, quantifiable, and had observable answers. Soft implies the opposite. Some studies included both and were classified as hard

means lesbian parenting) is based on some combination of weak empirical designs, small biased convenience samples, "snowballing," and low powered tests.[5]

This paper addresses these shortcomings by using the 2006 Canada census to study high school graduation probabilities of children who lived with both gay and lesbian parents in 2006, and to compare them with four other family types: married, common law, single mothers, and single fathers. Currently, the 2006 Canada census has several strengths compared to any other data set. First, it uses information from a country where same-sex couples have enjoyed all taxation and government benefits since 1997, and legal same-sex marriage since 2005.[6] As Biblarz and Savci note, such legalization reduces the stress and stigma of homosexuality, and encourages honest participation in census questions.[7] Second, not only does the census provide a large random sample, but married and common law same-sex

---

[5] "Snowballing" is the practice of asking individuals within a study to recruit their friends and associates to join the study.

[6] The first Canadian same-sex marriages took place on January 14, 2001 at the Toronto Metropolitan Community Church. These became the basis of a successful legal challenge which ended at the court of appeal on June 10, 2003. On July 20, 2005, the Federal government passed the Civil Marriage Act that made Canada the fourth country in the world to legalize same-sex marriage. Thus, different people date the arrival of same-sex marriage in Canada as 2001, 2003, or 2005.

[7] Biblarz and Savci, p. 490, 2010.

 Springer

couples and their children are self identified.[8] This is an important advantage over the US census. Third, because the child and parent records are linked together, the marital status and educational levels of the parents can be controlled for when analyzing child performance. Finally, because of the relatively large sample size, there is enough power to not only separate gay from lesbian households, but also enough to examine the gender mix of same-sex households.[9]

The point estimates for high school graduation show that there is a significant reduction in the odds of children living in same-sex homes completing high school. In the case of gay parents, children are estimated to be 69 % as likely to graduate compared to children from opposite sex married homes.[10] For lesbian households the children are 60 % as likely to graduate from high school. A breakdown of performance by the sex of the child shows a more dramatic result. Daughters of gay parents are only 15 % as likely to graduate, while daughters of lesbian parents are 45 % as likely to graduate. Both sets of results are estimated with precision. On the other hand, sons of lesbian parents are 76 % as likely to graduate, while sons of gay parents are 61 % *more* likely to graduate. However, neither of these results are statistically significant. In general, the results for gays and lesbians respond differently to different controls, and differ from the results for the other family types. This, and the different graduation rates for sons and daughters, suggest that the two types of same-sex couples are much different and should not be categorized together in empirical work.

These results survive several robustness checks. Graduation rates may be different because school attendance rates are different, yet no statistical difference in the probability of attending school across the different family types is found. In fact, the point estimates indicate children of opposite-sex married parents are less likely to attend school. Various changes in sample restrictions and controls also leave the results unchanged.

2 Context within the child development literature

Since most economists are unfamiliar with the literature on child performance in same-sex households, a brief review of its empirical problems is warranted. Generally speaking the literature is characterized by several different types of data bias and small samples that lack any power. Table 1 reports some information on the relevant fifty three studies conducted the past 15 years. With the exception of

---

[8] Unfortunately, it also lumps married and common law same-sex couples together, and I am unable to separate them.

[9] The census is not a panel, and provides only a snap shot of the population. As a result, this paper does not study the effect of *growing up* in a same sex household, but rather examines the association of school performance for those children who lived with same-sex parents in 2006.

[10] Rosenfeld (2010) stressed the importance of controlling for a child's home life stability. He restricted the sample to households that remained in one place for the past 5 years. Here mobility is controlled for with a fixed effect on whether or not the child has remained in the home for 1 year. Results reported in the text all refer to this mobility control. The "Appendix" shows the results of the alternative control: did the child move residences in the past 5 years.

 Springer

two of the last three, the others have serious empirical problems that render them exploratory in nature.

2.1 Random samples

Although a proper probability sample is a necessary condition for making any claim about an unknown population, within the same-sex parenting literature researchers have studied only those community members who are convenient to study. This point has been raised by others regarding the literature on gay parenting, including many within the literature.[11] Of the fifty-three studies reviewed here, only seven used probability samples.[12] All of the other studies arrived at their samples through means that introduced various levels of bias. Some studies recruited individuals from sperm bank data sources or other types of reproduction technology providers.[13] Other studies used Internet surveys where the respondents were recruited by various methods: parent forums, gay and lesbian web-sites, and online advocacy organizations.[14] Many studies recruited through LGBT events, bookstore and newspaper advertisements, word of mouth, networking, and youth groups.[15] A common method of recruitment was to use a combination of the above methods to form a sample base, and then recruit friends of the base.[16] Still other studies failed to even mention how their samples were arrived at.[17] Each different procedure has a different and unknown source of bias.

Of the studies before 2010, there are only four that use a random sample, and each has a trivial sample size. For example, consider the three studies by Wainright and Patterson.[18] These are not three independent studies, but rather three separate publications utilizing the same data source: the National Longitudinal Survey of Adolescent Health. Even though the survey contains 12,105 households, Wainright and Patterson were only able to identify 6 gay households and 44 lesbian ones. The

---

[11] Andersson et al. (2006) note:

> The lack of representative samples is the most fundamental problem in quantitative studies on gays and lesbians, which commonly rely on self-recruited samples from an unknown population. [p. 81]

See also Sweet (2009) or Stacey and Biblarz (2001).

[12] These were Allen et al. (2013), Regnerus (2012), Rosenfeld (2010), Wainright et al. (2004), Wainright and Patterson (2006, 2008), and Golombok et al. (2003). One study used a population: Rothblum et al. (2008).

[13] For example: Bos et al. (2007), Bos and Van Balen (2008), Chan et al. (1998a), Brewaeys et al. (1997) and Chan et al. (1998b).

[14] For example: Lehmiller (2010), Bos (2010), or Power et al. (2010).

[15] For example: Wright and Perry (2006), Oswald et al. (2008), Lehmiller (2010), Goldberg (2007), Bailey et al. (1995), Flaks et al. (1995), Fairtlough (2008), Dundas and Kaufman (2000), Power et al. or Fulcher et al. (2008).

[16] For example: Balsam et al. (2008), Golombok et al. (2003).

[17] For example: Stacey (2004, 2005) or Chrisp (2001).

[18] Wainright and Patterson (2006, 2008) and Wainright et al. (2006).

 Springer

other study by Rivers et al. (2008) used a similar British survey, and ended up with a sample of 18 lesbian households.[19]

The only study with a large random sample in the entire literature is Rosenfeld (2010), that used the 2000 US Census 5 % Public-use Micro-sample to examine the association between same-sex parenting and normal progress through school.[20] His study confirmed the findings of most earlier research, and he concluded that in terms of school grade progression children raised by same-sex couples "cannot be distinguished with statistical certainty from children of heterosexual married couples." Rosenfeld's study was the first to use a large random sample to support the finding that children of same-sex households were no different in a performance measure from children of married opposite sex couples.

However, a follow up study by Allen et al. (2013), found that Rosenfeld's conclusion was questionable. His estimates were so imprecise that the outcomes of children in same-sex households could not be distinguished with any statistical certainty from almost any other family type—not just opposite-sex married families. The imprecision came from Rosenfeld's decision to exclude from the sample any family who had moved within the past 5 years. Same-sex households turned out to be strongly correlated with mobility, and the result was a large reduction in the same-sex household sample, which led to an inability to statistically distinguish the children from these households with any others—including ones known to be poor environments for children. By controlling for mobility and restoring the sample to its full size, Allen et al. (2013) found that children from same-sex homes were about 35 % more likely to fail a grade compared to children from intact opposite sex married homes. About on par with children from single parent homes.[21]

2.2 Small sample sizes

Aside from the problem of non-random samples, most of the existing parenting studies contain tiny sample sizes.[22] Of the fifty-three studies examined here, only

---

[19] Golombok et al. (2003) uses a random sample from the Avon Longitudinal Study of Parents and Children—a local British study—and comes up with 18 lesbians. They then use snowball methods to bring their numbers up to 39 lesbians.

[20] The 2000 US Census does not directly identify same-sex couples. Rosenfeld, like others, did the best he could by indirectly identifying them. He did this by selecting those couples who indicated they were a couple and who identified their sex as being the same. This procedure requires the correct answer of three questions, and a small chance of error on the part of heterosexuals can lead to a large measurement error for the same-sex couple sample, given the large size of the former and the small size of the latter. Black et al. (2006) suggest a procedure for correcting this statistical problem; however, there is no indication in the Rosenfeld paper that he followed it.

[21] The Regnerus study (2012) also used a random sample; however, it was still too small to identify a sufficient sample of same-sex parents. To increase his sample size he decided to use a broader definition of same-sex parent.

[22] Of the fifty-three studies examined here, only a few dealt with gay male parents. Almost all of the studies are done on lesbians. This is another source of bias that warrants caution in drawing any conclusions about non-lesbian families.

 Springer

two had sample sizes larger than 500.[23] Much more common were sample sizes between 30-60.[24] The problem with such small sample sizes is that the data cannot generate any power for statistical testing, and low power means there is a small chance of rejecting a false null hypothesis.

Hence, the very small sample sizes found in many of these studies creates a bias towards accepting a null hypothesis of "no effect" in child outcomes between same- and opposite-sex households. This is well recognized, but it is exacerbated in the context of gay parenting because avenues through which these households are formed are many and complicated. As noted by Stacey and Biblarz (2001), Biblarz and Staccy (2010), these families often have experienced a prior divorce, previous heterosexual marriages, intentional pregnancies, co-parenting, donor insemination, adoption, and surragacy. These channels may have different effects on boys or girls, and may differ in gay or lesbian homes. Empirical work needs to control for the various selection effects that arise from the number of parents, sexual identity, marital status, gender, and biological relationships with children. That is, child performance is affected by all these channels and they need to be statistically identified, but this requires large sample sizes.

A review of the same-sex parenting literature inevitably leads to the conclusion that it is a collection of exploratory studies. Even the two most recent studies by Rosenfeld (2010) and Allen et al. (2013) suffer from several drawbacks. First, they have to rely on indirect identification of same-sex couples within an environment where same-sex marriage was illegal in all fifty states. Second, neither paper distinguishes between gay and lesbian households, and there is no reason to think their parental performance should be the same. Third, both papers fail to control for the marital history of the parents. The increased chance of failing a grade—especially when the correlation magnitude is so close to that of single parents—could likely be the result of a previous divorce or separation since many children in same-sex households were initially born into opposite sex families that later broke apart. The "same-sex" aspect of these parents may have nothing to do with slower grade progress.

And so, within the context of this uniform literature based on small biased samples, this study intends to examine high school graduation rates of children who lived within either gay or lesbian households in 2006, using a large random data set that links parent and child records.

---

[23] These were Rosenfeld (2010) and Allen et al. (2013). According to Nock (p. 37, 2001), to properly test any hypothesis regarding gay parenting, a sample size of 800 is required.

[24] Often the problem of small sample size comes from low response rates. Many of the fifty-two studies are silent on the question of response rates to their surveys, but when information is provided it often shows that response rates are very low. For example, in Bos (2010) the gay males were recruited from an Internet mail list for gay parents. Although the list had 1,000 names, only 36 replied and participated in the study. This amounts to a 3.6 % response rate. Other studies (e.g., Chan et al. and Fulcher et al.) have reductions in their samples similar in relative size to Rosenfeld. Response rates lower than 60 % are usually taken to mean the presence of a strong selection bias—even when the initial list is random.

 Springer

3 Data

Data come from the 2006 Canada census 20 % restricted master file.[25] From this file all children *living with* a parent within the home were selected.[26] It is important to note that the census identifies children living with their *parents*, and not just adults. Hence, children of same sex parents are those who respond affirmative to the question: "Are you a child of a male (female) same-sex married or common law couple?" This implies that the results below address the association of having two same-sex parents with a given sexual orientation, rather than just the association of having two parents of the same-sex. That is, the two parents are not same-sex roommates, friends, or other relatives.[27]

Restricting the sample to children living with parents allowed a matching of the child files with the parent files. Children over the age of 22 were dropped because of a likely selection bias in children who live at home well into adulthood.[28] Although the Census identifies children living with *two* same-sex parents, it does not identify children living with a gay or lesbian *single* parent. These families are inadvertently included with the single mothers and fathers.[29]

Table 2 defines the variables used in the analysis, and Tables 3 and 4 report some unconditional means for children between the ages 17–22 across the six family types. Table 3 reports graduation rates for the different family types, not just for the full sample, but also on three sub samples. In terms of the full sample three things stand out: children of married opposite-sex families have a high graduation rate compared to the others; children of lesbian families have a very low graduation rate compared to the others; and the other four types are similar to each other and lie in between the married/lesbian extremes. The three sub samples (both parents are high school graduates; the family never changed dwellings in the previous 5 years; and the family did change dwellings in the previous 5 years) show that even though the

---

[25] This file is not a public use data set. To use the data, a proposal is screened by the Social Sciences Research Council of Canada, an RCMP criminal check is conducted, and the researcher becomes a deemed employee of Statistics Canada subject to the penalties of the Statistics Act. Empirical work was conducted at the SFU Research Data Center, and all results were screened by Statistics Canada before release. Statistics Canada does not allow any unweighted observations or descriptives to be released, nor any maximums or minimums of weighted estimates, nor sample sizes for the weighted regressions.

[26] Because the procedure starts by selecting the children, and then matches the parents of the child to the file, the problem of having a non-biological parent *not* report a child in the household who is biologically related to their spouse is avoided.

[27] Statistics Canada does not allow the sample sizes to be released; however, there are approximately ten million children in Canada, and so the sample has close to two million children in it.

[28] There's no reason to believe this selection bias would be correlated with family type, however. All regressions were run with various restrictions on the child's age within the sample, including keeping everyone, and none of the gay or lesbian family results in the paper change, in terms of magnitudes or levels of significance, in an important way.

[29] Many children in Canada who live with a gay or lesbian parent are actually living with a single parent. About 64 % of children in gay homes have a single father, and about 46 % of children in lesbian homes have a single mother (see Allen and Lu, "Marriage and children: differences across sexual orientations," (unpublished, 2013). The number of gay and lesbian single parent homes is so small compared to all other single parent homes, however, that it likely causes little bias. In any event, the children analyzed here are a distinct subset of all children raised by a gay or lesbian parent.

 Springer

Table 2 Definitions of variables

Variable name	Definition
Human capital variables	
Highschool grad	1 if child has graduated from highschool
Province	10 if located in Newfoundland, 12 if PEI...62 if Nunavut
Visible minority	1 if a member of a visible minority
Disabled	1 if physically or mentally disabled
Moved within 1 year	1if family changed dwelling within past year
Moved within 5 years	1if family changed dwelling within the past 5 years
Urban	1 if child lives in urban area
Age	Age of child in years
Family size	Number of family members
Female	1 if child is a girl
Family income	Before tax income in dollars
Same race	1 if child is the same race as resident parent(s)
Father HSG	1 if father graduated from highschool
Mother HSG	1 if mother graduated from highschool
Father grad degree	1 if father has a graduate degree
Mother grad degree	1 if mother has a graduate degree
Father attended	1 if father ever attended school
Mother attended	1 if mother ever attened school
Parent's current marital status	
Father married	1 if father is legally married
Father divorced	1 if father is divorced
Father separated	1 if father is separated
Father never married	1 if father has never legally married and single
Father widowed	1 if father is widowed
Mother married	1 if mother is legally married
Mother divorced	1 if mother is divorced
Mother separated	1 if mother is separated
Mother never married	1 if mother has never legally married and single
Mother widowed	1 if mother is widowed
Family type	
Common law	1 if couple is living common law
Gay parents	1 if couple is two gay men
Lesbian parents	1 if couple is two lesbian women
Single mother	1 if only parent in the home is the mother
Single father	1 if only parent in the home is the father

level of graduation rates may change, the relationship between the groups remains the same.

Some of the results from Table 4 are fascinating. In terms of sample sizes, it is striking how few same-sex couples with children (between ages 17–22) there are. The country estimates for gay families is just 423, and for lesbian families 969;

 Springer

which together make up just over half of 1 % of all couples with children in this age group. There are a higher number of visible minority children for gay households (28 % compared to 13 % for common law couples), and a higher number of disabled children (13 % compared to 6 % for opposite sex married parents). This may imply a high number of adopted children in gay households, but interestingly there are no cases of inter-racial same-sex families within the 20 % sample.[30] Both lesbian and gay parents are well educated with well over 19 % of them graduating from high school. Finally, lesbians are much more likely to have moved dwellings, with 60 % having moved within the past 5 years.

The next section estimates the association of family type on high school graduation rates, controlling for individual and family characteristics. One contribution of this paper is to control for parental marital status.[31] However, the census, of course, is not a panel or even a retrospective data set. All it records is the current marital status of the parents. Unfortunately, this introduces measurement error into the marital status control for married individuals because the census only identifies if a spouse is currently married, common law, never married, divorced, separated, or widowed. Hence a married spouse may have *previously* been divorced, but is recorded as married; that is, the married category contains couples who have been divorced. This is not a problem for those currently cohabiting, since they are accurately coded as divorced, separated, never married (single), or widowed. Since the marriage rate is lower for gays and lesbians, this measurement error is likely to bias the opposite-sex family type effect on child school performance downwards.[32]

4 Estimation

4.1 School graduation

Table 5 reports on three logit regressions, where the dependent variable equals 1 if the child has graduated from high school.[33] All of the regressions in this table control for whether or not the family moved with the past year. Table 8 in the appendix reports on another three logit regressions with the same dependent variable and the same right hand side variables, except for the variable used to control for family mobility—it uses the mobility measure "did child move within

---

[30] The census identifies many visible minorities, but only has a broad based question on race. Hence, the same race variable likely contains significant measurement error.

[31] This control is lacking in other large sample studies on same-sex parents. It is important because a previous marriage disruption is likely to have a negative impact on high school performance. This is particularly important with same-sex couples given the evidence that their relationships are less stable [see Andersson et al. (2006)].

[32] Using current parental marital status is a decent *control* for family history (as used here), but the coefficients estimated are biased measures of the *correlation* of parental marital history on child school performance. For this reason, and to keep the tables to one page, these coefficients are not reported.

[33] Rosenfeld (2010), and Allen et al. (2013) use normal progress through school as their measure of child performance. The Canada census does not identify the grade of the student in 2006, and therefore, this measure is not possible. It does, however, identify if the child has graduated from high school or not.

 Springer

Table 3 Estimated population averages for child high school graduation (weighted observations, children ages 17–22)

	Opposite sex married parents	Opposite sex common law parents	Gay parents	Lesbian parents	Single father	Single mother
Full sample						
Highschool grad	0.72	0.59	0.60	0.52	0.62	0.61
Both parent high school grad						
Highschool grad	0.75	0.68	0.64	0.55	0.67	0.65
Never moved						
Highschool grad	0.73	0.62	0.59	0.58	0.65	0.64
Did move						
Highschool grad	0.69	0.55	0.60	0.48	0.58	0.57

past 5 years."[34] There is no qualitative difference in the estimates when using the different mobility controls.

Table 5 only reports the logit coefficient, its standard error, the odds ratio, and marginal effects, for the household type variables in order to keep the tables a reasonable size. The log of the odds ratio is the logit, which is a linear combination of the parameters and exogenous variables. The odds ratio is found by taking the exponential of both sides of the logit equation. The odds ratio has the nice property of an easy interpretation.[35] The marginal effect equals $(\partial y/\partial x)$, where y is the graduation rate and x is one of the right hand side variables.

The different columns result from different types of controls. Column (1) includes controls for child characteristics, and these include: province, visible minority, disabled, mobility, urban, age, family size, family income, female, and same race. Column (2) adds the parental education controls: did the mother/father graduate from high school, and did the mother/father have a graduate degree. Column (3) adds the parental marital status variables found in Table 2.

Before examining the results of Tables 5, some comment on the unreported results is warranted. Among the child characteristics, being disabled or having moved in the recent past reduces the odds of graduation (on average, to about 50 and 75 % respectively). Living in an urban area, being female, and having all family members the same race raises the odds of graduation (on average, by 30, 60, and 35 % respectively). Parental education matters a great deal: if the parents have

---

[34] Two mobility measures are used because of the important role mobility played in Rosenfeld (2010). He decided to restrict his sample by removing households that moved within the past 5 years. This procedure was also performed here. No qualitative difference was made in terms of the point estimates. Rather than controlling for whether or not the child had moved residences over the past one or 5 years, the regressions were also run controlling for whether or not the child changed census metropolitan areas over the past 1 or 5 years. No qualitative difference in the point estimates on type of household resulted, although they were estimated with more precision. All regressions cluster by province to provide robust standard errors.

[35] The key to interpreting the odds ratio is to compare it to the odds of 1 (equally likely). Hence, an odds ratio of 1.2 means that a unit change in an independent variable, others held constant, increases the chance of a positive outcome by 20 %.

 Springer

Table 4 Estimated population averages of other variables for children (weighted observations, children ages 17–22)

	Married parents	Common law parents	Gay parents	Lesbian parents	Single father	Single mother
Child characteristics						
% of total pop.	71.16	6.60	0.02	0.04	5.08	17.07
School attendance	0.76	0.67	0.73	0.68	0.64	0.69
Province	36.58	32.2	29.32	36.9	35.5	35.9
Visible minority	0.23	0.13	0.28	0.17	0.19	0.28
Disabled	0.06	0.06	0.13	0.08	0.08	0.09
Moved within 1 year	0.07	0.13	0.08	0.19	0.15	0.15
Moved within 5 years	0.24	0.38	0.39	0.60	0.42	0.44
Urban	0.78	0.74	0.72	0.91	0.79	0.88
Age	19.26	18.91	18.96	18.79	19.20	19.15
Family size	4.30	4.05	3.34	3.77	2.72	2.98
Female	0.48	0.45	0.43	0.54	0.41	0.47
Family income	119,172	95,656	91,357	88,600	68,473	49,874
Same race	0.99	0.98	1	1	1	1
Father HSG	0.81	0.70	0.94	0.93	0.73	na
Mother HSG	0.84	0.77	0.96	0.93	na	0.79
Father grad degree	0.08	0.03	0.05	0.08	0.05	na
Mother grad degree	0.04	0.02	0.00	0.04	na	0.03
Parent's current legal marital status						
Father married	1.00	na	0.45	0.20	0.03	na
Father divorced	0.00	0.38	0.40	0.37	0.44	na
Father separated	0.00	0.08	0.01	0.11	0.27	na
Father never married	0.00	0.51	0.13	0.32	0.14	na
Father widowed	0.00	0.03	0.01	0.00	0.12	na
Mother married	1.00	na	0.45	0.20	na	0.03
Mother divorced	0.00	0.40	0.24	0.22	na	0.43
Mother separated	0.00	0.09	0.01	0.05	na	0.24
Mother never married	0.00	0.47	0.29	0.52	na	0.17
Mother widowed	0.00	0.04	0.01	0.01	na	0.13
Estimated N	1,400,074	129,991	423	969	99,978	336,036

For gay and lesbian households the "father" is the survey respondent who self-identified as the household head

graduated from high school, the child is almost twice as likely to do so. Finally, marital history has the expected effects. Any marital disruption reduces the odds of a child graduating from high school.[36] For any given household type variable the odds ratio and level of statistical significance is generally robust to the different

---

[36] The odds are reduced to around 70–80 %, but keep in mind this variable contains measurement error.

 Springer

Table 5 Odds ratios of high school graduation (weighted observations, children ages 17–22, dependent variable: 1 if child graduated from high school controlling for moved within past year)

	(1)	(2)	(3)
Gay parents			
Coefficient	**−0.446**	**−0.618**	**−0.374**
Std. error	**(0.255)**	**(0.234)***	**(0.191)***
Odds ratio	**0.64**	**0.54**	**0.69**
Marginal effect	**−0.08**	**−0.13**	**−0.06**
Lesbian parents			
Coefficient	**−0.816**	**−0.925**	**−0.511**
Std. error	**(0.221)***	**(0.240)***	**(0.336)**
Odds ratio	**0.44**	**0.41**	**0.60**
Marginal effect	**−0.17**	**−0.19**	**−0.09**
Common law			
Coefficient	−0.466	−0.338	0.124
Std. error	(0.079)*	(0.066)*	(.111)
Odds ratio	0.63	0.71	1.13
Marginal effect	−0.09	−0.06	0.03
Single mother			
Coefficient	−0.661	−0.672	−0.471
Std. error	(0.041)*	(0.038)*	(0.123)*
Odds ratio	0.51	0.51	0.62
Marginal effect	−0.13	−0.13	−0.09
Single father			
Coefficient	−0.633	−0.685	−0.454
Std. error	(0.039)*	(0.039)*	(0.161)*
Odds ratio	0.53	0.50	0.63
Marginal effect	−0.13	−0.14	−0.09
Child controls	Yes	Yes	Yes
Parent education controls	No	Yes	Yes
Marital status controls	No	No	Yes
Pseudo R^2	.21	.23	.23

The variables of interest are highlighted in bold

* Significant at the 5 % level

specifications. That is, changing the controls does not change the parameter estimates for the association of graduation rates and household type in large ways.

Table 5 shows the associations between family type and child graduation. In all cases, the odds of a child with gay or lesbian parents completing high school are lower, by a considerable margin, compared to children of married opposite sex parents. For gay and lesbian households, adding the parental education controls to the base controls lowers the odds of a child graduating for same-sex families. This is because gay and lesbian homes are characterized by high levels of parent education which contributes to child graduation, and so conditional on this the odds of a child

 Springer

graduating are even lower. When all controls are used, including those for parental marital status, the conditional graduation rate odds ratios are reasonably similar between the two types of same-sex couples: 0.69 for gays and 0.60 for lesbians using the 1 year mobility measure.[37] The difference between the two point estimates for gay and lesbian parents in column (3) is not significant. To put this in another context, the marginal effect on the probability of graduating for children of same-sex homes is a reduction of approximately 6–9 % points.[38] The point estimates for gay households are always statistically significant at the 5 % level, but the estimate for lesbian households in column (3) is not.[39]

Table 6 repeats the column (2) and (3) regressions of Table 5, but this time separating girls and boys. This table shows that the particular gender mix of a same sex household has a dramatic difference in the association with child graduation. Consider the case of girls first. Regardless of the controls and whether or not girls are currently living in a gay or lesbian household, the odds of graduating from high school are considerably lower than any other household type. Indeed, girls living in gay households are only 15 % as likely to graduate compared to girls from opposite sex married homes. In all cases for girls the estimates are measured with precision.

The point estimates for boys are considerably different. Looking at equation (4) in Table 6, boys in lesbian homes are 76 % as likely to graduate, while boys in gay homes are 61 % *more* likely to graduate compared to boys in opposite sex married homes. However, none of these estimates are statistically significant. the results from Table 5 mask this gender difference, and the significant effect found in Table 5 column (3) for gay households is clearly being driven by the strong daughter effect.

The different results for the household gender mix are fascinating, especially since this difference is not found in single parent households. Table 6 shows that boys do better than girls in single parent homes, but the difference is not nearly as pronounced as in same sex households. Looking at the unconditional graduation rates (with standard errors in parentheses) for gay households, sons achieve 0.72 (0.074), while daughters achieve 0.43 (0.090). For lesbian households, son's graduation rates are 0.48 (0.060), and daughter's have 0.55 (0.055). Based simply on these unconditional measures, sons do better with fathers, and daughters do better with mothers.

---

[37] They are also reasonably close to the unconditional estimated average graduation rates found in Table 3. The odds ratios are .71 and .64 for the 5 year mobility measure.

[38] The reported odds ratios are relative to children from opposite sex married parents. Compared to children of opposite sex cohabiting parents, the children of same-sex parents do even worse. This can be seen indirectly from Table 5. If cohabiting parents are the left out category, the odds ratio (standard error) for high school graduation from a gay home is 0.61 (0.132), and 0.53 (0.138) from a lesbian home—when all controls are used.

[39] In order to further test the idea that lower graduation rates for children of gay and lesbian parents may be the result of a negative environment, more controls were used for location. Rather than just control for the province of residence, in an alternative specification the census metropolitan area was also controlled for. For gay parents the odds ratio changes from 0.69 to 0.68 if the 1 year mobility control is used with all other controls, and remains unchanged if the 5 year mobility control is used. For lesbian parents the odd ration changes from 0.60 to 0.57, and from 0.64 to 0.58 depending on the mobility control. These estimates have slightly lower standard errors.

 Springer

Table 6 Odds ratios of high school graduation (weighted observations, children ages 17–22, dependent variable: 1 if child graduated from high school controlling for moved within past year)

	Girls		Boys	
	(1)	(2)	(3)	(4)
Gay parents				
Coefficient	**−1.939**	**−1.860**	**0.225**	**0.476**
Std error	**(0.109)***	**(0.244)***	**(0.510)**	**(0.491)**
Odds ratio	**0.14**	**0.15**	**1.25**	**1.61**
Marginal effect	**−0.42**	**−0.40**	**0.04**	**0.08**
Lesbian parents				
Coefficient	**−0.913**	**−0.796**	**−0.883**	**−0.269**
Std error	**(0.165)***	**(0.365)***	**(0.441)***	**(0.519)**
Odds ratio	**0.40**	**0.45**	**0.41**	**0.76**
Marginal effect	**−0.17**	**−0.14**	**−0.20**	**−0.06**
Common law				
Coefficient	−0.180	−0.072	−0.450	0.214
Std error	(0.053)*	(0.313)	(0.079)*	(0.109)
Odds ratio	0.83	0.93	0.64	1.23
Marginal effect	−0.027	−0.010	−0.099	0.042
Single mother				
Coefficient	−0.663	−0.672	−0.723	−0.371
Std error	(0.031)*	(0.350)	(0.049)*	(0.064)*
Odds ratio	0.55	0.51	0.48	0.68
Marginal effect	−0.099	−0.112	−0.160	−0.079
Single father				
Coefficient	−0.615	−0.761	−0.721	−0.274
Std error	(0.048)*	(0.379)*	(0.042)*	(0.092)*
Odds ratio	0.54	0.46	0.48	0.76
Marginal effect	−0.106	−0.113	−0.164	−0.058
Child controls	Yes	Yes	Yes	Yes
Parent education controls	Yes	Yes	Yes	Yes
Marital status controls	No	Yes	No	Yes
Pseudo R^2	.26	.26	.21	.21

The variables of interest are highlighted in bold

* Significant at the 5 % level

At this state, such a result is an interesting empirical finding, and one worthy of further investigation. On the one hand, it seems this result is inconsistent with any type of discrimination theory for the lower graduation rates among children of same-sex households. Or, a discrimination theory would have to be modified to include the household gender mix. Within the child development literature and pop culture, there is the belief that mothers and fathers provide different parenting inputs

 Springer

that are not perfectly substitutable.[40] These results would be consistent with this notion, but further research is necessary to show any causality.

4.2 School attendance

Any difference found in graduation rates may be the result of a selection bias—children of same-sex families may be less likely to attend school. In this section, school attendance is investigated. Table 7 reports on four logit regressions, where the dependent variable equals 1 if the child attended school between September 2005 to May 2006; that is, if the child was in school during the previous year. School attendance is mandatory in Canada until age 15, thus children between 17–22 who do not attend have either quit, been expelled, or graduated already. The structure of the first three regressions of Table 7 is the same as Table 5.[41] The last regression in column (4) controls for the gender mix of the household.

In terms of the odds ratios results for unreported controls, being disabled or moving residences both lead to a reduced chance of attending school, while being a visible minority, older, and urban increase the odds of attending.[42] Having a parent who graduated school significantly increases the odds of a child attending.

In terms of the odds ratios reported in the table, once all controls are in place, column (3) shows that each family type is more likely to have their children in school compared to married parents (the omitted category). Indeed, lesbian households are 23 % more likely, while gays are about 16 % more likely. None of the column (3) coefficients are statistically significant; that is, there is little statistical confidence in the difference between married opposite sex and other family types when it comes to child school attendance. Indeed, none of the odds ratios for any family type are statistically different from each other. The bottom line from Table 7 is that in terms of school attendance, a conclusion of "no difference," between children of gay, lesbian, and married families is reasonable, and therefore, any difference in graduation rates is unlikely caused by a selection bias based on attendance.

---

[40] Within the literature, see Chrisp (2001), which addresses sons in lesbian homes. Within the popular culture, see *Modern Family*, Season 4, Episode 19, where the gay couple Cam and Mitchell decide their daughter Lily needs the input of aunt Gloria to discuss "girl issues."

[41] For school attendance only the results for the 1 year mobility control are reported. The results for controlling for 5 year mobility were virtually identical. An unreported regression on primary school attendance found no difference between the different household types

[42] It might seem odd that the effect of Age is positive. However, the dependent variable is 1 if the child *ever* attended school, or is now attending. Given that some students start school later than age 5, and that many children are home schooled in primary divisions, a positive effect of Age is expected. If the regression is run restricting the sample to students older than 12, the age effect is greatly removed. When the sample is restricted to various age ranges (e.g., starting at ages 6–12, or ending at ages 17–22, the odds ratios for the family type variables barely change at all and remain statistically indistinguishable.

 Springer

Table 7 Odds ratios of school attendance (weighted observations, children ages 17–22, dependent variable: 1 if child graduated from high school controlling for moved within past 5 years)

	(1)	(2)	(3)	(4)
Gay parents				
Coefficient	−0.019	0.006	0.149	
Std error	(0.259)	(0.260)	(0.311)	
Odds ratio	0.980	1.05	1.16	
Marginal effect	0.004	0.009	0.034	
Daughter of gay parents				
Coefficient				0.166
Std error				(0.437)
Odds ratio				1.18
Marginal effect				0.038
Son of gay parents				
Coefficient				0.737
Std error				(0.287)*
Odds ratio				1.14
Marginal effect				0.031
Lesbian parents				
Coefficient	−0.020	−0.013	0.208	
Std error	(0.084)	(0.083)	(0.137)	
Odds ratio	0.979	0.986	1.23	
Marginal effect	−0.004	−0.003	0.047	
Daughter of lesbian parents				
Coefficient				0.277
Std error				(0.144)
Odds ratio				1.31
Marginal effect				0.063
Son of lesbian parents				
Coefficient				0.143
Std error				(0.250)
Odds ratio				1.15
Marginal effect				0.033
Common law				
Coefficient	−0.179	−0.186	0.093	0.092
Std error	(0.042)*	(0.040)*	(0.076)	(0.076)
Odds ratio	0.835	0.829	1.09	1.09
Marginal effect	−0.043	−0.044	0.022	0.021
Single mother				
Coefficient	−0.106	−0.100	0.091	0.091
Std error	(0.025)*	(0.277)*	(0.076)	(0.076)
Odds ratio	0.898	0.904	1.090	1.090
Marginal effect	−0.025	−0.0249	0.021	0.021

 Springer

Table 7 continued

	(1)	(2)	(3)	(4)
Single father				
Coefficient	−0.213	−0.192	0.112	0.112
Std error	(0.036)*	(0.037)	(0.082)	(0.082)
Odds ratio	0.806	0.825	1.120	1.120
Marginal effect	−0.041	−0.046	0.026	0.026
Child controls	Yes	Yes	Yes	Yes
Parent education controls	No	Yes	Yes	Yes
Marital status controls	No	No	Yes	Yes
Pseudo R^2	.11	.11	.12	.12

The variables of interest are highlighted in bold

* Significant at the 5 % level

5 Conclusion

A casual reading of the literature on child performance would suggest that no-difference in child outcomes exists between children in same-sex or opposite-sex households. Indeed, the unanimous opinion of so many studies would appear conclusive—as noted by Justice Walker. However, a closer inspection reveals that there are really fifty-plus "preliminary" studies, and no general conclusion about child performance differences is warranted based on the literature. The samples used in these studies are often biased in some way, and the sample sizes are often very small. The one study that did use a large random sample and address a reliable performance measure (Rosenfeld 2010), turned out to draw the wrong conclusion, did not compare gay versus lesbian homes, did not examine the gender mix of the household, and did not control for parental marital status. As a result, there is little hard evidence to support the general popular consensus of "no difference."

I have argued that the 2006 Canada census—though not perfect—is able to address most of these issues, and the results on high school graduation rates suggest that children living in both gay and lesbian households struggle compared to children from opposite sex married households. In general, it appears that these children are only about 65 % as likely to graduate from high school compared to the control group—a difference that holds whether conditioned on controls or not.[43] When the households are broken down by child gender it appears that daughters are struggling more than sons, and that daughters of gay parents have strikingly low graduation rates.

This paper confirms the findings of Allen et al. (2013), and taken together they cast doubt on the ubiquitous claim that no difference exists in child outcomes for children

---

[43] As mentioned, the census data has an imperfect measure of marital status. Those "currently married" could be divorced from an earlier marriage. Given the higher marriage rate for opposite sex couples, the estimated odds ratio on graduation rates for children of same-sex families may be biased *upwards*. The true effect may be larger and more troubling.

 Springer

raised by same-sex parents compared to married opposite sex parents. That is, both the US census and Canada census show that children living with same-sex parents perform poorer in school when compared to children from married opposite sex families.

The question is: why? This study suggests further work is necessary to narrow down the source of this difference. This will require an exceptional data set that not only identifies sexual orientation of parents, but also has a retrospective or panel design to completely control for marital history. A better data set would also be able to test for the reasons behind any difference. An economist may be inclined to think that fathers and mothers are not perfect substitutes and that there must be some gains from a sexual division of labor in parenting. Others may suspect that children of same-sex parents are more likely to be harassed at school, and therefore, less likely to graduate. In any event, it is time to investigate the difference and reject the conventional wisdom of "no difference."

Acknowledgments Thanks to Sonia Oreffice, Krishna Pendakur, and three journal referees for their comments. This project was funded by the Social Sciences Research Council of Canada.

Appendix

See Table 8.

Table 8 Odds ratios of high school graduation (weighted observations, children ages 17–22, dependent variable: 1 if child graduated from high school controlling for moved within past 5 years)

	(1)	(2)	(3)
Gay parents	**0.66**	**0.55**	**0.71**
Marginal effect	**−0.08**	**−0.13**	**−0.05**
	(0.208)	**(0.132)***	**(0.135)**
Lesbian parents	**0.47**	**0.42**	**0.64**
Marginal effect	**−0.16**	**−0.18**	**−0.08**
	(0.085)*	**(0.095)***	**(0.205)**
Common law	0.65	0.73	1.17
Marginal effect	−0.09	−0.06	0.04
	(0.208)*	(0.048)*	(0.131)*
Single mother	0.53	0.52	0.65
Marginal effect	−0.13	−0.13	−0.06
	(0.007)*	(0.021)*	(0.082)*
Single father	0.55	0.51	0.66
Marginal effect	−0.14	−0.13	−0.06
	(0.012)*	(0.021)*	(0.106)*
Child controls	Yes	Yes	Yes
Parent education controls	No	Yes	Yes
Marital status controls	No	No	Yes
Pseudo R^2	.21	.23	.23

* Significant at the 5 % level. z scores in parentheses

 Springer

References

Allen, D. W. (2012). More heat than light: A critical assessment of the same-sex parenting literature, 1995–2012. Working paper, Simon Fraser University

Allen, D. W.., Pakaluk, C., & Price, J. (2013). Nontraditional families and childhood progress through school: A comment on Rosenfeld. *Demography, 50*(3), 955–961.

Andersson, G., Noack, T., Seierstad, A., & Weedon-Fekjaer, H. (2006). The demographics of same-sex marriages in Norway and Sweden. *Demography, 43*(1), 79–98.

Badgett, M. V. L., Gates, G., & Maisel, N. (2008). Registered domestic partnerships among gay men and lesbians: The role of economic factors. *Review of Economics of the Household, 6*(4), 327–346.

Bailey, J. M., Bobrow, D., Wolfe, M., & Mikach, S. (1995). Sexual orientation of adult sons of gay fathers. *Developmental Psychology, 31*(1), 124–129.

Balsam, K., Beauchaine, T., Rothblum, E., & Solomon, S. (2008). Three-year follow-up of same-sex couples who had civil unions in Vermont, same-sex couples not in civil unions, and heterosexual married couples. *Developmental Psychology, 44*(1), 102–116.

Barrett, H., & Tasker, F. (2001). Growing up with a gay parent: Views of 101 gay fathers on their sons' and daughters' experiences. *Educational and Child Psychology, 18*(1), 62–77.

Becker, G. (1981). *A treatise on the family*. Cambridge: Harvard University Press.

Biblarz, T., & Stacey, J. (2010). How does the gender of parents matter?. *Journal of Marriage and Family, 72*, 3–22.

Biblarz, T., & Savci, E. (2010). Lesbian, gay, bisexual, and transgender families. *Journal of Marriage and Family, 72*, 480–497.

Black, D., Sanders, S., & Taylor, L. (2007). The economics of lesbian and gay families. *Journal of Economic Perspectives., 21*(2), 53–70.

Black, D., Sanders, S., & Taylor, L. (2006). The measurement of same-sex unmarried partner couples in the 2000 US Census. California Center for Population Research Working Paper, 2007b.

Booth, A., & Frank, J. (2008). Marriage, partnership and sexual orientation: A study of British university academics and administrators. *Review of Economics of the Household, 6*(4), 409–422.

Bos, H. (2010). Planned gay father families in kinship arrangements. *Australia and New Zealand Journal of Family Therapy, 31*(4), 356–371.

Bos, H., & van Balen, F. (2008). Children in planned lesbian families: Stigmatisation, psychological adjustment and protective factors. *Culture, Health, and Sexuality, 10*(3), 221–236.

Bos, H., van Balen, F., & van den Boom, D. (2007). Child adjustment and parenting in planned lesbian parent families. *American Journal of Orthopsychiatry, 77*(1), 38–48.

Bos, H., van Balen, F., van den Boom, D., & Sandfort, Th. (2004). Minority stress, experience of parenthood and child adjustment in lesbian families. *Journal of Reproductive and Infant Psychology, 22*(4), 1–14.

Bos, H., van Balen, F., Gartrell, N., Peyser, H., & Sandfort, T. (2008). Children in planned lesbian families: A cross-cultural comparison between the United States and the Netherlands. *American Journal of Orthopsychiatry, 78*(2), 211–219.

Brewaeys, A., Ponjaert, I., Van Hall, E. V., & Golombok, S. (1997). Donor insemination: Child development and family functioning in lesbian mother families. *Human Reproduction, 12*(6), 1349–1359.

Carpenter, C., & Gates, G. (2008). Gay and lesbian partnership: Evidence from California. *Demography, 45*(3), 573–590.

Chan, R., Brooks, R., Raboy, B., & Patterson, C. (1998a). Division of labor among lesbian and heterosexual parents: Associations with children's adjustment. *Journal of Family Psychology, 12*(3), 402–419.

Chan, R., Raboy, B., & Patterson, C. (1998b). Psychosocial adjustment among children conceived via donor insemination by lesbian and heterosexual mothers. *Child Development, 69*(2), 443–457.

Chrisp, J. (2001). That four letter word–sons: Lesbian mothers and adolescent son. *Journal of Lesbian Studies, 5*(1-2), 195–209.

Clarke, V., Kitzinger, C., & Potter, J. (2004). Kids are just cruel anyway: Lesbian and gay parents talk about homophobic bullying. *British Journal of Social Psychology, 43*, 531–550.

Cloughessy, K. (2010). Sorry, but you're not a mother: An examination of the validity of the de facto threshold in determining motherhood for the non-birth mother in lesbian-parented families. *Gay& Lesbian Issues and Psychology Review, 6*(2), 82–90.

Dundas, S., & Kaufman, M. (2000). The Toronto lesbian family study. *Journal of Homosexuality, 40*, 65–79.

Fairtlough, A. (2008). Growing up with a lesbian or gay parent: Young people's perspectives. *Health and Social Care in the Community, 16*(5), 521–528.

Flaks, D., Ficher, I., Masterpasqua, F., & Joseph, G. (1995). Lesbians choosing motherhood: A comparative study of lesbian and heterosexual parents and their children. *Developmental Psychology, 31*(1), 105–114.

Fulcher, M., Sutfin, E., & Patterson, C. (2008). Individual differences in gender development: Associations with parental sexual orientation, attitudes, and division of labor. *Sex Roles, 58*, 330–341.

Fulcher, M., Chan, R., Raboy, B., & Patterson, C. (2002). Contact with grandparents among children conceived via donor insemination by lesbian and heterosexual mothers. *Parenting: Science and Practice, 2*(1), 61–76.

Gartrell, N., Bos, H. (2010). US national longitudinal lesbian family study: Psychological adjustment of 17 year old adolescents. *Pediatrics*, doi:10.1542/peds.2009-3153.

Gartrell, N., Deck, A., Rodas, C., & Peyser, H. (2005). The national lesbian family study 4: Interviews with the 10-year old children. *American Journal of Orthopsychiatry, 75*(4), 518–524.

Gartrell, N., Banks, A., Reed, N., Hamilton, J., Rodas, C., & Deck, A. (2000). The national lesbian family study 3: Interviews with mothers of five-year olds. *American Journal of Orthopsychiatry, 70*(4), 542–548.

Gartrell, N., Banks, A., Reed, N., Hamilton, J., Rodas, C., & Biship, H. (1999). The national lesbian family study: 2. Interviews with mothers of toddlers. *American Journal of Orthopsychiatry, 69*(3), 362–369.

Gershon, T., Tschann, J., & Jemerin, J. (1999). Stigmatization, self-esteem, and coping among the adolescent children of lesbian mothers. *Journal of Adolescent Health, 24*, 437–445.

Goldberg, A. (2010). *Lesbian and gay parents and their children: Research on the family life cycle*. Washington, DC: American Psychological Association.

Goldberg, A. (2007). (How) does it make a difference? Perspectives of adults with lesbian, gay, and bisexual parents. *American Journal of Orthopsychiatry, 77*(4), 550–562.

Goldberg, A., Downing, J., & Sauck, C. (2008). Perceptions of children's parental preferences in lesbian two-mother households. *Journal of Marriage and Family, 70*, 419–434.

Golombok, S., Perry, B., Burston, A., Murray, C., Mooney-Somers, J., Stevens, M., Golding, J.et al. (2003). Children with lesbian parents: A community study. *Developmental Psychology, 39*(1), 20–33.

Golombok, S., & Tasker, F. (1996). Do parents influence the sexual orientation of their children? Findings from a longitudinal study of lesbian families. *Developmental Psychology, 32*(1), 3–11.

Golombok, S., Tasker, F., & Murray, C. (1997). Children raised in fatherless families from Infancy: Family relationships and the socioemotional development of children of lesbian and single heterosexual mothers. *Journal of Child Psychology and Psychiatry, 38*, 783–791.

Jepsen, C., & Jepsen, L. (2009). Does home ownership vary by sexual orientation?. *Regional Science and Urban Economics, 39*(3), 307–315.

Klawitter, M. (2008). The effects of sexual orientation and marital status on how couples hold their money. *Review of Economics and the Household, 6*(4), 423–446.

Lehmiller, J. (2010). Differences in relationship investments between gay and heterosexual men. *Personal Relationships, 17*(1), 81–96.

Leung, P., Erich, S., & Kanenberg, H. (2005). A comparison of family functions in gay/lesbian, heterosexual and special needs adoptions. *Children and Youth Services Review, 27*, 1031–1044.

Lev, A. (2008). More than surface tension: Femmes in families. *Journal of Lesbian Studies, 12*(2-3), 126–143.

Lewin, E. (2006). Book review: 'The family of woman: Lesbian mothers, their children and the undoing of gender' by Maureen Sullivan. *Theory and Society, 35*, 601–605.

MacCallum, F., & Golombok, S. (2004). Children raised in fatherless families from infancy: A follow-up of children of lesbian and single heterosexual mothers at early adolescence. *Journal of Child Psychology and Psychiatry, 45*(8), 1407–1419.

Marks, L. (2012). Same-sex parenting and children's outcomes: A closer examination of the American Psychological Association's brief on lesbian and gay parenting. *Social Science Research, 41*(4), 735–751.

 Springer

McNeill, K., & Rienzi, B. (1998). Families and parenting: A comparison of lesbian and heterosexual mothers. *Psychological Reports, 82*, 59–62.

Negrusa, B., & Oreffice, S. (2011). Sexual orientation and household financial decisions. Evidence from couples in the United States. *Review of Economics of the Household, 18*(2), 445–463.

Nock, S. L. (2001). Sworn affidavit of Stephen Lowell Nock. Ontario Superior Court of Justice. Between Hedy Halpern et al. and the Attorney General of Canada et al.: Court File No. 684/00.

Oreffice, S. (2010). Sexual orientation and household decision making. Same-sex couples balance of power and labor supply choices. *Labour Economics, 18*(2), 145–158.

Oswald, R., Goldberg, A., Kuvalanka, K., & Clausell, E. (2008). Structural and moral commitment among same-sex couples: Relationship duration, religiosity, and parental status. *Journal of Family Psychology, 22*(3), 411–419.

Patterson, C. (1995). Families of the lesbian baby boom: Parent's division of labor and children's adjustment. *Developmental Psychology, 31*(1), 411–419.

Patterson, C. (2001). Families of the lesbian baby boom: Maternal mental health and child adjustment. *Journal of Gay & Lesbian Psychotherapy, 4*(3/4), 91–107.

Patterson, C., Hurt, S., & Mason, C. (1998). Families of the lesbian baby boom: Children's contact with grandparents and other adults. *American Journal of Orthopsychiatry, 68*(3), 390–399.

Patterson, C., Sutfin, E., & Fulcher, M. (2004). Division of labor among lesbian and heterosexual parenting couples: Correlates of specialized versus shared patterns. *Journal of Adult Development, 11*(3), 179–189.

Power, J., Perlesz, A., Brown, R., Schofield, M., Pitts, M., Mcnair, R., Bickerdike, A.et al. (2010). Diversity, tradition and family: Australian same sex attracted parents and their families. *Gay& Lesbian Issues and Psychology Review, 6*(2), 66–81.

Regnerus, M. (2012). How different are the adult children of parents who have same-sex relationships? Findings from the New Family Structures Study. *Social Science Research, 41*(4), 752–770.

Rivers, I., Poteat, V. P., & Noret, N. (2008). Victimization, social support, and psychosocial functioning among children of same-sex and opposite-sex couples in the United Kingdom. *Developmental Psychology, 44*(1), 127–134.

Rothblum, E., Balsam, K., & Solomon, S. (2008). Comparison of same-sex couples who were married in Massachusetts, had domestic partnerships in California, or had civil unions in Vermont. *Journal of Family Issues, 29*(1), 48–78.

Rosenfeld, M. (2010). Nontraditional families and childhood progress through school. *Demography, 47*(3), 755–775.

Sarantkos, S. (1996). Children in three contexts: Family, education, and social development. *Children Australia, 21*, 23–31.

Scheib, J., Riordan, M., & Rubin, S. (2005). Adolescents with open-identity sperm donors: Reports from 12–17 year olds. *Human Reproduction, 20*(1), 239–252.

Stacey, J. (2005). The families of man: Gay male intimacy and kinship in a global metropolis. *Journal of Women in Culture and Society, 30*(3), 1911–1937.

Stacey, J. (2004). Cruising to familyland: Gay hypergamy and rainbow kinship. *Current Sociology, 52*(2), 181–197.

Stacey, J., & Biblarz, T. (2001). (How) does the sexual orientation of parents matter?. *American Sociological Review, 66*, 159–183.

Sutfin, E. L., Fulcher, M., Bowles, R. P., & Patterson, C. J. (2008). How lesbian and heterosexual parents convey attitudes about gender to their children: The role of gendered environments. *Sex Roles, 58*, 501–513.

Sweet, M. (2009). The science of unisex parenting: A review of published studies. (unpublished manuscript).

Tasker, F., & Golombok, S. (1995). Adults raised as children in lesbian families. *American Journal of Orthopsychiatry, 65*(2), 203–215.

Vanfraussen, K., Ponjaert-Kristoffersen, I., & Brewaeys, A. (2002). What does it mean for youngsters to grow up in a lesbian family created by means of donor insemination?. *Journal of Reproductive and Infant Psychology, 20*(4), 237–252.

Wainright, J., & Patterson, C. (2006). Delinquency, victimization, and substance use among adolescents with female same sex parents. *Journal of Family Psychology, 20*(3), 526–530.

Wainright, J., & Patterson, C. (2008). Peer relations among adolescents with female same-sex parents. *Developmental Psychology, 44*(1), 117–126.

 Springer

Wainright, J., Russell, S., & Patterson, C. (2004). Psychosocial adjustment, school outcomes, and romantic relationships of adolescents with same sex parents. *Child Development, 75*(6), 1886–1898.

Wright, E., & Perry, B. (2006). Sexual identity distress, social support, and the health of gay, lesbian, and bisexual youth. *Journal of Homosexuality, 51*(1), 81–110.

Zavodny, M. (2008). Is there a 'marriage premium' for gay men?. *Review of Economics of the Household, 6*(4), 369–389.

 Springer

Summary of Walter R. Schumm's

"Comparative Relationship Stability of Lesbian Mother and Heterosexual Mother Families: A Review of Evidence"

Marriage & Family Review 46:8 (2010): 499–509,
http://dx.doi.org/10.1080/01494929.2010.543030

Schumm begins by noting that the scholarly literature on lesbian relationship stability is varied but tends toward the conclusion that either very little is known about lesbian relationship stability or (more optimistically) that lesbian relationships are just as stable—if not more stable—than opposite-sex relationships.[1] In 2010, however, Biblarz and Stacey published a paper in which they claimed that lesbian parents were more at risk of separation than were heterosexual parents. They cited only one paper in support of this thesis, so the claim seemed questionable.[2]

Schumm suggests that scholars do not want to acknowledge what is already known about lesbian relationship instability: "Do we really know so little about the stability of same-sex parents versus heterosexual parents? In fact, we *already* have numerous studies from English speaking countries. . . ."[3] He divides the available research into three groups and argues that there is more evidence than is acknowledged for the view that relationships of lesbian parents are less stable than those of opposite-sex parents.

The three groups of research papers are (1) studies that look at the stability of same-sex-couple relationships by themselves, without comparing them to those of opposite-sex couples, (2) studies that look at the stability of opposite-sex relationships by themselves, without comparing them to same-sex relationships, and (3) studies that look at both the stability of same-sex relationships as well as of a control group of opposite-sex relationships.

Separation Rates for Same-Sex Parenting Couples (no Comparison Group)

Schumm reports the findings of eight research papers on lesbian separation rates. After summarizing the findings of each, he averages the separation rates together and concludes: "It appears that instability rates for lesbian parents range from as low as 13% over 6 years to as high as 75% over 15 years, with an average of 42.9% breaking up over an average of 9.4 years."[4]

Average Separation Rate for Lesbian Parenting Couples

Separation Rates for Opposite-Sex Married Parents
(no Comparison Group)

Next, Schumm reports the findings of seventeen research papers on heterosexual relationships that also do not include a comparison group. While total divorce estimates for married couples in the United States range from 40 to 44 percent,[5] the figures are lower for those who are parents: "For heterosexual parents separation rates appear to range between 6% at 3 years and 31% at 25 years with an average across studies of about 15.5% at an average of about 13 years."[6]

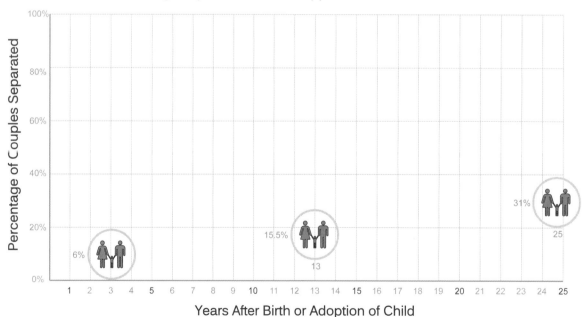

Average Separation Rate for Opposite-Sex Married Parents

Schumm notes that higher education and paternity (being a parent) promote relationship stability among married couples and that the method of conception of the child (whether natural, adoptive, donor inseminated, or in vitro) does not appear to make any difference in later breakup rates.

Separation Rates for Lesbian Parenting Couples
(with a Comparison Group of Opposite-Sex-Parenting Couples)

The paper that Biblarz and Stacey cite on lesbian parent instability had reported a 43-percent separation rate for lesbian parenting couples, compared to a 13-percent separation rate for opposite-sex parenting couples, for parents of children six to twelve years old.[7] Schumm notes that Biblarz and Stacey overlooked at least three additional studies that corroborate this trend. One of those studies is the famous National Longitudinal Lesbian Family Study (NLLFS). Gartrell and colleagues reported that 31 percent of these lesbian couples had separated by five years and that 56.3 percent had separated after seventeen years.[8]

Schumm reports the findings of additional studies and concludes,

> Across these four studies over similar periods of time, it appears that the odds of lesbian couples breaking up are over three times greater than the odds of heterosexual couples breaking up. Regardless of methodology used, it appears that 15% to 20% of heterosexual parents are likely to break up by 10 years compared with about 40% to 45% of lesbian parents.[9]

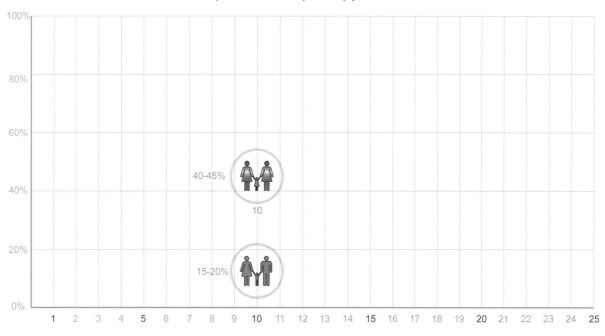

Average Separation Rate for Two Female Parents with Comparison Group of Opposite-Sex Parents

Why Might Lesbian Couples Be Less Stable?

Schumm discusses five possible reasons that could explain why lesbian parenting relationships are less stable than those of opposite-sex couples.

First, the lesbian parents appear to adhere less to traditional moral values. Schumm notes that research on gay, lesbian, and heterosexual couples has found that while heterosexual couples cite "moral values" as a deterrent for instability, same-sex couples score zero on moral values as a deterrent for instability. Schumm explains why this is noteworthy: "'None' is a pretty remarkable and rare occurrence in attitudinal research; usually, someone checks an infrequently checked box merely because of fatigue, confusion, or indifference."[10] His hypothesis is that traditional moral values— which encourage couples to stay together—influence opposite-sex couples more than they influence same-sex couples. He emphasizes, however, that further research is needed to confirm this possibility.

A second possibility is that lesbian-parenting-couple instability is related to "being in a second or third relationship," and the associated stresses that come with that.[11]

A third possibility is that lesbian parents may have greater financial independence in general than do opposite-sex couples, making them better able to handle the financial consequences of a breakup and so less deterred from separating.

A fourth possibility relates to the biological asymmetry lesbian couples experience when one of the mothers has a biological connection to the child while the other does not. A biological mother looking to separate from a lesbian partner may have less fear of custody battles than would a biological mother married to the biological father of her child. In this case, the biological connection of *two* parents to a child may serve as a greater deterrent to separation.

And fifth, Schumm considers that the civil institution of marriage may help opposite-sex couples achieve greater stability. Since the legal landscape is changing on this matter, "the research situation will probably remain fluid"[12] for quite some time, and it will be difficult to test this hypothesis.

In the end, Schumm calls for more research to better understand the various underlying factors related to instability for both lesbian and heterosexual couples: "However controversial this review may prove to be, hopefully it will stimulate further such research from a wide range of diligent scholars, an outcome that most scholars can probably support."[13]

Notes

1. From 2003 to 2010, six researchers argued that there was little to no research available on the subject, one (Richard Redding) claimed that there were no differences between the stability of lesbian families and heterosexual families, and one (Abbie Goldberg) claimed that lesbian relationships might be more stable than those of heterosexual couples. See Richard E. Redding, "It's Really about Sex: Same-Sex Marriage, Lesbigay Parenting, and the Psychology of Disgust," *Duke Journal of Gender Law & Policy* 15:127 (2008): 127–193; Abbie E. Goldberg, *Lesbian and Gay Parents and Their Children: Research on the Family Life Cycle* (Washington, DC: American Psychological Association, 2010).
2. See Timothy J. Biblarz and Judith Stacey, "How Does the Gender of Parents Matter?" *Journal of Marriage and Family* 72 (February 2010): 3–22.
3. Schumm, 501 (original emphasis).
4. Ibid., 502.
5. Ibid., 503, citing Robert Schoen and Nicola Standish, "The Retrenchment of Marriage: Results from Marital Status Life Tables for the United States, 1995," *Population and Development Review* 27 (September 2001): 553–563.
6. Schumm, 503.
7. Biblarz and Stacey cite Fiona MacCallum and Susan Golombok, "Children Raised in Fatherless Families from Infancy: A Follow-up of Children of Lesbian and Single Heterosexual Mothers at Early Adolescence," *Journal of Child Psychology and Psychiatry* 45 (November 2004): 1407–1419.

8. Schumm, 504. He cites Nanette Gartrell and Henny Bos, "US National Longitudinal Lesbian Family Study: Psychological Adjustment of 17-year-old Adolescents, *Pediatrics* 126: 28–36; Nanette Gartrell et al., "The National Lesbian Family Study: 3. Interviews with Mothers of Five-Year-Olds," *American Journal of Orthopsychiatry* 70: 542–548.

9. Schumm, 504–505.

10. Ibid., 505.

11. Ibid. Here, Schumm cites Kristin P. Beals, Emily A. Impett, and Letitia Anne Peplau, "Lesbians in Love: Why Some Relationships Endure and Others End," *Journal of Lesbian Studies* 6:1: 53–63; Ramona Faith Oswald et al., "Structural and Moral Commitment Among Same-Sex Couples: Relationship Duration, Religiosity, and Parental Status," *Journal of Family Psychology* 22 (June 2008): 411–419.

12. Schumm, 506.

13. Ibid.

Marriage & Family Review, 46:499–509, 2010
Copyright © Taylor & Francis Group, LLC
ISSN: 0149-4929 print/1540-9635 online
DOI: 10.1080/01494929.2010.543030

Comparative Relationship Stability of Lesbian Mother and Heterosexual Mother Families: A Review of Evidence

WALTER R. SCHUMM

*School of Family Studies and Human Services,
Kansas State University, Manhattan, Kansas, USA*

It has been concluded from a review of the literature involving only one study that lesbian parents were more likely to have unstable relationships. Other scholars have struggled with considerable controversy over how much was or was not known about the stability of lesbian parent relationships as well as whether such relationships were more or less stable than heterosexual parent relationships. Arguments have been made on all sides of the issues. A careful review of the literature suggests that more is known about the stability of lesbian parent relationships than previously suspected and that, on average, such relationships tend to be less stable than those of married heterosexual parents. Less is understood about the factors that may influence relationship stability for gay or lesbian parents, creating a critical need for additional research, especially with different demographic subgroups of lesbian and gay parents.

KEYWORDS bisexual, development or outcomes, family structure, fathering, gay, gender, lesbian, parenting and parenthood

Biblarz and Stacey desired "to revive conversation among scholars about research on gender differences in parenting and child development" (2010a, p. 4), and they reviewed considerable evidence on the effects of same-sex parenting on children. One of their conclusions was that lesbian parents had less stable relationships than heterosexual parents, a hypothesis

---

Address correspondence to Walter R. Schumm, School of Family Studies and Human Services, Kansas State University, Justin Hall, 1700 Anderson Avenue, Manhattan, KS 66506-1403, USA. E-mail: schumm@ksu.edu

supported by only one cited study (MacCallum & Golombok, 2004). Basing a conclusion on only one study would seem unwarranted in most situations (Schumm, 2010b); thus, Biblarz and Stacey's conclusion might seem doubtful. At the same time, delving into a controversial area of the literature may seem risky—witness the Internet furor over a recent article (Schumm, 2010a). However, an editor should lead by example; I have asked for controversial articles and for review articles, so it would be an issue for me to shy away from them myself. Comments on this review of the literature are, as always, welcomed!

METHODS

Social science literature was reviewed to determine if there were additional studies that might have addressed the relative stability of lesbian versus heterosexual mother families. Searching the literature is challenging in some areas because controversial outcomes often do not find their way into article summaries or abstracts; in other words, something close to detective work is required to find much of the information. The convention of .20, .50, and .80 for, respectively, small, medium, and large effect sizes (ES) are used throughout the discussion in addition to levels of statistical significance (Cohen, 1988; Lippa, 2005). A small effect size does not mean that it is unimportant; even if its associated significance level is not significant, that may only reflect the use of a small sample size with low statistical power. As Cohen, Cohen, West, and Aiken (2003) observed, "Yet many research reports, at least implicitly, confuse the issues of effect size and level of statistical significance, using the latter as if it meant the former" (p. 5).

RESULTS OF THE REVIEW

Background Controversy

Many would agree with Kurdek's (2005) statement that "Perhaps the most important 'bottom-line' question asked about gay and lesbian couples is whether their relationships last" (p. 252). Recent research suggests that multiple structural changes in the family can impact children adversely, regardless of the family form (Strohschein, 2010), so the issue has important implications for the long-term welfare of children. However, controversy remains regarding (1) whether we know anything about such relationship stability and (2) about the direction of effects, if any. Goldberg (2010a) has noted that research on the stability of gay and lesbian relationships was "quite slim" (p. 114); Peplau and Fingerhut (2007) regretted that "we currently know little about the longevity of same-sex relationships" (p. 412).

Ball (2003, p. 726) reported being unaware of any study ever done on the relative stability of lesbian and heterosexual parents. Baetens and Brewaeys (2001) dismissed any idea that lesbian couples had greater instability than heterosexual couples as a myth. Redding (2008) in his major review of the literature on gay and lesbian parenting concluded "that lesbi-gay families are just as stable for childrearing as heterosexual families" (p. 164). In contrast, however, Kurdek (2005) reviewed the literature and concluded that "The limited data available indicate that gay and lesbian couples may be less stable than married heterosexual couples" (p. 251). On the other hand, Goldberg (2010a, p. 26) suggested that relationships consisting of two women might have *enhanced* stability. Goldberg's idea may find some support from Kurdek (2008), who found a lower instability rate ($p < .02$, two-sided Fisher's exact test) for lesbians in civil unions (0.7%) than for gay men in civil unions (3.7%).

Some research has found that for both lesbian and heterosexual mothers, single parenthood is characterized, respectively, for lesbian *and* heterosexual mothers by lower parenting quality ($ES = 0.39$, 0.28), more severe disputes ($ES = 0.57$, 0.28), and less enjoyment of motherhood ($ES = 0.48$, 0.26) (Golombok et al., 2003). Therefore, lower stability would have implications for children of both heterosexual and lesbian women. Consequently, it is not surprising that Tasker (2010) indicated that "Future work could investigate whether Biblarz and Stacey (2010a) are justified in saying that lesbian coparents are more at risk of separation" (p. 39). Unfortunately, there appear to have been no published articles yet that report separation rates for same-sex marriages or civil unions as a function of both gender and parental status (Balsam, Beauchaine, Rothblum, & Solomon, 2008; Kurdek, 2008).

However, do we really know so little about the stability of same-sex parents versus heterosexual parents? In fact, we *already* have numerous studies from English speaking countries showing evidence of (1) the stability of same-sex couples or parents without comparisons to heterosexual couples, (2) the stability of heterosexual couples or parents without comparisons to same-sex couples, and (3) the stability of same-sex parents *with* comparisons to heterosexual couples; information on stability in Scandinavian nations has been reported elsewhere (Andersson, Noack, Seierstad, & Weedon-Fekjaer, 2006; Kurdek, 2005; Noack, Seierstad, & Weedon-Fekjaer, 2005; Rothblum, 2009).

Studies Without Heterosexual Parent Comparison Groups

Numerous studies have considered separation rates for same-sex parents without having a true comparison group of heterosexual parents. These reports are reviewed here in order of the duration of the study. Golombok, Tasker, and Murray (1997) appeared to indicate that 5 of 15 lesbian parents

(33%) had separated by the time their child was 6 years old. Vanfraussen, Ponjaert-Kristoffersen, and Brewaeys (2002) reported that 6 of 24 lesbian couples (25%) had separated between the time their child, conceived through donor insemination, was about 5 years old and then about 10 years old; it appears the comparison group of heterosexual couples had a similar separation rate (25%) that was by design, because the heterosexuals were selected as to create an equivalent comparison group.

In another study of lesbian parents with a child about 6 years old, Patterson (2001) reported that 4 of 30 couples (13%) had separated since the birth of the child. Stevens, Perry, Burston, Golombok, and Golding (2003), using the same sample from Golombok et al. (2003), reported that 4 of 10 lesbian couples (40%) who had conceived a child by donor insemination had separated by age 7 of the child and that 17 of 28 lesbian couples (61%) with non–donor inseminated children had separated within an average of 4 years. Kuvulanka and Goldberg (2009) interviewed 18 queer youth with bisexual or lesbian mothers; of the 17 mothers who appeared to have had partners at some point, it seems that 9 (53%) did not keep the same partner throughout the child's childhood and adolescence.

Tasker and Golombok (1997) in their longitudinal study in England indicated that "In the present study, the majority of lesbian mothers were no longer with the same partner they had been with at the time of the first investigation 14 years earlier" (p. 57). However, only 25% of the young adult children surveyed "recalled their mother having…one long-term mono-gamous cohabiting relationship" (p. 57), indicating an instability rate as high as or higher than 75% over 15 years. Without heterosexual comparison groups, it appears that instability rates for lesbian parents range from as low as 13% over 6 years to as high as 75% over 15 years, with an average of 42.9% breaking up over an average of 9.4 years.

Studies Without Lesbian Parent Comparison Groups

Turning to research on heterosexual relationships, using data from the Fragile Families Study, designed to study relationships at especially high risk for separation, fewer than 6% of White married mothers had separated over a 3-year period (Osborne, Manning, & Smock, 2007). Kurdek (2006b) reported an instability rate for married heterosexual parents over 18 months of only 1.6% (2.7% for married heterosexual couples without children). Balsam et al. (2008) reported a 2.7% divorce rate and a 3.6% divorce or separation rate over 3 years for heterosexual married couples. Veroff, Douvan, and Hatchett (1995, p. 13) reported an 8% divorce rate over 4 years for White couples. Orbuch, Veroff, Hassan, and Horrocks (2002) reported divorce rates for White couples in their longitudinal study as 9%, 20%, and 29% at 3, 7, and 14 years, respectively. Manning, Smock, and Majumdar (2004) reported a 15% and 28% breakup rate for heterosexual parents over 5 and 10 years, respectively.

U.S. Census data appear to yield a 27% breakup rate for heterosexual married women in a first marriage by 10 years and a 36% breakup rate for heterosexual married women in a second marriage by 10 years (Kreider & Fields, 2002, p. 5). Furthermore, the cumulative percent of first marriages ending in divorce by 10 years appears to vary little between Blacks (~22%) and non-Hispanic Whites (~20%) (Kreider & Fields, 2002, p. 18). Bramlett and Mosher (2002, pp. 27 and 55), using data from the 1995 National Survey of Family Growth, found a 28% to 32% breakup rate over 10 years for first marriages of non-Hispanic Whites; for women who became mothers after their marriage, the rate was 26% over 10 years (p. 56).

Goodwin, Mosher, and Chandra (2010, p. 32) using data from the 2002 National Survey of Family Growth found divorce rates of 3% (1 year), 9% (3 years), 14% (5 years), and 22% (10 years) for women with at least a college education. Using data from the 1990 Current Population Survey, Raley and Bumpass (2003) found 30% of White marriages dissolved after 10 years and 20% of the marriages of college graduates or those who had married after age 29 dissolved after 10 years; however, they did not account for post-marital parenthood status. Martin (2006, p. 546) found that among women who completed college before marriage, only 14% dissolved their first marriage within 10 years. Kurdek (2004) reported a breakup rate of less than 15% (70/483) for married heterosexual couples with children over 11 to 12 years of first marriage. Kposowa (1998) estimated divorce rates of 12%, 17%, 24%, and 33% for White women in the United States at 10, 15, 20, and 25 years, respectively, whereas the rates for *mothers* of all races with young children were lower: 12%, 16%, 20%, and 31% at the corresponding times.

Owen and Golombok (2009) reported low breakup rates for heterosexual parents over 18 or more years, regardless of method of conception: natural (9/63, 14%), donor insemination (6/26, 23%), adoptive (1/38, 3%), or in vitro fertilization (2/26, 8%). It appears that none of the relationships had broken up between when the child was 12 years old and at 18 years of age (Golombok, MacCallum, Goodman, & Rutter, 2002). Thus, method of conception does not by itself appear to produce high rates of separation or divorce for heterosexual parents, even over periods as long as 18 or more years.

Schoen and Standish (2001) estimated that 40% to 44% of marriages in the United States would end in divorce. For heterosexual couples in general, separation rates appear to range between 4% to 9% at 3 years and 44% lifetime, with an average across studies of about 18.8% at about an average of 9.5 years. For heterosexual parents separation rates appear to range between 6% at 3 years and 31% at 25 years with an average across studies of about 15.5% at an average of about 13 years. Regardless of the exact estimates, it appears that higher education and maternity each promote relationship stability, suggesting that both factors should be considered when evaluating relationship stability across different groups.

Studies With Lesbian and Heterosexual Parent Comparison Groups

With respect to research that compared the stability of lesbian with hetero-sexual parents, Biblarz and Stacey (2010a) cited one study (MacCallum & Golombok, 2004) in which 6 of 14 lesbian couples (43%) had broken up compared with 5 of 38 heterosexual couples (13%) (odds ratio [OR] = 4.95, $p < .05$) between when the focal child was about 6 and about 12 years of age, raising the possibility that lesbian parents might provide children with less parental stability. Even so, Golombok and Badger (2010), using the same longitudinal data, did not report stability rates for the original 10 birth couples or the remaining 7 (one mother had died) couples from the child's age of 12 to when the child was in early adulthood (ages 18–20); they only reported that 11 of 20 mothers (55%) had a current cohabiting partner.

Other studies have been published. Fulcher, Chan, Raboy, and Patterson (2002) reported results from early data in the Contemporary Families Study involving 49 lesbian couples and 17 heterosexual couples as well as single parents. By the time the focal child was 7 years old, Chan, Brooks, Raboy, and Patterson (1998) indicated that 1 heterosexual couple (6%) and 19 lesbian couples (39%) had separated (OR = 10.1, $p < .05$). Bos, Gartrell, Peyser, and van Balen (2008) compared relationship stability for lesbian parents with married heterosexual siblings; it appears that 34 of 71 lesbian parents (48%) broke up over 10 years compared with 22 of 74 married heterosexual couples (30%) (OR = 2.17, $p < .05$). From the same set of subjects, Bos, Gartrell, van Balen, Peyser, and Sandfort (2008) reported a 44% breakup rate, but that was calculated by including seven lesbian mothers who had always been single parents in the denominator (34/78). However, Gartrell and Bos (2010) reported that after 17 years, 40 of 71 couples (56.3%) had separated. Gartrell and colleagues (2000) also reported that 31% of their lesbian couples had separated after 5 years.

Brewaeys, Ponjaert, Van Hall, and Golombok (1997) found that by age 5 of their child, 3 of 30 lesbian couples (10%) had separated compared with 3 of 68 heterosexual couples (4%) (OR = 3.26, not significant). Thus, in nearly every comparison of same-sex lesbian parents with same-sex heterosexual parents, outcomes have indicated greater stability for heterosexual parents, even without statistical controls for substantial and often statistically signifi-cant advantages in terms of education, income, and fewer children (i.e., greater per capita income per household) for lesbian parents who partici-pated in these studies. If the results of the four studies are combined, 37.8% of lesbian couples (62/164) separated compared with 15.7% of heterosexual couples (31/197) (OR = 3.26, $p < .001$) over an average of 8.4 years for each group. In other words, across these four studies over similar periods of time, it appears that the odds of lesbian couples breaking up are over three times greater than the odds of heterosexual couples breaking up. Regardless of methodology used, it appears that 15% to 20% of heterosexual parents are likely to break up by 10 years compared with about 40% to 45% of lesbian parents.

Goldberg (2010b, p. 29) discussed interaction effects in the literature; one possibility is an interaction among several factors, including gender, parenthood, sexual orientation, and legal marital status, among others. As Strohschein (2010) concluded, "Indeed, the task of distinguishing between the effects of parental gender, sexual identity, marital status, biogenetic relationship to children, number of parents in the household, and family structure history has hardly begun" (p. 27).

DISCUSSION

Lower rates of stability among some same-sex couples might be related to an interesting finding by Kurdek (2006a, p. 531). In a study of 66 gay male, 104 lesbian, and 144 heterosexual couples, he found that *none* of the 170 non-heterosexual participants scored other than *zero* on moral values as a deterrent for instability compared with that deterrent being important for many of the heterosexual participants. "None" is a pretty remarkable and rare occurrence in attitudinal research; usually, someone checks an infrequently checked box merely because of fatigue, confusion, or indifference. Family and children were also cited far more frequently by heterosexuals as deterrents. The most important deterrent for same-sex couples was intimacy (an attraction). Bigner and Jacobsen (1989) found that heterosexual fathers were more likely ($p<.01$) to agree that having a child would reduce extradyadic sexual activity than were gay fathers, suggesting perhaps that traditional moral values were less likely to play a role in the latter's decisions. In other words, traditional social norms may constrain heterosexual parents more than lesbian or gay parents with respect to maintaining long-term relationship stability, if not other aspects of family life. Further research here would be very helpful.

CONCLUSION

Biblarz and Stacey's (2010a) conclusion that lesbian parents may have less stable relationships appears to have been a valid conclusion, even though they overlooked much of the available evidence in the literature. These results are still sketchy because the higher separation rates for lesbian mothers could be related to being in a second or third relationship, which might be related to a variety of selection effects or associated stressors that might account for lower stability rates (Beals, Impett, & Peplau, 2002; Oswald, Goldberg, Kuvalanka, & Clausell, 2008). Higher separation rates might reflect greater financial independence among lesbian parents, who might be better able to manage any financial consequences of a separation. The lesbian mother with a biological connection to a child might fear legal issues over child custody less because the social comother might have less claim for custody rights than would a biological father in a heterosexual divorce process.

The greater availability of the institution of marriage itself might be part of what gives heterosexuals an apparent advantage in terms of stability. Social changes, such as a growing number of states providing for nonheterosexual marriages, might change the variables at play at the same time further research was ongoing. In other words, the research situation will probably remain fluid. Clearly, much more research is needed to identify factors that are related to instability for both lesbian and heterosexual parents, especially among different demographic groups of such parents (e.g., different socioeconomic levels, different racial/ethnic backgrounds, different religious affiliations, different per capita household income levels, different methods of conception, different levels of parental impulsivity or delayed gratification values). However controversial this review may prove to be, hopefully it will stimulate further such research from a wide range of diligent scholars, an outcome that most scholars can probably support (Biblarz & Stacey, 2010b).

REFERENCES

Andersson, G., Noack, T., Seierstad, A., & Weedon-Fekjaer, H. (2006). The demographics of same-sex marriages in Norway and Sweden. *Demography*, *43*, 79–98.

Baetens, P., & Brewaeys, A. (2001). Lesbian couples requesting donor insemination: An update of the knowledge with regard to lesbian mother families. *Human Reproduction Update*, *7*, 512–519.

Ball, C. A. (2003). Lesbian and gay families: Gender nonconformity and the implications of difference. *Capital University Law Review*, *31*, 691–749.

Balsam, K. F., Beauchaine, T. P., Rothblum, E. D., & Solomon, S. E. (2008). Three-year follow-up of same-sex couples who had civil unions in Vermont, same-sex couples not in civil unions, and heterosexual married couples. *Developmental Psychology*, *44*, 102–116.

Beals, K. P., Impett, E. A., & Peplau, L. A. (2002). Lesbians in love: Why some relationships endure and others end. *Journal of Lesbian Studies*, *6*, 53–63.

Biblarz, T., & Stacey, J. (2010a). How does the gender of parents matter? *Journal of Marriage and Family*, *72*, 3–22.

Biblarz, T., & Stacey, J. (2010b). Ideal families and social science ideals. *Journal of Marriage and Family*, *72*, 41–44.

Bigner, J. J., & Jacobsen, R. B. (1989). The value of children to gay and to heterosexual fathers. *Journal of Homosexuality*, *18*, 163–172.

Bos, H. M. W., Gartrell, N. K., Peyser, H., & van Balen, F. (2008). The USA National Longitudinal Lesbian Family Study (NLLFS): Homophobia, psychological adjustment, and protective factors. *Journal of Lesbian Studies*, *12*, 455–471.

Bos, H. M. W., Gartrell, N. K., van Balen, F., Peyser, H., & Sandfort, T. G. M. (2008). Children in planned lesbian families: A cross-cultural comparison between the

United States and the Netherlands. *American Journal of Orthopsychiatry, 78,* 211–219.

Bramlett, M. D., & Mosher, W. D. (2002). Cohabitation, marriage, divorce, and remarriage in the United States. *Vital Health Statistics, 23*(22), 1–63.

Brewaeys, A., Ponjaert, I., Van Hall, E. V., & Golombok, S. (1997). Donor insemination: Child development and family functioning in lesbian mother families. *Human Reproduction, 12,* 1349–1359.

Chan, R. W., Brooks, R. C., Raboy, B., & Patterson, C. J. (1998). Division of labor among lesbian and heterosexual parents: Associations with children's adjustment. *Journal of Family Psychology, 12,* 402–419.

Cohen, J. (1988). *Statistical power analysis for the behavioral sciences* (2nd ed.). Hillsdale, NJ: Lawrence Erlbaum.

Cohen, J., Cohen, P., West, S. G., & Aiken, L. S. (2003). *Applied multiple regression/ correlation analysis for the behavioral sciences* (3rd ed.). Mahwah, NJ: Lawrence Erlbaum.

Fulcher, M., Chan, R. W., Raboy, B., & Patterson, C. J. (2002). Contact with grandparents among children conceived via donor insemination by lesbian and heterosexual mothers. *Parenting: Science and Practice, 2,* 61–76.

Gartrell, N., Banks, A., Reed, N., Hamilton, J., Rodas, C., & Deck, A. (2000). The National Lesbian Family Study: 3. Interviews with mothers of five-year-olds. *American Journal of Orthopsychiatry, 70,* 542–548.

Gartrell, N., & Bos, H. (2010). US National Longitudinal Lesbian Family Study: Psychological characteristics of 17-year-old adolescents. *Pediatrics, 126,* 1–9.

Goldberg, A. S. (2010a). *Lesbian and gay parents and their children: Research on the family life cycle.* Washington, DC: American Psychological Association.

Goldberg, A. S. (2010b). Studying complex families in context. *Journal of Marriage and Family, 72,* 29–34.

Golombok, S., & Badger, S. (2010). Children raised in mother-headed families from infancy: A follow-up of children of lesbian and single heterosexual mothers, at early adulthood. *Human Reproduction, 25,* 150–157.

Golombok, S., MacCallum, F., Goodman, E., & Rutter, M. (2002). Families with children conceived by donor insemination: A follow-up at age twelve. *Child Development, 73,* 952–968.

Golombok, S., Perry, B., Burston, A., Murray, C., Mooney-Somers, Stevens, M., & Golding, J. (2003). Children with lesbian parents: A community study. *Developmental Psychology, 39,* 20–33.

Golombok, S., Tasker, F., & Murray, C. (1997). Children raised in fatherless families from infancy: Family relationships and the socioemotional development of children of lesbian and single heterosexual mothers. *Journal of Child Psychology & Psychiatry, 38,* 783–791.

Goodwin, P. Y., Mosher, W. D., & Chandra, A. (2010). *Marriage and cohabitation in the United States: A statistical portrait based on Cycle 6 (2002) of the National Survey of Family Growth.* Washington, DC: National Center for Health Statistics.

Kposowa, A. J. (1998). The impact of race on divorce in the United States. *Journal of Comparative Family Studies, 29,* 529–548.

Kreider, R. M., & Fields, J. M. (2002). Number, timing, and duration of marriages and divorces: 1996. *Current Population Reports, P70–80*. Washington, DC: U.S. Census Bureau.

Kurdek, L. A. (2004). Are gay and lesbian cohabiting couples really different from heterosexual married couples? *Journal of Marriage and Family, 66*, 880–900.

Kurdek, L. A. (2005). What do we know about gay and lesbian couples? *Current Directions in Psychological Science, 14*, 251–254.

Kurdek, L. A. (2006a). The nature and correlates of deterrents to leaving a relationship. *Personal Relationships, 13*, 521–535.

Kurdek, L. A. (2006b). Differences between partners from heterosexual, gay, and lesbian cohabiting couples. *Journal of Marriage and Family, 68*, 509–528.

Kurdek, L. A. (2008). A general model of relationship commitment: Evidence from same-sex partners. *Personal Relationships, 15*, 391–405.

Kuvulanka, K. A., & Goldberg, A. E. (2009). "Second generation" voices: Queer youth with lesbian/bisexual mothers. *Journal of Youth and Adolescence, 38*, 904–919.

Lippa, R. A. (2005). Sexual orientation and personality. *Annual Review of Sex Research, 16*, 119–153.

MacCallum, F., & Golombok, S. (2004). Children raised in fatherless families from infancy: A follow-up of children of lesbian and single heterosexual mothers at early adolescence. *Journal of Child Psychology and Psychiatry, 45*, 1407–1419.

Manning, W. D., Smock, P. J., & Majumdar, D. (2004). The relative stability of cohabiting and marital unions for children. *Population Research and Policy Review, 23*, 135–159.

Martin, S. P. (2006). Trends in marital dissolution by women's education in the United States. *Demographic Research, 15*, 537–560.

Noack, T., Seierstad, A., & Weedon-Fekjaer, H. (2005). A demographic analysis of registered partnerships (legal same-sex unions): The case of Norway. *European Journal of Population, 21*, 89–109.

Orbuch, T. L., Veroff, J., Hassan, H., & Horrocks, J. (2002). Who will divorce: A 14-year longitudinal study of black couples and white couples. *Journal of Social and Personal Relationships, 19*, 179–202.

Osborne, C., Manning, W. D., & Smock, P. J. (2007). Married and cohabiting parents' relationship stability: A focus on race and ethnicity. *Journal of Marriage and Family, 69*, 1345–1366.

Oswald, R. F., Goldberg, A., Kuvalanka, K., & Clausell, E. (2008). Structural and moral commitment among same-sex couples: Relationship duration, religiosity, and parental status. *Journal of Family Psychology, 22*, 411–419.

Owen, L., & Golombok, S. (2009). Families created by assisted reproduction: Parent-child relationships in late adolescence. *Journal of Adolescence, 32*, 835–848.

Patterson, C. J. (2001). Families of the lesbian baby boom: Maternal mental health and child adjustment. In D. F. Glazer & J. Drescher (Eds.), *Gay and lesbian parenting* (pp. 91–107). Binghamton, NY: Haworth Press.

Peplau, L. A., & Fingerhut, A. W. (2007). The close relationships of lesbians and gay men. *Annual Review of Psychology, 58*, 405–424.

Raley, R. K., & Bumpass, L. (2003). The topography of the divorce plateau: Levels and trends in union stability in the United States after 1980. *Demographic Research, 8*, 245–260.

Redding, R. E. (2008). It's really about sex: Same-sex marriage, lesbigay parenting, and the psychology of disgust. *Duke Journal of Gender Law & Policy*, *15*, 127–193.

Rothblum, E. D. (2009). An overview of same-sex couples in relation ships: A research area still at sea. In D. A. Hope (Ed.), *Contemporary perspectives on lesbian, gay, and bisexual identities* (pp. 113–139). Nebraska Symposium on Motivation. New York, NY: Springer Science + Business Media.

Schoen, R., & Standish, N. (2001). The retrenchment of marriage: Results from marital status life tables for the United States, 1995. *Population and Development Review*, *27*, 553–563.

Schumm, W. R. (2010a). Children of homosexuals more apt to be homosexuals? A reply to Morrison and to Cameron based on an examination of multiple sources of data. *Journal of Biosocial Science*, *42*(6), 721–742.

Schumm, W. R. (2010b). How science is done. *Marriage and Family Review*, *46*, 323–326.

Stevens, M., Perry, B., Burston, A., Golombok, S., & Golding, J. (2003). Openness in lesbian-mother families regarding mother's sexual orientation and child's conception by donor insemination. *Journal of Reproductive and Infant Psychology*, *21*, 347–362.

Strohschein, L. (2010). Generating heat or light? The challenge of social address variables. *Journal of Marriage and Family*, *72*, 23–28.

Tasker, F. L. (2010). Same-sex parenting and child development: Reviewing the contribution of parental gender. *Journal of Marriage and Family*, *72*, 35–40.

Tasker, F. L., & Golombok, S. (1997). *Growing up in a lesbian family: Effects on child development*. New York, NY: Guilford Press.

Vanfraussen, K., Ponjaert-Kristoffersen, I., & Brewaeys, A. (2002). What does it mean for youngsters to grow up in a lesbian family created by means of donor insemination? *Journal of Reproductive and Infant Psychology*, *20*, 237–252.

Veroff, J., Douvan, E., & Hatchett, S. J. (1995). *Marital instability: A social and behavioral study of the early years*. Westport, CT: Praeger.

NONTRADITIONAL FAMILIES AND CHILDHOOD PROGRESS THROUGH SCHOOL*

MICHAEL J. ROSENFELD

I use U.S. census data to perform the first large-sample, nationally representative tests of outcomes for children raised by same-sex couples. The results show that children of same-sex couples are as likely to make normal progress through school as the children of most other family structures. Heterosexual married couples are the family type whose children have the lowest rates of grade retention, but the advantage of heterosexual married couples is mostly due to their higher socioeconomic status. Children of all family types (including children of same-sex couples) are far more likely to make normal progress through school than are children living in group quarters (such as orphanages and shelters).

What types of outcomes can be expected for children raised by same-sex couples, relative to children in other types of families? The answer is vitally important both for public policy relating to same-sex marriage and adoption (Eskridge 2002; Koppelman 2002) and for theories of how family structure matters. Supporters and opponents of same-sex marriage rights agree that the legal issue of same-sex marriage rights should revolve around the question of childhood outcomes for children raised by same-sex couples (Alvaré 2005; Patterson 2002). In this article, using data from the 2000 U.S. Census, I examine progress through school—that is, normal progress versus grade retention—for children of same-sex couples compared with children of other family types.

The debate over same-sex unions and their children draws from and informs a more general literature concerning family structure's effect on children. The literature on family structure has generally focused on structural variations within heterosexual-parented families, contrasting heterosexual married couples, heterosexual remarried couples, and (presumably heterosexual) single mothers (Cherlin 1992; McLanahan and Sandefur 1994). Even though same-sex couples are a small minority of all couples (1% of all couples in Census 2000 were same-sex couples), the inclusion of same-sex couples can provide researchers with more leverage over the key question of how family structure matters in general.

Studies of family structure and children's outcomes nearly universally find at least a modest advantage for children raised by their married biological parents. The question that has bedeviled researchers, and that remains essentially unresolved, is *why* (Cherlin 1999). Some results have indicated that socioeconomic status explains most or all of the advantage of children raised by married couples (Biblarz and Raftery 1999; Gennetian 2005; Ginther and Pollak 2004), while other scholars have found that family structure has an enduring effect on children net of all other factors (McLanahan and Sandefur 1994; Zill 1996). Married couples tend to be the most prosperous type of family unit, and this economic prosperity undoubtedly has certain advantages for children (but also see Mayer 1997).

LITERATURE REVIEW
Same-Sex Parenting

The modern reality of same-sex couples raising children long postdates the classical psychological theories of child development (e.g., Freud [1905] 1975). Recent research on

---

*Michael J. Rosenfeld, Department of Sociology, Stanford University, 450 Serra Mall, Bldg. 120, Stanford, CA 94305; e-mail michael.rosenfeld@stanford.edu. Thanks are due to Diana Baumrind, Michael Wald, Paula England, Judith Seltzer, Tim Biblarz, and anonymous reviewers for helpful comments.

Demography, Volume 47-Number 3, August 2010: 755–775

childhood socialization to gender roles has emphasized peer groups and genetics as much as direct parental influence (Harris 1998; Maccoby 1990). In-depth studies of the psychosocial development of children raised by lesbians and gay men has found that these children are normal and well adjusted (Chan, Raboy, and Patterson 1998; Flaks et al. 1995; Golombok et al. 2003). The existing studies have universally small sample sizes of children, and as I discuss shortly, the literature has critics for this reason.

Same-sex couples become parents in three main ways: through one partner's (generally prior) heterosexual relationship; through adoption; or through donor insemination or surrogate parenting (Stacey 2006). Same-sex couples cannot become parents through misuse of or failure of birth control as heterosexual couples can. Parenthood is more difficult to achieve for same-sex couples than for heterosexual couples, which implies a stronger selection effect for same-sex parents. If gays and lesbians have to work harder to become parents, perhaps those gays and lesbians who do become parents are, on average, more dedicated to the hard work of parenting than their heterosexual peers, and this could be beneficial for their children.

In Judith Stacey's (2006:39) discussion of gay adoption, she describes the gay men of Los Angeles as having to search through the state's "...overstocked warehouse of 'hard to place' children, the majority of whom . . . have been removed from families judged negligent, abusive, or incompetent. Most of the state's stockpiled children . . . are children of color, and disproportionately boys with 'special needs.'" If it is the case that same-sex couples who adopt mainly have access to "special needs" children, the special needs of these children could exert a downward bias on the average outcomes for children of same-sex couples. Fortunately, the census distinguishes between the head of household's "own children," adopted children, stepchildren, and foster children.

Nearly all children of gay and lesbian parents attend schools and live in neighborhoods in which other children overwhelmingly come from families with heterosexual parents. In other words, children of same-sex couples share a common peer and school environment with children of heterosexual couples. To the extent that peer environment is a primary socializing environment for children (Harris 1998; Maccoby 1990; for a survey, see Rutter 2002), whatever differences sexual orientation of parents makes within the home may well be mediated and diffused by the common peer and school environments that children share regardless of the gender or sexual orientation of their parents.

How the Census Complements the Existing Literature

In 45 empirical studies of outcomes of children of same-sex couples—including all studies listed in Tasker's (2005) comprehensive survey that examined childhood outcomes, several more recent studies listed by Wald (2006), all four studies listed by Meezan and Rauch (2005) as the highest-quality studies in this field,[1] and all the more recent studies that cite the earlier ones—none found statistically significant disadvantages for children raised by gay and lesbian parents compared with other children. These studies are listed in table form in a supplement posted on *Demography*'s Web site (http://www.populationassociation.org/publications/demography).

The uniform finding of no significant disadvantage for children raised by gay or lesbian parents has been convincing to some scholars (Ball and Pea 1998; Meezan and Rauch 2005; Stacey and Biblarz 2001; Wald 2006), although others remain unconvinced (Lerner and Nagai 2001; Nock 2001; Wardle 1997). Several points are worthy of comments. First, as the critics have noted, convenience sampling dominated this literature in the past (Nock 2001). More recent scholarship has answered this criticism by using nationally representative probability samples derived from the National Longitudinal Study of Adolescent Health (Add

---

1. The four articles featured in Meezan and Rauch (2005) are Wainright, Russell, and Patterson (2004); Golombok et al. (2003); Chan, Raboy, and Patterson (1998); and Brewaeys et al. (1997).

Health; see Wainright and Patterson 2006, 2008; Wainright et al. 2004) as well as studies constructed from a hybrid of probability sampling and convenience sampling (Golombok et al. 2003; Perry et al. 2004).

A second critique of the literature—that the sample sizes of the studies are too small to allow for statistically powerful tests—continues to be relevant. The mean number of children of gay or lesbian parents in these studies is 39, and the median is 37; both numbers would be slightly lower if studies without comparison groups were excluded. The nationally representative studies in the series found only 44 children who were raised by lesbian couples in the Add Health survey. Golombok et al. (2003) found only 18 lesbian mothers of 14,000 mothers in the Avon Longitudinal Study of Parents and Children, which is why they supplemented this sample with snowball sampling and their own convenience sample. The universally small sample sizes of the studies in the existing literature has left room for several critiques, including the argument that small sample studies would not have the statistical power to identify the effects of homosexual parents on childhood outcomes even if such effects did exist (Lerner and Nagai 2001; Nock 2001).

A third potential weakness of this literature is the narrowness of family structures under study (Tasker 2005). Of the 45 studies listed, only 7 examined the children of gay fathers, and only 2 of these 7 studies had a more traditional family control group built into the study.

Among the convenience sample studies, several of the most important have been based on samples of women who became parents through assisted reproductive technology (ART; Brewaeys et al. 1997; Chan, Raboy, and Patterson 1998; Flaks et al. 1995). Because individuals who become parents through assisted means can be identified through reproductive clinics—and are therefore easier to recruit than the general population of same-sex couple parents—the literature on same-sex couple parenting has tended to feature studies of the kind of women who can afford ART: white, upper-middle-class women. Nationally representative data tend to paint a different picture: in the U.S. census, same-sex couple parents tend to be more working class and are much more likely to be nonwhite compared with heterosexual married couples.

The debate over same-sex marriage and gay and lesbian adoption rights revolves around many competing sets of assumptions with political, religious, and ideological axes that cannot be resolved or even fully addressed in this article. To the extent that the debate is empirical—that is, to the extent that disagreement remains over the meaning of the empirical literature on the development of children of same-sex couples—this article offers a new perspective.

To supplement the existing small-scale studies, I offer a large-sample study of children from the 2000 U.S. census, including 3,502 children of same-sex couples who had been living with both parents for at least five years (2,030 children living with lesbian mothers and 1,472 children living with gay fathers; see Table 1) and more than 700,000 children in Grades 1–8 from other family types. This sample size more than satisfies Nock's (2001) criteria of 800 as the minimum number of gay and lesbian couples required for statistically useful study.

Using data from the U.S. census has several major disadvantages: normal progress through school is the only available children's outcome, and even this outcome is measured with less precision than one would hope for. Although the census data have several important limitations for the research questions considered here, the strengths of the census data (large sample, national representativeness, and a full array of family structures) address important lacunae in the literature; as such, this study offers a potentially useful new perspective on how family structure matters to children. The census data are far from ideal for the subject under study here, but better data are nowhere on the horizon.[2]

---

2. The 2010 census will reportedly not include the long form that was used to produce census microdata in the past (U.S. Census Bureau 2002). The American Community Surveys (ACS), which are supposed to replace

Grade Retention

Grade retention (the opposite of normal progress through school) has been increasing in U.S. schools since former President Bill Clinton proposed ending social promotion in schools in his State of the Union Address in 1998 (Alexander, Entwisle, and Dauber 2003:viii; Hauser 2001). Grade retention is an important childhood outcome because retention in the primary grades is a strong indicator of a lack of childhood readiness for school, and effective parenting is a crucial ingredient in school readiness (Brooks-Gunn and Markman 2005). Brooks-Gunn and Markman argued that the lower school readiness of racial minority children is due, in part, to parenting practices that differ from the authoritative parenting style favored in middle-class white homes (Baumrind 1966; Lareau 2003).

Guo, Brooks-Gunn, and Harris (1996) studied grade retention among urban black children and found that some indicators of parental stress, such as unemployment and welfare participation, were associated with increased grade retention for children; in other words, they found childhood grade retention to be a useful measure of difficulties that the students were experiencing at home. Guo et al. (1996:218) identified three potential sources of grade retention: "weak cognitive ability, behavioral problems, and lack of engagement in school." Of these three causes of childhood grade retention, the latter two might be partly associated with the quality of the home environment. Students with learning disabilities or physical disabilities that impact learning are also at risk of grade retention, and this type of grade retention would not be indicative of parenting deficits.

Grade retention is closely associated with more serious problems later in the life course. Students who are held back at least once are at much higher risk for eventually dropping out of high school (Alexander, Entwisle, and Horsey 1997; Guo et al. 1996; Moller et al. 2006; Roderick 1994; Rumberger 1987; Tillman, Guo, and Harris 2006). Failure to graduate from high school is associated with low earnings, high unemployment, low self-esteem, and high mortality rates (Guo et al. 1996; McLanahan 1985; Tillman et al. 2006). Even when grade retention takes place in the early grades, the "crystallization" of behaviors and academic abilities implies that the difficulties a child experiences when he or she is 7 or 8 carry forward (more so for girls than for boys) into adolescence and young adulthood (Kowalesi-Jones and Duncan 1999).

There are several theoretical reasons for supposing that children of same-sex couples might have lower school readiness (and therefore higher rates of grade retention) than own children of heterosexual married couples, net of race, parental income, and parental education. First, the legal privileges of marriage are numerous and have direct consequences for the well-being of children (Eskridge 1996; Pawelski et al. 2006). Second, evolutionary theory suggests that parents invest more in their own biological children (Wilson 2002; but see also Hamilton, Cheng, and Powell 2007), and same-sex couples (absent a prior sex change) cannot both be the biological parents of any one child. Third, the large majority of children of same-sex couples from the 2000 census were children from prior heterosexual relationships (only 11% were stepchildren, adopted children, or foster children of the head of household); thus, most of the children being raised by same-sex couples at the time of the 2000 census had previously lived through divorce or parental break-up, which research has shown to be traumatic for some children (Amato and Cheadle 2005; Chase-Lansdale, Cherlin, and Kiernan 1995; McLanahan and Sandefur 1994; Wallerstein and Kelly 1980; Wallerstein, Lewis, and Blakeslee 2000).

---

the census long form, have not included the five-year mobility question that I use in this article to determine family stability.

The Benefits of Legal Marriage

Legal marriage confers a host of protections and advantages to the couples who marry and to their children. Married couples generally share joint legal custody of their coresident children. In a system of employer-based health care insurance, either spouse in a married couple can usually provide health insurance for both spouses and all their children. Marriage is a long-term contract that allows and encourages parents to make long-term investments in their children (Waite and Gallagher 2000). Divorce rights, which are a corollary to marriage rights, provide guarantees for child support and visitation that are intended to minimize the damage of a breakup to a couple's children. Given the many practical, legal, economic, and social advantages of marriage as a child-rearing family structure, it should come as no surprise that children of long-term married couples have the best outcomes (McLanahan and Sandefur 1994). The various benefits of marriage extend far beyond income, so one would generally expect children in married couples to have advantages, even after socioeconomic status (SES) is accounted for in regressions.

The moral claim for same-sex marriage rests in part on the many practical and psychological benefits of marriage, benefits for which conservative family scholars have made the most careful and enthusiastic case (Waite and Gallagher 2000; Wilson 2002). The benefits of marriage, combined with the exclusion of gays and lesbians (and their children) from those benefits, together form one cornerstone of the case for same-sex marriage (Eskridge 1996).

Relevant Comparison Sets for Same-Sex Couples

Along with the standard comparison group of heterosexual married couples, heterosexual cohabiting couples are a second logical comparison group for same-sex cohabiting couples. Both heterosexual cohabiters and same-sex cohabiters are two-parent families living without the rights and benefits of marriage. Certainly, there are differences: for example, heterosexual cohabiting couples can marry if they want to, whereas in the United States at the time of the 2000 census, same-sex couples could not marry. The comparison between children of same-sex cohabiting couples and children of heterosexual cohabiting couples allows for a more specific test of the effect of same-sex parenthood on children, while holding constant legal rights and the number of parents.

A third relevant comparison for children of same-sex couples are the children living in group quarters because these are the children presumably available for adoption, and because same-sex couples are more likely than heterosexual couples to participate in the adoption market. Some of the difference between children in group quarters and children living with parents and guardians must be due to selection effects: the most troubled children available for adoption may not be adopted and may do poorly in school as a result of emotional or physical disabilities. On the other hand, if gay and lesbian adoptive parents are choosing from the middle or the bottom of the adoptive pool (Stacey 2006), rather than from the population of the most desirable potential adoptees, then the selection effect will be less important. In either case, the census, as a cross-sectional survey, is poorly suited to the analysis of selection effects. Nonetheless, 2000 census data provide strong controls for individual student disabilities, and any comparison between children living with families and children living in group quarters will be made after individual disabilities have been controlled for.

DATA AND MEASURES

I use age and current grade (variable GRADEATT) from the 2000 U.S. census obtained from the Integrated Public Use Microdata Series (IPUMS; see Ruggles et al. 2004) to create a measure of prior grade retention.[3] Delayed progress through school (also known

---

3. Later educational milestones, such as college attendance, cannot be used in this analysis because college students do not generally live with (and therefore cannot be associated with) their parents in a household survey

as *age-grade retardation*) is a widely used proxy for prior grade retention (Hauser 2001; Hauser, Pager, and Simmons 2001). A strong correlation between being older than one's classmates and having been retained a grade in the past can be documented using the October supplements to the Current Population Survey, which has more precise questions about childhood grade retention (although, unfortunately, a much smaller sample size). For example, for 8th grade students in October 2004, 2% of the 13-year-olds had ever been held back a year in school, but 31% of the 14-year-olds had ever been held back (author's tabulation). The census survey, which occurs 6 months later in the school year (April rather than October), requires a later age cutoff, so I use age 15 as the cutoff age at which 8th graders are considered too old to be making normal progress through school.[4]

The 2000 U.S. census question about current grade for students collapsed Grades 1–4 into a single category and Grades 5–8 into a single category. Students attending Grades 1–4 can be identified as over-age only if they are too old to be in the 4th grade (i.e., at least age 11), and students attending Grades 5–8 can be identified as over-age only if they are too old to be in the 8th grade (i.e., at least age 15).

The 2000 census did not include a question about the number of times respondents had been married, so married coresident couples cannot, in general, be distinguished from remarried couples. This problem is mitigated somewhat by the ability of the census to distinguish the head of household's "own children" from the head of household's "stepchildren." The census provides only a cross-sectional snapshot of family structure, which fails to capture the ways in which family changes over time can affect children (Wolfe et al. 1996; Wu and Martinson 1993).

Children's tenure within their current family structure can be reasonably assured by limiting the analysis to children and parents who all have at least five years of coresidential stability. If the child and both parents all lived at the same address in 2000 as they did five years earlier, it is likely that the family structure at the time of the 2000 census was also in place five years earlier. For children living in group quarters, five years at the same address indicates long-term residence rather than a brief stay at a shelter. Five years with the same family structure at the same address is long enough to imply that the child's primary school career through Grade 4, and most of the child's primary school career through Grade 8, are likely to have been undertaken within the family structure reported to the census in 2000. For children living with single parents, five-year residential stability of child and parent is a bit more ambiguous because we do not know whether or when a partner or ex-spouse moved out of the home.

Unmarried partners were first distinguished from roommates in the 1990 census. For the 2000 census, the Census Bureau changed its long-standing policy by counting self-reported same-sex "married" couples as unmarried partners (Rosenfeld and Kim 2005; U.S. Census Bureau 2001). The recoded "married" couples accounted for roughly one-half of the same-sex partners and 80% of the children of same-sex couples in the 2000 census. The inclusion of the self-reported "married" couples among the same-sex partnered couples is thought to yield a more accurate population count of same-sex couples (U.S. Census Bureau 2001; but see also O'Connell and Gooding 2006).

In the 2000 U.S. census same-sex couple cohabiting data, self-reported married and self-reported partnered same-sex couples differ in some systematic ways. Not only do the self-reported same-sex married couples have more children than the self-reported

---

such as the U.S. census. Even secondary school students (especially students who are over-age for their grade) are old enough to live apart from their parents, which is why my analysis focuses on the primary grades.

4. Children ready to start kindergarten as young 5-year-olds are sometimes held back from school for one year by affluent parents so that their child might be one of the oldest students when they start kindergarten at age 6 rather than one of the youngest students in the class, a process known as "redshirting." The late age cutoff that I use to define grade retention—11 years old for 4th grade (and, correspondingly, 7 years old for kindergarten)—places the redshirted children among those making normal progress.

same-sex partnered couples, but the self-reported same-sex married couples are more similar to heterosexual married couples along several other key dimensions. For example, the self-reported same-sex married couples are more likely to be white, less likely to be geographically mobile, and more likely to have high incomes (Rosenfeld and Kim 2005). Because the population of same-sex partners in the 2000 census is composed of these two rather distinctive subgroups, every table that includes statistics on same-sex couples and their children includes alternative versions of the same statistics calculated omitting the couples (and their children) whose dual marital status was recoded to indicate whether the results are robust with respect to this underlying diversity.

In the census data, all married couples are heterosexual married couples by Census Bureau definition. Since the 2000 census, however, several U.S. states and other countries have acknowledged married same-sex couples, so I add the modifier "heterosexual" to "married couples" for clarity.

First-Order Predictors of Childhood Grade Retention

Because denominator school populations cover four years (Grades 1–4, Grades 5–8), but the students who can be identified as over-age for their grade come only from the last grade of each four-year span (Grades 4 and 8),[5] the implied grade retention rate is four times higher than the observed grade retention rate. Table 1 shows both the observed grade retention rate and the implied grade retention rate for primary school students using weighted data from the 2000 census.

Table 1 suggests that childhood grade retention is correlated with family type. Children of heterosexual married couples had the lowest implied rate of grade retention: 6.8%. Children of lesbian mothers and gay fathers had grade retention rates of 9.5% and 9.7%, respectively. Children of heterosexual cohabiting parents had a grade retention rate of 11.7%, while children of single parents had grade retention rates between 11.1% and 12.6%

The differences in childhood grade retention between all types of non–group quarters households were dwarfed by the high rates of grade retention of children living in group quarters. According to Table 1, children living in group homes, many of them awaiting adoption or foster parents, had an implied grade retention rate of 34.4%. Children who were incarcerated had a grade-retention rate of 78.0%. Later in this article, I show that the enormous difference in grade retention between children raised in families and children living in group quarters remains even after individual-level student disabilities are accounted for.

One way to gauge the advantage of living with families is to note that adopted children (10.6% grade retention) who spent the five years prior to the census living with their adoptive parents and foster children (20.6% grade retention) with five years of residential stability performed considerably better than children who spent the same five years living at a single group-quarters address (34.4% grade retention for noninmates). The performance hierarchy that favors own children, and then (in declining order of school performance) adopted children, foster children, and children in group quarters, confirms the long-standing research finding that children do best when living with parents who make a long-term commitment to the children's development (Bartholet 1999). Selection bias (wherein the children with the most severe disabilities or children who have suffered the worst abuse are the least likely to be adopted) must also play a role, which unfortunately cannot be quantified with these data.

The rest of Table 1 shows implied grade retention along several other dimensions. Asian American children had the lowest rates of grade retention, and non-Hispanic black children had the highest. Girls were less likely to be held back in the primary grades than

---

5. This assumes that no children are held back more than one year in the primary grades, which is a fairly safe assumption based on October, CPS data.

Table 1. Selected First-Order Predictors of Childhood Grade Retention for Children With Five Years of Residential Stability

Variable	Unweighted Number of Children in Grades 1–8 (A)	% Over-age at Grades 4 or 8 (B)	Implied % Retained in Grades 1–8 (C = 4B)
Family Type			
Heterosexual, married (ref.)	612,790	1.71	6.8
Lesbian, cohabiting	2,030	2.38*	9.5
Gay male, cohabiting	1,472	2.42*	9.7
Separated, divorced, widowed women	81,876	2.78***	11.1
Separated, divorced, widowed men	21,019	2.86***	11.4
Heterosexual, cohabiting	14,199	2.92***	11.7
Never-married women	28,242	2.93***	11.7
Never-married men	2,365	3.15***	12.6
Group quarters, noninmates	436	8.59***	34.4
Group quarters, inmates	352	19.50***	78.0
Child's Relationship to Householder			
Own child (ref.)		1.86	7.4
Adopted child		2.64***	10.6
Stepchild		3.47***	13.9
Foster child		5.15***	20.6
Child's Race/Ethnicity			
Asian American		1.44**	5.8
Non-Hispanic white (ref.)		1.70	6.8
Hispanic		2.24***	9.0
Non-Hispanic black		3.14***	12.6
Household Income (in 1999 $)			
>100,000 (ref.)		1.33	5.3
50,000–99,999		1.53***	6.1
25,000–49,999		2.17***	8.7
<25,000		3.15***	12.6

(continued)

boys. Suburban schools had lower rates of grade retention than city schools, which in turn were lower than rural schools. Household SES was a crucial predictor of childhood school performance. In households with income less than $25,000, 12.6% of the primary school students were held back, compared with only 5.3% for children in households with incomes more than $100,000. Householder's education had an even stronger effect on children's progress through school: parents who had less than a high school diploma had primary school children who were retained 14.3% of the time, whereas householders with college degrees had children who were retained only 4.4% of the time.

Table 1 shows that the strongest factor in making normal progress through elementary school is living with a family rather than living in group quarters. For children living in a family, whether the family is headed by a heterosexual married couple or by some less-traditional parenting arrangement, the second–most-important factor in childhood progress through school appears to be parental educational attainment.

(Table 1, continued)

Variable	Unweighted Number of Children in Grades 1–8 (A)	% Over-age at Grades 4 or 8 (B)	Implied % Retained in Grades 1–8 (C = 4B)
Metro Status			
Suburban (ref.)		1.49	6.0
Urban		2.15***	8.6
Rural		2.58***	10.3
Child's Gender			
Female (ref.)		1.63	6.5
Male		2.25***	9.0
Head of Household's Education			
BA+ (ref.)		1.10	4.4
Some college		1.58***	6.3
High school diploma		2.18***	8.7
Less than high school		3.58***	14.3

Notes: Coefficients reflect census weights. Children include own children, adopted children, stepchildren, and foster children plus children in group quarters, where appropriate. All parents and children have at least five years of residential stability. With the omission of children of couples whose dual marital status was recoded, children of same-sex couples are more likely to be over-age (3.7%) and have a significantly higher implied grade retention rate (14.8%).

Source: Census 2000 microdata, via IPUMS.

$*p < .05; **p < .01; ***p < .001$ (two-tailed tests; significance compared with the reference category, determined by logistic regressions separately for each variable)

Consistency With Prior Findings

Although the U.S. census data have some limits for the purpose of studying grade retention, the first-order predictors of grade retention from the census are reassuringly consistent with the published research on normal progress through school using other sources. The gender and racial gradients for normal progress through school in Table 1 are similar to the gender and racial gradients found by the Census Bureau in its analysis of progress through school using data from the educational supplement of the October Current Population Surveys (CPS; Heubert and Hauser 1999:147–54; Jamieson, Curry, and Martinez 2001:3, Table A; Shin 2005:7, Table C). Table 1's gradients of normal progress through school (versus grade retention) by family type (specifically, single parent versus married parents), household income, student gender, and parental education are entirely consistent with the broad existing literature on grade retention from other data sources, including the following: Dawson's (1991) study using the 1988 National Health Interview Survey, Tillman et al.'s (2006) study using the Panel Study of Income Dynamics and the National Longitudinal Study of Adolescent Health, Moller et al.'s (2006:171) results using the National Educational Longitudinal Study, Bianchi's (1984) analysis of the CPS, and Zill's (1996) analysis of the National Household Education Survey. I show (in an extended analysis available on request) that the multivariate analysis of grade retention from this same literature is consistent with my multivariate analysis of grade retention using U.S. census data. In all the studies, family SES plays a crucial role in shaping children's educational experience.

Socioeconomic Status by Family Type

Table 2 shows that educational attainment for gays and lesbians was higher than average at 13.6 years (i.e., 1.6 years of college) compared with 13.4 years for heterosexual married

Table 2. Characteristics of Households With and Without Children

Variable	Number of Households	Head of Household's Mean Education	Median Household Income (in 1999 $)	Head of Household's Mean Age	% of Households That Have Children	% of Children Who Were Adopted, Step-, or Foster Children	% of Children Who Were Black or Hispanic
All Households							
Heterosexual, married	55,477,124	13.4	57,640	48.7	44.8		
Heterosexual, cohabiting	4,566,338	13.0	44,200	36.0	37.2		
Gay male, cohabiting	331,747	13.6	61,000	44.6	22.7		
Lesbian, cohabiting	328,406	13.6	55,000	42.8	35.4		
Separated, divorced, widowed men	9,071,563	12.7	30,500	54.3	10.7		
Separated, divorced, widowed women	20,626,824	12.4	22,200	59.6	20.3		
Never-married men	7,456,114	13.7	30,500	36.7	2.6		
Never-married women	7,700,852	13.7	24,500	37.3	26.0		
Households With Children							
Heterosexual, married	24,862,111	13.4	58,000	39.0		8.9	22.9
Heterosexual, cohabiting	1,699,954	12.0	36,600	33.2		11.4	44.5
Gay male, cohabiting	75,414	12.2	50,000	37.6		10.2	41.6
Lesbian, cohabiting	116,329	12.8	47,000	37.0		12.4	37.1
Separated, divorced, widowed men	973,714	13.0	37,000	41.5		5.2	24.6
Separated, divorced, widowed women	4,180,122	12.8	23,000	38.0		3.4	40.3
Never-married men	191,988	11.9	28,600	34.3		9.8	54.9
Never-married women	2,002,598	12.1	14,000	31.4		2.6	75.1

Notes: In families with children, head of household's mean education, median household income, and head of household's mean age are weighted by number of children. Children include own children, adopted children, stepchildren, and foster children. With the omission of couples whose dual marital status was recoded, 11% of gay couples and 26.6% of lesbian couples have children; median household income is $42,000 for gay fathers and $43,350 for lesbian mothers. For children of gay fathers, 13.7% are adopted, step-, or foster children, and 53.7% are black or Hispanic; the corresponding figures for children of lesbian mothers are 18% and 42.0%.

Source: Census 2000 microdata, via IPUMS.

heads of household. Across family types, gay couples had the highest median household income at $61,000 per household. It should also be noted that men have higher earnings than women, and gay male couples are the only household type that relied on the earnings of two men. The second four family types are all single-parent (i.e., single-income) families, so their household incomes were roughly half as high as the household incomes of the first four family types.

Despite the fact that the cost of becoming parents may be higher for gays and lesbians than for heterosexual couples, Table 2 shows that gay and lesbian couples who did have children had substantially lower income and educational attainment than gay and lesbian couples in general. Although gay and lesbian cohabiters had relatively high household incomes, gay and lesbian parents had lower SES than heterosexual married parents ($50,000 per household for gay parents compared with $58,000 for heterosexual married parents). Excluding recodes for dual marital status, the income and educational level of gay and lesbian parents was even lower. Among gay and lesbian couples, those with lower incomes are more likely to be raising children.

Not only were heterosexual married parents economically advantaged, but the heterosexual married couples were also racially/ethnically advantaged. Only 22.9% of children of heterosexual married couples were black or Hispanic, whereas 41.6% of children of gay men were black or Hispanic, and this percentage rose to 53.7% when recodes for dual marital status were excluded. The children of lesbians were similarly likely (37.1%) to be black or Hispanic. Never-married mothers were the most likely parenting family type to have black or Hispanic children. The racial/ethnic breakdown of parents was similar to the racial breakdown of children described in Table 2. Among heterosexual married heads of household, 22.2% were black or Hispanic, while 40.4% of gay fathers and 36.1% of lesbian mothers were black or Hispanic (not shown in Table 2).[6]

Among all family types, children of lesbian mothers were the most likely (more than 12%) to be adopted children, stepchildren, or foster children. Because economic disadvantage, minority racial/ethnic status, and experience with the adoption or foster care system are all challenges for children, a careful analysis of the school performance of children of gay and lesbian parents must take these disadvantages into account.

MULTIVARIATE ANALYSES

Comparisons With Children of Heterosexual Married Couples

Table 3 presents a series of multivariate logistic regression coefficients (for normal progress through primary school versus grade retention), of the following type:

$$\text{Log}\left(\frac{P_i}{1-P_i}\right) = \alpha + \beta_k X_{k,i},$$

where P_i is the predicted probability that the ith primary school student was making normal progress through school.[7] The constant term is α, and β_k represents a column of k coefficients

---

6. Rosenfeld and Kim (2005) showed that same-sex couples were also more likely than heterosexual couples to be interracial.

7. Because of the four-year categories for current grade, only one-fourth of the actual cases of grade retention are identified in the data set. In the data, the category "over-age" includes only students who were demonstrably over-age, but the category "making normal progress" is a mixed category whose components include 91%–95% (depending on the grade retention rate by family type) of students who truly were making normal progress through school, and the remainder are students who were over-age but are misclassified as making normal progress because of the four-year-wide categories in the census question GRADEATT.

Table 3. Predictors of Making Normal Progress Through Primary School, for Own Children of Nontraditional Family Types Compared With Own Children of Heterosexual Married Couples: Selected Coefficients From Logistic Regressions

Variable	Model 1	Model 2	Model 3	Model 4	Model 5
Family Type (heterosexual, married)					
Same-sex couple cohabiting	−0.267*	−0.112	−0.116	−0.128	−0.142
Separated, divorced, widowed women	−0.529***	−0.422***	−0.321***	−0.312***	−0.311***
Heterosexual, cohabiting	−0.547***	−0.271***	−0.202***	−0.207***	−0.236***
Separated, divorced, widowed men	−0.558***	−0.467***	−0.427***	−0.402***	−0.397***
Never-married women	−0.623***	−0.319***	−0.088*	−0.116**	−0.145***
Never-married men	−0.675***	−0.400***	−0.274*	−0.308*	−0.354**
Ln of Household Income		0.035***	0.026***	0.021***	0.013*
Head of Household's Education (less than high school)					
High school diploma		0.507***	0.518***	0.515***	0.511***
Some college		0.828***	0.839***	0.804***	0.767***
College degree+		1.118***	1.105***	1.026***	0.988***
Child Is U.S.-Born			0.622***	0.599***	0.629***
Child's Gender: Female			0.283***	0.282***	0.280***
Child Has Disability					
Difficulty with memory			−0.911***	−0.899***	−0.893***
Physical disability			−0.376***	−0.363***	−0.362***
Hearing or vision disability			−0.401***	−0.394***	−0.377***
Personal care limitation			−0.207**	−0.235***	−0.244***
Child's Race/Ethnicity (non-Hispanic white)					
Non-Hispanic black			−0.342***	−0.371***	−0.270***
Hispanic			0.181***	0.111***	0.009
Asian American			0.275***	0.199***	0.006
Metropolitan Status (rural)					
City				0.301***	0.152***
Suburbs				0.377***	0.235***
Grade Attending: Grades 5–8				−0.248***	−0.248***
School Type: Private School				0.154***	0.172***
State Dummy Variables					Yes
Constant	4.094***	3.092***	2.524***	2.532***	2.723***
Unweighted *N*	716,764	716,764	716,764	716,740	716,740
df	7	11	21	27	77
Log-Likelihood	−65,352	−64,284	−63,315	−63,080	−62,561

Notes: Comparison categories are in parentheses. Some categories of metro status and race/ethnicity are excluded for clarity. With the omission of children of couples whose dual marital status was recoded, and combining gay and lesbian couples, coefficients for children of same-sex couples would be −0.691*, −0.452, −0.361, −0.392;, and−0.427 in Models 1–5, respectively (statistically significant only in Model 1).

Source: Census 2000 microdata, via IPUMS.

*p < .05; **p < .01; ***p < .001

in the model.[8] Positive coefficients imply better outcomes (i.e., higher probability of making normal progress through school) for the students. Negative coefficients imply higher rates of grade retention. The sample in Table 3 includes only "own children" (excluding stepchildren, foster children, and adopted children) to reduce the number of children who are the result of previous relationships and to minimize the potential selection bias that could result from the nonrandom way in which children become available for adoption or fostering (Stacey 2006). This narrowing of the sample of children, along with the inclusion of household income and parental education (in Models 2–5), excludes children living in group quarters (by far, the worst performers in school) from the analysis. In a later section of this article, I present an analysis that includes the group-quarters children.

Model 1 of Table 3 shows the raw log odds ratios of normal progress through school for children of all less-traditional family types compared with heterosexual married couples. Similar to the result from Table 1, Model 1 shows that children from all nontraditional family types were less likely to be making good progress through school, with coefficients varying from –0.267 for children of same-sex couples (the most modest disadvantage among the nontraditional family types) to –0.675 for children living with never-married men.

Model 2 introduces controls for household SES, including the natural logarithm of household income, and a categorical variable for the head of household's educational attainment. The presence of these controls for household SES reduces the magnitude of the negative coefficients for children of all types of nontraditional families compared with Model 1. For children of same-sex parents, the introduction of household SES in Model 2 reduces the grade retention gap (compared with children of heterosexual married couples) by 58% (from –0.267 in Model 1 to –0.112 in Model 2), which renders the contrast with children of heterosexual married couples statistically insignificant in Model 2 and all subsequent models.

Model 3 introduces student gender (girls were more likely to be making good progress), U.S. nativity, student race/ethnicity, and four dichotomous measures for disabilities among the students. The most influential type of disability was memory deficits, which reduced the odds of making good progress through school by more than half ($e^{-0.911} = 0.40$).

Model 4 adds controls for urban, rural, or suburban residence; for grade attending; and for private school versus public school. Model 5 adds dummy variables for the 50 U.S. states (plus the District of Columbia) to account for differences in social promotion policy between states. The introduction of new controls in Models 3–5 reaffirms the core finding that the disadvantage in progress through school of children raised by same-sex couples (compared with children of heterosexual married couples) is statistically insignificant when general predictors of school progress are included in the models.

Table 3 does not nullify the importance of family structure. Family structure remains a significant predictor of childhood progress through school, even after every available sociodemographic control is applied, as other scholars have found with other outcomes and other data sets (McLanahan and Sandefur 1994). What Table 3 does show, however, is that the gap in one particular children's outcome (normal progress through school) is small between family types, and that the apparent disadvantage of children of same-sex couples (compared with children of heterosexual married couples) is especially small. After parental SES is accounted for, the disadvantage of children of same-sex couples (when compared with children of the most advantaged family group) is too small to be statistically significant.

---

8. Coefficients are based on weighted census microdata, with weights renormed to average 1, so that model likelihoods and coefficient standard errors reflect the real unweighted sample size. In general, children of same-sex cohabiting parents appear to do slightly better in these multivariate tests when the models are run without taking the census weights into account.

When examining small minority populations, such as children raised by same-sex couples, sample size and statistical power are fundamental limitations of empirical research. The relatively large sample size of children raised by same-sex couples is the fundamental advantage of the census data in this case, but the question remains, Is the sample size large enough to provide sufficient statistical power? There are several ways of addressing the question of statistical power.[9] One approach is to randomly reduce the sample of children from all the other family types to 3,174 children (the sample size of children of same-sex couples used in Table 3) to determine whether other relationships in the data remain significant (Cheng and Powell 2005). These results (available upon request) show, reassuringly, that the sample size of 3,174 is large enough to retain most of the important statistically significant predictors of grade retention in the data. The difference between children raised by same-sex couples and children raised by heterosexual married couples in making normal progress through school remains statistically insignificant.

It is also useful to compare the smaller group (children of same-sex couples) with the part of the larger group (other children) to which they are most similar. The process of finding and comparing the most similar subpopulations is known as *propensity score matching* (Lechner 2002; Lundquist 2004; Rubin 1979). In the first stage, children of same-sex couples are matched to the most similar children of heterosexual married parents via probit regression on a set of covariates, with ties randomly resolved. The resulting two groups, with equal sample sizes, are compared on grade retention by means of a two-sample t test. The t tests are nonparametric because no assumptions are made about how the control variables affect grade retention, and whether the shape of those effects might be different across family types.[10]

Model 1 of Table 4 matches the samples without using any covariates—that is, the sample of children raised by heterosexual married parents is a random sample—reflecting the unadjusted means of both groups. As expected, the unadjusted means show that own children of heterosexual married couples are significantly less likely to be left back in school than own children of same-sex couples. After the samples are matched on household income and householder educational attainment (Model 2), children of same-sex couples actually are less likely than their most similar peers among children of heterosexual married couples to be held back in school (9.07% compared with 9.45%), although the difference is not statistically significant. Introduction of additional controls into the matching process in Models 3–5 results in no significant differences in grade retention between children of same-sex couples and children of heterosexual married couples. The comparisons after propensity score matching, reported in Table 4, are entirely consistent with the large sample regressions reported in Table 3. After parental income and education are taken into account, the differences between children

---

9. If the odds of making normal progress through school were twice as high for children of heterosexual married couples as for children of same-sex couples, the existing census sample from Table 3 would provide a power of 0.999 (near certainty) to reject the null hypothesis of no difference. None of the family types in any of the models of Table 3 had a disadvantage this large. If the odds of grade retention were 1.5 times higher for children of heterosexual married parents than for children of same-sex couples, the power to detect the difference would be lower, but still substantial at 0.83. Children raised by divorced single mothers or divorced single fathers had this great a disadvantage, across several models. The main reason that the coefficients for children raised by same sex couples were not significantly different from zero in Models 2–5 of Table 3 is that their estimated disadvantage was relatively small. Power calculations assume alpha of .05, two-tailed tests, and Bernoulli distributions (for normal progress versus grade retention) with variance of $p(1 - p)$.

10. In fact, the effect of parental education on children's grade retention does differ across family types. Among same-sex couples, parental education has little effect on children's grade retention; among heterosexual married couples, there is a strong positive correlation between parental education and children's normal progress through school. At low parental educational levels, children of same-sex couples make better progress in school than children of heterosexual married couples. Among children raised by highly educated parents, the children of heterosexual married couples make better progress in school than the children of same-sex couples.

Table 4. Grade Retention Comparisons Between Own Children of Same-Sex Couples ($N = 3,174$) and Own Children of Heterosexual Married Couples ($N = 3,174$), Matched by Propensity Score

Variable	Model 1	Model 2	Model 3	Model 4	Model 5
Controls	None	Household income, head of household's education	Model 2 plus child is U.S.-born, child's gender, child has disability, child's race/ ethnicity	Model 3 plus metro status, grade, school type	Model 4 plus state
Implied Grade Retention Rate (%)					
Children of same-sex couples	9.07	9.07	9.07	9.07	9.07
Children of heterosexual married couples	6.81	9.45	8.95	8.57	7.94
Difference in Implied Grade Retention Rate	−2.27**	0.38	−0.12	−0.50	−1.13

Notes: The propensity-score–matched comparison set varies across models. Actual measured grade retention is one-fourth as large as implied grade retention; see the text. With the omission of children of couples whose dual marital status was recoded, N = 412, and implied grade retention rate difference would be −5.82**, −1.94, −2.92, 1.94, and −1.94 in Models 1–5, respectively (significantly different only in Model 1).

Source: Census 2000 microdata, via IPUMS.

*$p < .05$; **$p < .01$; ***$p < .001$

of same-sex couples and children of heterosexual married couples are small enough to be indistinguishable from zero.

Comparisons With Children of Unmarried Heterosexual Couples

Table 5 revisits the regressions from Table 3 (with the same models, covariates, and summary statistics), comparing children raised by same-sex couples with children raised by heterosexual cohabiting couples. Table 5 shows that children raised by same-sex couples are more likely to make normal progress through school than children raised by heterosexual cohabiting couples, but the difference is statistically significant only in Model 1, before parental SES has been accounted for. If children living with dual marital status–recoded couples are excluded, the signs are reversed (meaning that children raised by heterosexual cohabiting couples fare better), but none of the coefficients are statistically significant. These results suggest that for the outcome of normal progress through school, children raised by same-sex cohabiting couples are no different, and perhaps slightly advantaged, compared with children raised by heterosexual cohabiting couples. The similarity in school performance between children of same-sex couples and children of heterosexual cohabiting couples fails to support the gender essentialist theories of parenting, which argue that child development depends on having parental role models from both gender groups (Alvaré 2005; Popenoe 1996; Wardle 1997).

Comparisons With Children in Group Quarters

Table 6 represents a different variation on the type of analysis from Tables 3–5. In Table 6, the sample of children includes children in group quarters, and these children are the comparison category for the analysis. Because neither household income nor parental education can be associated with children in group quarters, these variables are dropped from the analysis. The sample of children in Table 6 includes own children, adopted children,

Table 5.   Normal Progress Through School for Children of Same-Sex Couples Compared With Children of Heterosexual Cohabiting Couples (coefficients adapted from Table 3)

Family Type	Model 1	Model 2	Model 3	Model 4	Model 5
Heterosexual Couple, Cohabiting (ref.)					
Same-Sex Couple, Cohabiting	0.281*	0.159	0.085	0.079	0.094

Notes: Models, covariates, and summary statistics are identical to those in Table 3. Sample size is the same as in Table 3: 716,764 in Models 1–3, and 716,740 in Models 4 and 5. With the omission of children of couples whose dual marital status was recoded, the coefficients are reversed in sign but remain insignificant: –0.138, –0.175, –0.155, –0.181, and –0.186 for Models 1–5, respectively.

Source: Census 2000 microdata, via IPUMS.

*p < .05

stepchildren, children living in group quarters, and foster children. Because the children in group quarters have no head of household to have a relationship with, it seems appropriate to use the broadest definition of "children" for children who were living with families. Furthermore, the adopted and foster children probably include some children who formerly lived in group quarters.

Table 6 confirms the robustness of a previous finding, from Table 1, that children who live with parents, regardless of family type, are much more likely to make normal progress through school than children living in group quarters. Even after student disabilities (more common among group quarters children than among children living with families) are taken into account, the difference remains between children raised by families and children living in group quarters. Children living at least five years with same-sex couples and children living at least five years with heterosexual cohabiting couples have odds of making good progress through school that are twice as high as noninmate children who spent the previous five years in group quarters. Based on coefficients from Model 2 of Table 6, which controls for children's race/ethnicity and disabilities, children raised by same-sex couples have odds of making good progress through school that are 2.43 times higher than children living in group quarters ($e^{0.886} = 2.43$). Children raised by heterosexual cohabiting couples are similarly advantaged compared with children in group quarters ($e^{0.810} = 2.25$). The advantage of children raised by same-sex couples over children living in group quarters remains positive and statistically significant across all four models even after children of those whose marital status was recoded are excluded.

DISCUSSION

Children raised by same-sex couples are one of the most difficult populations in the United States to study systematically because of their small numbers and their geographic dispersion. Census data are far from ideal, and better data would, of course, be welcome. However, currently, the U.S. census is the only nationally representative data set with a large enough sample of children raised by same-sex couples to allow for statistically powerful comparisons with children of other family types.

To the extent that normal progress through primary school is a useful and valid measure of child development, the results confirm that children of same-sex couples appear to have no inherent developmental disadvantage. Heterosexual married couples are the most economically prosperous, the most likely to be white, and the most legally advantaged type of parents; their children have the lowest rates of grade retention. Parental SES accounts for more than one-half of the relatively small gap in grade retention between children of heterosexual married couples and children of same-sex couples. When one controls for parental SES and characteristics of the students, children of same-sex couples cannot be distinguished with statistical certainty from children of heterosexual married couples.

Table 6. **Predictors of Making Normal Progress Through Primary School for Residentially Stable Children Compared With Children Living in Noninmate Group Quarters: Selected Coefficients From Logistic Regressions**

Variable	Model 1	Model 2	Model 3	Model 4
Family Type (group quarters, noninmates)				
Same-sex couple, cohabiting	1.321***	0.886***	0.888***	0.988***
Heterosexual, married	1.676***	1.191***	1.194***	1.302***
Separated, divorced, widowed women	1.181***	0.851***	0.880***	0.998***
Heterosexual, cohabiting	1.141***	0.810***	0.844***	0.932***
Separated, divorced, widowed men	1.142***	0.698***	0.746***	0.864***
Never-married women	1.115***	0.983***	0.991***	1.088***
Never-married men	1.058***	0.785***	0.785***	0.851***
Group quarters (inmates)	−0.948***	−0.801***	−0.732**	−0.657***
Child Is U.S.-born		0.675***	0.654***	0.678***
Child's Gender: Female		0.278***	0.276***	0.275***
Child Has Disability				
Difficulty with memory		−0.944***	−0.929***	−0.922***
Physical disability		−0.407***	−0.388***	−0.385***
Hearing or vision disability		−0.403***	−0.384***	−0.364***
Personal care limitation		−0.187***	−0.218***	−0.231***
Child's Race/Ethnicity (non-Hispanic white)				
Non-Hispanic black		−0.512***	−0.524***	−0.398***
Hispanic		−0.175***	−0.221***	−0.318***
Asian American		0.240***	0.151**	−0.032
Metropolitan Status (rural)				
City			0.376***	0.218***
Suburbs			0.531***	0.372***
Grade Attending: Grades 5–8			−0.245***	−0.245***
School Type: Private School			0.271***	0.285***
State Dummy Variables				Yes
Constant	2.365***	2.219***	2.305***	1.716***
Unweighted N	764,781	764,781	764,757	764,757
df	8	18	24	74
Log-Likelihood	−72,171	−70,885	−70,454	−69,788

Notes: Comparison categories are in parentheses. The sample includes own children, stepchildren, adopted children, foster children, and children living in group quarters. All children and all present parents have five years of residential stability. Some categories of metro status and race/ethnicity are excluded for clarity. With the exclusion of children of couples whose dual marital status was recoded, coefficients for children of same-sex couples would be 0.895**, 0.595*, 0.595*, and 0.661* for Models 1–4, respectively.

Source: Census 2000 microdata, via IPUMS.

**p < .01; ***p < .001

Children not living in group quarters, including children in households headed by same-sex couples, are dramatically more likely to make normal progress through school than students living in group quarters. Any policy that would deny gay and lesbian parents the right to adopt or foster children would force some children to remain in group quarters. A longer stay in group quarters would seem to be contrary to the best interest of the children. In recent years, scholars have arrived at a consensus that moving children out of group homes and into adoptive families should be the goal of public policy. Families, even suboptimal families, are better equipped than the state to raise children (Bartholet 1999; Goldstein, Freud, and Solnit 1979).

Historical restrictions against interracial adoption in the United States represent one relevant historical precedent for the current debate over the adoption rights of same-sex couples. Randall Kennedy (2003) argued that even though restrictions against interracial adoption have been proposed as a way of protecting children, such restrictions have victimized children by taking them away from loving homes or by forcing children to remain in group quarters for too long. Policies limiting the kinds of families that can adopt or foster children ignore the enormous advantages of personal attention that families have (even single parents and other nontraditional family types) over the state in raising children well.

The prior literature has found no evidence that children raised by same-sex couples suffer any important disadvantages (Chan, Raboy, and Patterson 1998; Patterson 1995; Stacey and Biblarz 2001; Wald 2006), yet this same literature has been heavily criticized on the methodological grounds that universally small sample sizes prevent the studies from having the statistical power to identify differences that might actually exist (Alvaré 2005; Lerner and Nagai 2001; Nock 2001). The analysis in this article, the first to use large-sample nationally representative data, shows that children raised by same-sex couples have no fundamental deficits in making normal progress through school. The core finding here offers a measure of validation for the prior, and much-debated, small-sample studies.

REFERENCES

Alexander, K.L., D.R. Entwisle, and S.L. Dauber. 2003. *On the Success of Failure: A Reassessment of the Effects of Retention in the Primary Grades*. Cambridge, England: Cambridge University Press.

Alexander, K.L., D.R. Entwisle, and C.S. Horsey. 1997. "From First Grade Forward: Early Foundations of High School Dropout." *Sociology of Education* 70:87–107.

Alvaré, H.M. 2005. "The Turn Toward the Self in the Law of Marriage and Family: Same-Sex Marriage and Its Predecessors." *Stanford Law and Policy Review* 16:135–96.

Amato, P.R. and J. Cheadle. 2005. "The Long Reach of Divorce: Divorce and Child Well-being Across Three Generations." *Journal of Marriage and Family* 67:191–206.

Ball, C.A. and J.F. Pea. 1998. "Warring With Wardle: Morality, Social Science, and Gay and Lesbian Parents." *University of Illinois Law Review* 1998:253–339.

Bartholet, E. 1999. *Nobody's Children: Abuse and Neglect, Foster Drift, and the Adoption Alternative*. Boston: Beacon Press.

Baumrind, D. 1966. "Effects of Authoritative Parental Control on Child Behavior." *Child Development* 37:887–907.

Bianchi, S. 1984. "Children's Progress Through School: A Research Note." *Sociology of Education* 57:184–92.

Biblarz, T.J. and A.E. Raftery. 1999. "Family Structure, Educational Attainment, and Socioeconomic Success: Rethinking the 'Pathology of Matriarchy'." *American Journal of Sociology* 105:321–65.

Brewaeys, A., I. Ponjaert, E.V. Van Hall, and S. Golombok. 1997. "Donor Insemination: Child Development and Family Functioning in Lesbian Mother Families." *Human Reproduction* 12:1349–59.

Brooks-Gunn, J. and L.B. Markman. 2005. "The Contribution of Parenting to Ethnic and Racial Gaps in School Readiness." *The Future of Children* 15:139–68.

Chan, R.W., B. Raboy, and C.J. Patterson. 1998. "Psychosocial Adjustment Among Children Conceived Via Donor Insemination by Lesbian and Heterosexual Mothers." *Child Development* 69:443–57.

Chase-Lansdale, P.L., A.J. Cherlin, and K.E. Kiernan. 1995. "The Long-Term Effects of Parental Divorce on the Mental Health of Young Adults: A Developmental Perspective." *Child Development* 66:1614–34.

Cheng, S. and B. Powell. 2005. "Small Samples, Big Challenges: Studying Atypical Family Forms." *Journal of Marriage and Family* 67:926–35.

Cherlin, A.J. 1992. *Marriage, Divorce, Remarriage*. Cambridge, MA: Harvard University Press.

————. 1999. "Going to Extremes: Family Structure, Children's Well-being, and Social Science." *Demography* 36:421–28.

Dawson, D.A. 1991. "Family Structure and Children's Health and Well-being: Data From the 1988 National Health Interview Survey on Child Health." *Journal of Marriage and the Family* 53:573–84.

Eskridge, W.N., Jr. 1996. *The Case for Same Sex Marriage: From Sexual Liberty to Civilized Commitment*. New York: Free Press.

————. 2002. *Equality Practice: Civil Unions and the Future of Gay Rights*. New York: Routledge.

Flaks, D.K., I. Ficher, F. Masterpasqua, and G. Joseph. 1995. "Lesbians Choosing Motherhood: A Comparative Study of Lesbian and Heterosexual Parents and Their Children." *Developmental Psychology* 31:105–14.

Freud, S. [1905] 1975. *Three Essays on the Theory of Sexuality*. New York: Basic Books.

Gennetian, L.A. 2005. "One or Two Parents? Half or Step Siblings? The Effect of Family Structure on Young Children's Achievement." *Journal of Population Economics* 18:415–36.

Ginther, D.K. and R.A. Pollak. 2004. "Family Structure and Children's Educational Outcomes: Blended Families, Stylized Facts, and Descriptive Regressions." *Demography* 41:671–96.

Goldstein, J., A. Freud, and A.J. Solnit. 1979. *Before the Best Interests of the Child*. New York: Free Press.

Golombok, S., B. Perry, A. Burston, C. Murray, J. Mooney-Somers, M. Stevens, and J. Golding. 2003. "Children With Lesbian Parents: A Community Study." *Developmental Psychology* 39:20–33.

Guo, G., J. Brooks-Gunn, and K.M. Harris. 1996. "Parents' Labor Force Attachment and Grade Retention Among Urban Black Children." *Sociology of Education* 69:217–36.

Hamilton, L., S. Cheng, and B. Powell. 2007. "Adoptive Parents, Adaptive Parents: Evaluating the Importance of Biological Ties for Parental Investment." *American Sociological Review* 72:95–116.

Harris, J.R. 1998. *The Nurture Assumption: Why Children Turn Out the Way They Do*. New York: Touchstone.

Hauser, R.M. 2001. "Should We End Social Promotion? Truth and Consequences." Pp. 151–78 in *Raising Standards or Raising Barriers? Inequality and High Stakes Testing in Public Education*, edited by G. Orfield and M.L. Kornhaber. New York: Century Foundation.

Hauser, R.M., D.I. Pager, and S.J. Simmons. 2001. "Race-Ethnicity, Social Background, and Grade Retention: An Analysis of the Last Thirty Years." *CEIC Review* 10(5):11–12.

Heubert, J.P. and R.M. Hauser. 1999. "High Stakes: Testing for Tracking, Promotion, and Graduation." Washington, DC: National Academies Press.

Jamieson, A., A. Curry, and G. Martinez. 2001. "School Enrollment in the United States—Social and Economic Characteristics of Students: October 1999." *Current Population Reports* P20-533. U.S. Census Bureau, Washington, DC.

Kennedy, R. 2003. *Interracial Intimacies: Sex, Marriage, Identity and Adoption*. New York: Pantheon.

Koppelman, A. 2002. *The Gay Rights Question in Contemporary American Law*. Chicago: University of Chicago Press.

Kowalesi-Jones, L. and G.J. Duncan. 1999. "The Structure of Achievement and Behavior Across Middle Childhood." *Child Development* 70:930–43.

Lareau, A. 2003. *Unequal Childhoods: Class, Race, and Family Life*. Berkeley: University of California Press.

Lechner, M. 2002. "Program Heterogeneity and Propensity Score Matching: An Application to the Evaluation of Active Labor Market Policies." *The Review of Economics and Statistics* 84:205–20.

Lerner, R. and A.K. Nagai. 2001. "No Basis: What the Studies *Don't* Tell Us About Same-Sex Parenting." Washington, DC: Marriage Law Project.

Lundquist, J.H. 2004. "When Race Makes No Difference: Marriage and the Military." *Social Forces* 83:731–57.

Maccoby, E.E. 1990. "Gender and Relationships: A Developmental Account." *American Psychologist* 45:513–20.

Mayer, S. 1997. *What Money Can't Buy: Family Income and Children's Life Chances*. Cambridge, MA: Harvard University Press.

McLanahan, S. 1985. "Family Structure and the Reproduction of Poverty." *American Journal of Sociology* 90:873–901.

McLanahan, S. and G. Sandefur. 1994. *Growing Up With a Single Parent: What Hurts, What Helps*. Cambridge, MA: Harvard University Press.

Meezan, W. and J. Rauch. 2005. "Gay Marriage, Same-Sex Parenting, and America's Children." *The Future of Children* 15:97–115.

Moller, S., E. Stearns, J.R. Blau, and K.C. Land. 2006. "Smooth and Rough Roads to Academic Achievement: Retention and Race/Class Disparities in High School." *Social Science Research* 35:157–80.

Nock, S.L. 2001. "Affidavit in the Ontario Superior Court in the Case of Halpern et al. v. Attorney General of Canada." Available online at http://www.marriagelaw.cua.edu/Law/cases/Canada/ontario/halpern/aff_nock.pdf.

O'Connell, M. and G. Gooding. 2006. "The Use of First Names to Evaluate Reports of Gender and Its Effect on the Distribution of Married and Unmarried Couple Households." Presented at Population Association of America, Los Angeles, March 30–April 1.

Patterson, C.J. 1995. "Families of the Lesbian Baby Boom: Parents' Division of Labor and Children's Adjustment." *Developmental Psychology* 31:115–23.

———. 2002. "Lesbian and Gay Parenthood." Pp. 317–38 in *Handbook of Parenting*, edited by M.H. Bornstein. Mahwah, NJ: Lawrence Erlbaum Associates.

Pawelski, J.G., E.C. Perrin, J.M. Foy, C.E. Allen, J.E. Crawford, M. Del Monte, K. Miriam, J.D. Klein, K. Smith, S. Springer, J.L. Tanner, and D.L. Vickers. 2006. "The Effects of Marriage, Civil Union, and Domestic Partnership Laws on the Health and Well-being of Children." *Pediatrics* 118:349–64.

Perry, B., A. Burston, M. Stevens, H. Steele, J. Golding, and S. Golombok. 2004. "Children's Play Narratives: What They Tell Us About Lesbian-Mother Families." *American Journal of Orthopsychiatry* 74:467–79.

Popenoe, D. 1996. *Life Without Father: Compelling New Evidence That Fatherhood and Marriage Are Indispensable for the Good of Children and Society*. New York: Free Press.

Roderick, M. 1994. "Grade Retention and School Dropout: Investigating the Association." *American Educational Research Journal* 31:729–59.

Rosenfeld, M.J. and B.-S. Kim. 2005. "The Independence of Young Adults and the Rise of Interracial and Same-Sex Unions." *American Sociological Review* 70:541–62.

Rubin, D.B. 1979. "Using Multivariate Matched Sampling and Regression Adjustment to Control Bias in Observational Studies." *Journal of the American Statistical Association* 74:318–28.

Ruggles, S., M. Sobek, T. Alexander, C.A. Fitch, R. Goeken, P.K. Hall, M. King, and C. Ronnander. 2004. *Integrated Public Use Microdata Series: Version 3.0* [Machine-readable database]. Minneapolis, MN.: Minnesota Population Center. Available online at http://www.ipums.org.

Rumberger, R.W. 1987. "High School Dropouts: A Review of Issues and Evidence." *Review of Educational Research* 57:101–21.

Rutter, M. 2002. "Nature, Nurture, and Development: From Evangelism Through Science Toward Policy and Practice." *Child Development* 73:1–21.

Shin, H.B. 2005. "School Enrollment—Social and Economic Characteristics of Students: October 2003." *Current Population Reports* P20-554. U.S. Census Bureau, Washington, DC.

Stacey, J. 2006. "Gay Parenthood and the Decline of Paternity as We Knew It." *Sexualities* 9:27–55.

Stacey, J. and T.J. Biblarz. 2001. "(How) Does the Sexual Orientation of Parents Matter?" *American Sociological Review* 66:159–83.

Tasker, F. 2005. "Lesbian Mothers, Gay Fathers, and Their Children: A Review." *Journal of Developmental and Behavioral Pediatrics* 26:224–40.

Tillman, K.H., G. Guo, and K.M. Harris. 2006. "Grade Retention Among Immigrant Children." *Social Science Research* 35:129–56.

U.S. Census Bureau. 2001. "Technical Note on Same-Sex Unmarried Partner Data from the 1990 and 2000 Censuses." Available online at http://www.census.gov/sdc/chap7pums.txt.

———. 2002. "2010 Census Re-Engineering." Available online at http://www.census.gov/Press-Release/www/2002/2_4_02Waite.html.

Wainright, J.L. and C.J. Patterson. 2006. "Delinquency, Victimization, and Substance Use Among Adolescents With Female Same-Sex Parents." *Journal of Family Psychology* 20:526–30.

———. 2008. "Peer Relations Among Adolescents With Female Same-Sex Parents." *Developmental Psychology* 44:117–26.

Wainright, J.L., S.T. Russell, and C.J. Patterson. 2004. "Psychosocial Adjustment, School Outcomes, and Romantic Relationships of Adolescents With Same-Sex Parents." *Child Development* 75:1886–98.

Waite, L.J. and M. Gallagher. 2000. *The Case for Marriage: Why Married People Are Happier, Healthier, and Better Off Financially*. New York: Doubleday.

Wald, M. 2006. "Adults' Sexual Orientation and State Determinations Regarding Placement of Children." *Family Law Quarterly* 40:385–439.

Wallerstein, J.S. and J.B. Kelly. 1980. *Surviving the Breakup: How Children and Parents Cope With Divorce*. New York: Basic Books.

Wallerstein, J.S., J.M. Lewis, and S. Blakeslee. 2000. *The Unexpected Legacy of Divorce: A 25 Year Landmark Study*. New York: Hyperion.

Wardle, L.D. 1997. "The Potential Impact of Homosexual Parenting on Children." *University of Illinois Law Review* 1997:833–920.

Wilson, J.Q. 2002. *The Marriage Problem: How Our Culture Has Weakened Families*. New York: Harper Collins.

Wolfe, B., R. Haveman, D. Ginther, and C.B. An. 1996. "The 'Window Problem' in Studies of Children's Attainments: A Methodological Exploration." *Journal of the American Statistical Association* 91:970–82.

Wu, L.L. and B.C. Martinson. 1993. "Family Structure and the Risk of a Premarital Birth." *American Sociological Review* 58:210–32.

Zill, N. 1996. "Family Change and Student Achievement: What We Have Learned, What It Means for Schools." Pp. 139–84 in *Family-School Links: How Do They Affect Educational Outcomes?*, edited by A. Booth and J.F. Dunn. Mahwah, NJ: Lawrence Erlbaum Associates.

Acknowledgments

Often, the language of social science is difficult for the nonspecialist to follow, and so *No Differences?* aims to serve as a bridge between that specialized research language and the everyday citizen interested in learning about the developing scholarly debate on children's outcomes in same-sex households.

Although research is still in its early stages and much has yet to be learned, this book displays the work of those scientists who have endeavored especially hard to identify large, random samples of children and study the pathways they face toward later-life outcomes.

This work has benefited from the careful review of many readers, including Betsy Stokes, who served as assistant editor, Alicia Grimaldi, who served as managing editor, and Margaret Trejo, our book design and layout artist. Thanks especially to Luis Tellez, president of the Witherspoon Institute, whose promotion of this work will serve to increase the public's awareness of these studies.

John Londregan is professor of politics and international affairs at the Woodrow Wilson School at Princeton University and director of the graduate program in political economy. He specializes in the development and application of statistical methods in political science.

Ana Samuel, Ph.D., is a research scholar at the Witherspoon Institute, where she works on family structure studies.